MADNESS, DISABILITY AND SOCIAL EXCLUSION

The One World Archaeology (OWA) series stems from conferences organized by the World Archaeological Congress (WAC), an international non-profit making organization, which provides a forum of debate for anyone who is genuinely interested in or has a concern for the past. All editors and contributors to the OWA series waive any fees they might normally receive from a publisher. Instead all royalties from the series are received by WAC Charitable Company to help the wider work of the World Archaeological Congress. The sale of OWA volumes provides the means for less advantaged colleagues to attend WAC conferences thereby enabling them to contribute to the development of the academic debate surrounding the study of the past.

The World Archaeological Congress would like to take this opportunity to thank all editors and contributors for helping the development of world archaeology in this way.

ONE WORLD ARCHAEOLOGY

Series Editor (Volumes 1–37): Peter J. Ucko
Academic Series Editors (Volume 38 onwards): Martin Hall and Julian Thomas
Executive Series Editor (Volume 38 onwards): Peter Stone

MADNESS, DISABILITY AND SOCIAL EXCLUSION

The archaeology and anthropology of 'difference'

Edited by

Jane Hubert

London and New York

First published 2000 by Routledge
2 Park Square, Milton Park, Abingdon, Oxon, OX14 4RN

Simultaneously published in the USA and Canada
by Routledge
270 Madison Ave, New York NY 10016

Routledge is an imprint of the Taylor & Francis Group

Transferred to Digital Printing 2010

Selection and editorial matter © 2000 Jane Hubert
Individual chapters © 2000 individual contributors

Typeset in Bembo by Keyword Typesetting Services Ltd

British Library Cataloguing in Publication Data
A catalogue record for this book is available from the British Library

Library of Congress Cataloging in Publication Data
Madness, disability, and social exclusion: the archaeology and anthropology of
"difference" / edited by Jane Hubert.
    p. cm. – (One world archaeology; 40)
    Includes bibliographical references and index.
    1. Social isolation – Cross-cultural studies. 2. Handicapped – Cross-cultural studies.
3. Mental illness – Cross-cultural studies. 4. Human remains (Archaeology) –
Cross-cultural studies. 5. Ethnopsychology – Cross-cultural studies.
    6. Difference (Psychology) – Cross-cultural studies. I. Hubert, Jane. II. Series.
HM1131.M33 2000
302.5′45–dc21   00-056029

ISBN10: 0–415–23002–0 (hbk)
ISBN10: 0–415–58907–X (pbk)

ISBN13: 978–0–415–23002–5 (hbk)
ISBN13: 978–0–415–58907–9 (pbk)

Publisher's Note
The publisher has gone to great lengths to ensure the quality of this reprint
but points out that some imperfections in the original may be apparent.

Contents

CONTENTS

Figures and table

Contributors

Sandra Blakely is Assistant Professor of Classics at Emory University in Atlanta, Georgia. She is currently working on a study of the Greek myths of the metallurgical daimones, who were credited with the invention of iron, attendance on the great mother goddess of Anatolia, and the patronage of mystery initiations at Samothrace, Lemnos and Boiotian Thebes. Her work combines anthropological, philological and archaeological data in the study of Greek religion. Publications include 'Smelting and sacrifice', in the *Proceedings of the Conference on Metals in Antiquity*, and 'Myth and models of production', in the SIMA publication of *Trade and Production in Premonetary Greece (VIII)*.

Lois Bragg is Professor of English at Gallaudet University, Washington, DC, where she teaches literature, mythology, and historical linguistics to Deaf undergraduates. She has published widely on Old English and Old Icelandic literature and literacy (including runic literacy), and on disability in medieval Celtic and old Norse literature. She also pursues research in Deaf history and the historical linguistics of signed languages. Her most recent book is *Deaf World: a historical reader and primary sourcebook* (New York University Press, 2000).

Robert A. Brooks is a graduate of the University of Detroit School of Law, and practised as an attorney for a number of years. He obtained an M.A. in Clinical Psychology, and worked as a social worker and counsellor before returning to the American University in Washington, DC to work on a Ph.D. in Sociology, specializing in social stratification and justice issues. His dissertation examines the relationship between civil commitment laws and civil commitment rates across the US, and will include a survey directed to judges and psychiatrists. He has presented papers at a number of conferences in the US and elsewhere.

Patrick J. Devlieger teaches in the Department of Social and Cultural Anthropology at the Katholieke Universiteit Leuven, in Belgium, and is a research professor in the Department of Disability and Human Development at the University of Illinois at Chicago. His research interests include cross-cultural, historical and semiotic analysis of disability. Recent publications include 'Why disabled? the cultural understanding of physical disability in an African society' (1995), 'Physical "disability" in Bantu languages' (1998), 'Mental retardation in American film' (2000), 'Your experience is not my experience: the concept and experience of disability on Chicago's near west side' (with G.L. Albrecht, 2000).

Ruth Gilbert is Lecturer in English at the University of Southampton. Her research focuses on early modern gender, sex, the body and monstrosity. She is co-editor with Erica Fudge and Sue Wiseman of *At the Borders of the Human: beasts, bodies and natural philosophy in the Early Modern period* (Macmillan, 1999). She is currently completing a book, *Early Modern Hermaphrodites: sex and other stories in English culture 1558–1741* (Macmillan, 2001).

Kathryn Hollins has lived briefly in India, France and Cameroon. She trained as a doctor, then undertook an M.Sc. in Medical Anthropology (at University College London) in order to develop her understanding of health within a broad variety of cultural perspectives. Her dissertation was on the meaning of deafness and the use of cochlear implantation in children born deaf. She is now training to be a psychiatrist and plans to specialize in child and adolescent psychiatry. Currently she is conducting full-time research (based at St Ann's Hospital in Haringey, London) into the mental health problems of refugee adolescents in inner city London.

Sheila Hollins is Professor of Psychiatry of Learning Disability at St George's Hospital Medical School, University of London. She is currently a member of the Minister's Advisory Committee on Learning Disability at the Department of Health. From 1994 to 1998 she was Chair of the Executive Committee of the Faculty of Psychiatry of Learning Disability at The Royal College of Psychiatrists. She has many publications on learning disability and mental health. Her particular interests are undergraduate medical education, the post-qualifying education of healthcare professionals, specialist mental health care for people with learning disabilities, and development of the academic infrastructure in learning disability nationally.

Jane Hubert is Senior Research Fellow and Honorary Senior Lecturer in Social Anthropology in the Department of Psychiatry of Disability, St George's Hospital Medical School. Her current research is with men living in a locked ward of an old 'mental handicap' hospital. She has published a number of books arising from her research with families caring for adult children with severe learning disabilities, and with severe head injury. She has also published on issues involved in indigenous claims for the return of ancestral remains, and is currently co-editing another OWA book on this subject. She co-authored *Sacred Sites, Sacred Places* (Routledge, 1994).

Jeanette Hyland worked in Nepal from 1969 to 1995 as Health Services Administrator and Health and Nurse Educator in general health and leprosy control and training. Her doctoral work there examined patients' experience of leprosy, their communities and the role of health workers, using an ethno-medical approach. She returned to the University of Tasmania and taught in the Centre for Research and Learning in Regional Australia. Now semi-retired, she writes, paints, propagates native plants and is active in Green politics. Her interest in cultural perceptions of health and illness, and involvement in leprosy worldwide, continues through The Leprosy Mission Australia.

David Jeffreys is Lecturer in Egyptian Archaeology, Institute of Archaeology, University College London. Current research interests are landscape archaeology and topography of the Nile Valley, especially the region of Memphis, and the history of Egyptian archaeology, especially the work of Joseph Hekekyan (mid-1850s). He regularly directs fieldwork at Memphis. Recent publications include articles on Memphis and related topics in *Mitteilungen des Deutschen Archaologischen Instituts Abteilung Kairo* and *Journal of Egyptian Archaeology*; site reports of excavations at Kom Rabi'a, Memphis; and sources for the Survey, including the Hekekyan manuscripts. He is on the editorial board of *Egyptian Archaeology*, and the *Bulletin of the Egyptian Exploration Society*.

Murray Last is Professor of Anthropology at University College London and co-Director of its Centre for Medical Anthropology. He has been editor of the International African Institute's journal, *AFRICA* since 1986. He first went to Nigeria in 1961 as a post-graduate at University College Ibadan; subsequently he taught at Ahmadu Bello and Bayero Universities, and still runs collaborative research projects with Nigerian colleagues. He published *The Sokoto Caliphate* (1967) and articles on northern Nigerian precolonial history; he also works on traditional health and healing, editing *The Professionalisation of African Medicine* (1986) and a special issue of *Kano Studies* on youth and health (1991).

Eileen M. Murphy is a post-doctoral Research Fellow at Queen's University Belfast. Her Ph.D. focused on a biocultural analysis of Iron Age semi-nomads from south Siberia. Her main research interest is in human osteology and palaeopathology, particularly Irish and prehistoric Russian populations. She is co-editor of *Kurgans, Ritual Sites, and Settlements: the Eurasian Bronze and Iron Age* (BAR International Series, 2000). Recent publications include 'A possible case of hydrocephalus in a medieval child from Doonbought Fort, Co. Antrim, Northern Ireland' (*International Journal of Osteoarchaeology*, 1996) and (as co-author) *Possible Neurofibromatosis in an Individual of the Scythian Period from Tuva, South Siberia* (*International Journal of Osteoarchaeology*, 1998).

John K. Papadopoulos is Associate Curator of Antiquities at the J. Paul Getty Museum in Los Angeles, USA. He is a classical archaeologist interested in many aspects of Aegean and Mediterranean archaeology. He has worked on excavations and surveys in Australia and Greece and was Field Director of the excavations at Torone in northern Greece. He has many publications, and is currently working on the publication of a three volume study on the Early Iron Age in the Athenian Agora. He was Deputy Director of the Australian Archaeological Institute at Athens (1987–1991), and Lecturer in Classical Archaeology at the University of Sydney (1991–1994).

Oyepeju Raji is a Specialist Registrar and Honorary Lecturer in Psychiatry of Disability at St Georges Hospital Medical School, University of London. She carries out research and teaches medical students, junior doctors and other medical professionals. Her clinical work is in a specialist community mental health service for people with learning disabilities who have challenging behaviour. Her main interest is in promoting the mental health of people with learning disabilities and reaching the wider public through clinical, academic and research work. Publications include (with O. Gureje and R. Bamidele) 'Early brain trauma and schizophrenia in Nigerian patients', *American Journal of Psychiatry* (1994).

Charlotte A. Roberts, a former nurse, is a biological anthropologist. She is Reader in Archaeology at the University of Durham, and her main research interest is in biocultural approaches to the history of disease and medicine. Her current work is focused on the infectious diseases in antiquity, and the effects of biological sex, environment, diet and climate on human health. She co-authored *The Archaeology of Disease* (2nd edition, 1995), and is currently completing a book on the antiquity of tuberculosis. She is also co-editing the proceedings of the *Third International Congress on the Evolution and Palaeoepidemiology of Infectious Diseases: the past and present of leprosy.*

John Tait is Edwards Professor of Egyptology at the Institute of Archaeology, University College London. He works chiefly on ancient Egyptian texts and languages, especially Demotic and Coptic. He has published editions of numerous texts, notably in *The Saqqara Demotic Papyri* and *The Carlsberg Papyri*. He has particular interests in the workings of literary and scribal traditions. Recent studies include: 'Demotic literature: forms and genres' in A. Loprieno (ed.) *Ancient Egyptian Literature: history and forms* (Brill, 1996); three chapters in J. Turner (ed.) *The Dictionary of Art*, (Grove, 1996); and (with B. Leach) 'Papyrus' in P. Nicholson and I. Shaw (eds.) *Ancient Egyptian Materials and Industries* (CUP, 2000).

Jonathan N. Tubb is Curator for Syria–Palestine in the Department of the Ancient Near East at the British Museum. He trained in Levantine archaeology at the Institute of Archaeology in London, and began his field career in Syria and Iraq in the 1970s. He has directed excavations on behalf of the Institute and for the British Museum. He is the author of many articles and several books on Levantine archaeology, including the recently published *Canaanites* (British Museum Press, 1998). He lectures internationally and for several years was Program Chair of the American Schools of Oriental Research. He is currently Chairman of the Palestine Exploration Fund.

Tony Waldron is a Consultant Physician at St Mary's Hospital, Paddington, and Visiting Lecturer at the Institute of Archaeology, University College London. His main interests are in palaeopathology and palaeoepidemiology, particularly joint and malignant disease in antiquity and changes in prevalence over time. Difficulties in applying modern epidemiological methods have led him to develop more appropriate methods for use in palaeoepidemiology. He has published many papers on palaeopathology and was awarded a D.Sc. based on his publications. Published books are: *Counting the Dead: the epidemiology of skeletal population* (Wiley & Sons, 1994;); (with J. Rogers) *A Field Guide to Joint Disease in Archaeology* (Wiley & Sons, 1995).

Foreword

One World Archaeology is dedicated to exploring new themes, theories and applications in archaeology from around the world. The series of edited volumes began with contributions that were either part of the inaugural meeting of the World Archaeological Congress in Southampton, UK in 1986 or were commissioned specifically immediately after the meeting – frequently from participants who were inspired to make their own contributions. Since then WAC has held three further major international congresses in Barquisimeto, Venezuela (1990), New Delhi, India (1994), and Cape Town, South Africa (1999); and a series of more specialized Inter-Congresses focusing on: *Archaeological ethics and the treatment of the dead* (Vermillion, USA, 1989); *Urban origins in Africa* (Mombasa, Kenya, 1993), and *The destruction and restoration of cultural heritage* (Brac, Croatia, 1998). In each case these meetings have attracted a wealth of original and often inspiring work from many countries.

The result has been a set of richly varied volumes that are at the cutting edge of – frequently multi-disciplinary – new work. They aim to provide a breadth of perspective that charts the many and varied directions that contemporary archaeology is taking.

As series editors we should like to thank all editors and contributors for their hard work in producing these books. We should also like to express our thanks to Peter Ucko, inspiration behind both the World Archaeological Congress and the One World Archaeology series. Without him none of this would have happened.

Martin Hall, Cape Town, South Africa
Peter Stone, Newcastle, UK
Julian Thomas, Manchester, UK
June 2000

Preface

This book derives from the symposium: *The Archaeology and Anthropology of Madness, Disability and Social Exclusion*, which formed part of the *Mind and Body in Society* symposium at WAC4 in Cape Town, in January 1999. I am very grateful to all the participants, and especially to those who later contributed chapters for this book. I would also like to thank others, including Robert Layton, Michael Rowlands and Peter Ucko, whose wide-ranging and critical contributions added immeasurably to the debate in Cape Town.

The theme of this book is central to the tradition of the *One World Archaeology* (OWA) series, and adds new perspectives to the themes of a number of other books in the series that are concerned with social exclusion and 'domination' in other contexts. Furthermore, it is essentially interdisciplinary, and is not confined to a particular area of the world, nor to one time period. It breaks down traditional academic disciplinary boundaries, and adopts a comparative perspective, demonstrating new approaches to the understanding of why societies incorporate categories of people that other societies exclude. These characteristics place it firmly within the parameters of the OWA series.

I am aware that the terminology used in a few of the chapters is not consistent with current politically correct practices. However, to have changed the terminology in the context of the historical texts and myths would have rendered the chapters incomprehensible; I hope that these chapters will be read without causing offence.

There were many ways, each sensible and defensible, that the chapters could have been ordered, and the last chapter could equally well have been the first.

I am very grateful to Olivia Forge for her help and patience in producing the final manuscript. I am indebted to Peter Ucko for his critical comments on the manuscript and, as always, for his insight, help and support throughout – and for his vision, which was the driving force behind the *One World Archaeology* series.

Jane Hubert, London
May 2000

Introduction: the complexity of boundedness and exclusion

JANE HUBERT

This book focuses on certain categories of people who have been deemed by the majority population, at any one time, to be 'other': those groups of individuals who have been, and are still socially and even physically excluded on the basis of being considered to be 'mad' – whether mentally ill or intellectually disabled[1]; those who have physical disabilities, and those who are perceived as 'deformed' or disfigured. It is not concerned with others who are excluded solely on the basis of their ethnic background, caste or class, religion, occupation, lack of money (i.e. the 'poor') and so on. However, these are not strictly bounded categories, and any discussion of people who are physically and socially excluded from society is bound to incorporate other issues, and be a reminder of the way in which the dominant elements in a society can treat disempowered groups – by marginalizing them, oppressing them or even eliminating them altogether.

Since its conception, the book has developed in diverse and unexpected ways. To begin with, it has become extremely clear that terms such as 'disability', 'madness' and 'mental illness' are, and have been in the past, defined, used and understood in many different ways, or they have not been used at all, depending on the disciplinary traditions and cultures concerned, and the sensitivities involved in the categorizing of people's physical and mental characteristics. Furthermore, when I began work on this book, I had assumed that what archaeologists might have to say about the past of madness, disability and social exclusion would be relatively straightforward, on the assumption that the past would get progressively simpler the further one goes back. But this, too, was an oversimplification of a very complex situation. The chapters in this book, therefore, reflect the subtlety and complexity of this whole field of study.

Over recent decades there has been a growing interdisciplinary body of literature which has investigated the nature and modes of creation of 'otherness', as well as material which has been designated as evidence for 'exclusion'. Anthropologists and archaeologists are among those who have turned their attention to these issues, not least as a result of the earlier writings of such people as Goffman (e.g. 1961, 1963), and Foucault (e.g. 1967, 1974), and their critics (e.g. Scull 1993).

The book investigates both evidence for, and consequences of, the recognition that the criteria given for exclusion of any specific group of people from a society have not been static or unique but changing. It demonstrates that both physical and social exclusion are not recent social developments, nor associated only with literacy, complex societies and state organization. For the first time, perhaps, in a book which aims to be relevant to the contemporary world, it investigates, and shows the relevance of, the evidence for exclusion and inclusion within prehistoric and other societies known only from archaeological remains, texts or iconography.

Some of the chapters present ethnographic material about the present and recent past, documenting cultures and sub-cultures that can be observed and participated in directly. Others seek an answer to the question: what kind of material evidence, whether the location and configuration of an archaeological site, burial or artefact, must be sought and interpreted in order to establish the existence and nature of social exclusions in the past? Other contributors discuss disability and madness in the context of texts and myth.

Evidence from a number of specialist disciplines is brought together here to create a new perspective on social and physical exclusion from society. A range of archaeological, historical, mythical and anthropological evidence throws light on such things as the causes and consequences of social exclusion, stigma, marginality, dangerousness and ritual power of the 'other' in society. In addition, there is discussion of the emotional and intellectual effects of social and/or physical exclusion on those who are subjected to it in contemporary society.

What determines whether an individual or a group is thought of as 'different', and to what extent any such 'difference' results in social exclusion, are two questions that underlie many of the chapters in the book. Last (Ch. 16), describes a culture in Nigeria in which there are many categories of 'excluded' people – but these do not include those people who are physically or intellectually disabled. In this culture the body is believed to be 'housing', and is seen as distinct from the self which lives within it. Thus madness is simply the occupation of the body, and what happens does not reflect upon the individual. In this Nigerian society, unlike in the west, physical disabilities and deformities are accommodated within the social group: the rights and recognition of the self as a full person in the community are unaffected. This is almost the antithesis of British society, for example, in which the body and the mind are inextricably bound up with the 'self'.

Last (Ch. 16) points out the dangers inherent in making assumptions about other cultures on the basis of one's own cultural beliefs, and reiterates the question: what kind of evidence is needed to be able to make statements about the place and role of madness and disability in other cultures, past and present?

The book makes it obvious that who is excluded from society is not an *a priori* category, but arises from a dynamic body of socio-cultural law (see Brooks Ch. 1). Different cultures interpret different things as 'abnormal', different or dangerous – as 'other'. A well-known example is the variation in cultural beliefs about the significance of the birth of twins: according to different cultural belief systems one, or both, or neither should be killed at birth. In this context, day-to-day decisions are not made at random, but are rooted in a range of concepts about dangerousness, spiritual power, good and evil, and the health of the social group (Devlieger Ch. 11). This same theme of dangerousness attributed to 'others' also occurs in several other chapters, but sometimes the message is a complex one. For example, Hubert (Ch. 14), suggests that people who are believed to be 'unknowable', such as those who live in locked wards of mental institutions, and who cannot speak, are often perceived as both vulnerable *and* dangerous. The material from Icelandic myths (Bragg Ch. 9) illuminates a relationship between physical disability and powerfulness, in a mythical world in which lack of physical wholeness does not carry with it the impotence with which it is widely invested in the real world, or, at least, the contemporary world of today. Blakely (Ch. 8), describing a different mythology, suggests that in Greek myth, madness may be constructed through arts, institutions, religious sanction or political act, in order to constrain and contain 'the energies of the uncontrollable', i.e. to render dangerous forces less destructive.

Within a particular society the evidence for social exclusion must be sought in the complexities of social structures, and ethical and legal systems. Brooks' (Ch. 1) comparison of the laws passed to enforce involuntary commitment of people deemed to be 'mad' throughout the world, indicates that such laws arise from various combinations of law and medicine, and are the subject of constant controversy and change. The law with regard to physical exclusion in any society will depend primarily on that culture's conceptions about mental illness and dangerousness, both of which are (to at least some extent) socio-cultural views, rather than inherent in an individual's behaviour.

In all societies some set or sets of individuals are excluded, and this is often assumed to occur in order that the main body of the group can better define itself. As Marks (1999: 153) writes: 'Our sense of citizenship and community is defined by boundaries which demarcate zones of inclusion and exclusion'. Thus, in all social groups there will be a concept of 'otherness'. Whoever is unwanted, for whatever reason, is liable to be labelled by the dominant population as 'other', and when a category is thus formed, it will be vested with a mythology and a set of rules regarding who is to be excluded or not, i.e. who is perceived as the same or different from a culturally defined 'we/us'.

The creation of new categories is a continuing process. Hollins (Ch. 13), for example, shows that current British society is creating a new category of socially excluded children – as a result of an advance in medical technology. Though this technology may marginally improve the functioning of the ear in children born deaf, its use may in fact catapult such children into a social limbo: they will not grow up as part of the Deaf culture nor hear well enough to join the hearing world. This is a graphic example of the misunderstanding between those who seek to reduce 'normality' to one dominant social category, and others who value their own different categories of normality. The relevance and validity of such categories is emphasized by Hollins' report that deaf parents may *prefer* to have a deaf child, rather than a hearing one.

If a group is socially excluded at one point in time, this does not mean that it will necessarily stay excluded, nor that the boundaries are not permeable. In this context it is essential to identify what it is that changes which makes it possible for those who have been excluded to be brought back into the fold. It is not clear, however, whether or not people who have been excluded can always be reintegrated into society. When cultural rules are changed, social attitudes and beliefs do not necessarily keep pace with the changes. Hyland's (Ch. 12) study of leprosy in Nepal, for example, shows that people who are medically cured in western terms do not return to 'social' health or social integration, and she questions whether it is possible to identify the mechanisms that would enable people with leprosy to come back from 'social death'.

In all cultures social and political practices change over time, for various social, moral and/or political reasons. Thus some people who had previously been socially excluded may begin to be incorporated into the wider social group. However, the members of the majority (or dominant) population do not necessarily adapt to such changes. Stigma is an insidious concept, and although there may be social and even individual claims of acceptance of those who have been brought into the fold, stigma and prejudice against them often remains. An example of this, in Britain, is the frequently hostile attitude towards people who move out of institutions into a community environment. They often continue to be stigmatized and, furthermore, are frequently labelled as 'dangerous'.

Even within a family group, people with intellectual disabilities who live as 'part of the family', may nevertheless be excluded from significant family and group rituals, and thus are excluded, at least at some levels, from the category of 'social beings'. Raji and Hollins (Ch. 15) discuss the frequent exclusion of people with intellectual disabilities from funerary rituals, presumably on the assumption that they do not need to have any individual or social right to 'say goodbye', and to internalize their separation from the person who has died. There is a considerable literature (e.g. Davies 1997) to show that death rituals are of supreme importance, and that participation in them is vital for those who are left behind.

The social (and often physical) exclusion of people who are classified as mentally ill, and/or intellectually or physically disabled, is an extreme example of the way in which human beings act in order to separate themselves from those who are considered 'different'. Such exclusion of madness, disability and disease occurs not only because such people (however defined in any particular culture) can be claimed to embody 'difference', but also because such categories threaten everyone throughout their life, from birth to death. At any point an individual can become, or be categorized as, mad, diseased, intellectually or physically impaired, through internal or external trauma, and as a result, may become stigmatized and socially excluded. It could, therefore, be claimed that these socio-cultural reasons for being categorized as 'other' make it more immediate to each one of us than social exclusion based on such things as ethnic or political difference. Of course, the parameters of ethnic and political groups change, either gradually or suddenly, as witnessed in Eastern Europe in recent years. But in these situations it is a group which is put beyond the pale (though it is the individuals who suffer). In the case of acquired madness or disability it is a single individual who is abruptly forced out of one category into another, and moves from being an accepted member of a group to being an isolated 'other' – though this may well implicate a family group as well. Jeffreys and Tait (Ch. 6) suggest that differences apparent at birth may be better tolerated, perhaps because they do not suddenly strike unawares in later life, and are therefore less threatening.

Gilman (1988: 1) suggests that we try to rid ourselves of the fear of our own mental and physical disintegration by locating it in someone else, who we can then separate from us, and say that they are 'other': '[T]he fear we have of our own collapse does not remain internalized. Rather, we project this fear on to the world in order to localize it ... For once we locate it, the fear of our own dissolution is removed'.

In many cultures physical difference may evoke negative reactions, including pity and embarrassment. However, a global 'disability movement' is trying to change this; it has acquired a powerful political voice, which challenges the stereotypes of physically disabled people as helpless and dependent. In this respect such groups of disabled people differ from those who have intellectual disabilities, who may not have the skills to organize campaigning groups, and, as a result, do not often have a voice, and are thus dependent on others to interpret and represent their needs. In fact, many people with severe intellectual disabilities literally have no voice, which is a further reason why they are sometimes perceived as being on the margins of humanity, even animal-like. Bragg (Ch. 9) discusses the blurring of human/animal categories within myth, and discusses the symbolism of a powerful man becoming a stranded seal, impotent and 'unmanly'. Sibley (1995: 27), from another perspective, suggests that 'the relegation of some groups to nature, where they are "naturally" wild, savage, uncivilized, is also expressed in the representation of people as animals' and proposes that 'to dehumanize through claiming animal attributes for others is one way of legitimating exploitation and exclusion from civilized society'. This finds resonances in Hubert's (Ch. 14) description of the way that the dehumanizing process of people living segregated lives in institutions pervades all aspects of their selfhood, and by so doing, propels them further and further into psychological and social states that are perceived negatively by others.

This book reveals that some attributes categorized as 'physical differences' have been perceived and treated as far more than simply abnormalities of the body or lack of physical abilities. Gilbert's (Ch. 10) discussion of hermaphrodites demonstrates how difficult, perhaps impossible, it is (and has been) to come to terms with the concept of a fellow human who does not fall clearly within one of two categories, male and female, into which at least the western world believes itself to be divided. In some respects this is the most extreme example of the 'other', a person who cannot be referred to as either a man or a woman, as 'he' or 'she', 'him' or 'her'. The English language, at least, has no way to tackle this except by using the neutral term 'it', which in English refers to objects or animals, i.e. non-humans.

In the seventeenth and eighteenth centuries, one of the ways of dealing with hermaphrodites was to eroticize them. At this level of analysis little seems to have changed: now, in the twenty-first century, a search for hermaphrodites on the Internet will lead first to pornographic sites, consisting of pictures of 'hermaphrodites' (outwardly female) in erotic poses.

Papadopoulos (Ch. 7) describes the 'invisibility' of social exclusion in the more distant past, but his discovery of socially excluded people buried, not in normal burial grounds, but in wells, suggests that more evidence of social exclusion could be found through a closer consideration of human remains excavated outside community burial grounds. Most of the burials of people with disabling conditions have been found within community burial grounds, but the numbers are relatively small, and not all the disabling conditions that are assumed to have been present in the past appear to be represented. In some cases the correct interpretation of human remains may be vitiated by assumptions about disabilities in the past. It is vital that archaeologists are aware of the possibility of disabled people in burials (Tubb Ch. 5), and that they have the complex skills to correctly identify conditions from detailed studies of bone material (Murphy Ch. 4).

Tubb (Ch. 5) describes Middle Bronze Age burials which suggest that our current western ethnocentric assumptions, that people with disabilities would have been disadvantaged both socially and economically, may be wrong. He also demonstrates that at least some disabled people were buried in the same tombs as other people. However, the conclusions that can be drawn from this about the extent of social and economic advantages or disadvantages that someone had in life, solely from the evidence of their inclusion in death, must remain tentative. In contemporary British society, for example, people living segregated lives in total institutions are no longer buried in mass graves on the hospital site, but in individual graves in community cemeteries (even among the graves of their families). In these circumstances archaeologists of the future will learn nothing about an individual's segregation in life from the location of their burial.

There is considerable evidence in a variety of past cultures in different parts of the world that some people with disabling conditions died and were buried in later life, in spite of the fact that they would have been dependent on others to provide them with food, drink and shelter, and possibly help in moving around. An example from predynastic Egypt is given by Podzorski (1990: 88–89), who describes three individuals with traumatic injury to the femur so severe that they would have been rendered immobile for the rest of their lives, and in one example 'the injury almost certainly occurred when the woman was an older juvenile or young adult, yet she lived to be an old woman and bore more than one child'.

Such an example may suggest that at least one person cared enough about the disabled person to provide the necessary support but, equally, it may indicate that there were certain social rules which dictated whether a person should be supported throughout life or not, rather than this being dependent on the strength of individual relationships. For example, in Britain (and many other countries) there is now a category of 'carers'. These range from people who are paid to deal with someone's physical needs, a kind of 'processing', to the sort of caring for and about someone which is typified by the love and attention given by parents to their children (and by children to their parents). People who live in institutions have 'carers', but many of these may have little or no sympathy for the people they wash and dress and feed. The physical care may be adequate, but emotionally and socially the people cared for may be ignored.

It is difficult to identify the nature of relationships from the evidence of the past, or even to determine the existence and extent of social acceptance. The fact that someone lives within a particular social group is not necessarily an indication that they are really accepted by others. As both Roberts (Ch. 3) and Murphy (Ch. 4) point out, even if people lived within their family or wider social group, there is no way of identifying what people actually felt about them. There is no way to determine, as Dettwyler (1991) has pointed out, whether people in the past felt any 'compassion' for deformed or disabled people.

Discussion about whether carers in the past felt 'compassion' to some extent simply reflects our own ethnocentric prejudices. It cannot be assumed in relation to the past (or even with regard to an unfamiliar contemporary culture) that a society had, or has, any concept of the *need* for compassion for people with disabling conditions. What is perceived as a 'disability' or as 'madness' in one society, in another may be considered as just one attribute among many which make up an individual, or may not be perceived as part of the individual at all. In such circumstances the concept of compassion is irrelevant. Similarly, with regard to pain, it cannot be assumed that past or unfamiliar current cultures have the same pain thresholds as current western ones.

This book makes it clear that it may be possible to identify certain diseases and injuries from skeletal remains, and to speculate on the effects which they may have had on the mobility of the individual; it may also be possible to make certain assumptions about social inclusion or exclusion from the content and location of burials. However, without secondary evidence, there is no foolproof way of identifying social attitudes, or even how people behaved during life – there is only what remains in death. Where and how the bodies of people who were mad or disabled were disposed of will have depended on the wishes of the living. In the context of madness, disability and sickness, the wishes of the living may depend on many complex and conflicting emotions, including relief, guilt, the desire to make amends, to restore the wholeness of the family, and the wish to remember – or to forget.

Obviously, the source of material about past practices and beliefs is not always limited to burials. Often there is secondary evidence, such as iconography and texts (Papadopoulos, Ch. 7; Waldron, Ch. 2), to extend and illuminate the knowledge of madness and disability in the past. To some extent, of course, the interpretation of the past as portrayed in words and iconography is also coloured by current attitudes and beliefs. For example, in the interpretation of ancient texts, it is often the case that the meaning of words is not known, nor how much the denotation and connotation of terms used have changed over time. Furthermore, there is often insufficient information about the social context of the distant past to be able to interpret what was written and portrayed. This is also relevant to the interpretation of the relatively recent past – less than a century ago in Britain, for example, concepts of mental illness and intellectual disability carried with them such attributes as promiscuity, criminality and moral degeneracy. As Last (Ch. 16) points out, 'social categories vary over time even within a single community; our own past can be "another country"'. Last suggests that it should be the task of ethnography to record the present in order to provide future generations with contemporary interpretations of concepts such as madness, disability and social exclusion.

Even today, concepts, definitions and interpretations are changing continuously, sometimes in leaps and bounds, but perhaps more often almost imperceptibly. Future generations will inevitably encounter problems in the construction of the social context of twenty-first century material culture, and in the identification and interpretation of 'madness' and disability both in their present and past. However, this book is the first to examine this whole area diachronically, synchronically and comparatively. It is hoped that it will stimulate a fresh approach to the understanding of the context and conditions of those who are excluded from society, for whatever 'reasons', past and present.

ACKNOWLEDGEMENT

I am extremely grateful to Peter Ucko for his constructive criticism of this Introduction.

NOTE

1 The term 'intellectual disability' is used throughout the book. It is the least offensive term which can be used, and will also be understood in different parts of the world, to refer to people variously described as having learning disabilities, mental handicap, mental retardation, mental impairment or intellectual impairment.

REFERENCES

Davies, J.D. 1997. *Death, Ritual and Belief: the rhetoric of funerary rites*. London: Cassell.
Dettwyler, K.A. 1991. Can paleopathology provide evidence for 'compassion'? *American Journal of Physical Anthropology* 84, 375–84.
Foucault, M. 1967. *Madness and Civilization: a history of insanity in the age of reason*. London: Tavistock Publications Ltd.
Foucault, M. 1974. *The Order of Things: archaeology of the human sciences*. London: Tavistock.
Gilman, S. 1988. *Disease and Representation: images of illness from madness to AIDS*. Ithaca, New York: Cornell University Press.
Goffman, E. 1961. *Asylums: essays on the social situation of mental patients and other inmates*. London: Penguin Books.
Goffman, E. 1963. *Stigma: notes on the management of spoiled identity*. New Jersey: Prentice Hall.
Marks, D. 1999. *Disability: controversial debates and psychosocial perspectives*. London: Routledge.
Podzorski, P.V. 1990. *Their Bones shall not Perish: an examination of human skeletal remains from Naga-ad-Dar in Egypt*. New Malden: SIA.
Scull, A. 1993. *The Most Solitary of Afflictions: madness and society in Britain 1700–1900*. New Haven and London: Yale University Press.
Sibley, D. 1995. *Geographies of Exclusion: society and difference in the west*. London: Routledge.

1 Official madness: a cross-cultural study of involuntary civil confinement based on 'mental illness'

ROBERT A. BROOKS

Involuntary commitment[1] laws usually contain two components, first that the person in question be diagnosed with a 'mental illness',[2] and second that they either: (a) pose a danger to themselves or others, (b) are in need of treatment, or (c) cannot see to their basic necessities of life. Involuntary commitment laws are said to serve three social functions: protection of society ('police power'), looking after the patient's 'own good' (*parens patriae*), and meeting people's basic needs ('custodial confinement') (Stromberg and Stone 1983: 279–80).

Involuntary commitment laws exist at the crossroads of two potent social forces, law and medicine, and are the subject of constant controversy. Terms such as 'mental illness' and 'dangerousness' are social constructs arising from political arguments among various constituencies regarding the classification of deviant behaviours. Involuntary commitment laws in different jurisdictions[3] thus reflect a wide variety of conceptions about mental illness, and offer different justifications for incarcerating the 'mentally ill'. However, the effect of differing wordings of involuntary commitment laws is not clear because various extra-legal factors may 'trump' the intentions behind carefully worded statutes.

THE MEDICAL MODEL AND 'MENTAL DISORDER'

During the modern age the field of medicine has attained a monopoly over the assessment and treatment of mental illness (Foucault 1965). The 'medical model' of mental illness claims that psychological disorders are 'sicknesses'; mental illness is seen as an objective disorder arising within the person that may be diagnosed and treated (or cured) through therapeutic intervention (Sanua 1994). The first psychiatric classification system of mental disorders was developed just over 100 years ago (Murthy and Wig 1993: 388). Since then, diagnostic manuals have been subject to continuous revision; new disorders are identified and old ones put to rest (Aderibigbe and Pandurangi 1995). Such revisions are ostensibly grounded in medical 'science'; however, the debate over some disorders reflects more the socio-cultural environment of psychiatric practice. For example, in 1973, members of the American Psychiatric Association (APA), after several years of highly charged discussions, voted to remove homosexuality from the Association's list of mental disorders (Greenberg 1997). Some saw the decision as a reversal of the inappropriate inclusion of homosexuality in the first place, while others contended that psychiatry had caved in to political demands of 'activists' (Bayer 1987). Other battles have been waged over such diagnoses as 'passive–aggressive syndrome' (Wetzler and Morey 1998), 'premenstrual syndrome' (Lorber 1997), and 'attention-deficit hyperactivity disorder' (Searight and McLaren 1998).

Typically, psychiatry defines mental disorder as arising in the individual; Wakefield's (1997, 1992a, 1992b) definition of 'harmful dysfunction' and Ossorio's (1985) 'inability to engage in deliberate action' are two prominent models. Wakefield (1992a) distinguishes six other accounts of mental disorder: the sceptical anti-psychiatric view, the value approach, the idea that disorder is whatever professionals treat, two scientific approaches (statistical deviance and biological disadvantage), and the operational definition of disorder as 'unexpected distress or disability'. The two major contemporary psychiatric classification systems – the Diagnostic and Statistical Manual of Mental Disorders (currently the DSM-IV) (American Psychiatric Association (APA) 1994) and the International Classification of Diseases (currently the ICD-10) (World Health Organization (WHO) 1992) – define and explain a multitude of specific syndromes, illnesses, and disorders.

Yet the broader concepts of 'mental illness' or 'mental disorder' are not fixed psychiatric definitions. The DSM-IV recognizes that 'no definition adequately specifies precise boundaries for the concept of "mental disorder"'. However, mental disorder is broadly conceptualized as a clinically significant behavioural or psychological syndrome that is associated with present distress, disability, or with an increased risk of suffering death, pain, disability, or an important loss of freedom (APA 1994: xxi). Such dysfunction must occur in the individual; a disturbance limited to conflict between the individual and society is not in itself a mental disorder (APA 1994: xxi–xxii; Bennett 1986: 80–1).

The reasons for the ascendance of the 'medical model' are complex and outside the scope of this chapter. However, it is worth noting that psychiatric explanations of mental illness came to predominate long before psychiatry had offered any explanations for the causes of mental illness or developed any successful treatments for it (Conrad and Schneider 1980). Thus, some (e.g. Foucault 1965; Conrad and Schneider 1980) conclude that the early rise of the medical model was more a social and political phenomenon than a medical one.

THE SOCIAL CONSTRUCTION OF MENTAL DISORDER

Every known society employs some conception of 'madness' (Conrad and Schneider 1980: 38). However, societies differ – culturally, contextually, and temporally, as to their conceptions of exactly what constitutes madness (Lillard 1998), what causes madness, and what ought to be done with the mad (Conrad and Schneider 1980).

For example, while there is wide consensus as to the core symptoms of schizophrenia (Brislin 1993; Draguns 1990), other disorders are 'culture-bound' (Hughes *et al.* 1996). These include *susto* in Latin America (typified by extreme anxiety, restlessness and fear of Black Magic) (Castro and Eroza 1998), *taijin-kyofusho* in Japan (marked by social anxiety, easy blushing, and fear of eye contact) (Kleinknecht *et al.* 1997), and anorexia and bulimia in western (or westernized) cultures (DiNicola 1990).

In fact, a medical explanation is only one of many possible axes on which to place mental illness (Siegler and Osomond 1966: 1193–203). During the 1960s and 1970s 'sociogenic' factors began to be emphasized over 'egocentric' ones (Murthy and Wig 1993: 395), leading to 'bio-psycho-social' models of mental illness. Adding to this shift is increasing recognition of promoting mental health, rather than simply treating mental illness (Desjarlais *et al.* 1995). Under these models, the psychiatrist is viewed as one of several people on a treatment team (Symonds 1998). However, some perceive a 'new medicalization' of mental illness over the past few years (Zaumseil 1998).

The socio-cultural view conceptualizes mental disorder as usually identified with behaviours that are bizarre, irrational, or unusually distressful (Mechanic 1999). Under the social view, mental illness cannot be said to arise in persons' behaviours, as such; rather, mental illness is a 'quality' attributed to persons and behaviours by others (Conrad and Schneider 1980). The 'social' view of madness is not altered by consideration of biological 'causes' of mental disease. Illness does not exist in nature (Sedgwick 1973); rather, illness is a negative human value judgement of objectively neutral conditions. Under this view, psychiatrists do not classify diseases or disorders; rather, they classify 'the kinds of problems which psychiatrists currently deal with' (Kendall 1988: 339). Also, the fact that there is widespread agreement at a certain place and time as to the nature of a particular illness does not change the fact that illness is a judgement; it only obscures the process of consensus (Conrad and Schneider 1980: 31). This is so even without recognizing that mental illness may have sociogenic causes as well as social definitions.

Some critics of psychiatry, notably Szasz (1974a, 1974b), go a bit further, claiming that 'mental illness', as such, is a 'myth', a social construction designed for the control of individuals deemed socially deviant. Szasz acknowledges that personal suffering exists, and that people should be afforded treatment when they request it. However, Szasz emphasizes the harmful effects of the labelling process – the means by which certain people or groups of people are determined to be disordered or deviant – and argues that it is essentially political (Szasz 1974b, 1963). Because labelling is a political process, labels ultimately reflect the view of the dominant social institutions and forces. When the Church was the pre-eminent institution, mental illness was considered punishment for sin (Conrad and Schneider 1980: 41–42). In contemporary society, mental illness is a medical affliction.

CIVIL COMMITMENT: LEGALIZED EXCLUSION OF THE MENTALLY ILL

Notwithstanding the wide variety of cultural conceptions of mental illness, almost all cultures have viewed mental illness as a deviant form, subject to negative social sanctions. The mentally ill are viewed as 'the other' (Foucault 1965). This has been true whether mental illness has been explained by sin, possession by spirits, heredity, or bio-physiological factors (Simon 1992). Even in the relatively sophisticated western world at the end of the twentieth century, the mentally ill remain highly stigmatized and subject to discrimination (Sayce 1998). Media portrayals misrepresent mental illness, falsely depict the mentally ill as violent, and 'poke fun' at mental illness in ways that would be unthinkable of 'physical' illness (Wahl 1995; Philo et al. 1996).

While the mentally ill have been socially excluded in most societies, physical exclusion is a phenomenon of the modern age (Foucault 1965). Beginning in the 1700s in the West, in what has been dubbed the 'First Wave', states enacted involuntary commitment laws, incarcerating mental deviants alongside convicted criminals, and treating alike 'idiots', 'lunatics', and those found to be 'of unsound mind'. The focus was on the preservation of law and order, and treatment was non-existent or minimal (Conrad and Schneider 1980).

Later, in the 'Second Wave' of reforms, separate asylums for the mentally ill were constructed, and various 'treatments' were offered for the first time (Noble 1981: 17). The asylum system remained dominant until the middle of the twentieth century, when, in response to a number of factors (including the introduction of powerful medications, public outcry over asylum conditions, and fiscal motivations), states began to shift treatment from asylums to community mental health centres, at least in theory (e.g. Curran and Harding 1978: 44 (generally); Burti and Benson 1996 (Italy); Bottomley 1987 (New South Wales)). However, the legacy of physical exclusion remains, as many communities object to placing the mentally ill in their midst (Sayce 1998). This 'Third Wave' of reforms saw major substantive and procedural revisions to involuntary commitment statutes. In the United States, California was the first to enact reform legislation, in 1968; most other states followed shortly thereafter. Diagnostic categories were sharpened; for example, those with epilepsy, mental retardation, dementia, and other 'organic' brain disorders were now categorized and treated differently from those with 'mental illness', and, in some cases, more specific, legalistic criteria further delineating 'mental illness' were developed and introduced (Curran and Harding 1978: 35). More significantly, many of the new involuntary commitment laws changed involuntary commitment requirements by eliminating the 'need for treatment' standard, leaving only the 'dangerousness' standard, and perhaps the 'disability' criterion as well.

However, the greater focus of reforms – Gostin (1983) calls this the 'new legalism'– was in regard to procedural rights rather than being concerned with substantive changes. The new laws guaranteed the right to a judicial hearing, to appointed counsel, and to an appeal. Similar changes were instituted in other western jurisdictions. However, the procedural reforms may have had limited effect, as many of the substantive decisions remained with medical personnel (Gostin 1983). Many claim that these reforms resulted in dramatic increases in the homeless mentally ill, and the diversion of many mentally ill into the criminal justice system (Miller 1992a; Bonovitz and Bonovitz 1981). In response, some jurisdictions in recent years have re-instituted a 'need for treatment' basis in their involuntary commitment statutes (Miller 1992b).

Most developing countries were left out of the Third Wave. Many did not have mental health laws to begin with. Others inherited the antiquated laws of their colonial forebears. In many cases, such laws remain in effect today while having been repealed and replaced in the colonizing country. Many Asian countries particularly have been slow to adopt mental health legislation. Taiwan's law was first submitted in 1983, and became law in 1990 (Salzberg 1993: 171). China and Thailand have no involuntary commitment law; nevertheless, compulsory admissions take place in those countries (Pearson 1996 (China); Soothill et al. 1981 (Thailand)). Chinese families are willing to endure great hardship to avoid committing a family member. However, once the family identifies a member as 'crazy', the decision is sealed (Pearson 1996: 452).

Many middle-eastern countries also do not have involuntary commitment laws (Curran and Harding 1978) but operate under similar 'informal systems' of compulsory admission, wherein the patient's family acts as the social control agents, rather than the state or psychiatrists. Curran and Harding (1978: 20) identified twelve of the forty-three countries they surveyed as having no involuntary commitment law. Eight of the twelve were countries in the eastern Mediterranean region. In most such countries, the stigma of mental illness is very strong, and psychiatric hospitalization affects the family very directly (for example, single women with known psychiatric histories are not 'marriageable'). Given these strong cultural forces, it is not surprising that state involvement with psychiatry is strictly limited.

Maintenance of a separate legislative framework for those considered mentally disordered is difficult to justify (Campbell and Heginbotham 1991; Szasz 1963). Such disparate treatment only serves to institutionalize 'society's unfounded prejudice and fear regarding madness' (Campbell and Heginbotham 1991, in Symonds 1998: 949). The 'dangerousness' justification is particularly weak. Monahan (1992) points out that the mentally ill are less dangerous than other groups within society (such as young disadvantaged males). However, such systems are now deeply ingrained and have achieved 'taken for granted' status.

STATUTORY DEFINITIONS OF MENTAL ILLNESS

One of the basic functions of any mental health law is to define mental illness (Salzberg 1993: 174). Such a task is obviously not a simple one. However, law, as a normative science, requires a definition (Kruger 1980: 50). Definitions serve at least three important functions: they guide the relevant decision-makers, provide notice to those possibly subject to the statute, and affect public confidence in the legal system (Rees 1993/4: 23).

In nearly every jurisdiction, legal definitions of 'mental illness' differ from psychiatric diagnostic criteria. This can be explained by the divergent purposes of law and medicine. Within a jurisdiction's laws, there may actually be several definitions. For example, the definition of 'insanity' in a criminal trial is very different from the definitions of 'mental illness' for the purpose of civil commitment or for determining work disability. The goal of psychiatry, on the other hand, is much broader: to identify and then to treat all individuals who appear to be suffering from mental disorders. Ostensibly, the goal of the law is threefold: to protect the interests of 'society' against 'dangerous' persons, to offer treatment and prevent suicide (in many jurisdictions, attempting suicide is a criminal act), and to make provisions for the care of those who cannot care for themselves. In western countries, these aims are balanced against the individual's claim to liberty. Thus, under the law, a diagnosis of 'mental disorder' is insufficient to establish mental illness (APA 1994: xxiii), while a court finding of 'insanity' or 'mental illness' may not be consistent with any classified psychiatric disorder (Errington 1987).

Involuntary commitment laws have dealt with the challenges of defining mental illness in one of four ways. Many offer a broadly worded, vague, or tautological definition. Some use a definition based on scientific or quasi-scientific criteria; others provide no definition at all, and a rare few directly incorporate psychiatric classification systems.

No definition

Early involuntary commitment laws did not define mental illness, due perhaps to the undeveloped state of psychiatric classification systems, or as some (e.g. Briscoe 1968) contend, to the existence of a 'commonsense' understanding of the types of people subject to such laws. Pakistan's 1912 Lunacy Act was typical in its failure to define 'lunacy'. (A new mental health act proposed in 1992 still contains no definition of mental illness, as well as no standards for civil commitment) (Yousaf 1997: 299–300).

Most contemporary involuntary commitment laws contain some definition of mental illness. However, a few, such as The Northern Territories and Queensland, Australia; Uruguay (see Moncada 1994), and the USA states of California and Pennsylvania, do not. Queensland's then Minister of Health explained the omission when introducing that state's Mental Health Act:

> The question of mental illness is not decided on whether a person can be given a certain diagnostic label. *Mental illness can refer to any degree of mental or emotional defect or aberration, whether from physical or psychological causes.* Whether the provisions of the Act should apply depends on a medical assessment of the nature and degree of the disorder, and its effects on the person and on other people. (Queensland Parliamentary Debates (emphasis supplied))
>
> (Errington 1987: 185)

The United Nations 'Principles for the Protection of Persons with Mental Illness and for the Improvement of Mental Health Care' (UN Principles)[4] provide, among other things, a set of involuntary commitment standards. They do not, however, define mental illness, providing only that the determination of mental illness should be made according to 'internationally accepted medical standards' (UN Principle 4(1)). An earlier version had defined mental illness as 'a disturbance of thought, mood, volition, perception, orientation, or memory which impairs judgement or behaviour to a significant extent'. Rees (1993–94: 30) notes that there are no 'internationally accepted medical standards' defining mental illness, and finds it 'regrettable' that the final version is so inconclusive.

Broad, circular, or vague definitions

Some early involuntary commitment laws did provide definition of mental illness; however, they were vague, broad, or tautological. For example, South Africa's Cape Lunacy Act (1891) defined an insane person as also being an 'idiot' and a 'mentally defective person'. The succeeding law, the 1916 Mental Disorders Act, listed seven categories of insane persons. However, the 'umbrella clause' defined a 'mentally disordered person' as any person 'suffering from mental disorder' (Kruger 1980: 48). The Indian Lunacy Act of 1912 (which is still in effect) defines a 'lunatic' as 'an idiot or person of unsound mind' (Mestrovic 1986: 431). Tautological definitions were also found in the laws of New South Wales (see Durham 1988; Errington 1987), Tasmania (Mental Health Act 1963, §4(1)) and Victoria (Mental Health Act 1959, §3).

Unfortunately, many contemporary statutes retain imprecise language that is infinitely flexible. Some state courts in the United States have struck down statutory definitions as unconstitutionally vague, including those contained in the laws of Arkansas ('any person [who is] an idiot, lunatic, or of unsound mind'), Colorado ('of such a mental condition that he is in need of medical supervision, treatment, care or restraint'), and Texas ('person whose mental health is substantially impaired') (Stromberg and Stone 1983: 313). England's current law broadly defines 'mental disorder' as 'mental illness, arrested or incomplete development of mind, psychopathic disorder and any other disorder or disability of mind ...' (Mental Health Act 1983, §1(2)). 'Mental illness' itself is not defined, and 'psychopathic disorder' is defined very broadly as 'a persistent disorder or disability of mind ... which results in abnormally aggressive or seriously irresponsible conduct on the part of the person concerned'. New York's Mental Hygiene Law provides a circular definition of mental illness as 'an affliction with a mental disease ... *to such an extent that* the person afflicted requires care, treatment and rehabilitation' (34A McKinney's Consol. Laws of New York, §1.03(20), emphasis supplied).[5] 'Mental disease' is not defined.

Higher specificity does not necessarily lead to 'better' laws. The involuntary commitment law of British Columbia, Canada, defines 'mentally ill person' as 'a person who is suffering from a disorder of the mind that seriously impairs the person's ability to react appropriately to his or her environment and to associate with others' (R.S.B.C. 1979, c. 256, §1). However, the terms 'disorder of the mind', 'appropriately', and 'seriously impair' are not defined and are subject to broad interpretation and potential abuse. Ironically, the USSR is credited with having had perhaps the most precise definition of mental illness (Heginbotham 1987: 2). Thus, someone with a genuine mental illness might have been well served by the Soviet system; however, Soviet psychiatrists also 'treated' 'perfectly ordinary sane' people (Heginbotham 1987: 2). Opposition to the Soviet system was considered in itself an indication of mental illness, and diagnoses such as 'sluggish schizophrenia' were used to shut away political dissidents (Bonnie 1990; Bloch and Reddaway 1984, 1987).

Such abuses are not limited to totalitarian nations. Japan's involuntary commitment law has been sharply criticized for its alleged lack of attention to human rights (Salzberg 1991: 137). In the USA, a relatively recent phenomenon is the enactment of statutes governing 'sexual predators'. Minnesota's law allows commitment of persons identified as possessing a broadly defined 'psychopathic personality'. Such a person may be held for an indefinite period but need not be found to suffer from a mental illness of any kind (Erlinder 1993: 100).

Psychiatric or quasi-psychiatric definitions

The law of the state of Utah (USA) is perhaps unique in its explicit incorporation of a psychiatric diagnostic manual to define mental illness, defining mental illness as any disorder in the current DSM 'which substantially impairs a person's mental, emotional, behavioural or related functioning' (Utah Code Ann. §64-7-28 (Supp. 1981)). (As noted below, a similar definition was created in California through court decision.)

More typical are laws that set out certain psychiatric symptomatology as conditions for the existence of mental illness. Such definitions typically contain three parts. The first requires the existence of a mental disorder (whether termed an 'impairment', 'abnormal state of mind', or 'psychiatric illness'). Second, such disorder must affect some aspect of the person's psyche (including thought, mood, perception, orientation, memory, emotion, control, or volition). Third, the disorder must 'grossly impair' or 'substantially interfere with' a person's functioning (this may involve judgment, thinking, feeling, behaviour, capacity to recognize reality, reasoning and understanding, or meeting the ordinary demands of life).[6]

Some involuntary commitment laws limit mental illness strictly to psychosis. However, 'psychosis' is frequently undefined or ill defined. Japan's 1987 law defines a 'mentally disordered person' as 'a psychotic person or a psychopathic person' (Salzberg 1993: 175, n. 61). Neither 'psychotic' nor 'psychopathic' are further defined. Denmark's law is more ambiguous, authorizing commitment of persons who are psychotic or whose states of mind 'are analogous to psychosis' (Vestergaard 1994: 194).

Other laws emphasize psychotic symptomatology, but frequently include nonpsychotic measures as well. Israel's 1991 law defines mentally ill persons as those who are 'suffering from an illness as a result of which their capacity for judgement or for assessment of reality is severely impaired' (Bar El et al. 1998). Only the second half of this definition would arguably define a psychotic symptom. The law of the Australian

Capital Territory is much more specific, defining a 'psychiatric illness' as including any of the following: delusions, hallucinations, serious disorder of thought form, or a severe disturbance of mood (Mental Health (Treatment and Care) Act 1994, §4). New South Wales has a similar provision (Mental Health Act 1990, Sch. 1). Only the first three symptoms are characteristic of psychosis.

Defining who is not mentally ill

Some legislation, in addition to defining what mental illness is, also declares what it is not. Such limitations fall into three categories. The first is the separation of certain mental disorders, such as dementia or mental retardation, from mental illnesses, as discussed above. This limitation is arguably the most 'medical' one, as it was motivated largely by differing treatment needs of various mental conditions. The second regards the more socio-cultural question of whether such 'deviant' behaviours as alcohol and drug abuse constitute 'mental illness'.[7]

The third category has a human rights focus, with the aim of protecting people who hold unpopular views or engage in deviant behaviours. The exclusions in the UN Principles are one example; they exclude consideration of a person's political, economic, or social status as well as the person's 'non-conformity with community moral or political values or religious beliefs' in diagnosing 'mental illness' (UN Principles 4(1)–(3)). The laws of several Australian jurisdictions provide similar limitations, as does Russia's new law (Polubinskaya and Bonnie 1996: 157). The involuntary commitment laws of The Australian Capital Territory and New South Wales also preclude courts from considering a person's sexual orientation, and certain immoral or illegal behaviours, such as sexual promiscuity and alcohol or drug abuse, which England's law also excludes (Mental Health Act 1983, §1(3); Mental Health (Treatment and Care) Act 194 (ACT), §5; Mental Health Act 1990 (NSW), §11(1)).

Other criteria: 'dangerousness', 'disability' and 'need for treatment'

As discussed above, a finding of mental illness is a necessary but insufficient ground for civil commitment. A further finding – usually either 'dangerousness'[8] or 'grave disability' – is required (Ross et al. 1996). Some statutes, such as New York's, add a 'need for treatment' ground as well. New Zealand's 1992 law is slightly different, providing a 'one-step' process. A finding of 'mental disorder' rests upon quasi-scientific criteria as well as a determination of either dangerousness or need for treatment (Rogers 1994: 404). Thus, without a finding of dangerousness or need for treatment, a person is not deemed 'mentally ill'.

The typical measure of 'dangerousness' is whether the person is 'reasonably expected to inflict serious physical harm upon himself or herself or another in the near future' (405 Illinois Compiled Statutes Annotated 5/1–119 §§1, 2 (1997)).[9]

However, laws may differ as to four particulars: (1) the specificity of danger, (2) the level of proof, (3) the putative object of the danger and (4) whether the criterion is worded as protecting the patient or preventing harm. For example, some laws (e.g. New South Wales (Mental Health Act 1990 (NSW), §9(1)), Ontario (Canada) (Mental Health Act, §32), and Germany (see Rössler *et al.* 1996: 405)) require a 'clear' showing of danger, as opposed to the standard burden of proof ('more likely than not'). Other laws, such as those of Florida and Pennsylvania, require proof of recent violent acts or threats (Fla. Stat. Ann. §394.467(1) (Supp. 1997); 50 Penn. Stat. §7301(b)(1), (2)). Japan has enacted a very detailed set of requirements, by regulation. However, some of the acts listed therein include seemingly minor offences such as eating at a restaurant without paying (Salzberg 1991: 150). Last, some laws contemplate a wider view of potential 'victims'. The laws of the Netherlands (Smit 1987: 254) and Japan (Salzberg 1991) consider possible danger 'to the public order'.

The dangerousness criterion has been widely criticized as overly broad and utterly unrealistic (Mestrovic 1986; Rogers 1994). Even when there is conceptual agreement as to the meaning of 'dangerousness', psychiatric predictions are highly unreliable. Mestrovic (1986) makes the analogy between the western model's prediction of dangerousness and the Indian idea of possession by demons. Both cases involve 'magic', Mestrovic (1986: 447–8) claims, because

> these phenomenon cannot be "observed", predicted or exorcised. "Dangerousness" is constrained by chemical means in the West and "possession" by chains in India – both means have been criticized as being inhumane, at least in part. The "treatment" for either affliction is unscientific.

While the 'dangerousness' criterion is the one most subject to debate and controversy, the far more common involuntary commitment justification, at least in the United States, is disability. California is one of many jurisdictions that provide for commitment of the mentally ill if they are 'gravely disabled', meaning 'unable to provide for . . . basic personal needs for food, clothing, or shelter' (Cal. Welf. and Inst. Code §5008(h)(1)). A review (Turkheimer and Parry 1992: 647) of seven studies found that more than three-quarters of persons who were involuntarily committed were committed on the basis of disability.[10]

THE RISKS OF VAGUENESS

In the absence of clear legislative direction the power to define mental illness devolves to one of three decision-makers: administrative agencies, courts, or psychiatrists. (In turn, any of the three may defer to one of the others.) The California courts, in the absence of a statutory definition of mental disorder, have held that the term includes all those disorders contained in the DSM (*Estate of Chambers*, 71 Cal. App. 3d 277, 139

Cal. Rptr. 357 (1977)). The result is a definition of mental disorder that is much broader than that of most jurisdictions.

However, the ruling of the California court is atypical. In jurisdictions with a common law history, courts have been more likely to defer to a 'lay definition' of mental illness. Such is the case in England (Errington 1987) and most of Australia (Hogget 1990). Expert opinion is frequently introduced and considered as well. This 'commonsense' approach has been termed the 'man-must-be-mad' test and arises from a famous English case, in which the court ruled:

> [O]rdinary words of the English language should be construed in the way that ordinary sensible people would construe them. [Therefore] I ask myself what would the ordinary sensible person have said about [the respondent's condition and behaviour]? In my judgement such a person would have said: 'Well, that fellow is obviously mentally ill'.
>
> (*W v. L*, 1 Q.B. 711 (1974), in Errington 1987: 184)

This test may have a certain 'natural' appeal; however, there are dangers in relying on 'commonsense' conceptions of mental illness. First, it is possible that there is not a single 'commonsense' agreement as to what constitutes mental illness. Research has shown that lay conceptions of mental illness differ widely based upon such factors as education, socio-economic status, exposure to the mentally ill, and place of residence (i.e. urban versus rural) (Murthy and Wig 1993: 392). Second, there is the real possibility that judges and juries will decide to commit the merely peculiar rather than the truly mentally ill. Behaviour which is 'abnormal' or even extremely repulsive should not be a determining factor in finding mental illness. In addition, members of minority racial and ethnic groups, and the lower classes, may endure higher rates of commitment because of the majority's ignorance or prejudice. Warren (1979: 359) concluded that 'persons involuntarily committed to mental hospitals tend to be lower class and to have engaged in annoying behaviours rather than criminal activity'. The majority may attribute 'elevated perceptions of dangerousness' to members of certain groups, such as young black men in Britain (Symonds 1998: 951). In parts of London, the rate of emergency detention is significantly higher for Afro-Caribbeans than for whites (Bean *et al.* 1991), and in Great Britain as a whole, the proportion of Afro-Caribbeans increases at each successive point in the mental health system.

At the same time, leaving the determination of mental illness solely in the hands of psychiatrists presents other problems. Doctors' opinions may go unchallenged, as there is no 'check' on their authority (Heginbotham 1987). More generally, 'medicalization' of mental illness tends to ignore social, familial, and biological origins; thus, non-psychiatric treatment options – and the involvement of other professionals – may be thwarted (Symonds 1998). Rogers (1994) and Høyer (1988) argue that psychiatrists are unable to appreciate that their interventions may not be wanted, and therefore do not balance their patients' competing interests. Commentators in various jurisdictions, including Denmark (Vestergaard 1994), Israel (Levy 1992), Norway (Høyer 1988), and Russia (Polubinskaya and Bonnie 1996) have criticized the broad discretion afforded psychiatrists.

WHAT *SHOULD* MENTAL ILLNESS MEAN?

There is surprisingly little commentary regarding the meaning of 'mental illness' in mental health legislation (Arrigo (1993) analysed the multiple meanings given to mental illness by the appellate court in the USA). Two notable exceptions are a number of analyses of various laws in Australia (e.g. Rees 1993/94; Bottomley 1989; Durham 1988; Errington 1987; Briscoe 1968) and a great deal of commentary criticizing the politicization of mental illness in the former Soviet Union (e.g. Bloch and Reddaway 1984, 1987; Bonnie 1990). The only large-scale international studies of compulsory admission practices (Curran and Harding 1978; World Health Organization 1955) paid little attention to legislative definitions of mental illness *per se*. Curran and Harding (1978: 34–38) devote less than four pages of their 161-page report to statutory definitions of mental illness, and the WHO (1955) study about two pages. Most of Curran and Harding's discussion concerns whether 'special categories', such as alcoholism or drug abuse, are included in involuntary commitment legislation.

Some (e.g. Ellard 1990) suggest that a suitable definition is practically impossible. However, most commentators who have addressed the question (e.g. Rees 1993/94; Bennett 1986; Stromberg and Stone 1983) advocate a narrow definition, as have some administrative agencies, including Britain's Department of Health and Social Services (Peng et al. 1994: 21). However, justifications vary. Some (e.g. Rees 1993/94; Bennett 1986) are concerned that a broadly-worded definition inappropriately encourages the 'medicalization' of deviant (criminal) behaviour. Others are motivated by civil liberties concerns. Stromberg and Stone (1983: 313) support the restricted definition of 'severe mental disorder' in the APA's model law (which they claim 'corresponds roughly to a psychotic disorder') because of the 'serious social decision that underlies commitment'. Others support a stringent definition (or the abolition of involuntary commitment altogether), because of the questionable benefits of forced treatment (Høyer 1988: 300–1).

DO DEFINITIONS MATTER?

In the midst of continuing controversy over the content of involuntary commitment laws, some researchers have asked what effects, if any, do differences in, or changes to, the specific wording of involuntary commitment statutes have on actual clinical populations (whether measured by increases or decreases in overall populations, changes in the ratio of voluntary to involuntary admittees, or the numbers of mentally ill persons in the prison population). Such studies (e.g. Ross et al. 1996; Peters et al. 1987; Applebaum 1984) have typically examined the effects of differences in the 'dangerousness' and 'need for treatment' standards. However, it appears that no research has been conducted regarding the effect on patient populations of differing definitions of mental illness.

A study by Ross *et al.* (1996) is illustrative. The researchers set out to compare the relative 'strictness' of states' involuntary commitment laws in the USA. They considered only two components: (1) whether the 'dangerousness' or 'gravely ill' standard, or both, were required to commit, and (2) what level of evidence was required to prove the foregoing. Differing definitions of mental illness were not considered; the only reference to a diagnosis of mental illness was that it was a component of all state statutes (Ross *et al.* 1996: 346).

Other research suggests that cultural norms as to what 'mental illness' is, or what 'ought to be done' with the mentally ill may be deeply imbedded and relatively impervious to change through legislative manipulation. For example, in many cultures, such as those of India, China, Japan, and Singapore, the family often decides where and when (or if) a mentally ill member receives psychiatric intervention. Less savoury cultural pressures, such as the profit-driven private hospital system in Japan, concerned with filling as many beds as possible, may influence outcomes regardless of the letter of the law. More basically, there may exist a collective consensus as to what constitutes mental illness (Scheff 1984; Warren 1982). As Warren (1982) (quoted in Bottomley 1989: 294) states:

> [P]sychiatric or legal models of madness merely add to, and do not cancel out, commonsense concepts. [In fact, commonsense conceptions] are as legitimate as the use of unproven psychiatric or genetic theories, or contextually absurd legal assumptions concerning rationality, choice, and free will.

Results of research regarding changes in the components of involuntary commitment laws (i.e. from a 'need for treatment' to a 'dangerousness' standard or vice versa) are mixed. Some (e.g. Ross *et al.* 1996; Segal 1989; Fisher and Pierce 1985; Lambrinos and Rubin 1981) suggest that statutory language is an important – even *the* most important, variable – in determining patient populations. However, such conclusions must be tempered by a number of factors. First, the studies explain only some of the variance in admission rates (e.g. 52 per cent in Ross *et al.* 1996). Second, they may depend upon somewhat subjective rankings of the 'strictness' of involuntary commitment statutes (e.g. Ross *et al.* 1996). Last, the effects of other variables cannot be effectively isolated. Wanck (1984) reported that changes in statutory language had a direct impact on changing patient ratios in public hospitals. However, the states involved in that study had made deliberate changes in their statutes with the purpose of reducing their patient populations. Thus, it is conceivable that this policy was communicated (directly or indirectly) to judges, psychiatrists, and others in the mental health system, who may have aligned themselves (intentionally or not) with the states' goals.

Other studies (e.g. Applebaum 1984; Miller 1992b) have suggested that changes in laws do not necessarily result in changes in patient populations. Miller (1992b) studied changes in compulsory admissions in several states that returned to a 'need for treatment' criteria and concluded that '[c]hanges in admission and census rates are multi-determined and cannot be simplistically attributed to a single cause, such as changes in commitment criteria' (Miller 1992b: 1383).

Indeed, many commentators have argued that extra-legal social–structural factors, such as administrative concerns, fiscal constraints, specifics of locale, and organizational settings, are more significant impacts upon decision-making than the precise wording of statutes (Aviram 1990: 165, citing studies). The availability of alternate forms of treatment (and the extent of the patient's actual resources) may well 'trump' strict statutory criteria (Vestergaard 1994: 200; Turkheimer and Parry 1992: 647; Mestrovic 1986: 434).

A variety of 'micro' factors affects whether decision-makers adhere to statutory criteria. These include such things as the education and training of judges (Curran and Harding 1978: 30–1) and attorneys (Turkheimer and Parry 1992: 646–7), the effects of interactional courtroom processes (Arrigo 1992/93; Holstein 1987; Smit 1987), and the evaluations of clinicians (Engleman et al. 1998: 941; Høyer 1988). Researchers (Arrigo 1992/93; Holstein 1987) suggest that courts are influenced more by a person's being labelled as mentally ill than a person's 'actual' mental condition. A clinician's 'decision-making process is influenced by multiple factors, such as the evaluation setting, the clinician's tendency to detain patients, and the availability of detention beds' (Engleman et al. 1998: 941, citing studies). In addition, the medical imperative to presume sickness may lead to over-diagnosis of mental illness (Arrigo 1992/93: 144).

Vaguely worded statutes only serve to encourage varying interpretations. 'Dangerous to oneself' may mean imminent threat of suicide or other major harm, or may mean a suspected major deterioration in the person's mental condition if not hospitalized (Rogers 1994: 410). The 'need for treatment' standard has been interpreted as 'prevention of relapse', which might appear to exceed the statutory intent (Høyer 1988: 297). Judicial interpretations, which may not reflect legislative intent, may become 'frozen' through appellate court decisions; or in the absence of such court precedent, individual judges may act as 'mini-legislatures', resulting in as many interpretations of legislative criteria as there are judges.

Given the social complexities affecting involuntary commitment decisions, Turkheimer and Parry (1992: 653) state that solutions are 'unlikely to be found in the minutiae of legal requirements for involuntary commitment hearings, because the conduct of those hearings is governed as much by the system in which they operate as in the statutes that regulate them'. Nevertheless, most conclude that laws *do* matter. Specifically, as noted above, some research has suggested that the orientation of the system that defines the criteria for admission does result in a different mix of patient population. More generally, laws 'set up the boundaries within which we may operate and attempt improvements' (Aviram 1990: 174), and represent at least our collective ideals and goals for the treatment of the mentally ill. Ideally, the very process of law-making involves the consideration of multiple viewpoints. Curran and Harding (1978: 6) state that '[m]ental health legislation is now widely recognized as a critical factor which can either impede or facilitate development of mental health services'.

Such legislation will always arise from a dialectic process, both reflecting and influencing socio-cultural understandings about the meaning of mental illness and the proper place for the mentally ill.

NOTES

1   The term 'civil commitment' as used in this chapter refers to the detention of persons, against their will, to a mental health facility under a formal legal process. The term 'compulsory admission' has a broader meaning, namely, 'involuntary detention of a person in an institution designated as a mental [facility]' (Szasz 1963: 39), whether by legal or other means. Compulsory admission does not include those 'voluntary' admissions that are coerced through threat of court proceedings (see Hoge et al. 1998; Kjellin and Westrin 1998; Cascardi and Poythress 1997; Lewis et al. 1984).

2   The term 'mental illness' is used here when speaking in general terms, while recognizing that many statutes use alternative terminology such as 'mental disorder' or 'psychiatric illness'.

3   The term 'jurisdictions' rather than 'countries' is used to take into account the federal systems in several countries, including Australia, Canada, and the United States, in which mental health law is made at the level of state or territory rather than nationally.

4   The UN Principles were adopted by General Assembly Resolution on November 18, 1991, 46th Session, Item No. 98b. The intent of the UN Principles is to assure the human rights of persons thought to be, or determined to be, mentally ill. As of June 1999 no country had yet adopted the UN Principles in full.

5   Other jurisdictions using such a definition include: Ontario, Singapore (see Peng, Cheang, and Tsee 1994: 14), South Africa (see Kruger 1980: 49), and South Australia. Taiwan's mental health law defines mental illness according to fairly specific quasi-psychiatric criteria; however, it adds the catchall 'and such other mental illnesses as shall be recognized by the central organ having authority with respect to health' (see Salzberg 1993: 188).

6   This composite is based on the laws of Florida (USA), Indiana (USA), Mississippi (USA), The Northwest Territories (Canada), New Zealand, Taiwan and Victoria (Australia).

7   For example, Mississippi's (USA) statute excludes epilepsy, mental retardation, and 'brief periods of intoxication caused by alcohol or drugs' (Miss. Code Ann. Supp. 1998) while California's law excludes epilepsy and chronic alcoholism but includes drug abuse (see Leukfeld and Tims 1990). Some jurisdictions have very broad criteria. Taiwan's law states that mental illness 'shall include psychosis, neurosis, alcohol and drug addiction' (in Salzberg 1993: 188).

8   India's involuntary commitment law does not require a finding of dangerousness (Mestrovic 1986). Nevertheless, civil commitment is popularly understood to serve a police power function:

> In tune with the times in which it was enacted, the [statute] views mental illness as a 'law and order' problem. Therefore, the procedure of involuntary commitment is required to be activated in order to protect society from the disruptive and dangerous manifestations of mental illness. Mental hospitals, are in the main, required to function as custodial houses and not treatment centres (Dhanda 1993: 98).

Uruguay's law also contains no 'dangerousness' requirement for medical commitment, which is the route by which the vast majority of persons are compulsorily admitted. 'Emergency commitments', based on the standard 'dangerousness to himself or others' or 'imminent danger' to the peace and public morals, can be ordered for one day only, during which time a medical commitment must take place if the person is to be further detained (Moncada 1994: 603–4). Thus, this form of 'civil commitment' 'resembles an arrest for disorderly conduct more than it resembles proper commitment of a mental patient' (Moncada 1994: 604). In Japan, the route taken by the great majority of persons – the so-called 'consent admission', wherein the consenting party is a family member and not the patient – also does not require a finding of dangerousness (Salzberg 1991).

9 Some other jurisdictions with similarly worded provisions include Denmark (see Vestergaard 1994: 195), Germany (see Rössler *et al.* 1996: 405), and Ontario (Mental Health Act, §32).

10 The 'need for treatment' criterion, all but eliminated in the 1970s and 1980s, appears to be making a comeback. The UN Principles include that standard, as do the laws of New South Wales, Queensland and Denmark (see Vestergaard 1994: 195). Several states in the USA have re-adopted the criteria, including at least: Alaska, Arizona, Colorado, Kansas, North Carolina, South Carolina, and Texas (Miller 1992b).

REFERENCES

Aderibigbe, Y.A. and A.K. Pandurangi 1995. Comment. The neglect of culture in psychiatric nosology: the case of culture bound syndromes. *International Journal of Social Psychiatry* 41(4), 235–41.

American Psychiatric Association 1994. *Diagnostic and Statistical Manual of Mental Disorders* 4th edn. Washington, D.C.: APA.

Applebaum, P.S. 1984. Standards for civil commitment: a critical review of empirical research. *International Journal of Law and Psychiatry* 7, 133–44.

Arrigo, B.A. 1992/93. Paternalism, civil commitment and illness politics: assessing the current debate and outlining a future direction. *Journal of Law and Health* 7, 131–68.

Arrigo, B.A. 1993. *Madness, Language and the Law.* New York: Harrow and Heston.

Aviram, U. 1990. Care or convenience? On the medical-bureaucratic model of commitment of the mentally ill. *International Journal of Law and Psychiatry* 13, 163–77.

Bar El, Y.C., R. Durst, J. Rabinowitz, M. Kalian, *et al.* 1998. Implementation of order of compulsory ambulatory treatment in Jerusalem. *International Journal of Law and Psychiatry* 21(1), 65–71.

Bayer, R. 1987. *Homosexuality and American Psychiatry: the politics of diagnosis* 2nd edn. Princeton: Princeton University Press.

Bean, P.T., W. Bingley, I. Bynoe, A. Faulkner, *et al.* 1991. *Out of Harm's Way.* London: MIND.

Bennett, P.E. 1986. The meaning of "mental illness" under the Michigan Mental Health Code. *Cooley Law Review* 4, 65–100.

Bloch, S. and P. Reddaway 1984. *Soviet Psychiatric Abuse: the shadow over world psychiatry.* London: Victor Gollancz Ltd.

Bloch, S. and P. Reddaway 1987. *Russia's Political Hospitals.* London: Gallancz.

Bonnie, R.J. 1990. Soviet psychiatry and human rights: Reflections on the report of the U.S. delegation. *Law, Medicine, and Health Care* 18(1–2), 123–31.

Bonovitz, J.C. and J.S. Bonovitz 1981. Diversion of the mentally ill into the criminal justice system: the police intervention perspective. *American Journal of Psychiatry* 138, 973–6.

Bottomley, S. 1987. Mental health law reform and psychiatric deinstitutionalization: the issues in New South Wales. *International Journal of Law and Psychiatry* 10, 369–82.

Bottomley, S. 1989. The concept of mental illness and mental health law in New South Wales: a critical argument. *University of New South Wales Law Journal* 12, 284–302.

Briscoe, O.V. 1968. The meaning of 'mentally ill person' in the Mental Health Act, 1958–1965, of New South Wales. *Australian Law Journal* 42, 207–15.

Brislin, R. 1993. *Understanding Culture's Influence on Behavior.* Ft. Worth, Texas: Harcourt Brace.

Burti, L. and P.R. Benson 1996. Psychiatric reform in Italy: developments since 1978. *International Journal of Law and Psychiatry* 19(3/4), 373–90.

Campbell, T. and C. Heginbotham 1991. *Mental Illness, Prejudice, Discrimination and the Law.* Dartmouth: Aldershot.

Cascardi, M. and N.G. Poythress 1997. Correlates of perceived coercion during psychiatric hospital admission. *International Journal of Law and Psychiatry* 20(4), 445–58.

Castro, R. and E. Eroza 1998. Research notes on social order and subjectivity: individuals' experience of *susto* and fallen fontanelle in a rural community in central Mexico. *Culture, Medicine and Psychiatry* 22(2), 203–30.

Conrad, P. and J.W. Schneider 1980. *Deviance and Medicalization.* St. Louis, Missouri: The C.V. Mosby Company.

Curran, W.J. and T.W. Harding 1978. *The Law and Mental Health, Harmonizing Objectives.* Geneva: World Health Organization.

Desjarlais, R., L. Eisenberg, B. Good and A. Kleinman 1995. *World Mental Health: problems and priorities in low-income countries.* New York, Oxford: Oxford University Press.

Dhanda, A. 1993. Mental health law and policy: need for co-ordination. In *Mental Health in India: Issues and Concerns,* P. Mane, and K.Y. Gandevia (eds), 94–107. Bombay: Tata Institute of Social Sciences.

DiNicola, V.F. 1990. Anorexia multiforme: self-starvation in historical and cultural context: II. Anorexia nervosa as a culture-reactive syndrome. *Transcultural Psychiatric Research Review* 27(4), 245–86.

Draguns, J.G. 1990. Applications of cross-cultural psychology in the field of mental health. In *Applied Cross-cultural Psychology,* R.W. Brislin (ed.), 302–24. Newbury Park, California: Sage.

Durham, J. 1988. The gravely inadequate definition of a 'mentally ill' person in the Mental Health Act (NSW) 1983. *Australian and New Zealand Journal of Psychiatry* 22(1), 43–68.

Ellard, J. 1990. The madness of Mental Health Acts. *Australian and New Zealand Journal of Psychiatry* 14, 167–74.

Engleman, N.B., D.A. Jobes, A.L Berman and L.I. Langbein 1998 Clinicians' decision making about involuntary commitment. *Psychiatric Services* 49(7), 941–5.

Erlinder, C.P. 1993. Minnesota's gulag: involuntary treatment for the 'politically ill'. *William Mitchell Law Review* 19, 99–159.

Errington, M. 1987. 'Mental illness' in Australian legislation. *The Australian Law Journal* 61, 182–91.

Fisher, W.H. and G.L. Pierce 1985. Civil commitment reform: context and consequences. *Psychiatric Quarterly* 57, 217–29.

Foucault, M. 1965. *Madness and Civilization.* New York: Pantheon Books.

Gostin, L. 1983. Contemporary legal approaches to psychiatry. *Issues in Criminological and Legal Psychology* 4, 54–62.

Greenberg, G. 1997. Right answers, wrong reasons: revisiting the deletion of homosexuality from the DSM. *Review of General Psychiatry* 1, 256–70.

Heginbotham, C. 1987. *The Rights of Mentally Ill People.* London: Minority Rights Group.

Hoge, S.K., C.W. Lidz, M. Eisenberg, J. Monohan *et al.* 1998. Family, clinician, and patient perspectives of coercion in mental hospital admission: a comparative study. *International Journal of Law and Psychiatry* 21(2), 131–46.

Hogget, B. 1990. *Mental Health Law* 3rd edn, London: Sweet and Maxwell.

Holstein, J.A. 1987. Mental illness assumptions in civil commitment proceedings. *Journal of Contemporary Ethnography* 16(2), 147–75.

Høyer, G. 1988. Grounds for involuntary hospitalization according to the opinion of Norwegian Psychiatry. *International Journal of Law and Psychiatry* 11, 289–303.

Hughes, C.C., R. Littlewood, R.M. Wintrob and H.A. Pincus 1996. Culture-bound syndromes. In *Culture and Psychiatric Diagnosis: A DSM-IV Perspective,* J.E. Mezzich and A. Kleinman (eds), 289–323. Washington, DC: American Psychiatric Press, Inc.

Kendall, R.E. 1988. Priorities for the next decade. In *International Classification in Psychiatry: Unity and Diversity,* J.E. Mezzich and M. Von Cranach (eds), 332–40. New York: Cambridge University Press.

Kjellin, L. and C-G. Westrin 1998. Involuntary admissions and coercive measures in psychiatric care: registered and reported. *International Journal of Law and Psychiatry* 21, 31–42.

Kleinknecht, R.A., D.L. Dinnel, E.E. Kleinknecht and N. Hiruma 1997. Cultural factors in social anxiety: a comparison of social phobia symptoms and Taijin Kyofusho. *Journal of Anxiety Disorders* 11(2), 157–77.

Kruger, A. 1980. *Mental Health Law in South Africa*. Durban: Butterworth.

Lambrinos, J. and J. Rubin 1981. The determinants of average daily census in public mental hospitals: a simultaneous model. *Medical Care* 19, 895–906.

Leukfeld, C.G. and F.M. Tims 1990. Compulsory treatment for drug abuse. *The International Journal of the Addictions* 25(6), 621–40.

Levy, A. 1992. New Israeli psychiatric legislation. *International Journal of Medicine and Law* 11, 281–96.

Lewis, D.A., E. Goetz, M. Schoenfield, A.C. Gordon *et al.* 1984. The negotiation of involuntary civil commitment. *Law and Society Review* 18(4), 629–49.

Lillard, A. 1998. Ethnopsychologies: cultural variations in theories of mind. *Psychological Bulletin* 123(1), 3–32.

Lorber, J. 1997. *Gender and the Social Construction of Illness: Vol. 4 (The Gender Lens)*. Thousand Oaks, California: Sage Publications, Inc.

Mechanic, D. 1999. Mental health and mental illness: definitions and perspectives. In *A Handbook for the Study of Mental Health: social contexts, theories, and systems*, A.V. Horwitz, and T.L. Scheid (eds), 12–28. New York, NY: Cambridge University Press.

Mestrovic, S.G. 1986. Magic and psychiatric commitment in India. *International Journal of Law and Psychiatry* 9, 431–49.

Miller, R.D. 1992a. Economic factors leading to diversion of the mentally ill from the civil to the criminal commitment systems. *International Journal of Law and Psychiatry* 15, 1–12.

Miller, R.D. 1992b. 'Need-for-Treatment' criteria for involuntary civil commitment: Impact in practice. *The American Journal of Psychiatry* 149(10), 1380–4.

Monahan, J. 1992. Mental disorder and violent behaviour; perceptions and evidence. *American Psychologist* 47(4), 511–21.

Moncada, A.C. 1994. Comment: Involuntary commitment and the use of seclusion and restraint in Uruguay. *The University of Miami Inter-American Law Review* 25(3), 589–620.

Murthy, R.S. and N.N. Wig 1993. Evaluation of the progress in mental health in India since independence. In *Mental Health in India: issues and concerns*, P. Mane and K.Y. Gandevia (eds), 387–405. Bombay: Tata Institute of Social Sciences.

Noble, P. 1981. Mental health services and legislation – an historical overview. *Medical Science and the Law* 21(1), 16–24.

Ossorio, P.G. 1985. Pathology. *Advances in Descriptive Psychology* 4, 151–201.

Pearson, V. 1992. Law, rights, and psychiatry in the People's Republic of China. *International Journal of Law and Psychiatry* 15, 409–23.

Pearson, V. 1996. The Chinese equation in mental health policy and practice. *International Journal of Law and Psychiatry* 19, 437–58.

Peng, K.L., M. Cheang and C.K. Tsee 1994. *Mental Disorders and the Law*. Kent Ridge, Singapore: Singapore University Press.

Peters, T., K.S. Miller, W. Schmidt and D. Meeter 1987. The effects of statutory changes on the civil commitment of the mentally ill. *Law and Human Behavior* 11, 73–99.

Philo G., G. McGlaughlin and L. Henderson 1996. Media content. In *Media and Mental Distress*, G. Philo (ed.). London and New York: Longman.

Polubinskaya, S.V. and R.J. Bonnie 1996. The code of professional ethics of the Russian Society of Psychiatrists. *International Journal of Law and Psychiatry* 19, 143–72.

Rees, N. 1993/94. Mental illness: the Australian search for a workable definition. *International Journal of Mental Health* 22(4), 23–38.

Rogers, C. 1994. Proceedings under the Mental Health Act 1992, The legalisation of psychiatry. *New Zealand Law Journal* Nov., 404–11.

Ross, R.E., A.B. Rothbard and A.P. Schinnar 1996. A framework for classifying state involuntary commitment statutes. *Administration and Policy in Mental Health* 23(4), 341–56.

Rössler, W., H-J. Salize and A. Riecher-Rössler 1996. Changing patterns of mental health care in Germany. *International Journal of Law and Psychiatry* 19, 391–411.

Salzberg, S.M. 1991. Japan's new mental health law: more light shed on dark places? *International Journal of Law and Psychiatry* 14, 137–68.

Salzberg, S.M. 1993. Taiwan's mental health law. *China Law Reporter* 7, 161–205.

Sanua, V.D. 1994. Quo vadis APA? Inroads of the medical model. *Humanistic Psychologist* 22(1), 3–27.

Sayce, L. 1998. Stigma, discrimination and social exclusion: what's in a word? *Journal of Mental Health* 7, 331–43.

Scheff, T.J. 1984. *Being Mentally Ill: a sociological theory* 2nd edn. New York: Aldine.

Searight, R.H. and L.A. McLaren 1998. Attention-deficit hyperactivity disorder: the medicalization of misbehavior. *Journal of Clinical Psychology in Medical Settings* 5(4), 467–95.

Sedgwick, P. 1973. Mental illness is illness. *Salmagundi* (Summer/Fall), 196–224.

Segal, S.P. 1989. Civil commitment standards and patient mix in England/Wales, Italy, and the United States. *American Journal of Psychiatry* 146(2), 187–93.

Siegler, M. and Osomond, A. 1966. Models of madness. *British Journal of Psychiatry* 112, 1193–203.

Simon, B. 1992. Shame, stigma, and mental illness in ancient Greece. In *Stigma and Mental Illness*, P.J. Fink and A. Tasman (eds), 29–39. Washington, DC: American Psychiatric Press.

Smit, J. 1987. Question or quarrel: an analysis of the dialogue between judge and patient in the involuntary commitment procedure. *International Journal of Law and Psychiatry* 10, 251–63.

Soothill, K.L., T.W. Harding, B.J. Adserballe, S. Enré et al. 1981. Compulsory admissions to mental hospitals in six countries. *International Journal of Law and Psychiatry* 4, 327–44.

Stromberg, C.D. and A.A. Stone 1983. A model state law on civil commitment of the mentally ill. *Harvard Journal on Legislation* 20, 275–396.

Symonds, B. 1998. The philosophical and sociological context of mental health care legislation. *Journal of Advanced Nursing* 27, 946–54.

Szasz, T. 1963. *Law, Liberty and Psychiatry*. Syracuse, NY: Syracuse University Press.

Szasz, T. 1974a. *Ideology and Insanity: essays on the psychiatric dehumanization of man*. Syracuse, NY: Syracuse University Press.

Szasz, T. 1974b. *The Myth of Mental Illness* (rev. edn). New York: Harper and Row Publishers.

Turkheimer, E. and C.D.H. Parry 1992. Why the gap? Practice and policy in civil commitment hearings. *American Psychologist* 47, 646–55.

Vestergaard, J. 1994. The Danish Mental Health Act of 1989: psychiatric discretion and the new legalism. *International Journal of Law and Psychiatry* 17, 191–210.

Wahl, O. 1995. *Media Madness*. New Brunswick, New Jersey: Rutgers University Press.

Wakefield, J.C. 1992a. Disorder as harmful dysfunction: a conceptual critique of DSM-III-R's definition of mental disorder. *Psychological Review* 99(2), 232–47.

Wakefield, J.C. 1992b. The concept of mental disorder: on the boundary between biological facts and social values. *American Psychologist* 47(3), 373–88.

Wakefield, J.C. 1997. Normal inability versus pathological disability: why Ossorio's definition of mental disorder is not sufficient. *Clinical Psychology – Science and Practice* 4(3), 249–58.

Wanck, B. 1984. Two decades of involuntary hospitalization legislation. *American Journal of Psychiatry* 141(1), 33–8.

Warren, C.A.B. 1979. The social construction of dangerousness. *Urban Life* 8, 359–84.

Warren, C.A.B. 1982. *The Court of Last Resort: mental illness and the law*. Chicago: University of Chicago Press.

Wetzler, S. and L.C. Morey 1998. Passive-aggressive personality disorder: the demise of a syndrome. *Psychiatry: Interpersonal and Biological Processes* 62(1), 49–59.

World Health Organization 1955. Hospitalization of mental patients: a survey of existing legislation. *International Digest of Health Legislation* 6, 3–100.

World Health Organization 1992. *The ICS-10 Classification of Mental and Behavioral Disorders.* Geneva: WHO.

Yousaf, F. 1997. Psychiatry in Pakistan. *International Journal of Social Psychiatry* 43(4), 298–302.

Zaumseil, M. 1998. The meaning of mentally ill in modern Western cultures. *Psychiatry* 61, 130–2.

2   Hidden or overlooked? Where are the disadvantaged in the skeletal record?

TONY WALDRON

So many vagabonds, so many beggars bold.

John Skelton

In *The Beggars*, Pieter Breughel the Elder shows a group of five men with deformities of the legs and a variety of curious crutches and prostheses to help them get around. Three of the group face forwards, whereas the others have their backs to the group, one looking into the distance towards a stone arch. We can assume that he is similarly afflicted as his comrades, since the shaft of a crutch under his right arm can just be glimpsed emerging from under his cloak, adorned with what look like fox tails (Figure 2.1). Three of the remaining four have lost their feet and all are armed with crutches and all have wooden devices attached to their lower legs. Two of these devices (of the first and fifth beggars) look like elaborate shin guards which were evidently used to shuffle along the ground; the beggar at the right of the group is on his knees indicating both how these rudimentary sleds were used and were attached to the leg. The shin guards of the third beggar have a long point projecting from the front which was used to support the knee, as he hobbled along with the aid of his crutches. The fifth beggar is standing with his right knee flexed and we may suppose the joint was fixed in this position, which would explain his need for crutches. His face has a rather vacuous expression and his eyes appear to be moving independently in the way those of a blind man move.

Breughel is by no means the only painter to include those with disabilities in his paintings, and other examples may be found, for example, in the works of Hieronymus Bosch. Bosch's paintings abound with bizarre figures and animals and while his depiction of the beggars may owe something to the idiosyncrasies of his style, they appear sufficiently frequently in his works to allow us to suppose that they were a common sight in the Low Countries in the late fifteenth and early sixteenth centuries. In his study of *Beggars and Cripples*, Bosch depicts more than two dozen individuals with varying deformities and mechanical aids for getting around. Some of the devices are similar to those shown by Breughel, but some are novel. To the right of the centre of the sketch is a portly man with bilateral, above-knee amputations, seeming to sit on a low stool. In fact, the 'legs' of the stool are separate

Figure 2.1 *The Beggars* by Pieter Breughel the Elder. (By courtesy Musée du Louvre)

supports by which he may have been able to shuffle along slowly. Opposite this figure is another leaning heavily on two four-legged supports. It is difficult to see what is wrong with this man, but he may have lost his left leg and he moves by advancing his supports and dragging his single leg forward. Just below the man on the stool and to the right is a man whose right leg is bandaged and swollen while his left is withered and twisted, perhaps as the result of poliomyelitis or cerebral palsy. There is, of course, no means of knowing how the individuals who featured in these paintings received their injuries, but it is likely that most of the amputations were traumatic in origin, although one cannot entirely rule out the possibility that some were surgical amputations for conditions such as compound fractures of the ankle or chronic osteomyelitis. Some trades would have been likely to carry a high risk of injury, particularly those engaged in building. In the medieval period, large numbers of workmen were engaged in building and maintaining the castles, monasteries and collegiate churches of the period; for example, during the reign of Edward I, employment was found for 400 masons, thirty smiths and carpenters, 1000 unskilled workers and 200 carters at Beaumaris Castle (Knoop and Jones 1949: 3).

The methods of construction are well-illustrated in medieval manuscripts of the period and leave little doubt of the potential for injury, but there are no actual accounts of this unless the victim was important. William of Sens, who was called to repair Canterbury Cathedral after the fire of 1174, was badly injured when the beams on which he was standing collapsed, and although he survived, he was not able to continue to supervise the works and had to return to France (Andrews 1976: 20).

There is no reason to suppose that William's injury was a unique, or even an unusual occurrence, but evidence for such injuries in the archaeological record is scarce, as is evidence for other physical disabilities, and presents a considerable challenge to palaeopathologists to explain. Dwarfism seems to be an exception to this general rule, certainly so far as the written record is concerned. Dwarfs, especially those with achondroplasia, seem to have held a special place in some cultures, particularly that of ancient Egypt where there are references to them in papyri and in tomb paintings (see Dasen 1988). Individuals with physical abnormalities were often the subjects of public curiosity; they were depicted on picture postcards in the early 1900s, the most common depictions being those of pituitary dwarfism and achondroplasia, and it has been suggested that being put on show provided, at least in some cases, some social benefit (Enderle 1998).

Disability and disadvantage have a number of antecedents including injury, disease and abuse. The apparent deficit of physical evidence for their presence in earlier times may be due to the fact that they occurred less frequently than now, that individuals with deformities may have been buried separately from the rest of the population, that they may have congregated in one place and have been buried in places which have not yet been excavated, or that the skeletons of those with physical deformities survive less well than others. Alternatively, the conditions may have been missed or mis-diagnosed by those examining assemblages of skeletons, or the deficit may be an outcome of the relatively small numbers of skeletons which become available for study. These possibilities will be explored with reference to three conditions: child abuse, tuberculosis and scoliosis. This chapter concentrates only on those with some kind of physical disability that would put them at a disadvantage compared with the general population. Disadvantage, however, is not to be found exclusively among the physically disabled; people who are deaf or blind, those with chronic heart or lung disease, those with brain damage and those who have no disability other than poverty, may be equally disabled, but their skeletons will provide no clues to their impairments or poverty.

CHILD ABUSE

Child abuse is the difference between a hand on the bottom and a fist in the face.

Henry Kempe

In modern Britain at least one child in a thousand under of the age of four years suffers severe physical abuse, including fractures, brain haemorrhage, severe internal injuries or mutilation, and the mortality rate of such children is at least one in 10,000 children (Meadow 1997: 3). Child abuse is often spoken of as a modern phenomenon and many paediatricians and other medical people tend to feel that it all started with Kempe's famous paper (Kempe et al. 1962), in which he coined the term 'the battered baby syndrome' to provoke his colleagues and the general public into taking notice of what was happening to young children. In fact, Caffey (1946; 1957) had pointed out some time before this that the combination of sub-dural haemorrhage and fractured bones might be the result of parental abuse, but this work seems largely forgotten. There is, however, plenty of documentary evidence that the phenomenon has a long and undistinguished history. Soranus of Ephesus, for example, writing in the AD early second century, was aware that infants might be neglected or abused. In his *Gynaecology* he gives advice on choosing a wet nurse and comments that she should be self-controlled, sympathetic and affectionate and not ill-tempered. Angry women, he writes:

> are like maniacs and sometimes when the newborn cries from fear and they are unable to restrain it, they let it drop from their hands or overturn it dangerously.
>
> (quoted in Temkin 1956: 116)

The Arab physician, Rhazes, who is the author of what is considered to be the earliest surviving treatise on paediatrics, was aware that some injuries in children may be caused intentionally (Radbill 1971). The literary record is then silent on the matter until the seventeenth century, although Knight records a revealing oral tradition from the Shetland Islands (Knight 1986). For many years children there sang what appears to have been a meaningless jingle:

> Barn vil ikka teea, barn vil ikka teea,
> Tak an leggen, slog an veggen,
> Barn vil ikka teea.

The words were eventually recognized to be Old Norse and were translated as: 'The child will not be quiet, the child will not be quiet; take it by the leg and hit it against the wall; the child will not be quiet'. There is no doubt that this method would have been very effective at silencing the child – for good. It would be interesting to know how frequently it was resorted to.

References to child abuse appeared in the medical literature again in England during the sixteenth century (Lynch 1985) and increased in frequency during the eighteenth and nineteenth centuries; in France, the condition came to be recognized and commented upon as the nineteenth century progressed (Knight 1986). Lynch suggests that it was the increasing awareness of child abuse which led to the foundation of Societies for the Prevention of Cruelty to Children first in Liverpool in 1883, and in London the following year. In its first three years, the London Society dealt with 762 cases of cruelty of which 333 were assaults, 81 starvations, 130 dangerous neglect, 30 desertions, 70 cruel exposure to excite sympathy and 116 other wrongs; of the total, 25 children died (Lynch 1985).

There seems no reason to suppose that human nature has altered in any important respect in the last two thousand years or so, or that it is only in recent times that adults have treated children cruelly, yet in no skeletal assemblage which I have examined – and in which children account for up to a fifth of the total population – has a single case been found in which the death could have been attributed to wilful abuse.

The criteria by which child abuse may be recognized have been frequently described by paediatricians and radiologists. In addition to the soft tissue signs of trauma, which are not available to those who study human remains, there are some well recognized radiological signs which can guide those who examine children's skeletons. The most revealing indication of deliberate abuse is the presence of multiple fractures at different stages of healing, indicating that they have occurred over a length of time (Figure 2.2). Fractures of the distal metaphysis – the so-called 'corner' fracture – in a child who has not started to walk should always raise the possibility of deliberate harm. Fractures of the ribs are common in abused children and they may also be found in the sternum, vertebrae and skull (Resnik 1989).

The signs which may be found radiologically can also be easily recognized in the skeleton. Kerley (1978) has recorded the case of three infants who were killed by their parents and buried in the basement and backyard of the house. The case came to light when two children who were being interviewed by their teacher as to the number of siblings they had, casually remarked that there had been three more of them but that their mother and father had killed them. Multiple fractures, some healed and some healing, were found in the skeletons of all three children, the sites affected including the mandible, ribs, clavicle, radius and ulna; the left clavicle of one of the children had two separate fractures in it. In addition to these fractures, Kerley noted some which he

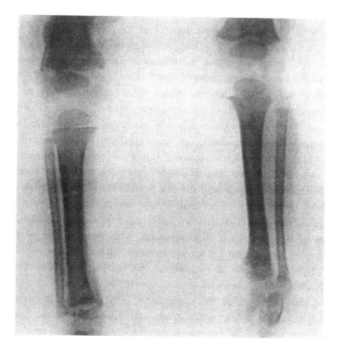

Figure 2.2 Radiograph of battered baby showing healing metaphyseal fracture of right femur and both tibiae.

Table 2.1 Peak times of morphological or radiological appearances of fractures in children.

Morphological or radiological appearance	Time from occurrence of fracture
Periosteal new bone formation[a]	10–14 days
Loss of definition of fracture line	14–21 days
Soft callus formation	14–21 days
Hard callus formation	21–42 days
Remodelling	1 year

Note: [a] A fracture without periosteal new bone is usually less than 7–10 days old and seldom more than 20 days. A fracture with only slight periosteal new bone formation could be only 4–7 days old.

considered had been caused at or around the time of death, and there were also some breaks in the bone which had occurred during excavation. The latter could be distinguished by the fact that the broken ends of the bones were of a lighter colour than the surface.

All three skeletons that Kerley examined had unequivocal evidence of ante-mortem fractures in various stages of healing and which had certainly been caused at different periods of the children's lives, confirming that they had been subject to repeated trauma (the age of fractures in the skeleton can be determined by the physical or radiological appearances as shown in Table 2.1). Kerley stressed the importance of x-raying suspected fractures as the increased density at the broken ends of the bones (indicating remodelling of bone) is evidence that the fracture occurred before death; while this might be a requirement in forensic cases, it is doubtful that an experienced osteologist would fail to differentiate an ante-mortem or peri-mortem fracture from one which had occurred during excavation.

It is unlikely that the kind of injuries which would be sustained by an abused child would escape notice among a skeletal assemblage, but perhaps the children who died, as the result of abuse, were buried covertly, as happened with the infants in the modern case which Kerley described. The most satisfactory explanation for their non-appearance in the archaeological record, however, seems certainly to do with numbers. Modern data suggest that although approximately 0.4 per cent of children suffer abuse, the mortality rate is only about 1 in 10,000 and, in those who survive, the injuries will heal, bones will remodel and, if they survive into adulthood, there will be no skeletal evidence to show that they were ever harmed during childhood. If the rates of child abuse in the past are at all comparable with those of the present day, the chances of finding an abused infant are remote indeed. Since the 95 per cent confidence intervals around the modern death rate are from $0.61-5.5/10^4$, approximately 2000 infant skeletons would have to be examined in order to detect death from child abuse even at the upper limit. The apparent absence of battered babies in the past, then, is the result of chance effects due to the small numbers involved. Even were such children to be discovered, the true prevalence of child abuse would be a substantial underestimate, since the majority of children who suffer intentional harm nevertheless survive and the stigmata of their injuries vanish as their skeleton matures and remodels.

TUBERCULOSIS

I can get no remedy against this consumption ... the disease is incurable.

William Shakespeare

Tuberculosis has some claims to be the oldest human bacterial infection. It is caused by the _Mycobacterium tuberculosis_, one of a large group of related organisms widespread in the environment. The disease seems to be rare in wild animals which are not in contact with domesticated animals, although some strains of mycobacteria do cause epizootics in wild animals (Francis 1958). The disease does occur in a wide range of domesticated animals and in wild animals kept in captivity (Kovalev 1980) and it was probably only when animals were kept in close proximity that the acute form of the disease was able to develop. It is generally considered that man originally contracted the disease from domestic cattle. The supposition is that the form of the organism which affects cattle, _M bovis_, probably evolved from saprophytic soil bacteria and that the human form (_M tuberculosis_) then evolved from the bovine form (Stead 1997), being especially prevalent in the post-medieval period. The two forms are certainly very closely related – and to the mycobacterium which causes leprosy (_M leprae_) (Frothingham 1999). _M bovis_ can infect an exceptionally wide range of hosts, including goats, cats, dogs, pigs, buffalo, badgers, deer and bison (O'Reilly and Daborn 1995). It is possible that the disease may have spread originally from other animals with which early man came into contact rather than cattle, although the latter seem a more likely source.

Human infection with _M bovis_ occurs through the ingestion of infected milk and milk products such as butter and cheese. The organism is absorbed from the gastro-intestinal tract and spreads to the abdominal lymphatic system and from there to other parts of the body, including the skeleton. Spread between infected animals occurs through droplet infection and this is also the mode of spread of the human organism. The target organ for _M tuberculosis_ is the lung and the natural history of the disease is different from that of the bovine form of the disease. Following the primary lung infection, the infection may lie dormant for several years, only to become re-activated by mechanisms which are not clearly understood. The infection may then spread widely throughout the lung and to other organs; the predominant symptoms are those relating to the lung infection, resulting in the condition widely referred to as consumption in nineteenth century literature.

Bone infections are relatively uncommon in patients with pulmonary tuberculosis, occurring in between 3–5 per cent of cases; it is much more common in those with extra-pulmonary disease, affecting perhaps up to 35 per cent of cases (Resnick and Niwayama 1988). It is this characteristic of the disease which probably gave rise to the notion that skeletal tuberculosis was present _only_ in bovine tuberculosis, but reference to the early literature on the disease, when it was very much more common than nowadays, suggests that anything between 40–97 per cent of cases of skeletal tuberculosis were _not_ due to infection with the bovine bacterium (e.g. Fraser 1914: 6).

Spinal disease accounts for between 25–45 per cent of all cases of skeletal tuberculosis and the lower half of the spine is most frequently involved. Although a single vertebra may be involved, it is more common to find a number of adjacent vertebrae and their intervertebral discs affected (Revell 1986). The disease leads to erosion and destruction of bone tissue; in the spine, the vertebral bodies are especially prone to infection. The destruction which follows may cause the spine to collapse, leading to an acute angulation of the spine which is referred to as Pott's disease (see Figure 2.3). Unusual forms of the disease may occur – it may be present in the cervical spine, for example (Slater *et al.* 1991), or affect the posterior parts of the vertebrae (Rahman *et al.* 1997), or there may be no disc involvement (Pertuisit *et al.* 1999) – and the disease may also be found in any bone or joint. In dry bones, the disease appears as an erosive lesion with very little proliferation of new bone. There is nothing which is specific to these lesions, so that in the absence of the classic Pott's spine, the diagnosis may present considerable difficulty. Indeed, more than thirty years ago, Morse *et al.* (1964) wrote that:

> If one were to attempt to make a diagnosis [of tuberculosis] from a dried bone specimen, the only chance of making even a good guess would be on the basis of involvement of the spine; bone tuberculosis in other locations would be indistinguishable from too many other diseases.

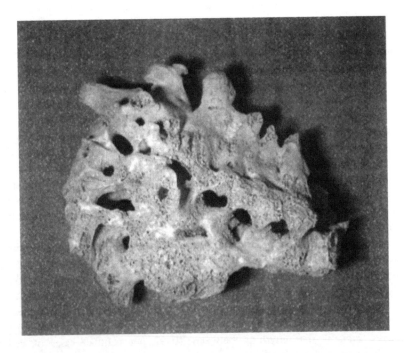

Figure 2.3 Cervical and upper thoracic spine of young boy recovered from a Byzantine site in Turkey. The cervical spine is uppermost and points to the right. The spine has collapsed and the cervical and thoracic spines have fused.

Kelley and El-Najir (1980) discussed the differential diagnosis of skeletal tuberculosis in considerable detail and suggested nineteen different conditions with which it might be confused. Although, in practice, many of these other conditions would not be too difficult to exclude from the differential, some certainly would be easily confused and Ortner has recently noted that the differential diagnosis of tuberculosis 'can be challenging and in some cases, not possible at all' (Ortner 1999: 257). The disease which would be likely to cause most confusion is brucellosis. This is another disease contracted from animals – most likely cattle in this country; in this case, the disease is contracted by contact with infected blood, as may occur when helping a cow in labour, for example. There seems no reason to suppose that this disease was not present in ancient herds or that those who tended them would not contract it themselves. The proportion of patients who develop skeletal brucellosis is variously reported and estimates range from 1–75 per cent but there is general agreement that the spine, particularly the lumbar spine, is commonly affected and the radiological and morphological appearances of spinal brucellosis and tuberculosis are similar (e.g. de Dios Colmonero *et al.* 1991).

Cases of Pott's disease have been recorded in antiquity, indeed it was one of the first diseases to appear in the palaeopathological literature, being described in 1910 by Elliot Smith and Ruffer in a mummy from the 21st dynasty (Figure 2.4) (Elliot Smith

Figure 2.4 Sketch of mummy from 21st dynasty from paper by Elliot Smith and Ruffer. Note the angulation of the spine typical of spinal tuberculosis.

and Ruffer [1910] 1921). The number of cases, however, is relatively small, especially when one considers that the disease was likely to have been common in the past, in earlier times from the drinking of contaminated milk or eating infected butter or cheese, and in more recent times, when pulmonary tuberculosis was common (for details of cases in the archaeological record see Ortner and Putschar 1981; Pálfi et al. 1999). The conclusion must be that the prevalence of tuberculosis in past populations will be greatly underestimated. There are two explanations for this, the first to do with the problems surrounding diagnosis referred to above, and the second to do with the small numbers of individuals who go on to develop skeletal tuberculosis. As noted above, probably no more than five per cent of those with pulmonary tuberculosis develop skeletal forms of the disease and not much more than 35 per cent of those with the extra-pulmonary form of the disease. It is not possible to know on morphological grounds whether individuals found with skeletal tuberculosis died from the pulmonary or the extra-pulmonary form of the disease, but even supposing that *all* those with skeletal lesions died from extra-pulmonary tuberculosis, then the prevalence of the disease would still be underestimated by up to 70 per cent. When one also considers that the only certain way of diagnosing the disease in skeletal remains depends upon the finding of the classic spinal changes and that these develop in no more than half the patients with skeletal tuberculosis, then it is obvious that the estimates of the prevalence of tuberculosis in the past will be substantially too low. An estimate of the order of magnitude of the number of expected cases of tuberculosis in the past can be made. At present, the prevalence of tuberculosis in the most badly affected countries is 100/100,000. If it is assumed that this figure applied in the past, and that between 5–30 per cent of cases develop bony lesions, then the number of cases detectable morphologically in the skeleton might be between 5–30/100,000. If only half develop spinal lesions, then Pott's disease of the spine would be found in between 2.5–15 cases per 100,000. It is, perhaps, not surprising that the number of reported cases remains small.

Recent advances in palaeopathology, however, do give some grounds for optimism and the hope that it may be possible, with adequate funding, to arrive at more reliable estimates of tuberculosis in the past, and also to test whether the human form derived from the bovine form or if the two have been co-existing from earliest times.

The advances referred to depend on the observation that the organic component of bone survives much better in archaeological remains than had previously been supposed. Bone consists of a crystalline matrix (hydroxyapatite), an organic phase, comprising collagen, bone, other proteins and DNA from various sources, and water. It had always been assumed that the organic component was broken down during the time that bones were buried, leaving only the inorganic matrix behind, and that usually much altered by diagenesis. This supposition was overturned when various authors were able to extract blood and plasma proteins from bone and then ancient DNA (aDNA), both human and that derived from bacteria, using the polymerase chain reaction (PCR) technique. The first recovery of aDNA of *M tuberculosis* was reported by Spigelman and Lemma (1993) from the spine of a young boy excavated from a Byzantine site in Turkey, followed shortly by the report of a similar extraction from the mummy of a 12 year-old girl from Peru, dating to about AD 1000 (Arriaza *et al.* 1995). It is possible now to differentiate *M tuberculosis* from *M bovis* and other strains of mycobacteria using a technique referred to as spoligotyping (Kamerbeek *et al.* 1997), and using this method Taylor *et al.* (1999) were able to show that aDNA from three medieval bone samples was from the human rather than the bovine form.

The use of PCR seems to offer a valuable means whereby the diagnosis of tuberculosis can be confirmed in human remains and by which the form of the disease can be identified. There are, however, some caveats which need to be entered. First, although aDNA seems to preserve well in bone – and, rather surprisingly, better in cremated than non-cremated bone (Brown *et al.* 1995), and apparently better in the bones of mummies than in the soft tissues, especially if the latter are degraded (Lassen *et al.* 1994) – the method is expensive and time-consuming and can only realistically be used in cases where tuberculosis is suspected on morphological grounds. Moreover, the preservation of aDNA varies from place to place; it is preserved better in skeletons from the Mediterranean than from Romano-British sites, for example (Burger 1997), and only positive results of PCR analysis are informative. A negative result cannot be taken as evidence that the individual did not have the disease since the possibility that the aDNA has disappeared cannot be ruled out.

Mycobacteria have a waxy coat which contains a number of mycolic acids. Using gas chromatography it is possible to extract these compounds from the tissues of patients with tuberculosis and differentiate between different strains (Garza-Gonzalez *et al.* 1998). The technique is relatively straightforward and much more likely than PCR to be applicable on a large scale, and it is much less susceptible to contamination than PCR. It has been used to demonstrate the presence of *M tuberculosis* in a fragment of calcified pleura some 1,400 years old (Donaghue *et al.* 1998) and it could be used to determine the prevalence of tuberculosis on a cemetery-wide basis. The application of the method to skeletons which did not have any morphological evidence of tuberculosis would provide a better indication of the frequency of the disease in the past, although even with this method, false negative results would be certain to occur, leading to an underestimate of the true prevalence.

SCOLIOSIS

> Crookbacked he was, tooth-shaken, and blear-eyed. Went on three feet, and sometime crept on four.
>
> Thomas Sackville

Scoliosis is the term given to spinal deformities in which there is lateral curvature of the spine. The condition may be accompanied by a posterior curvature (kyphosis) or by an anterior curvature (lordosis), or both. It may be congenital, in which case it is associated with defects in the vertebrae, or idiopathic, by far the most common variety (Winter and Lonstein 1992). The idiopathic form is generally divided into an infant form, which appears before puberty, and an adolescent form which appears after puberty, the latter being the more common. There is also a form which first appears in adulthood, and which is the consequence of other spinal disease such as osteoporosis, osteomalacia or degenerative change. Idiopathic scoliosis is more common in females than in males and epidemiological studies suggest that the overall prevalence in the general population is up to 4.5 per cent (Rogala *et al.* 1996). The prevalence varies considerably, however, with the degree of curvature present. Where curves greater than 10° are considered, the prevalence is 2–3 per cent, for those over 20° it is 0.3 to 0.5 per cent and for those over 30°, it is 0.2 to 0.3 per cent (Winter and Lonstein 1992). Only the most severe degrees of curvature result in significant debility. The aetiology of the condition is not understood – as the name implies – although twin studies have shown that it has some genetic basis (Ponsetti *et al.* 1976).

The condition is likely to progress during adult life, especially in those with the more pronounced degrees of curvature. Although the appearances may appear alarming, the condition does not result in a higher frequency of back pain than in the general population, but curves in the thoracic region interfere with pulmonary function and may lead to death from right-sided heart failure, secondary to raised pressure in the pulmonary vessels (Kolind-Sørensen 1973). The socio-economic effects of the condition may also be considerable; some studies have shown that those with scoliosis are likely to be unemployed or in receipt of disability pensions, and are self-conscious of, or embarrassed by their condition (Fowles *et al.* 1978). Victor Hugo's hunchback of Notre Dame exemplifies the social distress which can be caused by the condition, and it is inevitable that those with severe scoliosis would descend into vagrancy or beggary unless they enjoyed the support of their community, given that their condition would limit their opportunities for work.

There is no mistaking scoliosis in the skeleton (Figure 2.5); the spine may show one or more curves of varying magnitude, wedging of the vertebrae on the concavity of the curves and frequently osteoarthritis in the facet joints of the spine. It is not conceivable that the condition could be overlooked in a skeletal assemblage, no matter how inexperienced the examiner, but – again – the frequency with which it is reported appears low, compared with modern rates. From the crypt of Christ Church, Spitalfields in London, for example, a total of 311 adult males and 312 adult females buried during the 18th and early 19th centuries was recovered. Two of the males and three of the females had appearances consistent with idiopathic scoliosis, giving crude prevalence rates for the condition of 0.64 and 0.96 per cent respectively, and an overall crude prevalence rate of 0.8 per cent. These estimates are considerably lower than expected, even though the sample is, by osteological standards, a large one.

By contrast, Wells (1967) reported on a series of fifty burials which were recovered from the church of St Michael-at-Thorn in Norwich. Among this small group, of which only eight had well preserved spines, Wells (1967: 41) found three cases with spinal deformities, two (both female) with scoliosis and one (a male) with kyphosis. Finding two of eight spines with scoliosis is remarkable and prompted Wells to seek an explanation in the presumed occupation of the women by – as he put it – 'the integration of informed speculation based upon a wide experience of bone pathology with information gleaned from the contemporary art of the period and ancient city records.' He noted that Norwich had for centuries been a centre of

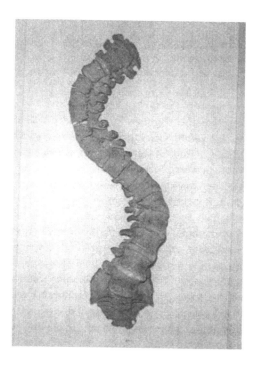

Figure 2.5 Spine with two very marked scoliotic curves. The upper curve is approximately 80° and the lower, approximately 70°.

weaving and he supposed that the two women with scoliosis had been employed as weavers and that this had been the cause of their deformity. (The man with kyphosis Wells decided had not been a weaver but a tailor.) Even supposing that Wells was correct in his assumptions, and there is no hard evidence to support him, a much more likely explanation for this unusual cluster of cases suggests itself, that is, that those who are disadvantaged tend to gravitate towards large centres of population and that Wells' findings are an example of this. Certainly, there can be no question of being able to determine an individual's occupation from skeletal pathology, even though a great many osteologists think that they can achieve this remarkable feat.

More recently Stirland (*pers. comm.*) has found another unusual cluster of cases of scoliosis in a group of skeletons recovered from the church of St Margaret in Magdalen Street in Norwich (sixteen cases among 368 adults). The graveyard was used from about 1240 to 1468 and was the poorest medieval parish in the city. This finding lends support to the view that people who were disadvantaged in some way moved to the poorest parts of the city where there would be better opportunity to support themselves by begging or other means.

CONCLUSION

And suppose we solve all the problems . . .? What happens? We end up with more
problems than we started with . . . A problem left to itself dries up or goes rotten.
But fertilize a problem with a solution – you'll hatch out dozens.

N.F. Simpson

The problem as to whether those who were disadvantaged are hidden or
overlooked in archaeology admits of a number of possible solutions, although none
may necessarily be correct. Unfortunately it is not possible to design the kind of
epidemiological study which would be required to provide a definitive solution – or at
least one as definitive as epidemiology can get – because of the nature of the material.
All skeletal assemblages have been subject to processes which attenuate their numbers
and degrade the bones which do remain. The resultant sample which is dug from the
ground and presented to the bone specialist is far from random, and may not even be
representative of the population of which it was originally a part, and a modern
epidemiologist would certainly not be in a rush to deal with it.

Nevertheless, using the examples discussed above, some solutions can be suggested,
and at least some could be tested. It is clear that the number of some disadvantaged
individuals is too small to be detected, given the small size of most skeletal assemblages.
This is the case in child abuse, where very few of the children who are deliberately
injured die from their injuries, and those who survive and enter adult life will have no
pathognomonic traces of their childhood trauma on their skeletons. It would require
the examination of many thousands of infant skeletons in order to be certain of finding
even a single case of multiple fractures, and battered babies are likely to remain hidden
from view, except through the medium of a chance finding.

The diagnosis of some conditions presents another problem to palaeopathologists,
indeed it may be the most serious problem they face, as there are very few diseases
which leave pathognomonic signs on the skeleton. This is certainly the case with
tuberculosis, except perhaps where there is a classic Pott's spine. An added difficulty
with tuberculosis is that the skeleton is affected in only a minority of cases so that even
where the disease is correctly diagnosed, the true prevalence in the population will be
underestimated. The use of PCR to detect bacterial DNA or gas chromatography for
the analysis of mycolic acids, however, offers an opportunity to confirm the diagnosis
in cases where the spine is not affected, and even to estimate the prevalence of the
disease in a group of skeletons which may show no evidence of skeletal lesions at all.
The detection of mycolic acids seems to offer the best prospect since it is a cheaper
technique and not subject to contamination during the collection of samples or during
analysis as is PCR. Some groups are already working on the development of protocols
for such a study and there is every hope that some results will be available in the next
two or three years.

There is no difficulty in detecting skeletons with severe physical deformities, such as
scoliosis, although for the sake of comparison it would be necessary for different
workers to agree on how to categorize the degree of disability. Minor degrees of
scoliosis and kyphosis can be found commonly due to vertebral collapse following

trauma or as a consequence of osteoporosis, for example, and these need to be differentiated from the gross changes resulting from idiopathic scoliosis. In orthopaedic practice, the magnitude of curvature of the spine is expressed in degrees, and it would be helpful if the same procedure were adopted when reporting scoliosis in the skeleton, as it is only the greater degrees of scoliosis which result in severe disability.

The suggestion has been made here that those with disabilities would be likely to migrate towards big towns or cities where they might better be able to support themselves. This could be tested by comparing the prevalence of scoliosis – or other conditions which might be of interest – in town and country settings and in poor and rich parishes with towns. The data required to carry out this analysis may already exist in published bone reports.

Finally, although it seems that the majority of individuals who were disadvantaged in life will remain hidden from archaeological gaze, diligent searching should reveal at least some to view.

ACKNOWLEDGEMENTS

I am grateful to those colleagues and students who have listened uncomplainingly to me discussing these matters over the years. I am also extremely grateful to Dr Ann Stirland for permission to quote data from her unpublished report on St Margaret's Church.

REFERENCES

Andrews, F.B. 1976. *The Medieval Builder and His Methods*. East Ardley: EP Publishing.
Arriaza, B.T., W. Salo, A.C. Aufderheide and T.A. Holcomb 1995. Pre-Columbian tuberculosis in northern Chile: molecular and skeletal evidence. *American Journal of Physical Anthropology* 98, 37–45.
Brown, K., K. O'Donoghue and T. Brown 1995. DNA in cremated bones from an early Bronze Age cemetery cairn. *International Journal of Osteoarchaeology* 5, 181–7.
Burger, J. 1997. DNA preservation under different burial conditions. In *Conference Proceedings, Ancient DNA IV*, Göttingen 5–7 June 1997.
Caffey, J. 1946. Multiple fractures of long bones in infants suffering from subdural hematoma. *American Journal of Roentgenology* 56, 163–9.
Caffey, J. 1957. Some traumatic lesions in growing bones other than fractures and dislocations; clinical and radiological fractures. *British Journal of Radiology* 30, 225–31.
Dasen, V. 1988. Dwarfism in Egypt and classical antiquity. *Medical History* 32, 253–76.
Dios Colmonero, J. de, J.M. Reguera, A. Fernández-Nebro and F. Cabrera-Franquelo 1991. Osteoarticular complications of brucellosis. *Annals of the Rheumatic Diseases* 50, 23–6.
Donaghue, H.D., M. Spigelman, J. Zias, A.M. Gernaey-Child and D.E. Minnikin 1998. *Mycobacterium tuberculosis* complex DNA in calcified pleura from remains 1400 years old. *Letters in Applied Microbiology* 27, 265–9.
Elliot Smith, G. and M.A. Ruffer [1910] 1921. Pott'sche Krankheit an einer Ägyptischen Mumie aus der Zeit der 21. Dynastie. In: *Studies in the Palaeopathology of Egypt*, R.L. Moodie (ed.), 3–11. Chicago: University of Chicago Press.
Enderle, A. 1998. Dwarfism and gigantism in historical picture postcards. *Journal of the Royal Society of Medicine* 91, 273–8.

Fowles, J.V., D.S. Drummond and S. L'Ecuyer 1978. Untreated scoliosis in the adult. *Clinical Orthopaedics and Related Research* 134, 212–17.

Francis, J. 1958. *Tuberculosis in Animals and Man*. London: Cassell.

Fraser, J. 1914. *Tuberculosis of the Bones and Joints*. London: Adam and Charles Black.

Frothingham, R. 1999. Evolutionary bottlenecks in the agents of tuberculosis, leprosy and paratuberculosis. *Medical Hypotheses* 52, 95–9.

Garza-Gonzalez, E., M. Guerro-Olazaran, R. Tijerina-Menchaca and J.M. Viader-Salvado 1998. Identification of mycobacteria by mycolic acid pattern. *Archives of Medical Research* 29, 303–6.

Kamerbeek, J., L. Schouls, A. Kolk, M. van Agterveld *et al.* 1997. Simultaneous detection and strain differentiation of *Mycobacterium tuberculosis* for diagnosis and epidemiology. *Journal of Clinical Microbiology* 35, 907–14.

Kelley, M. and M.Y. El-Najir 1980. Natural variation and differential diagnosis of skeletal changes in tuberculosis. *American Journal of Physical Anthropology* 52, 153–67.

Kempe, C.H., F.N. Silverman, B.F. Steele, W. Droegmueller and H.K. Silver 1962. The battered child syndrome. *Journal of the American Medical Association* 181, 17–24.

Kerley, E.R. 1978. The identification of battered-infant skeletons. *Journal of Forensic Sciences* 23, 163–8.

Knight, B. 1986. The history of child abuse. *Forensic Science International* 30, 135–41.

Knoop, D. and G.P. Jones 1949. *The Medieval Mason*. Manchester: Manchester University Press.

Kolind-Sørensen, V. 1973. A follow-up study of patients with idiopathic scoliosis. *Acta Orthopedica Scandinavica* 44, 98–103.

Kovalev, C.K. 1980. Tuberculosis in wildlife reviewed. *Journal of Hygiene, Epidemiology, Microbiology and Immunology* 24, 495–504.

Lassen, C., S. Hummel and B. Herrmann 1994. Comparison of DNA extraction and amplification from ancient human bone and mummified soft tissue. *International Journal of Legal Medicine* 107, 152–5.

Lynch, M.A. 1985. Child abuse before Kempe: an historical literature review. *Child Abuse and Neglect* 9, 7–15.

Meadow, R. 1997. Epidemiology. In *ABC of Child Abuse*. London: British Medical Association.

Morse, D., D.R. Brothwell and P. Ucko 1964. Tuberculosis in ancient Egypt, *American Review of Respiratory Disease* 90, 524–41.

O'Reilly, L.M. and C.J. Daborn 1995. The epidemiology of *Mycobacterium bovis* infections in animals and man: a review. *Tuberculosis and Lung Diseases* 76, Suppl. 1, 1–46.

Ortner, D. and W.G.J. Putschar 1981. *Identification of Pathological Conditions in Human Skeletal Remains*. Washington: Smithsonian Institution Press.

Ortner, D. 1999. Paleopathology: implications for the history and evolution of tuberculosis. In *Tuberculosis Past and Present*, G. Pálfi, O. Dutour, J. Deák and I. Hutás (eds), 257–65. Golden Book Publisher.

Pálfi, G., O. Dutour, J. Deák and I. Hutás (eds) 1999. *Tuberculosis Past and Present*. Golden Book Publisher.

Pertuisit, E., J. Beaudreuil, F. Liote, A. Horusitzky, *et al.* 1999. Spinal tuberculosis in adults. *Medicine (Baltimore)* 78, 309–20.

Ponsetti, I., V. Pedrini, R. Wynne-Davies and G. Duval-Beaupere 1976. Pathogenesis of scoliosis. *Clinical Orthopaedics and Related Research* 120, 268–80.

Radbill, S.X. 1971. The first treatise in pediatrics. *American Journal of Diseases of Children* 122, 369–76.

Rahman, N.U., A. Jampoon, Z.A. Jampoon and A.M. Al-Tahan 1997. Neural arch tuberculosis: radiological findings and their correlation with surgical findings. *British Journal of Neurosurgery* 11, 32–8.

Resnick, D. and G. Niwayama 1988. *Diagnosis of Bone and Joint Disorders*. Philadelphia: W.B. Saunders.

Resnik, C.S. 1989. Diagnostic imaging in pediatric skeletal trauma. *Radiologic Clinics of North America* 27, 1013–22.

Revell, P. 1986. *Pathology of Bone*, 245–7. Berlin: Springer-Verlag.

Rogala, E., D. Drummond and J. Gurr 1996. Scoliosis: incidence and natural history. *Journal of Bone and Joint Surgery* 78B, 314–17.

Slater, R.R., R.W. Beale and E. Bullitt 1991. Pott's disease of the cervical spine. *Southern Medical Journal* 84, 521–3.

Spigelman, M. and E. Lemma 1993. The use of the polymerase chain reaction to detect *Mycobacterium tuberculosis* in ancient skeletons. *International Journal of Osteoarchaeology* 3, 137–43.

Stead, W.W. 1997. The origin and erratic global spread of tuberculosis. How the past explains the present and is the key to the future. *Clinical Chest Medicine* 18, 65–77.

Taylor, G.M., M. Goyal, A.J. Legge, R.J. Shaw and D. Young 1999. Genotypic analysis of *Mycobacterium tuberculosis* from medieval human remains. *Microbiology* 145, 899–904.

Temkin, O. 1956. *Translation of Soranus' Gynecology*. Baltimore: Johns Hopkins Press.

Wells, C. 1967. Weaver, tinker or shoemaker? *Medical and Biological Illustration* 17, 39–47.

Winter, R.B. and L.E. Lonstein 1992. Juvenile and adolescent scoliosis. In *The Spine*, H.N. Herkowitz, S.R. Garfin, R.A. Balderson, F.J. Eismont et al. (eds), 373–430. Philadelphia: W.B. Saunders.

3 Did they take sugar? The use of skeletal evidence in the study of disability in past populations

CHARLOTTE A. ROBERTS

INTRODUCTION: THE COMPLEX NATURE OF DISABILITY

> A disability is only one aspect of an individual. In history, people have often forgotten that the individual always is more than the sum of their disabilities.
>
> (Covey 1998: 42)

Disability is present in all societies and every one of us may become disabled at some stage in our life. Perceptions and treatment of disability reflect, like disease, the social, cultural and political environment. Thus archaeologists and anthropologists should be inherently interested in this issue.

Disability is perceived by populations differently around the world, but the way disabled people are viewed will have also changed through time. Disability may be temporary, or more permanent and long-term, affecting the individual much more deeply. The disability may also be minor or major, and minor disabilities may not be deemed relevant or even noticed. A major disability may also be invisible to the outside world but be very disabling to the person concerned; for example, some forms of cancer, and AIDS. Disability is also a likely accompaniment of the ageing process, e.g. the development of joint degeneration. Disability can be adapted to, especially if it is a minor condition, but even people with major conditions may have access to supportive devices such as crutches, wheelchairs and artificial limbs to help them with their mobility.

The term 'disability' covers a wide range of conditions that lead to a person being perceived as 'different' by others in their social group. The nature of these perceptions will differ over time. Some diseases which may have been considered disabling in the past may not be today, perhaps because of medical control of the disease causing the disability. What is considered a disability will also vary in different social groups. Some groups may consider one condition a disability, while in another it is within the parameters of normality. For example, in Martha's Vineyard in the United States, congenital deafness, which in other parts of the same country is considered a severe disability, is the norm (Dettwyler 1991).

This chapter explores why archaeologists and anthropologists are starting to look at disability in a more critical way, and the possible methods and problems of reconstructing the archaeology of disability using skeletal evidence.

Disability must be considered in the context of the specific society and its belief system, taking account of all relevant factors, and many issues will be raised which interact with each other. The impact of physical (and mental) disabilities are also very much affected by the physical environment, both in the past and present.

In recent years disability has, in a sense, come out into the open: issues have been discussed readily and openly in the British media in the last few years (especially since the passing of the Disability Discrimination Act in 1995), and disabled people are now realizing their rights and are lobbying government for better resources, and an infrastructure for disabled people. Shakespeare (1998: 20) discusses the almost lemming-like rush to study disability by academics over the last few years:

> Perhaps the study of disability has at last "arrived" as a major academic field: publishers' catalogues are swelling with books on disability theory, disability and sexuality, disability and literary studies, disability and education ... For so long the poor relation to gender, sexuality and race, disability is finally being recognized as an exciting domain of study.

Apart from the physical aspects of disability, there are other related, less identifiable concepts, such as stigma, psychological factors, and how people with disabilities are perceived and treated within their social group. To what extent can these aspects be identified in the past?

EVIDENCE FROM THE PAST

> Each person ... has individual characteristics that go well beyond their outward appearance or physical disabilities.
>
> (Covey 1998: 87)

There are various sources of evidence which may be used to construct the archaeology of disability. The primary source of data is human remains from archaeological sites, while secondary evidence may serve to flesh out the bones. Both primary and secondary evidence have certain limitations which must be taken into account in interpretation.

In order to identify physical disabilities, it is necessary to work from a clinical base (e.g. Resnick and Niwayama 1988) to understand what could be disabling. There are many limitations of the use of skeletal remains to assess disease and disability. Those associated with disease have been outlined by Wood et al. (1992). With regard to disability, there are a number of questions to be asked. For example, are the skeletons under study a representative sample of the population, i.e. does the proportion of deformed/diseased skeletons match the proportion that would be found among the living population? Are the human remains of 'disabled' people found in communal burial sites, or elsewhere?

An important factor to be taken into account is that most human remains are skeletal and therefore any disabling condition affecting only the soft tissues would not be identifiable – and, in fact, most disabling conditions do only affect soft tissues (Lindemann 1981). Furthermore, a strong immune response to a disease will limit bone damage, thus it is possible that an individual may have been disabled even if this is not apparent from their skeletal remains. For example, medieval leprosy hospital cemetery sites contain a number of skeletons which do not show the common changes of leprosy. This does not necessarily mean that the people did not have the disease – it simply might not have affected the bones. However, it could also mean that the individuals had been misdiagnosed as having leprosy, or even that the hospital functioned as a general institution for the sick and not just for people with leprosy.

Fragmentary skeletal material will also hinder the recognition of disability; for example in both rheumatoid arthritis and leprosy the hands and feet may be affected (and in both cases can lead to severe malfunction), and these bones are the parts of the skeleton which are the least likely to survive burial and excavation (Waldron 1987). A complete skeleton is usually needed to even hazard a guess at a diagnosis. It is also common to use the signs and symptoms of specific diseases in the final interpretation of the changes seen. However, this may be misleading, because the symptoms experienced by different people will vary; deformity does not always lead to disability, and it has been shown that people with the most severe symptoms, e.g. pain, are not necessarily those who have the most bone damage (Rogers et al. 1990). A key point here is an individual's potential ability to adapt to a disabling condition both mentally and physically.

Hawkey (1998) suggests that establishing the timing of disease in a skeleton, estimating movement restriction at the joints, predicting activity pattern using musculo-skeletal markers of stress, establishing the degree of impairment, and then estimating disability is a good way of trying to identify disability in the past.

Some conditions which can be assumed to be potentially disabling are identifiable in the skeletal record. Cancer may affect bone (Figure 3.1). Non-specific infections such as chronic osteomyelitis (Figure 3.2), and specific infections caused by bacteria such as leprosy and tuberculosis are identifiable in skeletal remains, and may be disabling (Figure 3.3) although this is not necessarily so (Figure 3.4). Infections caused by viruses, such as poliomyelitis (which can affect the skeleton as a result of paralysis and wasting), and Paget's Disease (also believed to be caused by a virus) will leave characteristic changes in the skeleton, which may also be disabling. Conditions affecting the skeleton may be disabling, but this will depend on their chronicity, upon the ability of the person concerned to adapt both physically and mentally, and on the attitudes, beliefs and care systems of the social group concerned.

Other conditions which may be identifiable include tumours (e.g. those affecting structures of the body such as the spinal cord and leading to complications); injuries, such as fractures and dislocations; congenital conditions such as cleft lip and palate, achondroplasia, osteogenesis imperfecta, myositis ossificans progressiva, and spina bifida (although the more serious disabling form – cystica – is unlikely to have been compatible with survival in the past); cerebral palsy; talipes (clubfoot); spinal deformities (which could also develop as acquired conditions through disease or

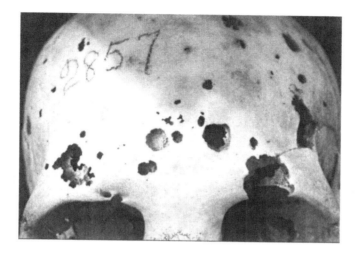

Figure 3.1 Anterior view of the skull of an individual with cancer affecting the bone, which could have resulted in disability due to the associated symptoms. [Photo: C. Roberts]

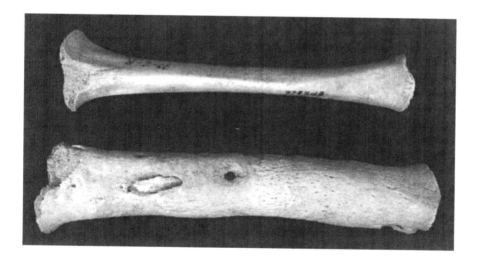

Figure 3.2 Tibia (and unaffected opposite side) with changes consistent with osteomyelitis, which can cause extreme pain and swelling of the affected limb. [Photo: C. Roberts]

trauma throughout life); diseases of the nervous system such as multiple sclerosis (which may be reflected in changes in the skeleton due to paralysis); cardiovascular system diseases (such as paralysis caused by blockage of a vessel with an embolism or thrombus); metabolic disorders such as rickets, leading to bowing deformities of the limbs; diabetes (potential damage to bones of the feet due to ulceration); osteoporosis,

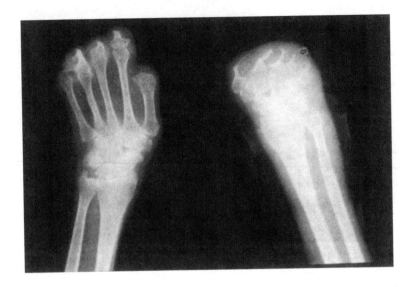

Figure 3.3 Radiograph of the hand and arm of a person with leprosy, showing loss of bones of the hand. [Photo: C. Roberts]

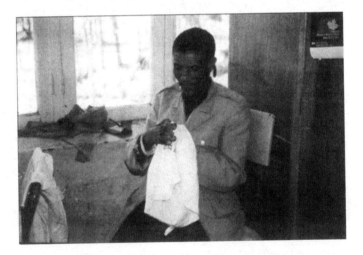

Figure 3.4 A person with leprous involvement of the hand and loss of fingers nevertheless managing to do needlework, and thus contribute to his social group. [Photo: C. Roberts]

which can lead to fractures and disability; blood forming diseases such as anaemia (leading to general fatigue and weakness), and sickle cell (leading to death of bone tissue due to blocking of blood vessels with abnormally shaped cells) and thalassaemia (leading to associated fractures), cancers of the blood such as myeloma and leukaemia, circulatory disorders which lead to death of bone tissue at joint surfaces; endocrine disease such as a pituitary disorder, causing dwarfism or gigantism; joint disease such as osteoarthritis which may lead to joint fusion (Figure 3.5), and rheumatoid arthritis. In all these conditions, it is also necessary to be aware of the implications for involvement of associated soft tissues.

Despite the fact that all these conditions have been identified archaeologically (Aufderheide and Rodriguez Martin 1998; Roberts and Manchester 1995), some are very rare today and are also not seen much in the past. Joint, infectious and traumatic conditions are probably the most common. In addition to disease, people who are abnormally tall, or short, may also have attracted adverse attention (as they do now), possibly leading to stigma and ostracism.

Ideally, studying the skeletal remains of people with known diseases and medical histories helps to correlate skeletal changes with signs and symptoms and therefore to potentially reconstruct disability. Mann et al. (1991) describe the remains of three skeletons, two from the Terry Collection (dating from 1910–1940) and the third from the National Museum of Health and Medicine (both in Washington DC). Long term flexion deformities were seen in all the skeletons, interpreted as such because of changes in the knees of all three, due to the effect of the quadriceps tendon on their surfaces (Figure 3.6). Such data collected from 'known' individual skeletons are useful because they may help to explain changes seen in archaeologically derived skeletons.

Clearly, each condition, and its associated disability (if there was one), are likely to have been perceived differently in different parts of the world, and these perceptions will also have changed over time. For example, in the eighteenth century, children with rickets were seen as changelings (idiots) to be mistreated or killed or abandoned (Haffter 1968), and people with spinal curvatures were seen as villains or deviants (Covey 1998: 62). At the other extreme, in the late eighteenth century, tuberculosis

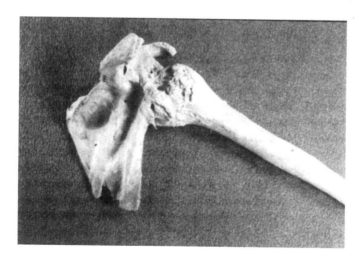

Figure 3.5 Humerus and scapula fused at the shoulder joint, probably from joint disease or underlying trauma. [Photo: C. Roberts]

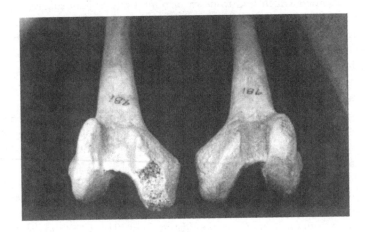

Figure 3.6 Femora from person with known long-term flexion at the knees; notice the groove on the anterior aspects. [Photo: C. Roberts]

was romanticized; some suggested that tuberculosis benefited the creative side of its victims (Covey 1998: 5), and it is said that Lord Byron wished to die from it to improve his poetry and prose. Later, however, until well into the nineteenth century, it was seen as a disease of the poor and 'inferior', and caused by misbehaviour.

INTERPRETATIONS OF THE EVIDENCE

> Much of coping with illness and disability involves development of cognitive
> defense mechanisms that buffer emotional stress and feelings of loss.
>   (McElroy and Townsend 1996: 105)

Despite the range of potentially disabling conditions visible in the skeleton, it is difficult to interpret their impact within the social group. Interpretations of skeletal data may be made which cannot be justified, because of the problems of inferring disease or disability from the skeleton (Wood et al. 1992). An attempt must be made to interpret changes in the skeleton and assess their impact on individuals and populations, without over-interpreting the data and making assumptions based on our own contemporary and ethnocentric ideas about what would have been disabling, and how it would have been perceived and treated. Misjudgements are often made about the present, and judgements about the past are likely to be even more flawed. It is also important not to make sweeping generalizations about the past:

> The great majority of disabled persons had no occupation, no source of
> income, limited social interaction, and little religious comfort ... abnormal
> persons were surrounded by superstition, myth and fatalism ... severely
> limited by widely held beliefs and superstitions that justified the pervasive

prejudice and callous treatment. Individuals seen as different were destroyed, exorcized, ignored, exiled, exploited...

(Winzer 1997: 80)

Extensive interpretation of physical data is not valid unless it is supported by other relevant material. Many biological anthropologists studying skeletal remains make unsubstantiated inferences from the physical evidence to the nature of individual experiences and circumstances, and social attitudes and behaviour. The following cases illustrate this point.

The late Calvin Wells, a Norfolk general practitioner with an interest in archaeology, was well known for making too much of the data (but it always made a good story!). For example, in a Romano-British cemetery (Wells 1982) he describes inhumation 278, a male with extensive pathological changes to his feet, including gout and osteoarthritis, with some fusion of bones. Here he says: 'Severe limitation of function must have resulted from these lesions and it is likely that walking would have been almost impossible at times' (Wells 1982: 185). He also describes inhumation 182, a female with severe osteoarthritis of the hip joints, and he makes an assumption that,

> If the permanent flexion and extremely limited movement possible in these two joints had not made it quite impossible for this woman to walk, it is likely that one or both femoral heads would have perforated the acetabular floor and gone through into the pelvic cavity.
>
> (Wells 1982: 191)

Kerr (1995: 197) likewise describes an adult male skeleton with a severe facial injury, from a 4th millennium BC short cist burial on the Isle of Lewis in the Outer Hebrides in Scotland. In interpreting the findings, he says, 'It is almost certain that some form of fibrous ankylosis had taken place following the injury, with consequent trismus and limitation of jaw movement'. Merbs (1989: 165), trying to make an interpretation of a poorly healed fracture in an individual from Arizona, suggests that: 'The fracture obviously made walking very difficult, particularly over the rough terrain of this site'. Knusel et al. (1992: 118) also infer pain from the condition they describe in an adult male skeleton of a priest with a slipped proximal femoral epiphysis; they conclude: 'Even suffering this painful and debilitating condition, however, this individual survived and came to assume an important position in the medieval community'. This may have been an accurate picture but, equally, may not have been.

Another group of studies links the apparent disability with presumed care of the afflicted. For example, Wakely (1993: 44) describes a female skeleton from a Medieval cemetery at Abingdon with congenital dislocation of the hip, spina bifida occulta and spondylolysis and says:

> [I]t is fair to assume that "5384" did spend the greater part of her infancy in this situation, to the detriment of her anatomical and locomotor development ... [and] ... she would have been dependent upon others to

some extent. Her survival to adulthood gives us some physical confirmation of the evidence from artistic sources of the existence of persons with disabilities in a medieval community and their place in society.

Frayer *et al.* (1987: 62) describe an adolescent skeleton with dwarfism from the Italian late Upper Palaeolithic, and interpret the reduced stature and problems with forearm extension as follows:

> [H]e must have been supported by members of his social group … the reduced stature and lack of complete forearm extension would have greatly limited this individual's ability to participate effectively in hunting … [and would have] … impinged on the individual to keep up with the group's periodic movements, especially in the rugged environment of southern Italy … [and] … he survived to about 17 years of age … [which illustrates] … acceptance by the group despite his severe handicaps and limited ability to contribute to subsistence and other economic activities.

Congenital conditions visible in the skeletal remains of an older person (or even older child) tend to lead to assumptions that some level of care must have been in operation, as in the case of Armelagos *et al.* (1992) who describe a ten-year old child from a Nubian cemetery dated to AD 350–550 with hydrocephalus and possible quadriplegia. They suggest that the child must have been cared for because s/he had reached ten years of age.

Trinkhaus and Zimmerman (1982: 70), describing the male skeleton of Shanidar I, suggest blindness due to a crushing fracture of one orbit, leading to cerebral motor cortex damage resulting in hemiplegia to the right side of the body, affecting the motor nerves to both upper and lower limb. As it is likely that these injuries would have made him more vulnerable to other trauma and also to infection, they concluded that his social group must have looked after him.

Another example comes from Hawkey (1998: 328) where skeletal changes are interpreted and an assumption made that 'movements [were] painful'. She also suggests that in later life the person would only have had movement in the head, neck, shoulder and hand, and although he would have been able to feed himself, he would not have been able to acquire food without help. She suggests that the person was not treated any differently from the rest of the group, and that he was 'well cared for, permitting him to survive into middle age' (Hawkey 1998: 338). Again, although such interpretations may be correct, it is important to be cautious in presenting any interpretation of this kind.

In addition to the primary evidence, the skeletal remains, there may be secondary evidence available to help in the interpretation of the archaeological data, consisting of historical, iconographic, and ethnographic material. Ethnographic evidence has a large part to play in the reconstruction of disease and disability in the past (Sargent and Johnson 1996), and historical and iconographic data can also serve to flesh out the bones. These sources also demonstrate that concepts of disability have varied considerably through time. For example, Covey (1998) cites a wide range of possible causes of disability, from punishment for sin, demons and witches to violence and accidents, and the normal process of ageing. Furthermore, people with disabilities have been viewed as subhuman, non-human, specially gifted, evil, pitiful, damned, morally weak, sick, sexually hyperactive, ugly, deviant, and as scapegoats. These perceptions reflected the nature and concerns of society at a particular time. In addition, as Covey (1998: 25) states: 'regardless of whether the perception is negative or positive, the perception nevertheless serves to separate and distinguish people with disabilities from those who lack them'.

EVIDENCE OF ATTITUDES, TREATMENT AND CARE

Medieval monasticism promoted care by establishing hospitals to take care of people who could not look after themselves, but they were not usually given any treatment (Covey 1998: 37). This situation has persisted in many institutions all over the world. For example, on Blackwell's Island in New York, a hospital known as 'consumptive's prison', was opened in 1893 to segregate sufferers and prevent the spread of tuberculosis to others, but no treatment was given (Covey 1998: 77). Leprosy hospitals were founded from the late medieval period onwards in Europe but they were also, originally, a means to segregate and not to treat and cure (Roberts 1986). In France, in the fifteenth century, laws were passed to expel leprous and syphilitic people, and in Scotland, in 1497, people with leprosy were given the choice to be banished to the island of Inch Keith or to be branded with a hot iron (Quetel 1990).

Devices were developed for people with disabilities (as seen from iconographic evidence) such as crutches, artificial limbs, devices to get people around in, such as litters, wheelbarrows, and bath-chairs. We also see swaddling being used to prevent limb deformities, but this also prevented normal bodily function and, for rickets, did more harm than good (Covey 1998: 59). There is also evidence of treatment such as amputations (Mays 1996) and trepanations (Aufderheide 1985), and even splinting (Elliott-Smith 1908).

Thus, there is evidence for treatment but little of it is primary evidence, although there have been some attempts to link the biological and historical data together to assess the availability of treatment of fractures (Grauer and Roberts 1996; Roberts 1991). Gaining first-hand evidence that people did care for the sick and disabled in the past is problematic, and even if there is evidence that a person who must have had a major disability was kept alive, it is not possible to determine whether they were well cared for: 'There is a wide gap between "survival" and being treated nicely' (Dettwyler 1991: 382).

In the present, it is usually possible to distinguish between the sort of caring that is simply the 'processing' of another individual and that which is carried out with compassion. Identifying this difference in the past is much more problematic. As Dettwyler (1991: 382) points out: 'Compassion, cruelty and indifference leave few traces in the archaeological record'.

It cannot be assumed that disabled people have always been stigmatized, ostracized and treated as 'different' in all cultures, and at all periods in the past, but what sort of information can gives us clues to this? One source is the demographic profile of a population at a particular time in the past, which will show, for example, which sections of the population were dying at an earlier age than the majority. This may reflect social attitudes, or even policies of a majority population to get rid of certain categories of people. In the case of infants, for example, Hill and Ball (1995) found that the majority of examples of (assumed) infanticide appeared to be related to deformity. However, Mays' (1993) study of skeletal material found no evidence of disability or deformity in the infants which he believed had been the victims of infanticide, suggesting that other socio-cultural factors were involved.

The study of human remains may be able to reveal whether more males or females became disabled (at a certain period and place in the past), and the age at which specific disabilities tended to develop. It may be possible to determine whether people living in non-industrialized or industrial areas were more likely to have disabilities and whether urban communities looked after and tolerated its disabled people more or less than rural groups. How do people living in agricultural societies compare with nomadic groups? Do higher status people always get better treatment?

What type of funerary contexts were disabled people buried in? Funerary context may highlight that disabled people were not buried in the normal cemetery of the people of a particular population. Lack of identifiable disabilities in a burial site may indicate that disabled people were left to die if they could not keep up with the rest of the group and they may have been buried or disposed of in unusual places. On the other hand excavations might show that such people were buried with the rest of their group. Body position in the grave (e.g. prone burials) may also indicate that there was something different about the person.

It has been suggested that people received more attention in small egalitarian groups in the past rather than from large-scale competitive goups. On the other hand, however, in a mobile hunter and gatherer group a physical disability might present problems (e.g. see Frayer et al. 1987 and Berger and Trinkhaus 1995).

With the development of agriculture around the world, and in theory a stable food supply which could support a large sedentary population, it is possible that disabled people may have been better supported. The Industrial Revolution shift to an economy based on industrial production by families meant that social value depended on whether a person could work or not. Disabled people were less tolerated and more laws were passed to restrict their lives.

In discussion of the archaeological record of disability, archaeologists are tempted to place the evidence in an assumed social context. Berger and Trinkaus (1995: 849), for example, describe trauma in Neanderthal human remains, and make a number of assumptions:

> Those no longer capable of keeping up with the social group, whether as a result of age or serious lower limb trauma, may have simply been left behind to die in localities where their remains were not preserved or recovered ... these hominids did not sacrifice the survival of the social group as a whole when it was threatened by an immobile individual.

Similarly, Webb (1995: 73) infers from a male skeleton with multiple injuries from Murrabit, on the southern side of the Murray River in Australia, that:

> The fact that this man lived some considerable time after sustaining them suggests that he must have received some nutritional and nursing care. After all, a man with two broken arms and a broken leg is not able to go hunting or provide for himself.

In another example of skeletal material with evidence of trauma (a femur with a comminuted fracture) from the Murray Valley, Webb (1995: 194) concludes that they had received long-term care because, for the fracture to heal, immobility would have been necessary, which would have been unusual for people who were constantly on the move.

CONCLUSION

In order to find answers about tolerance, care and treatment of people with disabilities using skeletons from archaeologically derived contexts, it is necessary first to establish what can be identified in the skeletal record as potentially disabling, and then to try to correlate symptoms with the conditions.

The attitudes to disease and disability at any particular time period must also be considered, and a multidisciplinary and holistic approach taken, because without one form of evidence, a vital part of the jigsaw may be missing.

The archaeology of disability is a relatively recent field of study, and has many pitfalls. Interpretation of archaeological data in this context must always be tentative, as Dettwyler (1991: 384) has warned:

> Those who interpret the fossil and archeological record, in their attempts to reconstruct past behavior, need to think about the assumptions underlying their interpretations and the implications of their statements. I urge them to be more cautious in their recreations of what life was like for disabled individuals in the past – how they were treated, how other people felt about them, and particularly whether their survival tells us anything about the moral standards of the population.

There are often many possible alternative interpretations of the evidence for disability, and certainly for the impact of the social context of disability on past human populations. Dettwyler's warning must be heeded by all who work in this field.

REFERENCES

Armelagos, G.J., T. Leatherman, M. Ryan and L. Sibley 1992. Biocultural synthesis in medical anthropology. *Medical Anthropology* 14, 35–52.

Aufderheide, A.C. 1985. The enigma of ancient trepanation. *Minnesota Medicine* 68, 119.

Aufderheide, A.C. and C. Rodriguez Martin 1998. *The Cambridge Encyclopedia of Human Paleopathology*. Cambridge: Cambridge University Press.

Berger, T.D. and E. Trinkaus 1995. Patterns of trauma among the Neanderthals. *Journal of Archaeological Science* 22, 841–52.

Covey, H. 1998. *Social Perceptions of People with Disabilities in History*. Springfield, Illinois: Charles C. Thomas.

Dettwyler, K. 1991. Can paleopathology provide evidence for "compassion"? *American Journal of Physical Anthropology* 84, 375–84.

Elliott-Smith, G. 1908. The most ancient splints. *British Medical Journal* 1, 732.

Frayer, D.W., W.A. Horton, R. Macchiarelli and M. Mussi 1987. Dwarfism in an adolescent from the late Upper Palaeolithic. *Nature* 330, 60–2.

Grauer, A.L. and C.A. Roberts 1996. Paleoepidemiology, healing and possible treatment of trauma in the Medieval cemetery population of St Helen-on-the-Walls, York, England. *American Journal of Physical Anthropology* 100, 531–44.

Haffter, C. 1968. The changeling: history and psychodynamics of attitudes to handicapped children in European folklore. *Journal of the History of the Behavioral Sciences* 4(1), 55–61.

Hawkey, D.E. 1998. Disability, compassion and the skeletal record: using musculo-skeletal stress markers (MSM) to construct an osteobiography from early New Mexico. *International Journal of Osteoarchaeology* 8, 326–40.

Hill, K. and H. Ball 1995. *Precarious Life, Predictable Death?* Paper presented at a conference on Difficult Births and Precarious Lives: biological perspectives on stresses of childhood, University of Durham, December 1995.

Kerr, N.W. 1995. Severe facial injury nearly 4000 years ago. *International Journal of Osteoarchaeology* 5, 196–7.

Knusel, C., Z. Chundun and P. Cardwell 1992. Slipped proximal femoral epiphysis in a priest from the Medieval period. *International Journal of Osteoarchaeology* 2, 109–19.

Lindemann, J.E. 1981. *Psychological and Behavioural Aspects of Physical Disability: a manual for health practitioners*. New York: Plenum Press.

Mann, R.W., C.A. Roberts, M.D. Thomas and D.T. Davy 1991. Pressure erosion of the femoral trochlea, patella baja, and altered patella surfaces. *American Journal of Physical Anthropology* 85, 321–7.

Mays, S. 1993. Infanticide in Roman Britain. *Antiquity* 67, 883–8.

Mays, S. 1996. Healed limb amputations in human osteoarchaeology and their causes. *International Journal of Osteoarchaeology* 6(3), 101–13.

McElroy, A. and P.K. Townsend 1996. *Medical Anthropology in Ecological Perspective*. 3rd edn. Boulder, Colorado: Westview Press.

Merbs, C. 1989. Trauma. In *Reconstruction of Life from the Skeleton*, M.Y. Iscan and K.A.R. Kennedy (eds), 161–89. New York: Alan R. Liss Inc.

Quetel, C. 1990. *History of Syphilis*. Baltimore: The Johns Hopkins University Press.

Resnick, D. and G. Niwayama 1988. *Diagnosis of Bone and Joint Disorders*. London: W.B. Saunders.

Roberts, C.A. 1986. Leprosy and leprosaria in Medieval Britain. *MASCA Journal* 4, 15–21.

Roberts, C.A. 1991. Trauma and treatment in the British Isles in the Historic Period: a design for multidisciplinary research. In *Human Paleopathology: current syntheses and future options*, D.J. Ortner and A.C. Aufderheide (eds), 225–40. Washington DC: Smithsonian Institution Press.

Roberts, C.A. and K. Manchester 1995. *The Archaeology of Disease*. Ithaca: Cornell University Press and Gloucester: Sutton Publishing.

Rogers, J., I. Watt and P. Dieppe 1990. Comparison of visual and radiographic detection of bony changes at the knee joint. *British Medical Journal* 300, 367–8.

Sargent, C.F. and T.M. Johnson (eds) 1996. *Medical Anthropology: contemporary theory and method*. London: Praeger.

Shakespeare, T. 1998. Able minds incarcerated by traditional attitudes. *Times Higher Educational Supplement* 24th April, 20.

Trinkaus, E. and M.R. Zimmerman 1982. Trauma among the Neandertals. *American Journal of Physical Anthropology* 57, 61–76.

Wakely, J. 1993. Bilateral congenital dislocation of the hip, spina bifida occulta and spondylolysis in a female skeleton from the medieval cemetery at Abingdon, England. *Journal of Paleopathology* 5(1), 37–45.

Waldron, T. 1987. The relative survival of the human skeleton: implications for palaeopathology. In *Death, Decay and Reconstruction: approaches to archaeology and forensic science*, A. Boddington, A.N. Garland and R.C. Janaway (eds), 55–64. Manchester: Manchester University Press.

Webb, S. 1995. *Palaeopathology of Aboriginal Australians: health and disease across a hunter-gatherer continent.* Cambridge: Cambridge University Press.

Wells, C. 1982. The human burials. In *Romano-British Cemeteries at Cirencester*, A.McWhirr, L. Viner and C. Wells (eds), 135–202. Cirencester: Cirencester Excavations Committee.

Winzer, M.A. 1997. Disease and society before the 18th century. In *The Disability Studies Reader*, L.J. Davies (ed.), 75–109. London: Routledge.

Wood, J.W., G.R. Milner, H.C. Harpending and K.M. Weiss 1992. The osteological paradox: problems of inferring health from the skeleton. *Current Anthropology* 33, 343–70.

4 Developmental defects and disability: the evidence from the Iron Age semi-nomadic peoples of Aymyrlyg, south Siberia

EILEEN M. MURPHY

INTRODUCTION

The cemetery complex of Aymyrlyg is located in the Ulug-Khemski region of the Autonomous Republic of Tuva, south Siberia.[1] Most of the burials were dated to between the third and second centuries BC and others from the first century BC to AD second century. The former, therefore, derived from within the Uyuk Culture of the so-called Scythian period (seventh to second century BC), and the latter from the so-called Hunno-Sarmatian period.[2]

Recent palaeopathological research on a corpus of approximately 800 skeletons from the cemetery has revealed the occurrence of a large number of developmental defects among both populations (Murphy 1998). The majority of the defects may be regarded as occult, since they would have had no obvious detrimental health effects on the affected individuals. Several congenital malformations which would have resulted in the individuals displaying physical disabilities and abnormal appearances were also evident.

DEVELOPMENTAL DEFECTS

Developmental defects are relatively common in modern populations, occurring with a frequency of between 1 and 5 per cent in all live births. The defects occur with even greater frequencies in stillbirths and natural abortions, and are one of the highest causes of neonatal and infant death (Kennedy 1967: 1). The causes of developmental defects in humans are many and complex, and each form of defect may arise for a number of reasons. It may occur as a result of specific dominant or recessive genes, or it may arise sporadically or follow a familial tendency (Fraser 1959: 97–9). In addition, environmental factors such as maternal dietary deficiencies (e.g. hypovitaminosis A and lack of riboflavin) and excesses (e.g. a fatty diet) during early pregnancy can result in the occurrence of developmental defects (Seller 1987: 227). It is generally considered that the majority of defects arise from complex interactions between genetic predispositions and subtle factors in the intra-uterine environment (Fraser 1959: 108). When one considers the immense complexities and the many factors involved during the formation, growth and development of a human being it is surprising that more abnormalities do not occur per head of population (Fishbein 1963: v).

Non-occult developmental defects: axial skeleton

Hypoplastic mandibles

Two Scythian period individuals displayed hypoplasia of the mandible, a defect which arises as a result of delay in growth during the development of the mandibular precursor (Barnes 1994: 161). Both individuals had been buried in the same log house tomb and it is probable that they were related. One of the individuals was a 25–35 year-old probable male, and the other was a 35–45 year-old probable female.

Hemimetamere hypoplasia-aplasia – Congenital scoliosis

Skeleton XXXI. 89, a 25–35 year-old female, displayed multiple unilateral hemimetameric hypoplasia which had resulted in scoliosis of the upper thoracic spine by approximately 30° to the right, and severe scoliosis of the lower thoracic region by approximately 90° to the left (Figure 4.1). The skeleton was very gracile with poorly developed muscle markings and no degenerative changes were apparent on any of the post-cranial bones with the exception of the vertebrae. It is probable, therefore, that the woman was generally immobile, since it would be expected that the scoliosis would have resulted in severe strain to the joints and muscles if she had possessed locomotory abilities.

It is also probable that the diameter of the vertebral foramina in the eighth to the eleventh thoracic vertebrae would have been reduced, and this may have caused damage to the spinal cord and/or its associated blood supply. Studies have shown that if the lumen of the spinal canal is narrowed between the fourth and the ninth thoracic vertebrae, maximal compromise of the spinal cord can arise as a result of minimal reduction of the lumen (Dommisse 1985: 244). It is therefore possible that the woman was, at least partially, paraplegic. Clinical studies have indicated that in congenital scoliosis the incidence of paraplegia is as high as 10 per cent (Winter 1985: 250). The scoliosis would have caused the thorax to have a grossly abnormal morphology and this would have resulted in stress and strain being placed on the internal vital organs. Cardiorespiratory failure is a common complication of progressive scoliosis and generally results in premature death (Milner and Milner 1985: 198). Individuals with congenital scoliosis are also likely to display abnormalities of the genito-urinary tract, congenital heart disease, undescended scapulae and abnormalities of the thumb (Ozonoff 1995: 4255).

Possible meningocele and hydrocephalus

In Skeleton VII. 13, a 4–5 year-old child, the cranium had a globular appearance with notable frontal and parietal bossing. Evidence of stretching was apparent in the sagittal and coronal sutures, numerous wormian bones were present in the lambdoid suture,

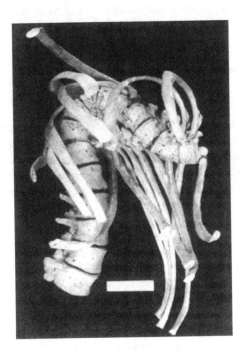

Figure 4.1 Reconstruction of the vertebral column and rib cage of the Hunno-Sarmatian period woman with congenital scoliosis due to multiple unilateral hemimetameric hypoplasia. Scale bar represents 6 cm. [Photo: E. Murphy]

and an ossicle was apparent in the right side of the coronal suture. In addition, the cranial capacity was 1400cc. The morphology of the cranium is indicative that the individual may have been suffering from hydrocephalus (Murphy 1996: 437). The individual also displayed an oval-shaped, well-defined depressed area at the midpoint of the frontal bone on the line of the metopic suture. A small perforation was apparent at the inferior aspect of the lesion, and it is possible that the depression is indicative of a meningocele.

A meningocele is a postneurulation defect of the neural tube which results in a section of the meninges protruding outside the cranium or vertebral column in a skin-covered cyst (Barnes 1994: 52). Individuals born with a cranial meningocele can survive into adulthood since it would have been covered by protective membrane and skin but it would still, however, have been vulnerable to irritation and trauma (Barnes 1994: 54). The size of the protruding sac can range from a small nubbin of tissue to a cyst which is larger than the cranium itself. Individuals with a meningocele have a generally good prognosis and can develop without motor or mental disabilities (Fishman 1991: 1697). They are commonly associated with hydrocephalus (Richards and Anton 1991: 196), the condition in which there is an abnormal accumulation of cerebrospinal fluid within the cranium due to an imbalance in the production and absorption of the fluid (Fishman 1991: 1697). Hydrocephalus can be either congenital or acquired, and in a study of relatively modern cases the aetiology of the condition was attributed to malformations, trauma, infection and tumours (Laurence 1958: 1152).

In modern situations there are numerous indicators that a child is suffering from hydrocephalus. There is usually a gradual increase in the size of the upper part of the head with the effect that it becomes out of proportion to the size of the face or the rest of the body, and the cranium develops a globular appearance (Fishman 1991: 1700). The increased pressure may cause a child to complain of headaches, to become dull, listless and irritable, and to undergo a general change in personality. In some cases the child may suffer from mental subnormality, gait disturbances, loss of balance and an inability to concentrate (McLone et al. 1987: 9). Since no evidence of tumours, infections or any other disease processes were apparent in the remains, it would seem that the hydrocephalus in the Aymyrlyg individual was either congenital or a genetically induced malformation. It is possible that the meningocele and the hydrocephalus were related conditions, and both abnormalities may be indicative of neural tube defects. Alternatively, the hydrocephalus may have been secondary to the meningocele.

Non-occult developmental defects: appendicular skeleton

Developmental dysplasia and congenital dislocation of the hip

Two Scythian period individuals displayed developmental dysplasia and dislocation of their hip joints. In Skeleton D. 5. Sk. 6, a 17–25 year-old possible female, developmental dysplasia of the right hip was apparent (Figure 4.2). The bones were generally atrophied with an abnormal morphology, and the acetabulum was triangular shaped. The femoral head had a flattened appearance supero-inferiorly, the femoral neck was very thin, and the lesser trochanter was quite pronounced. The shaft appeared to have undergone a degree of torsion and the gluteal tuberosity and linea aspera were positioned more laterally than normal. The abnormal morphology of the bones, and the lack of secondary degenerative joint disease or a false joint surface, suggests that the right hip joint and right leg were dysfunctional. A slight area of pitting positioned immediately above the superior margin of the ilium may indicate that the femoral head had been positioned against this part of the bone. Unfortunately, none of the other bones of the skeleton were available for analysis.

In Skeleton VI. 10. Sk. 1, a 25–35 year-old female, unilateral developmental dysplasia of the left hip was apparent. In general, the remains of the individual were very gracile, and all of the bones of the left innominate were atrophied relative to those of the right side. The acetabulum had a triangular shape and it would probably have been impossible for the femoral head to articulate with the acetabulum. It is likely that the left side of the pelvis would have been displaced inferiorly relative to the right side. The entire left femur was atrophied and the femoral head was abnormally small with a flattened appearance supero-inferiorly. The left tibia and fibula were also

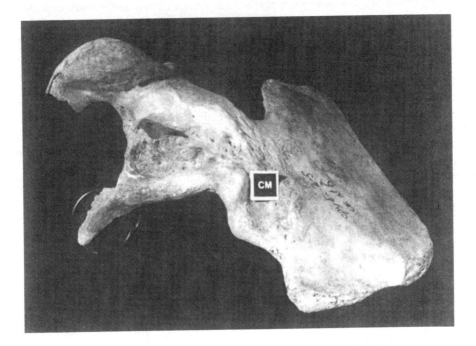

Figure 4.2 The right innominate of a Scythian period female displaying developmental dysplasia. [Photo: E. Murphy]

atrophied and no muscle markings were apparent. It is probable that the left leg would have been generally dysfunctional as a consequence of the dysplastic hip.

Marginal osteophytes were apparent on the proximal lateral condyle of the right tibia. A minor enthesophyte was also apparent (patellar ligament) although, in general, the muscle markings of the right leg bones were well developed, and this may indicate that the individual was able to use this limb for locomotion. The proximal end of the right humerus had a slightly different morphology to that of the left humerus. The head did not extend as far posteriorly on the right humerus as in a normal bone. Porosity was apparent on the postero-lateral surface of the anatomical neck, which may indicate that there was strain of the infraspinatus and teres minor. These changes may be indicative that the individual had used some form of crutches for locomotory purposes which would have involved the majority of stress being placed on the right side of her body. The occurrence of Schmorl's nodes may indicate that an excessive strain was being placed on her lower spine, perhaps as a result of her locomotory methods.

Genetic, mechanical, hormonal and social factors have all been implicated as possible factors which are responsible for susceptibility to dislocation of the hip in the embryo (Ferrer-Torrelles and Ceballos 1982: 21). In the majority of cases the dysplasia arises as a result of abnormalities in the developmental processes, indicating that the defect is genetically controlled (Inman 1963: 250). Factors which genetically predispose an individual to having a dislocated hip include the depth of the socket of the joint and generalized ligamentous laxity (Carter 1964: 308). Cases of developmental dysplasia of the hip also occur sporadically, however, and it has been suggested that these cases arise due to an intra-uterine position of the foetus in which either the hips are flexed or the knees are incompletely flexed and the feet are externally rotated. This posture commonly occurs in breech births, especially among the first-born (Carter 1964: 308).

Individuals with congenital dislocation of the hip will generally display the Trendelenburg gait, a limp which is characterized by an even timing of the two legs, but with a tilt towards the normal hip. From a distance, unilateral examples of the limp are observed as a lateral movement of the shoulders towards the normal side, or as a movement of the shoulders from side to side if the condition is bilateral (Gruebel Lee 1983: 78). If the dysplasia of the hip has not been treated in individuals over the age of three years then the femoral head will become deformed and the acetabulum will have a triangular morphology (Inman 1963: 252).

Slipped femoral capital epiphysis

Three Scythian and two Hunno-Sarmatian period individuals displayed evidence for slipped femoral capital epiphysis. This condition most typically occurs in children and adolescents, with a greater incidence occurring among males. A number of factors have been proposed as possible aetiologies for the condition, and a link is generally accepted between it and adolescent growth spurts since the growth plate is particularly vulnerable to shearing stresses during this period (Resnick *et al.* 1995: 2646). Associated with the adolescent growth period are the influences of a variety of sex hormones. Slipped femoral epiphysis is common in adolescents who are overweight and have delayed sexual maturation. A greater amount of growth hormones relative to sex hormones are present in these individuals, and this may increase the period of time when the proximal epiphysis is vulnerable to slippage (Gruebel Lee 1983: 176). In some families there may be a notable history of slipped epiphysis, and the condition has been observed in monozygotic twins (Resnick *et al.* 1995: 2646).

There are a number of main characteristics of slipped femoral capital epiphysis, which include the crumbling of inadequately ossified metaphyseal bone positioned just inferior to the epiphyseal plate. This results in a chronic slippage in which the bones of the femoral neck gradually bend and deform. Acute slippage occurs as a result of sudden shearing separation of the epiphysis from the metaphysis (Gruebel Lee 1983: 175). Chronic slippage occurs in approximately 70 per cent of cases, with acute slippage present among 30 per cent of affected individuals (Apley and Solomon 1988: 172). The sequelae of the condition include severe varus deformity, broadening and shortening of the femoral neck, flattening of the femoral head, osteonecrosis, chondrolysis and degenerative changes (Resnick *et al.* 1995: 2647). In an individual with slipped femoral epiphysis the affected leg will be shortened and externally rotated. A loss of abduction will be apparent, associated with increased adduction due to coxa vara. In addition, there is loss of internal rotation, increased external rotation and hyperextension with loss of flexion of the hip. The individual may also experience pain upon certain movements (Gruebel Lee 1983: 181).

Clubfoot (Equinovarus Congenita)

A possible case of clubfoot was noted from the remains of Skeleton XXXI. 182b, a 17–25 year-old Hunno-Sarmatian period female. The distal epiphysis of the right tibia was dysplastic, and when viewed from an inferior position the epiphysis had a triangular-shaped appearance. The articular surface had a concave morphology and existed only at the antero-lateral aspect of the epiphysis. The lateral malleolus was more prominent than normal, while the medial malleolus was reduced. A prominent tubercle was situated at the postero-inferior aspect of the epiphysis. The fibular notch was enlarged to form a distinct articular facet. This corresponded to a prominent oval-shaped articular facet, situated just superior to the normal distal tibio-fibular articular facet on the medial surface of the right fibula. The bones of the right leg were slightly more gracile than those of the left leg, which may suggest that the right leg was not as useful for locomotory purposes as its normal counterpart.

It is unfortunate that the right tarsals and metatarsals were not available for analysis, since without an understanding of their morphology it is difficult to deduce a definitive aetiology for the dysplasia of the right tibia. It is possible, however, that the individual had a clubfoot abnormality in her right foot. Two major theories have been proposed to account for the occurrence of this deformity. Extrinsic factors, such as an abnormal intrauterine position or decreased fluid within the amniotic sac (oligohydramnios), are considered to be possible aetiologies. The second theory proposes that intrinsic factors are responsible for the deformity, and these include developmental arrest, abnormal tendon and ligament attachments, neurological defects with associated muscle dysfunction, and primary germ plasm defects (Coleman 1983: 24). It is most widely accepted, however, that the deformity arises as a result of a primary defect in the development of the tarsal bones, particularly the talus (Coleman 1983: 26).

Clinical studies have indicated that the incidence of clubfoot deformity varies markedly between peoples. In Caucasians an incidence of 1 to 1.24 per 1000 births has been recorded, while among Orientals the incidence is only 0.57 per 1000 births. In general, males are twice as likely to have the abnormality than females (Coleman 1983: 28), and clubfoot is familial in a notable proportion of cases, which may indicate that the abnormality is genetically related. It is considered that congenital idiopathic clubfoot is inherited as a polygenic multifactorial trait, in which the mode of inheritance is extremely complicated (Turco 1981: 10).

Polytropic defects

Three Scythian period individuals displayed lesions which are considered indicative of polytropic developmental defects or syndromes. These defects are identified on the basis of multiple anomalies which occur in the same, or related morphogenetic fields as a consequence of a single disturbance, at a time when their precursor structures are all equally vulnerable. The majority of multiple-field defects recognized by clinicians have been classified as a result of the pattern of anomalies expressed in the phenotype (Turkel 1989: 112).

Neurofibromatosis

A possible case of neurofibromatosis was apparent in Skeleton XXIII. 10. Sk. 2, a 25–35 year-old female individual (Murphy *et al.* 1998). Only the skull of the individual was available for analysis. The left orbit had an abnormal appearance with hypertrophy of the superior orbital rim and expansion of the orbital walls (Figure 4.3). The right orbit was also larger than the average size recorded for other individuals from Aymyrlyg, a finding which may indicate that the person was suffering from a condition which affected both orbits. Inferior and medial displacement of the orbital floor was evident in the hypertrophied left orbit, and the lacrimal bone and the orbital surface of the maxilla also appeared expanded. The fossa for the lacrimal sac and the posterior lacrimal crest were not clearly defined and had a shallow elongated appearance. The optic canal and the superior and inferior orbital fissures appeared to

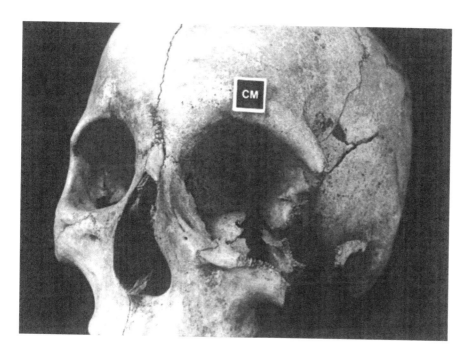

Figure 4.3 Grossly enlarged left orbit in a Scythian period female with possible neurofibromatosis. [Photo: E. Murphy]

be of normal size and morphology. All interior surfaces of the bones of the left orbit had a very smooth appearance, with the only exception being the presence of a bony exostosis at the lateral part of the orbital surface of the greater wing of the sphenoid bone, medial to the suture with the zygomatic. It is possible that the exostosis was an enthesopathy of the lateral palpebral raphe ligament. The frontal process of the maxilla and the right nasal bone were also dysplastic. The metopic suture was retained and may be another component of the facial dysplasia.

Neurofibromatosis is the term used to represent a wide range of abnormalities resulting from neuroectodermal dystrophy. It is a congenital condition with an autosomal dominant inheritance. Signs and symptoms reflect primary involvement of the central and peripheral nervous systems, with secondary involvement of many organs including the orbit, eye, skin, viscera, muscles and bone (Brazier 1994: 247). The condition may result in the development of tumours of the peripheral and central nervous system. Clinical characteristics of the condition include the appearance of numerous *café au lait* spots on the chest, back and thighs, skin tumours, lesions of the viscera and congenital absence of part of the sphenoid bone (Hoskins and Kass 1989: 386). In the majority of cases the early manifestations of the condition are not apparent until late childhood or early adult life (Brazier 1994: 247).

In the orbit, bone abnormalities and benign soft-tissue tumours, including neurofibromas, schwannomas, optical nerve gliomas and nerve sheath menin-giomas, may be apparent in neurofibromatosis. The secondary bone abnormalities most commonly found include a generalized enlargement of the orbit and thinn-ing of its margins (Burrows 1963: 552). The generalized enlargement is considered to be due to the presence of a soft-tissue tumour or to buphthalmos (enlarge-ment and distension of the eye globe) associated with neurofibromatosis. In some instances, however, the enlargement is regarded as part of the bony dysplasia (Brazier 1994: 249).

It is considered that the enlarged left orbit in the individual from Aymyrlyg was possibly caused by the presence of a plexiform neurofibroma. The abnormal appearance, with hypertrophy of the superior orbital rim and extension of the orbital walls, is considered to be compatible with the occurrence of a soft-tissue tumour in the orbital cavity. The slightly enlarged right orbit and the abnormal morphology of the nasal region indicate that the person was suffering from a condition in which the general facial area was involved, possibly indicative of systemic neurofibromatosis. Although the sphenoid and optic canal were of normal morphology, this does not exclude a diagnosis of neurofibromatosis, since the plexiform neurofibroma is the most typical orbital lesion in neurofibromatosis (Brazier 1994: 247).

The grossly enlarged and dysmorphic left orbit indicates that there would probably have been facial hemi-hypertrophy, proptosis, restriction of ocular movement, and possibly reduced vision in the individual from Aymyrlyg. To have caused such marked changes to the facial skeleton the condition would most likely have started in childhood while the bones were still developing. Since the individual survived into adulthood the condition could not have been aggressive and would have developed gradually over a substantial period of time.

Hemifacial microsomia/Goldenhar syndrome

A possible case of hemifacial microsomia/Goldenhar syndrome was apparent in the remains of Skeleton IV. 2. Sk. 7, an 8–10 year-old juvenile. Only the skull was available for analysis but this displayed unilateral hypoplasia which affected the left side of the face (Figure 4.4). The left maxilla, the left side of the nasal cavity and the left zygomatic were all hypoplastic relative to their right counterpart bones. The inferior portion of the metopic suture, the nasal bones, the palate and the left orbit all displayed marked lateral oblique deviation. In addition, the calvarium was asymmetrical with the left side having a reduced greatest length and greatest breadth relative to the right side. The left side of the mandible was also hypoplastic, the left mental tubercle was very pronounced, and there was a prominent enthesis between the mental tubercle and the coronoid process. The right molars displayed extensive attrition relative to the left

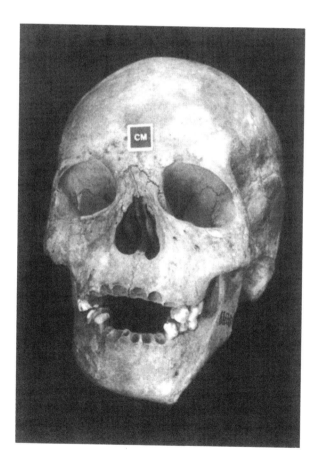

Figure 4.4 Unilateral hypoplasia of the left side of the skull in a Scythian period juvenile, possibly due to Goldenhar syndrome/hemifacial microsomia. [Photo: E. Murphy]

molars, which may indicate that the individual had predominantly chewed using the right side of the mouth. The hypoplasia of the left side of the skull may have made it difficult for the individual to use the left side of the mouth for mastication. The morphology of the socket of the right mandibular first incisor was abnormally small, and this may be indicative that either the deciduous first incisor had been retained, or that the permanent first incisor was peg-shaped. It is possible that this dental abnormality is related to the cranial hypoplasia. The morphology of the cranium suggests that the individual had one of the conditions of the oculo-auriculo-vertebral spectrum.

The malformations of the oculo-auriculo-vertebral spectrum are derived from disruptions in the development of the first and second branchial arches (Gorlin et al. 1990: 641). Malformations of the maxillary section of the first branchial arch results in down-slanting fissures, an abnormal contour of the lower eyelids, and zygomatic hypoplasia. Mandibular abnormalities are generally characterized by a receding chin. Faulty development of the second branchial arch results in abnormalities of the external ear, supernumerary auricular appendages, hypoplastic or aplastic auricles, and the occurrence of blind fistulas between the ear and the angle of the mouth. Deafness and dental abnormalities can arise from maldevelopment of both the first and second branchial arches (Sargent and Ousterhout 1983: 1040).

A wide variety of terms have been applied to the oculo-auriculo-vertebral complex and this reflects the variety of anomalies contained within this spectrum. Since only the skull of Skeleton IV. 2. Sk. 7 was available for analysis it is impossible to ascertain the full extent of the cranial and skeletal anomalies which would have been present in the individual. Consequently, it is difficult to know which term is most appropriate. Since the majority of medical texts consulted by the author opt for the use of Goldenhar syndrome to describe this condition, this term will be applied in the current discussion.

Goldenhar syndrome is a pattern of malformation with a variety of expressions characterized by ocular, auricular and skeletal defects (Sargent and Ousterhout 1983: 1040). The syndrome was first characterized by Goldenhar in 1952 when an infant with an epibulbar dermoid, auricular appendages and an auricular fistula was described (Duke-Elder 1964: 1021). In Goldenhar syndrome, hypoplasia of the mandible and maxilla is unilateral, which can result in malocclusion, abnormal positioning of the teeth and asymmetry of the palate. The gonial angle of the mandible is commonly flattened. The maxillary, temporal, and zygomatic bones on the affected side are reduced in size and have a flattened appearance. The orbit may be reduced in size and positioned at a lower level than the eye on the unaffected side (Gorlin et al. 1990: 646). In addition, vertebral anomalies including occipitalization of the atlas, block vertebrae, hemivertebrae, supernumerary vertebrae and cleft neural arch defect can occur (Feingold and Gellis 1968: 33). Hemivertebrae and block vertebrae are the most frequently encountered spinal anomalies (Rees et al. 1972: 15). Mental retardation is encountered in approximately 10 per cent of children with Goldenhar syndrome (Shokeir 1977: 67).

Researchers have attempted to differentiate between hemifacial microsomia and Goldenhar syndrome by stating that hemifacial microsomia is a complex dysmorphic syndrome which involves the first and second branchial arches and can be associated with cardiac, pulmonary, renal, genital and skeletal abnormalities, while Goldenhar syndrome is generally confined to hemifacial microsomia, dermoids of the eyes, coloboma of the upper eyelid, macrostomia, microtia, and vertebral abnormalities (Burck 1983: 292). Individuals displaying either pattern of anomalies are, however, generally referred to as having the Goldenhar syndrome. It is thought that the hemifacial microsomia syndrome and Goldenhar syndrome may represent gradations in severity of a similar error of development (Burck 1983: 291).

The aetiology of Goldenhar syndrome is uncertain but, since sporadic instances are most common, exogenous influences when the foetus is *in utero* have been postulated as a probable aetiology (Setzer *et al.* 1981: 90). Although the majority of cases of hemifacial microsomia are sporadic, there are occasional familial occurrences. A few examples have been reported in siblings, and the disorder appears as a dominant trait in a small number of families (Burck 1983: 296). The incidence of Goldenhar syndrome has been estimated at 1 per 3000 to 1 per 5000 births, with a slight predominance in males (3:2) (Smith and Jones 1982: 497).

The unilateral hypoplasia of the cranium and mandible, and the dental malocclusion are compatible with Goldenhar syndrome. In the more severe cases of the syndrome the entire half of the face, the orbit and the skull can be affected (Sargent and Ousterhout 1983: 1042). This appears to have been the case in this individual, and he or she may have had bulbar dermoids in the eyes, misshapen or low-set ears and vertebral skeletal anomalies (Sargent and Ousterhout 1983: 1042).

Frontometaphyseal dysplasia

The skull of Skeleton IV. 2. Sk. 3a, a 25–35 year-old adult male, displayed possible signs of frontometaphyseal dysplasia. Only the skull was available for analysis. The cranium was notably large and robust, and the supraorbital ridge was pronounced (Figure 4.5). Despite post-mortem damage, there appeared to have been a degree of ocular hypertelorism. The left maxilla was slightly hypoplastic relative to the right maxilla, giving the face an asymmetrical appearance. The left side of the palate was also hypoplastic relative to the right side. The mandible was dysplastic, with the left side displaying hypoplasia of the ascending ramus and the coronoid process, while the mandibular condyle was aplastic. All four third molars were genetically absent.

Frontometaphyseal dysplasia is characterized by the occurrence of prominent supraorbital ridges, micrognathia, a wide nasal bridge, a high arched palate, loss of hearing, problems with vision, a short trunk with long extremities, elongated fingers with ulnar deviation of the hands, genu valgum, and decreased joint mobility (McAlister and Herman 1995: 4207). Missing permanent teeth and retention of the deciduous teeth are also characteristic features of the condition (Gorlin *et al.* 1990: 237). The disorder was first reported by Gorlin and Cohen in 1969 (as quoted by Smith and Jones 1982: 288). Although many of the reported cases of frontometaphyseal dysplasia have been sporadic, x-linked recessive inheritance has been established (McAlister and Herman 1995: 4208).

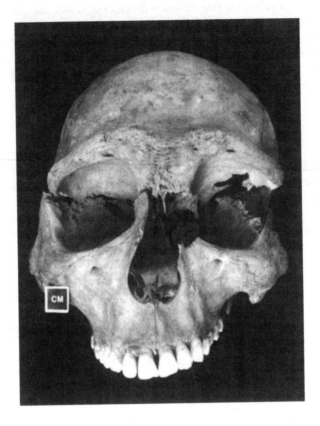

Figure 4.5 Possible frontometaphyseal dysplasia in a Scythian period male. [Photo: E. Murphy]

PHYSICAL IMPLICATIONS OF THE DEVELOPMENTAL DEFECTS

In the Scythian period group the two individuals with hypoplastic mandibles may have had abnormal appearance. The hypoplasia would probably not, however, have caused any significant disability. Both of the Scythian period individuals with developmental dysplasia and congenital dislocation of the hip would probably have had abnormal gaits, and less efficient locomotory powers than most unaffected members of society. The three Scythian and two Hunno-Sarmatian period individuals with possible slipped femoral capital epiphyses may also have had gait disturbances and less powerful locomotory capabilities relative to the unaffected members of society.

The Hunno-Sarmatian period female individual with hemimetameric hypoplasia-aplasia would have displayed severe scoliosis, whereby the upper thoracic spine would have been slightly angulated to the right and the lower thoracic spine would have displayed scoliosis of approximately 90° to the left. The Hunno-Sarmatian period child with a possible meningocele and hydrocephalus would probably have displayed an abnormally large head, possibly with an extra nubbin of tissue situated on the superior aspect of the forehead. The Hunno-Sarmatian period female with a clubfoot would certainly have displayed an abnormal gait and may have had problems with locomotion.

The three Scythian period individuals with polytropic defects would definitely have displayed abnormal facial characteristics. The female with possible neurofibromatosis would have had a dysplastic appearance with a grossly enlarged and probably exophthalmic eyeball. In addition, she would probably have had reduced vision in the affected eye. Other physical characteristics of neurofibromatosis include the occurrence of *café au lait* spots, skin tumours, kyphoscoliosis, pseudoarthroses as well as a large range of other abnormalities (Gorlin *et al.* 1976: 536–8). Since only the skull was preserved, however, the full extent of the lesions apparent in this individual remain unknown. The child with possible Goldenhar syndrome would have displayed unilateral hypoplasia of the left side of the skull. He or she may also have displayed abnormalities of the external ear and been deaf, had eye defects possibly including microphthalmia or anophthalmia, suffered from mental retardation, and vertebral anomalies (Gorlin *et al.* 1976: 548–50). Since only the skull of the individual was available for analysis, however, it is not possible to ascertain the full extent of skeletal involvement. The adult male with possible frontometaphyseal dysplasia would also have displayed abnormal facial characteristics. His facial features would have been coarse with large brow-ridges, widely spaced eyes and an asymmetrical face and chin. He may also have been deaf and had poor vision, as well as a number of other physical abnormalities, as described earlier. Again, unfortunately, only the skull was preserved and it is, therefore, impossible to determine the full extent of skeletal involvement.

SOCIAL ATTITUDES TO INDIVIDUALS WITH OBVIOUS MALFORMATIONS

It has been argued that in the past, as in many societies today, unwanted infants, in some cases with obvious physical abnormalities, were allowed to die from disease, or natural means or exposed to predators. Infanticide, for example, may have resulted in the disposal of such infants away from the main cemetery and, as a result, their remains are rarely present among archaeological skeletal populations (Gregg *et al.* 1981: 220). The appearance of individuals with developmental defects in an archaeological population group can, however, enable us to elucidate information on the society's attitude towards these affected individuals. When developmental defects are found, this suggests that the affected persons had the benefit of some life support measures (Gregg *et al.* 1981: 221). Aymyrlyg is one such site.

The majority of developmental defects discussed above would probably not have been apparent in the individuals at birth, although a proportion (for example, clubfoot) may have been evident at that time. Consequently, affected individuals would not have been regarded as abnormal at birth and for that reason were allowed the chance to grow and develop as normal members of society. The occurrence of adult individuals with prominent developmental defects in both population groups from Aymyrlyg indicates that, even after the development of observable physical disabilities and disfigurements, presumably during childhood, the majority of them were allowed to survive into adulthood.

Unfortunately, the incomplete nature of the excavation record for the site makes it impossible to discover whether affected members of society had been buried with grave goods similar to those buried with unaffected members of the population. As a consequence, it is not generally possible to use grave goods as a means of identifying differential treatment of these individuals by their peers. The inclusion of these individuals with possible abnormal appearances and disabilities in communal graves with unaffected people might suggest that they were held in similar regard to other members of society.

It is unlikely that disabled individuals would have been non-productive members of society, and ethnographic studies indicate that all societies have necessary jobs which can be undertaken by people with disabilities. Disabled individuals with reduced mobility or deafness among the !Kung San of the Kalahari, for example, contribute to cooking, gathering and childcare activities (Lee and DeVore 1976). Blind individuals in Mali have been recorded as being responsible for spinning cotton, cloth production and minding children (Dettwyler 1991: 380). Archaeology cannot tell us if Aymyrlyg's disabled individuals would have been treated with compassion simply from an examination of their skeletal remains and contexts, but their burial in communal tombs might provide evidence that they were accepted by their peers as having roles to play in society. The nature of these roles, however, remains hidden. They may have had very difficult lives, perhaps being ridiculed, beaten, treated as slaves, and constantly reminded of their physical differences. Ethnographic work in Mali, for example, has shown that the disabled people in the community under study were routinely stoned, beaten and taunted in the market for the entertainment of the crowd. These individuals were able to survive through the efforts of their families, but they were not treated compassionately (Dettwyler 1991: 382). The same may, or may not, have been true for the disabled in Iron Age Tuva.

What is clear is that these individuals were allowed to reach adulthood, and some effort must have been made to enable them to survive within a semi-nomadic lifestyle. The historical and ethnographic sources stress the semi-nomadic nature of both societies and it is probable that the individuals would have spent a proportion of their time travelling in wagons across the steppes between their seasonal camps (Watson 1961: 155; Sélincourt and Burn 1972: 286; Chadwick and Mann 1978: 163; Vainshtein 1980: 51–2). Consequently, individuals such as the Hunno-Sarmatian period woman with severe congenital scoliosis would probably have needed assistance with the most basic of activities such as getting in and out of the wagons. The gracile nature of her skeleton, in conjunction with the severe scoliosis, suggest that she would have been practically immobile.

The Scythian period child with possible Goldenhar syndrome, and the adult male with possible frontometaphyseal dysplasia recovered from Log House Tomb IV. 2, displayed polytropic defects which cannot be biologically related. It is, therefore, impossible to prove that a familial relationship existed between the two individuals. Consequently, although it is possible that the two individuals were related and simply displayed unusual congenital syndromes through coincidence, it is also possible that they were buried in the same tomb for social reasons.

The differential burial of people of 'unusual' appearance is known from a variety of populations. Ethnographic studies have indicated that the 'Bantu' of North Kavirondo had different burial rites for people with physical abnormalities, and that 'hunchbacks', for example, were denied the usual rites (Wagner 1949: 479). The Yoruba of Nigeria buried leprosy sufferers, albinos, 'hunchbacks', and women who had died during childbirth in 'sacred graves' so that the priests could ensure that there would not be a recurrence of these conditions and deaths (Bascom 1969: 66). The majority of the Amba people in East Africa were buried in the courtyards of their houses, but abnormal or dangerous people (including those with distended abdomens, twins and the mentally disturbed) were interred in forests (Winter 1967: 25). Special burial grounds in Ireland, known as cillíní, and dating from approximately AD seventh century until early this century, were reserved for the interment of the mentally retarded, strangers, the shipwrecked, criminals, famine victims, and suicides as well as stillborn and unbaptized infants (Donnelly et al. 1999).

It is possible that the two Scythian period individuals from Aymyrlyg had been deliberately buried together in the one tomb because of their unusual appearance. This argument is weakened, however, by the fact that the location of Log House Tomb IV. 2 did not appear unusual, and that the remains of at least ten other individuals were in the tomb. In addition, the grave goods associated with the individuals in the tomb were generally similar to those retrieved from other Scythian period tombs, and included the remains of weaponry which may be indicative of warrior burials. Bearing this in mind, however, the two individuals did display unusual developmental defects, which would have caused obvious facial disfigurement, and it cannot be dismissed out of hand that the other individuals buried in the tomb may also have been subject to differential burial, perhaps for social reasons which did not leave their mark on the skeletal remains.

AYMYRLYG'S NON-OCCULT DEVELOPMENTAL DEFECTS AND THE PALAEOPATHOLOGICAL RECORD

The corpus of congenital malformations from Aymyrlyg is valuable since it contains both common occult defects as well as a variety of rarer and serious anomalies. Barnes (1994: 60–1) recorded the existence of three known cases of hemivertebrae from England, New Mexico and Peru and a single case of hemimetameric hypoplasia–aplasia from Alaska, though of a much milder variant than that recovered from Aymyrlyg (Barnes 1994: 66). Approximately 30 cases of hydrocephalus are known from the palaeopathological record (Murphy 1996: 435), while six examples of meningoceles were recorded by Barnes (1994: 53–4). Palaeopathological cases of clubfoot are relatively rare, possibly because it is hard to identify (Roberts and Manchester 1995: 38).

Although the case from Aymyrlyg is not definitive, since the bones of the feet were not present, it should be considered as a possible example.

The three possible polytropic defects must be regarded as the most unusual palaeopathological cases among the entire Aymyrlyg population. As Turkel (1989: 125) stated, 'skeletons collected for study from individuals with rare syndromes are more rare than the syndromes'. Only one previous case of neurofibromatosis has been previously described in the palaeopathological record to date, an example from an AD 19th century context in England (Knüsel and Bowman 1996). Consequently, Aymyrlyg's Scythian period case of possible neurofibromatosis is, to the best of the author's knowledge, the first prehistoric example of this syndrome to have been discovered. The child with possible Goldenhar syndrome/hemifacial microsomia is also a rare palaeopathological finding. Barnes (1994: 161–3) discussed five cases of hemifacial microsomia. Only one of the individuals, however, was described as displaying slight facial asymmetry while the other cases displayed lesions more reminiscent of the two Scythian period individuals who had hypoplastic mandibles. The individual from Aymyrlyg with possible frontometaphyseal dysplasia is thought to be the first example of this syndrome to have been described in the palaeopathological literature. With only some 30 cases reported in modern clinical literature (Gorlin et al. 1990: 235), the condition is considered very rare. Consequently, the possible case from Aymyrlyg is an important clinical and palaeopathological finding since it could extend the earliest recorded cases of the condition back to between 300 and 200 BC.

CONCLUSIONS

The principal significance of the discovery of individuals in both population groups who had suffered from debilitating developmental conditions lies in the fact that it can provide us with an insight into the social attitudes of these particular Iron Age peoples. The survival in semi-nomadic populations of physically and, in some cases, possible mentally disabled individuals might suggest that they had received support during their lives. In addition, the burial of these individuals in communal tombs with apparently non-affected people may indicate that they were regarded as full members of society and were able to make a valid contribution to their society. Although the majority of developmental defects apparent in both populations may not have been evident at birth, it is probable that defects such as clubfoot may have been obvious at this time. It is possible, therefore, that individuals with obvious deformities were not considered abnormal and were not ostracized by their peers, but even so, the question of how others actually felt about them cannot be definitively answered.

ACKNOWLEDGEMENTS

I would like to thank Professors Yuri Chistov and Ilyia Gokhman, Department of Physical Anthropology, Peter the Great Museum of Anthropology and Ethnography,

St Petersburg, for granting me permission to examine the Aymyrlyg human remains. I would also like to thank Professor Jim Mallory, School of Archaeology and Palaeoecology, the Queen's University of Belfast, for supervising my doctorate research and Dr Colm Donnelly, of the aforementioned School, for his comments on the text. I am also grateful to Dr Robert Gorlin of the School of Dentistry at the University of Minnesota for verifying the identification of the possible cases of Goldenhar syndrome/hemifacial microsomia and frontometaphyseal dysplasia, and Dr Feldore McHugh for providing me with anthropological examples of differential burial practices.

NOTES

1 The cemetery complex was excavated in the period between 1968 and 1984 by archaeologists of the Sayano-Tuvinskaya expedition team from the Institute for the History of Material Culture of St Petersburg. The Director of the expedition for the period between 1968 and 1978 was Dr A.M. Mandelshtam, and Dr E.U. Stambulnik continued the research until the mid 1980s.

2 In the Scythian period the most common funerary monument was the rectangular log house tomb. The numbers of individuals buried within an Aymyrlyg log house tomb was considerable, with as many as 15 skeletons being recovered from individual tombs. Another funerary monument of the Scythian period was the stone cist, commonly encountered at Aymyrlyg (Mandelshtam 1983: 33). In the Hunno-Sarmatian period burial was in a composite wooden coffin or, less frequently, in a hollowed-out log. The majority of burials from this period consisted of a single individual, although several double and triple burials were encountered (Stambulnik 1983: 34).

On the basis of the Scythian artefacts from Tuva it is inferred that the peoples of this highland steppe practised a semi-nomadic form of pastoralism which was combined with cultivation, hunting and gathering (Vainshtein 1980: 51). Their economy is believed to have involved seasonal movements between mountains and steppes within borders of a defined territory (Mandelshtam 1992: 193). In the subsequent period semi-nomadic pastoralism continued but with a greater degree of mobility (Vainshtein 1980: 52).

In both periods the distribution of large tribal burial grounds in Tuva indicates cyclic migration with fixed routes and set winter camps (Vainshtein 1980: 96). Presumably, herds would have been pastured in the mountains during the summer and in the more low-lying land during the winter (Bokovenko 1995: 255).

REFERENCES

Apley, A.G. and L. Solomon 1988. *Concise System of Orthopaedics and Fractures*. Oxford: Butterworth-Heinemann Ltd.

Barnes, E. 1994. *Developmental Defects of the Axial Skeleton in Paleopathology*. Colorado: Colorado University Press.

Bascom, W. 1969. *The Yoruba of Southwestern Nigeria*. London: Holt, Rinehart and Winston.

Bokovenko, N.A. 1995. History of studies and the main problems in the archaeology of southern Siberia during the Scythian period. In *Nomads of the Eurasian Steppes in the Early Iron Age*, J. Davis-Kimball, V.A. Bashilov and L.T. Yablonsky (eds), 255–61. Berkeley: Zinat Press.

Brazier, J. 1994. Neurofibromatosis and optic nerve tumours. In *Pediatric Ophthalmology*, D. Taylor (ed.), 247–60. London: Blackwell Scientific Publications.

Burck, U. 1983. Genetic aspects of hemifacial microsomia. *Human Genetics* 64, 291–6.

Burrows, E.H. 1963. Bone changes in orbital neurofibromatosis. *The British Journal of Radiology* 36, 549–61.

Carter, C.O. 1964. The genetics of common malformations. In *Second International Conference on Congenital Malformations*, M. Fishbein (ed.), 306–13. New York: The International Medical Congress.

Chadwick, J. and W.N. Mann 1978. Medicine. In *Hippocratic Writings*, G.E.R. Lloyd (ed.), 61–276 revised edn. London: Penguin Classics.

Coleman, S.S. 1983. *Complex Foot Deformities in Children*. Philadelphia: Lea and Febiger.

Dettwyler, K.A. 1991. Can paleopathology provide evidence for 'compassion'? *American Journal of Physical Anthropology* 84, 375–84.

Dommisse, G.F. 1985. The Anatomy of Cord Ischemia. In *Scoliosis Prevention, Proceedings of the 7th Phillip Zorab Symposium 1983*, J.O. Warner and M.H. Mehta (eds), 233–46. New York: Praeger Publishers.

Donnelly, S., C. Donnelly and E. Murphy 1999. The forgotten dead: the *cillíní* and disused burial grounds of Ballintoy, County Antrim. *Ulster Journal of Archaeology* 58, 109–13.

Duke-Elder, S. 1964. *System of Ophthalmology* vol. III, *Normal and abnormal development Part 2, Congenital deformities*. London: Henry Kimpton.

Feingold, M. and S.S. Gellis 1968. Ocular abnormalities associated with first and second Arch Syndromes. *Survey of Ophthalmology* 14, 30–42.

Ferrer-Torrelles, M. and T. Ceballos 1982. Embryology of the hip in relation to congenital dislocation. In *Congenital Dislocation of the Hip*, M.O. Tachdjian (ed.), 1–25. London: Churchill Livingstone.

Fishbein, M. 1963. Introduction. In *Birth Defects*, M. Fishbein (ed.), v–ix. Philadelphia: J.B. Lippincott Company.

Fishman, M.A. 1991. Disturbances in neural tube closure and spine and cerebrospinal fluid dynamics. In *Rudolph's Pediatrics*, A.M. Rudolph, J.I.E. Hoffman and C.D. Rudolph (eds), 1696–705. London: Prentice-Hall International (UK) Limited.

Fraser, F.C. 1959. Causes of congenital malformations in human beings. *Journal of Chronic Disease* 10, 97–110.

Gorlin, R.J., J.J. Pindborg and M.M. Cohen 1976. *Syndromes of the Head and Neck*. 2nd edn. London: McGraw-Hill Book Company.

Gorlin, R.J., J.J. Pindborg and M.M. Cohen 1990. *Syndromes of the Head and Neck*. 3rd edn. Oxford: Oxford University Press.

Gregg, J.B., L. Zimmerman, S. Clifford and P.S. Gregg 1981. Craniofacial anomalies in the Upper Missouri river basin over a millennium: archaeological and clinical evidence. *Cleft Palate Journal* 18, 210–22.

Gruebel Lee, D.M. 1983. *Disorders of the Hip*. London: J. Lippincott Company.

Hoskins, H.D. and M.A. Kass 1989. *Becker-Shaffer's Diagnosis and Therapy of the Glaucomas*, 6th edn. Baltimore: The C. V. Mosby Company.

Inman, V.T. 1963. Clubfoot and other bony defects. In *Birth Defects*, M. Fishbein (ed.), 245–52. Philadelphia: J. B. Lippincott Company.

Kennedy, W.P. 1967. *Epidemiologic Aspects of the Problem of Congenital Malformations*. London: Birth Defects Original Article Series 3.

Knüsel, C.J. and J.E. Bowman 1996. A possible case of neurofibromatosis in an archaeological skeleton. *International Journal of Osteoarchaeology* 6, 202–10.

Laurence, K.M. 1958. The natural history of hydrocephalus. *The Lancet*, 29 November, 1152–4.

Lee, R.B. and I. DeVore 1976: *Kalahari Hunter-Gatherers: studies of the !Kung San and their neighbors*. Cambridge, MA: Harvard University Press.

Mandelshtam, A.M. 1983. Issledovaniye na mogilnom polye Aymyrlyg: Nekotoriye itovi i perspektii, *Drevniye Kulturi Euraziiskih Stepei*, 25–33. Leningrad: Institute for the History of Material Culture. (Research at the Aymyrlyg burial ground: some results and perspectives).

Mandelshtam, A.M. 1992. Ranniye kochevniki Skifskova perioda na territorii Tuvi, M.G. Moshkova (ed.), *Stepnaya Polosa Aziatskoi Chasti SSSR v Skifo–Sarmatskoye Vremya*, Archeologiya SSSR, Moskva, Nauka, 178–96. (Early nomads of the Scythian period in the territory of Tuva).

McAlister, W.H. and T.E. Herman 1995. Osteochondrodysplasias, dysostoses, chromosomal aberrations, mucopolysaccharidoses and mucolipidoses. In *Diagnosis of Bone and Joint Disorders* 3rd edn, vol. 6, D. Resnick (ed.), 4163–244. London: W.B. Saunders.

McLone, D.G., D. Riegel and F.J. Epstein 1987. *An Introduction to Hydrocephalus*. New York: Guardians of the Hydrocephalic Research Foundation.

Milner, A.D. and M.E. Milner 1985. The place of lung function in children with scoliosis. In *Scoliosis Prevention: proceedings of the 7th Phillip Zorab Symposium 1983*, J.O. Warner and M.H. Mehta (eds), 190–9. New York: Praeger Publishers.

Murphy, E.M. 1996. A possible case of hydrocephalus in a medieval child from Doonbought Fort, Co. Antrim, Northern Ireland. *International Journal of Osteoarchaeology* 6, 435–42.

Murphy, E.M. 1998. An osteological and palaeopathological study of the Scythian and Hunno-Sarmatian period populations from the cemetery complex of Aymyrlyg, Tuva, South Siberia. Unpublished PhD thesis, School of Archaeology and Palaeoecology, the Queen's University of Belfast.

Murphy, E.M., U.M. Donnelly and G.E. Rose 1998. Possible neurofibromatosis in an individual of the Scythian period from Tuva, South Siberia. *International Journal of Osteoarchaeology* 8(6), 424–30.

Ozonoff, M.B. 1995. Spinal anomalies and curvatures. In *Diagnosis of Bone and Joint Disorders* 3rd edn, vol. 6, D. Resnick (ed.), 4245–68. London: W.B. Saunders.

Rees, D.O., L.M.T. Collum and D.I. Bowen 1972. Radiological aspects of oculo–auriculo-vertebral dysplasia. *British Journal of Radiology* 45, 15–18.

Resnick, D., T.G. Goergen and G. Niwayama 1995. Physical injury: concepts and terminology. In *Diagnosis of Bone and Joint Disorders* 3rd edn, vol. 5, D. Resnick (ed.), 2561–692. London: W.B. Saunders.

Richards, G.D. and S.C. Anton 1991. Craniofacial configuration and postcranial development of a hydrocephalic child (*ca.* 2500 BC–AD 500): with a review of cases and comment of diagnostic criteria. *American Journal of Physical Anthropology* 85, 185–200.

Roberts, C. and K. Manchester 1995. *The Archaeology of Disease*. 2nd edn. Stroud: Alan Sutton Publishing Limited.

Sargent, R.A. and D.K. Ousterhout 1983. Ocular manifestations of skeletal disease. In *Pediatric Ophthalmology*, 2nd edn, R.D. Harley (ed.), 1030–52 London: W.B. Saunders.

Sélincourt, A. de and A.R. Burn 1972. *Herodotus: the histories* (revised edn). Middlesex: Penguin Books Ltd.

Seller, M.J. 1987. Nutritionally induced congenital defects. *Proceedings of the Nutrition Society* 46, 227–35.

Setzer, E., S.N. Ruiz-Castaneda, C. Severn, S. Ryden and J.L. Frias 1981. Etiologic heterogeneity in the oculoauriculovertebral syndrome. *The Journal of Pediatrics* 98, 88–90.

Shokeir, M.H. 1977. The Goldenhar syndrome: a natural history. In *Natural History of Specific Birth Defects: original article series*, vol. 13, D. Bergsma and R.B. Lowry (eds), 67–83. New York: Alan R. Liss Inc.

Smith, D.W. and K.L. Jones 1982. *Recognizable Patterns of Human Malformation* 3rd edn. London: W.B. Saunders.

Stambulnik, E.U. 1983. Noviye Pamyatniki Hunno-Sarmatskova Vremeni B Tyvye: Nekotoriye Itogi Rabot. In *Drevniye Kulturi Euraziiskih Stepei*, 34–41. Leningrad: Institute for the History of Material Culture. (New Monuments of the Hunno-Sarmatian period in Tuva: some results of the work.)

Turco, V.J. 1981. *Clubfoot*. London: Churchill Livingstone.

Turkel, S.J. 1989. Congenital abnormalities in skeletal populations. In *Reconstruction of Life from the Skeleton*, M.Y. Iscan and K.A.R. Kennedy (eds), 109–27. New York: Alan R. Liss Inc.

Vainshtein, S.I. 1980. *Nomads of South Siberia: the pastoral economies of Tuva*. Cambridge: Cambridge University Press.

Wagner, G. 1949. *The Bantu of North Kavirondo*, vol. I. London: Oxford University Press.

Watson, B. 1961. *Records of the Grand Historian of China Translated from the Shih Chi of Ssu-Ma Ch'ien*. London: Columbia University Press.

Winter, E.H. 1967. Amba Religion. In *Gods and Rituals: readings in religious beliefs and practices*, J. Middleton (ed.), 21–40. New York: The Natural History Press.

Winter, R.B. 1985. Spinal deformities at risk for neurological complications. In *Scoliosis Prevention, Proceedings of the 7th Phillip Zorab Symposium 1983*, J.O. Warner and M.H. Mehta (eds), 247–56. New York: Praeger Publishers.

5   Two examples of disability in the Levant

JONATHAN N. TUBB

In most archaeological contexts in the ancient Near East, disabled people have tended to be overlooked, or misinterpreted. The human bone reports attached to cemetery excavations will sometimes mention arthritis or dental peculiarities in detailed appendices, but the results of these investigations are rarely fed back into the social or demographic constructs. Representations of disabled people are also extremely rare – to such an extent indeed that this element of society tends to be disregarded completely. It is also possible that excavators working in the Near East have been conditioned by modern social stereotypes, and have assumed that the disabled would always have been disadvantaged, both socially and economically. In this chapter, I present two examples of disabled individuals which argue to the contrary.

The first example is from Jericho and dates to the Middle Bronze Age (eighteenth century BC). During Kathleen Kenyon's excavations at the site between 1952 and 1958, some twenty-seven shaft tombs of this period were explored, one of the most impressive being Tomb P19 (Kenyon 1965: 388–410, fig. 193 [plan and elevation] and pl. 18:1).

Tomb P19 (Figure 5.1) had a very large chamber, and in common with many of the Middle Bronze Age tombs, was constructed and first used in the preceding Early Bronze IV period (c. 2400–2000 BC). Remains of the earlier Early Bronze IV burial consisted of a single jar, some bronze scraps and a collection of fragmentary human bones which had been pushed to the front of the chamber and covered by a ramp of earth.

During the Middle Bronze IIB period (c. 1750–1650 BC), after a gap of some 300 or so years, the chamber was re-used to inter seven individuals. These were found arranged in a row with their heads to the rear (west) of the chamber. Six of the skeletons were intact, but one (Skeleton E) was seen to be very disarranged, as if it had greatly decayed and had been kicked about when the other six were interred. It was apparent to the excavators, therefore, that two phases of burial had occurred (Kenyon 1965: 388). Skeleton E was of a female, aged about twenty-eight years, and 'powerfully built', roughly 5 ft 2 in tall.

Of the other six skeletons, three were male; a man (Skeleton B) aged about twenty-six years, of normal build, about 5 ft 8 ins tall, another man (Skeleton F), aged about

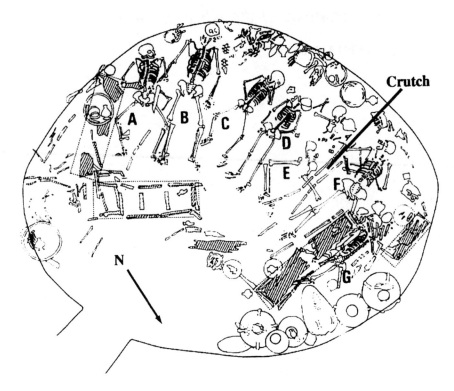

Figure 5.1 Plan of the interior of Tomb P19 at Jericho, showing the position of the seven individuals. (Adapted from Kenyon 1965: fig. 193)

twenty-four years, of 'particularly robust build', about 5 ft 9 ins tall (Figure 5.2), and a boy (Skeleton C) aged about eleven. The three females (Skeletons A, D and G) were all girls aged approximately fifteen, eleven and seventeen respectively.

All six of these individuals had been killed by one or more violent blows to the skull with a blunt instrument. They had been killed simultaneously and were buried simultaneously, at some time after the interment of Individual E. It was also noted that the three males (B, F and C) were missing their right hands.

Kenyon, in attempting to offer an explanation for what seemed to her to be evidence of a mass execution, suggested that the six individuals represented thieves caught in the act of robbing the tomb of individual E (1965: 390). This might, according to her, explain the 'kicked about' condition of Skeleton E and, pointing to the still current practice in some oriental countries, the missing right hands. She therefore proposed, as the most likely explanation, that tomb-robbers were caught, perhaps the males B, F and C actually in the act, and that they, and the rest of the family, were executed and placed in the tomb which they had desecrated.

Kenyon's explanation remains highly improbable. It is difficult to imagine a situation in which convicted criminals would be interred in the same tomb as the one

Figure 5.2 Interior of Jericho Tomb P19, showing Individual F. The top of the 'crutch' belonging to Individual E is seen to the left. (By courtesy of the British Museum)

which they had violated. More significantly, however, her theory seems entirely contrary to the lavish nature of the burial offerings. These consisted of pottery store jars, bowls, vases, juglets and lamps, alabaster vessels, wooden tables and stools, wooden platters, wooden boxes with delicately carved bone inlay, baskets, a decorated ostrich egg, beads and scarabs. Food offerings included two complete lambs or kids, together with other joints in the bowls and wooden platters.

If Kenyon's 'tomb-robber' hypothesis is correct, all of these items should be assigned to Individual E since convicted criminals would hardly have been provided with much in the way of grave goods. Examination of the tomb drawings, however, make it quite clear that this was not the case. This is most obviously observed with regard to the wooden furniture which, as with the tomb itself, demonstrates two clear phases of deposition. Some pieces of the furniture, presumably those associated with Individual E, seem to have been in the process of decay when the later burials were put in, for they were considerably disarranged. Other tables and stools, on the other hand, were found in the positions in which they ultimately deteriorated, and it would make sense to associate these items of furniture with the later burial of the six executed individuals. Such fine and expensive furniture would hardly be appropriate grave-goods for disgraced tomb-robbers.

A further point of incongruity lies in the fact that three of the 'tomb-robbers' (B, C and D) had been laid out on rush mats, in two cases with clearly associated personal ornaments. Again this would seem an improbably benevolent approach to the burial of criminals.

Altogether, a much more likely explanation for the situation found in Tomb P19 is that the six individuals interred simultaneously were killed or executed in a raid or skirmish and, being of the same family as Individual E, they were buried in the same tomb with all due honour and respect. Although it is undeniably true that the punishment for robbery in parts of the Near East was (and still is) the cutting off of the right hand, it is also the case that the Egyptians certainly, and possibly others, practised a similar mutilation in order to keep a tally of the dead.[1] Such mutilation and execution, following a raid or punitive attack on Jericho, could well account for the simultaneous interment and condition of the six individuals in P19, and in these circumstances rich grave goods for these unfortunate victims would not have been inappropriate. It is, of course, interesting to observe that the three executed girls (A, D and G) were buried with their right hands intact. Clearly, as in the case of Egyptian tallying procedures, only 'men' or 'warriors' counted, not women.

Returning now to Skeleton E, a recent re-examination of this individual prior to a reconstruction of part of P19 in the British Museum's new Raymond and Beverly

Figure 5.3 Interior of Jericho Tomb P19, showing Individual E with her wooden 'crutch'. (By courtesy of the British Museum)

Sackler Gallery of the Ancient Levant, has added an extra dimension to the story. Examination of the skeleton by human bone specialist, Stephanie Leach, revealed that the woman had a deformity of the left leg. Although more work needs to be undertaken in order to add definition to this observation, it was the opinion of Leach (*pers. comm.*) that the deformity was pronounced enough to have impaired mobility.

This recent observation helps to explain the presence of the two wooden staves, which were found beside Skeleton E, and which were interpreted by Kenyon as a 'sign of rank' (1965: 390). In point of fact, the two staves in question were found not just beside Skeleton E, but were quite clearly tucked beneath the left shoulder, and in this position, given the leg deformity, they should properly be interpreted as the constituent elements of a crutch (Figure 5.3).

The new evidence allows us to state that the first interment in Tomb P19 in the Middle Bronze Age was of a disabled lady, aged about 28, who probably died of natural causes. She was buried not only with her crutch, but also with a rich assemblage of grave goods, suggesting that far from being a beggar or social outcast, she was a person of high social status within Jericho society (Figure 5.4).

The second example of disability comes from the site of Lachish in the southern Levant. Found in one of the houses adjacent to the so-called 'Fosse Temple', was a small bronze statuette of a naked male (Tufnell 1940: pl. XXVI: 33). The figure

Figure 5.4 Interior of Jericho Tomb P19, showing well-preserved baskets and, from left to right, Individuals C, D and E. (By courtesy of the British Museum)

Figure 5.5 Bronze figure of disabled man from Lachish.

(Figure 5.5), which dates to the Late Bronze Age (fifteenth century BC), is missing part of the right arm and part of the left leg. Whereas the arm shows a clean, square break, the leg break terminates in a rounded end, suggesting that it had been deliberately fashioned to represent a severed limb.[2]

The figure was very plausibly a votive statue (the missing right arm might well have been extended forward in an act of submission), in which case, it can be assumed that it was intended to represent the supplicant accurately. What is significant, however, is that, whereas most votive figures of this period tend to be crudely fashioned in clay, this little figure was carefully modelled and well made – an unusual and expensive item. Again, it would seem to imply that the disabled man who made this offering was a person of some wealth and importance.

NOTES

1 For a very clear illustration of this practice, see the scene depicted on the east wall of the first court of the mortuary temple of Ramses III at Medinet Habu (Nelson 1932: pl. 78). Here, Egyptian scribes are recording the numbers of severed hands and also phalluses recovered from the enemy victims of a campaign.
2 This piece is now in the collections of the Western Asiatic Department of the British Museum (WA 1980-12-14, 12012), where it was available to the author for close examination.

REFERENCES

Kenyon, K.M. 1965. *Excavations at Jericho II: the tombs excavated in 1955–8*. London: British School of Archaeology in Jerusalem.
Nelson, H.H. 1932. *Medinet Habu II: Later Historical Records of Ramses III*. Oriental Institute Publication 9. Chicago: University of Chicago.
Tufnell, O. 1940. *Lachish II: The Fosse Temple*. London: Oxford University Press.

6   *Disability, madness, and social exclusion in Dynastic Egypt*

DAVID JEFFREYS and JOHN TAIT

Archaeological sources for exclusion or distinction, on grounds of physical attribute, of certain sections of the Egyptian population are plentiful but often ambivalent. While the elderly might normally expect some kind of social safety-net based largely on family support and succession into craft and administrative specialities, certain discrepant groups (dwarfs, clubfeet, hunchbacks, cleft palates) were accommodated differently. Unlike Greece (and perhaps Mesopotamia), Egypt seems, on the whole, to have been accepting, and even welcoming, towards such groups, except in the case of contagious or infectious disease (e.g. leprosy), when sufferers could face banishment from the community (Filer 1995: 73). The Egyptian 'wisdom texts' are in the main concerned with advice on achieving worldly success and knowing how to maintain your proper position in society by not overstepping the mark. However, the 'Instruction of Amenemope' (complete translation in Lichtheim 1973–80: vol. 2, 146–63) of the later New Kingdom (late second millennium BCE) contains several passages recommending tolerance: for example, towards the less fortunate or the aged (chapters 2, 11, and 27–29), and the blind, dwarfs, the lame, and the man 'who is in the hand of god' (chapter 25). The last expression has been interpreted as referring explicitly to mental illness (e.g. Westendorf 1977).

It is appropriate to ask whether Egypt's status as the earliest territorial state is connected to the treatment of such marginalized groups. Some have seen the seeds of incipient nationalism, or at least a common sense of identification on the basis of geographical residence, as the driving force behind the overwhelmingly 'primate' distribution of settlement from the end of the fourth millennium (Wenke 1989) and the resulting formation of a powerful and far-reaching distributive framework shared between state and temple organisms. Whether such a framework is an example of inclusive fitness in the evolutionary sense, and whether the formal apparatus reflects the same attitudes towards minorities on the part of groups and individuals, are points also worth considering.

The archaeological evidence is plentiful though not especially diverse, and in the case of the pictorial record (normally relief scenes and paintings in elite tombs) is subject to a tendency to formulaic 'borrowing'. Physical anthropology, and the spatial relations exhibited by the more populous cemeteries, are the most direct and valuable survivals in the archaeological record, though the need to present the deceased (both human and non-human) for burial in an idealized, ritually perfect condition frequently had a distorting or obscuring effect. Prosthetic limbs, limb parts, and other organs might be inserted or attached (Ikram and Dodson 1998: 130; David 1979: 91); in the case of some cult-animal burials offered on a mass scale, the deceased might be represented by an entirely different animal and even by bundles of textile or some other handy material. In general, so long as the norms of outward appearance were observed, and ritually essential items such as amulets and other body decoration were included, the deceased was considered to have been properly served by the funerary profession. The mummification procedure introduces other uncertainties into the physical record. Some conditions shown by some examples of exposed or x-rayed mummies, once thought to be of pathological or genetic origin, are now explained as features due to the binding process itself (Cockburn and Cockburn 1980: 63).

Several discrete groups (pygmies, dwarfs, clubfeet, hunchbacks, twins) seem to be represented by a firmer set of data with which to propose a distinctive treatment of anomalies (el-Aguizy 1987: 53–4). Egyptian attitudes towards physical-attribute minorities is in some ways comparable to the way in which ethnic-origin minorities were regarded. There is a certain ambivalence to both: in the case of foreigners, there was a need to observe ritual conventions relating to a perceived outside threat to the social and cultural integrity of Egypt. This seems to be at variance with the way in which the state evidently accommodated settlement by outsiders, whether through warfare and hostage-taking, group migration, or commerce, especially those with specific skills or new technologies to offer. An illustration of this ambivalence is provided by the two surviving texts placed on stelae by Sesostris III (early second millennium BCE) in the second cataract region. The Semna stela of regnal year 16 (and its duplicate from Uronarti) presents the Nubians in racist terms, and in metrical form, as vicious cowards, deserving only plunder and spiteful destruction (translation in Lichtheim 1973–80: vol. 1, 118–20). However, the stela from Semna of year 8 (Smith 1995: 40) had dealt very prosaically with the regulation of trade and communications. In technological terms, Egypt's conservatism may even have led to the conferring of elite status upon those whose presence promised to communicate unusual or esoteric areas of knowledge, as well as on their products. There is the example of the introduction of military hardware, including chariotry, during the sixteenth century BCE at a time when a new power base was being revived at Thebes, and when expertise in equine husbandry, metallurgy, and shipbuilding seems to have been at a premium.

Interestingly, at least one of the physical-attribute minorities – dwarfs – were also associated (as in other cultures) with certain craft specialisms, notably metalworking. Gold-working skills, in particular, were often demonstrated by dwarfs, to the extent that a specific late (first millennium BCE) form of the Memphite deity Ptah (Pataikos, significantly a cult of Levantine origin) was a kind of patron of this craft (Montet 1952). Other emblematic skills were also firmly attached to elite activities and concerns (expert care of animals, especially hounds and horses; as attendants in childbirth and as infant companions).

Dwarfs were doubly liminal in Egyptian society, regarded as being neither prepubescent nor properly adult (and perhaps had not enacted the puberty rite of circumcision), although they could be represented alongside family members of normal stature in otherwise characteristically Egyptian postures, as in the case of the famous group statue of Seneb, his wife and children (e.g. Tiradritti 1998: 74–5). Here the man's legs are folded and the son and daughter, perhaps in a visual reference to filial piety and support, stand where the legs of a normally proportioned figure would have been (Figure 6.1). Dwarfs are also shown as being both human in some contexts, and belonging to an animal realm in others; it is notable that they are sometimes iconographically interchangeable with domestic or 'pet' animals such as monkeys (e.g. in a scene in the tomb of Kaaper at Saqqara, Fischer 1959: 243 fig. 8; 251–4), although these animals clearly had a more restricted and very different range of functions and associations.

It is uncertain to what extent dwarfs could be regarded as a social group: in Egyptian iconography they appear as individuals attached to households with a range of skills and duties, although the proximity to one another of dwarfs' tombs in the Giza necropolis might suggest that they also shared a sense of community, if this clustering was not simply determined by the funerary space available to patrons. Since achondroplastic dwarfism is one of the commonest genetic mutations (Harer 1993: 19) it may simply be that these individuals were, in fact, born into elite families and occupied their privileged position in this way.

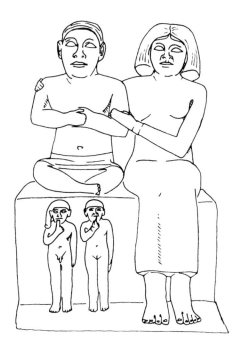

Figure 6.1 A 'dwarf' represented alongside family members of normal height in the group statue of Seneb, his wife and children. His legs are folded and the son and daughter stand where the legs of a normally proportioned figure would have been.

In at least one funerary scene, in the decorative repertoire of the tomb of Ti at Saqqara, dwarfs are shown in a context which clearly distinguishes them from other afflictions and deformities such as distended abdomens but associates them with particular features such as hunchbacks (e.g. Steindorff 1913: pl. 115). The mummified remains of the twelfth century ruler Siptah (e.g. Reeves and Wilkinson 1996: 155–6) show a clear case of club feet (in this case the deformity not being due to post-mortem treatment), which was clearly no bar to advancement in his case; and, in the curious example of the stela of Roma (Figure 6.2), the deceased is shown with a withered leg, using his staff as a crutch rather than as a badge of rank, in a scene otherwise conforming faithfully to the norms of mortuary iconography (Mogensen 1930: 99). In this case the physical peculiarity is even emphasized by the shape of the kilt, the horizontal baseline, and the fact that the staff passes unconventionally across the outline of the offering jar in the bottom left corner. It may be significant that the deity invoked in this stela is that of Astarte (not a native Egyptian cult), and that she does not appear in the scene.

Figure 6.2 The stela of Roma, on which the deceased is shown with a withered leg, using his staff as a crutch rather than as a badge of rank.

The case of 'blind musicians' presents a special, but related, category. The artistic convention generally associates this condition with expertise on the harp; but in other contexts unsighted (or partially sighted?) persons also perform the socially vital role of land measurers and cadastral recorders, in what is suggested as an early version of 'blind justice' (Dasen 1993: 103). In the Amarna period, male musicians are sometimes depicted blindfolded, which has been interpreted as symbolic blindness (Manniche 1978).

The iconographic treatment of all these groups – dwarfs, those with clubfeet or withered limbs, and even conditions resulting from traumatic accident (e.g. in the case of a dislocated hip, Harris and Wente 1980: fig. 2.4) – strongly suggests that they were not regarded as subnormal or in any way socially diminished. On the contrary, their particular conditions are paradoxically emphasized by the way in which the established modes of representation and systems of proportion accommodate the unfamiliar detail. In the case of the Old Kingdom (late third millennium BCE) statues of dwarfs, the execution is meticulous and the materials used are from a selected range of stones reserved for the elite (Figure 6.3).

Possibly such 'noble' deformities share at least two common characteristics: they are incurable, and they are conditions acquired before or during birth, and may be compared with other conditions noted, and associated with each other, by the Egyptians themselves. Multiple births (typically twins), cleft palates, and blindness may also have been singled out as special cases (Baines 1985). There are several examples of this, but most notably the well-known 'Two Brothers' Tomb' of Khnumhotep and

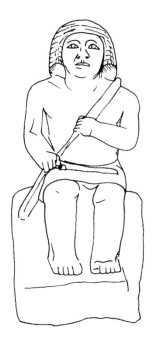

Figure 6.3 Late third millennium BCE statue of a dwarf [Pernankh] from Giza (Hawass 1991).

Niankhkhnum at Saqqara, evidently an elite funerary property with its unique scenes of same-sex intimacy in which, it is suggested, the individual identity of the tomb-owners is transcended by the special nature of the family association (Baines 1985: 465). It may be significant also that the tomb-owners specifically recognize, in their theophoric names, the personal importance of the cult of Khnum, the potter-creator deity. A later reference to multiple birth casts the siblings in the ritual role of the archetypal brothers Horus and Seth, and only later in the first millennium BCE does multiple birth become treated as a misfortune, when it is grouped together (perhaps because of the attendant health risks) with miscarriage and 'Horus birth' (cleft palate?), as evils against which oracular protection was sought (Dasen 1993: 99). The exposure of infants became common in Greco-Roman Egypt, but there is no evidence for the practice earlier, and it is possible that it was entirely an introduction from the Greek world.

While tolerance, and even social assistance from pious foundations or adoption into private households, may have been available to those with such relatively mild unobtrusive physical abnormalities, very different attitudes seem to have been held against serious conditions developed after birth. Spinal deformities due to tuberculosis, for example, were depicted in a very different way on medical votives, while leprosy certainly called not only for exclusion but even banishment, and for similar reasons is never represented in the standard repertoire of scenes. Other conditions, not necessarily occupational in nature, but emblematic of non-elite rank and activities, include grossly distended abdomens (umbilical hernia?) and genital hypertrophy (schistosomiasis?); similarly deformed knees and extreme emaciation are typically demonstrated by herdsmen (Figure 6.4, from Blackman 1915: pl. 3). While these

Figure 6.4 A herdsman with typically deformed knees and extreme emaciation.

associations may well not be specific, but drawn from a finite and prescribed repertoire of scenes, the regularity with which some conditions represent a privileged position, and others not, is striking.

Imprisonment does not seem to have been a regular mode of Egyptian punishment, although (unsurprisingly) there is good evidence for the detention of criminals awaiting judgement or sentence. The latter provided a literary topos: the Demotic wisdom text *The Instructions of Onchsheshonqy* (translated in full in Lichtheim 1973–80: vol. 3, 159–84), has an introductory narrative section, in which the supposed author of the 'wisdom text', Onchsheshonqy, learns of a plot against the king's life, in which a family friend is involved. He tries to dissuade the conspirators, but shrinks from denouncing them to the king. The plot fails; Onchsheshonqy escapes summary execution by fire, but is imprisoned far from his home in 'the houses of delay'. When he is the only prisoner who is not released on the anniversary of the king's accession, in his despair he obtains permission to write down on potsherds the wisdom material which forms the greater part of the surviving text, so that they can be taken to his son, whom he is unable to educate in person. Onchsheshonqy's detention is to all intents punishment by imprisonment, and may reflect the practice of the Saite Dynasty (mid first millennium BCE). Formal banishment is attested in the 'Banishment Stela' (Von Beckerath 1968) in which the crown prince, evidently after a coup, records the oracular approval of the god Amun for the recall of those allegedly banished by the god himself.

Mental illness by its nature is almost impossible to identify in the archaeological record. The Egyptian language in the dynastic period had no recognizable word for mental illness. In the Coptic stage of the language (from the third century CE onwards), there are two words for 'madness', one of which is in common use, and quite clearly can denote mental derangement. It is significant that the word is a loan-word imported from a Semitic language (first appearing in the Demotic stage of the Egyptian language only some two centuries earlier). The origin of the other term is quite unknown. It would be virtually impossible to disprove a hypothesis that mental illness was in no sense recognized in earlier Egypt, but it seems plausible to assume that the concept is embraced by a number of phrases found in the medical, wisdom, and other texts. For the Egyptians, the 'heart' was the seat of intelligence, rather than of emotion, and several idioms speak of the heart as for example 'flooded', or 'forgetful', or 'unaware' (Grapow 1956: 37–9).

In the Middle Kingdom narrative 'The Tale of Sinuhe' (complete translation in Parkinson 1997: 21–53), the hero narrates how a sudden attack of panic led him to flee into self-imposed exile in Syria-Palestine. The episode is referred to several times in the text, and the narrator vacillates between blaming himself and claiming that 'the god' was responsible (Baines 1982: 39–42).

The 'Report of Wenamun' (complete translation in Lichtheim 1973–80: vol. 2, 224–30) is a narrative set in the last years of the second millennium BCE, and was probably written close to the date of the events it purports to relate. The much-debated question as to whether it was a factual report or a work of literary imagination is of little importance here, as it plainly aims to relate credible events. Wenamun travels from Thebes in Egypt to the Levant with the mission of obtaining timber for the manufacture of a new sacred boat for the god Amun. After a number of misfortunes, Wenamun finds himself in the harbour of Byblos, alone and with no transport. The ruler of Byblos daily requests him to leave his territory, but abruptly adopts a more welcoming attitude when 'the god' puts a youth of his court into a trance, in which he communicates the command that Wenamun, and the image of the god Amun that he has with him, should be brought up to the court. The episode has been explained as an authentic picture of a Phoenician 'professional oracular medium' (Cody 1979), and as a phenomenon very foreign to the Egyptians – although it is narrated in a very matter-of-fact manner. The prohibition of the 'possessed' from entry to temples dates only from the Roman Period when different, perhaps imported, attitudes may have prevailed (Sauneron 1960).

The question remains whether Egypt, as the earliest recorded example of a territorial (nation) state, in contrast to the city- and town-based polities of south-western Asia, fostered a society and government which deliberately suppressed the differences between these selected marginal groups and the majority population, as part of a myth of cultural homogeneity (cf. Sibley 1995: 110). Since an alien (and allegedly hostile) 'other' is a prominent feature of the defining of the country's political identity, all those residents who belonged to physical minorities, but who were, at least, functionally contributing members of an internal society, may have been more easily accommodated. Little or no social stigma seems to have attached to any of these groups (at least in official contexts), and there is supplementary evidence from the didactic literature that society required the old, the sick, and the deformed to be tended. Thus the care, and even promotion, of those who were physically disadvantaged and outside the mainstream of society, may well have been regarded as official altruism and even as a solemn religious duty.

REFERENCES

el-Aguizy, O. 1987. Dwarfs and pigmies in ancient Egypt. *Annales du Service des Antiquités de l'Égypte* 71, 53–60.

Baines, J. 1982. Interpreting Sinuhe. *The Journal of Egyptian Archaeology* 68, 31–44.

Baines, J. 1985. Egyptian twins. *Orientalia* (Rome) 54, 461–82.

Blackman, A.M. 1915. *The Rock Tombs of Meir.* Part II: the tomb chapel of Senbi's son Ukhhotp (B, no. 2). London: Egypt Exploration Society.

Cockburn, A. and E. Cockburn (eds) 1980. *Mummies, Disease, and Ancient Cultures.* Cambridge: Cambridge University Press.

Cody, A. 1979. The Phoenician ecstatic in Wenamun: a professional oracular medium. *The Journal of Egyptian Archaeology* 65, 99–106.

Dasen, V. 1993. *Dwarfs in Ancient Egypt and Greece.* Oxford: Oxford University Press.

David, A.R. (ed.) 1979. *The Manchester Museum Mummy Project: multidisciplinary research on ancient Egyptian mummified remains.* Manchester: Manchester University Press.

Filer, J. 1995. *Egyptian Bookshelf: disease.* Austin: University of Texas Press.

Fischer, H.G. 1959. A scribe of the army in a Saqqara mastaba of the early Fifth Dynasty. *Journal of Near Eastern Studies* 18, 233–72.

Grapow, H. 1956. *Kranker, Krankheiten und Arzt: vom gesunden und kranken Ägypter, von den Krankheiten, vom Arzt und von der ärztlichen Tätigkeit.* Berlin: Akademie Verlag (Grundriss der Medizin der alten Ägypter 3).

Harer, B. 1993. Health in pharaonic Egypt. In *Biological Anthropology and the Study of Ancient Egypt*. W.V. Davies and R. Walker (eds), 19–23. London: British Museum Press.

Harris, J.E. and E.F. Wente (eds) 1980. *An X-ray Analysis of the Royal Mummies*. Chicago: University of Chicago Press.

Hawass, Z. 1991. The statue of the dwarf [Pernankh] recently discovered at Giza. *Mitteilungen des Deutschen Archäologischen Instituts, Abteilung Kairo* 47, 17–62.

Ikram, S. and A. Dodson 1998. *The Mummy in Ancient Egypt: equipping the dead for eternity*. London: Thames and Hudson.

Lichtheim, M. 1973–80. *Ancient Egyptian Literature: a book of readings*. 3 vols. Berkeley: University of California Press.

Manniche, L. 1978. Symbolic blindness. *Chronique d'Égypte* 53 (105), 13–21.

Mogensen, M. 1930. *La Glyptothèque Ny Carlsberg: la collection égyptienne*. Copenhagen: Levin & Munksgaard.

Montet, P. 1952. Ptah Patèque et les orfèvres. *Revue Archéologique* 40, 1–11.

Parkinson, R.B. 1997. *The Tale of Sinuhe and other Ancient Egyptian Poems 1949–1640 BC*. Oxford: Clarendon Press.

Reeves, C.N. and R.H. Wilkinson 1996. *The Complete Valley of the Kings: tombs and treasures of Egypt's greatest pharaohs*. London: Thames and Hudson.

Sauneron, S. 1960. Les possédés. *Bulletin de l'Institut français d'archéologie orientale au Caire* 60, 111–15.

Sibley, D. 1995. *Geographies of Exclusion: society and difference in the West*. London: Routledge.

Smith, S.T. 1995. *Askut in Nubia: the economics and ideology of Egyptian imperialism in the second millennium BC*. London: Keegan Paul.

Steindorff, G. 1913. *Das Grab des Ti*. Leipzig: J C Hinrichs.

Stol, M. and S.P. Vleeming 1998. *The Care of the Elderly in the Ancient Near East*. Leiden: Brill.

Tiradritti, F. (ed.) 1998. *The Cairo Museum: masterpieces of Egyptian art*. London: Thames and Hudson.

Von Beckerath 1968. Die 'Stele der Verbannten' im Museum des Louvre. *Revue d'Égyptologie* 20, 7–36.

Wenke, R.J. 1989. Egypt: origins of complex societies. *Annual Review of Anthropology* 18, 129–55.

Westendorf, W. 1977. Geisteskrankheiten. In *Lexikon der Ägyptologie*, vol. 2. W. Helck and E. Otto (eds). Wiesbaden: Harrasowitz.

7 Skeletons in wells: towards an archaeology of social exclusion in the ancient Greek world

JOHN K. PAPADOPOULOS

INTRODUCTION

In dealing with the bog bodies of northwest Europe, particularly against the backdrop of ritual killing or sacrifice, Bahn (1997: 62; see also van der Sanden 1996) recently remarked:

> Most scholars now agree that bog bodies are not the remains of ill-fated people who fell into stagnant pools after losing their way home. There is simply too much evidence pointing to the involvement of others. But if they were killed, who killed them? And why? Sacrifices to ensure good crops, to celebrate military victories, to recover from illness, or as punishment for crimes or perceived social imperfections such as homosexuality (as Heinrich Himmler believed) have all been proposed.

Whereas human sacrifice has been established in many parts of the world, especially in the New World (Boone 1984; also Suhler and Freidel 1998), and critically discussed in the context of ancient Greece (Hughes 1991), the issue of the visibility of social exclusion in the archaeological record has not received the attention it deserves. A notable exception has been the notion of archaeologically invisible burials: the forgotten dead, those who would defy the material record. In dealing with neolithic England, for example, Richard Atkinson deduced, on the basis of some adroit calculations, that only a selected part of the population received formal burial in chambered tombs and that some, if not the majority, of the dead were disposed of in ways that left no archaeological trace (Atkinson 1968; cf. Ucko 1969: 269). In the context of ancient Greece, Morris deployed the notion of archaeologically invisible death to great effect. He argued that in the unstable political climate of the Aegean Early Iron Age, the social group which he labelled as *agathoi* (aristocrats and wealthy but non-governing peasants) received formal burial, whereas in two quantifiable periods the *kakoi* (the poor) were excluded from formal burial on the basis of social rank (Morris 1987: 95–6; cf. Papadopoulos 1993). Morris drew a distinction between formal disposal, in subterranean facilities discovered in archaeological excavations, and informal disposal, 'still constituting a rite of passage for all the actors, but in a manner very different from that of the observed burials, and leaving little or no identifiable material residue' (Morris 1987: 105). Despite an attempt to list examples of the latter, such as certain types of mass burials, cenotaphs and informal surface cremation, even mausolea as argued by Themelis (1976), Morris was hard-pressed to point to incontrovertible evidence for this sort of disposal in Greece, particularly in Attica, and concluded: '. . . but then it is never easy to find positive evidence for a negative argument' (Morris 1987: 109). Although archaeologically invisible burials have been established for many cultures around the world (Metcalf and Huntington 1991), and classical Greek literature is full of references to the 'unburied' – the *ataphoi* (Garland 1985: 103, 165; Lawson [1910] 1964: 457) – there are nevertheless various categories of exclusion to formal burial that not only survive in the material record, but are blatantly visible.

The purpose of this chapter is to point to the wealth of evidence for social exclusion, including madness and disability, in classical literature and iconography, and from there to explore a neglected category of archaeological evidence. Skeletons in wells are a phenomenon common to both Aegean prehistory and classical archaeology. Although a variety of ingenious interpretations have been suggested for this manner of disposing of the dead and for attempting to explain the identity of the deceased, as in the case of the bog bodies of northwest Europe, formal social exclusion has rarely been considered as a central defining issue.

SOCIAL EXCLUSION IN CLASSICAL LITERATURE AND ICONOGRAPHY

In any attempt to detect social exclusion or deviant social behaviour in the ancient world, classical antiquity in general and the Greek world in particular offers a wealth of information by way of literature, which is often complemented by iconographic representations. The literary testimonies are particularly rich, for example, on strangers, foreigners and aliens (Clerc 1893; Hall 1989), lunatics and epileptics (Lloyd 1979; Grmek 1989; Temkin 1991, 1994; von Staden 1992), religious madness (Evans 1988), suicides and the blind (Buxton 1980), criminals, sinners, prisoners – including such luminaries as Socrates – and slaves (Hager 1879; Saller and Shaw 1984; Morris 1987: 93–6, 173–9; 1992: 160–1; MacMullen 1987; Samson 1989; Little and Papadopoulos 1998: 394–5). There are numerous other categories, including social issues of marginality to do with gender (Gould 1980; Richlin 1992; Rabinowitz and Richlin 1993; DuBois 1988; Veyne *et al.* 1998) and sexuality (Richlin 1983; Dover 1989; Halperin *et al.* 1990; Halperin 1990), including hermaphrodites (Ajootian 1990).

Ancient Greek literature is full of references to subjects such as infanticide and the exposure of abnormal births, particularly of girls (Golden 1981, 1990; Dasen 1993: 205–10), scapegoats, bastardy and deformity (Ogden 1997), dwarfs, disabled citizens and other physical minorities (Dasen 1993: 205–42), including Siamese twins (Dasen 1997; Papadopoulos 1999a), vampires (Lawson [1910] 1964: 361–484; cf. Barber 1988), and even those individuals who were simply hated and reviled, especially characters like Thersites. The latter appears in the very heart of Homer's heroic epic as the worst of the Achaians (Nagy 1979: 259–65, 279–81; Thalmann 1988); Homer (*Iliad* 2.216–220) describes him thus:

> Evil-favoured was he beyond all men who came to Ilios: he was bandy-legged and lame in the one foot, and his two shoulders were rounded, stooping together over his chest, and above them his head was warpen, and a scant stubble grew thereon. Hateful was he to Achilles above all, and to Odysseus . . .

The literary Thersites is a useful poetic device, providing a pivotal contrast with the best of the Achaians. Nevertheless, when passages such as Homer are scanned not for what their authors wished to say, but for the unarticulated assumptions they carry (Papadopoulos 1999b), then we have a useful starting point for the manner in which social imperfections were viewed in the ancient world. Similarly, the social status of a variety of disabilities can be gleaned from the statements of ancient authors (Little and Papadopoulos 1998). Epilepsy, for instance, provides a useful example, with references to it scattered throughout numerous ancient authorities, even from the Latin term for epilepsy: *morbus comitialis*, thus designated because an epileptic attack spoiled the day of the *comitia* (Temkin 1994: 8). Theophrastos, for example, in his *Characters* (16.14), states that when a superstitious man sees a madman or epileptic he shudders and spits down at his chest. For Pliny the Elder (*Naturalis Historia* 28.7.36), spitting on epileptics while they were in a fit was one recommended way of averting infection; the use of blood was another (Eitrem 1915: 441–7; Parker 1983: 233–4; Temkin 1994: 22–3). Indeed, the manner in which epileptics were treated in ancient society is well covered by Temkin (1994: 9), who writes:

> The magic conception according to which epilepsy was a contagious disease was one of the factors which made the epileptic's life miserable and gave him a social stigma. For it was a disgraceful disease . . . To the ancients the epileptic was an object of horror and disgust.

In the same manner that the literary Thersites is portrayed as bandy-legged, stooped-shouldered and pointed- or warpen-headed, so too are other social imperfections depicted in art. Not only mythology, but Greek geography and history conventionally located people distinguished by some oddities, physical or mental, in distant countries (Dasen 1993: 178). Thus was the land of the pygmies always at the end of the inhabited world. This was a world, as Dasen (1993: 178) explains, inhabited by other marvellous peoples: 'some one-legged, others one-eyed; without lips, tongue or neck; or with eyes on their shoulders, or with heads of dogs and a bark.' In Greek art pygmies are only depicted in their struggle against cranes: a battle popular in Greek, Etruscan and Roman art from the sixth century BC through late antiquity (Dasen 1993: 182–8, 1994). This was a perpetual struggle pitting tall birds against short men (Figures 7.1–7.2). Pygmy otherness is further contrasted against the Greek – European – ideal in the clearly rendered negroid facial features (cf. Snowden 1970). Pygmy physical deformities, particularly size, are marked: small bodies, large penises.

Similar proportions are found in other mythologically marginal figures, such as the Kerkopes, a pair of malefactors, highwaymen who committed many evil deeds, who

Figure 7.1 Pygmies fighting cranes on a Boiotian black-figure kantharos from the Kabeirion at Thebes. Berlin, SM 3159. (After Wolters and Brun 1940, pl. 29: 3–4)

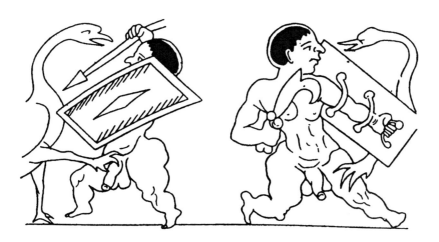

Figure 7.2 Detail of pygmies fighting cranes on an Etruscan red-figure column-crater from Volterra, Florence. (Mus. Arch., inv. 4084)

a

b

c

Figure 7.3a–c Lucanian red-figure pelike depicting Herakles and the Kerkopes, the J. Paul Getty Museum, inv. 81. AE. 189, including details of the Kerkopes. (By courtesy of the J. Paul Getty Museum, Malibu, California)

were finally overcome by the quintessential Greek hero, Herakles (Dasen 1993: 188–94). A typical Greek representation is that on a Lucanian red-figure pelike (Figure 7.3a–c). It depicts a tall, handsome Herakles, fully equipped with all his attributes, which include lion's skin and club, and ideally proportioned genitals. In contrast, the Kerkopes are short and dwarf-like, with marked animal features: one has pointed ears (Figure 7.3b), like those of a satyr, the other a monkey-like face (Figure 7.3c); both have oversized genitals contrasting to those of Herakles (Brommer 1985: 203–4; Jentoft-Nilsen and Trendall 1991: 31–2, pls. 216–17; Dasen 1993: 193). It should be stressed that representations of dwarfism and primitivism are not a male preserve, since female dwarfs are also commonly depicted, as the representation on the drinking cup now in Munich (Figure 7.4) shows (Robertson 1979: pl. 34: 3–4; Dasen 1988: 271, pl. 5: b; Dasen 1993: pl. 51: a). Such primitivism and ethnocentrism is not limited to

Figure 7.4 Athenian red-figure skyphos, Staatliche Antikensammlungen, inv. 8934, depicting a naked female dwarf wearing a headband adorned with branches and holding out a pot (skyphos). (By courtesy of the Staatliche Antikensammlungen, Munich)

classical antiquity. As Dasen (1993: 179) notes:

> Stories about races of short people are found in many parts of the world, even in North America where no pygmies ever existed. This need is still present; the limits of our known world have now expanded to space and galaxies whose furthest inhabitants are imagined as small green men. . .

There are numerous other categories of disability, including madness, depicted in Greek art, which would easily form the subject of a monograph (cf. Gilman 1988 for later periods). I have pointed to only a few of these above. Greek art is also full of references to non-Greeks – Barbarians – including, among many others, Persians (Miller 1997), Scythians (Minns 1913) and Thracians (Tsiafakis 1998), distinguished either physically, or by attributes, including dress. The Greek and the Barbarian, whether in literature or in art, are poignant cultural constructs, like all ethnicities (Hall 1997; Jones 1997), and ultimately like all definitions of deviancy, as they highlight self-conceptualizations that underlie identity.

DEATH, SOCIAL EXCLUSION AND THE MATERIAL RECORD

Against such a backdrop of literary and iconographic information for social marginality – whether real or perceived – and social exclusion, archaeologists have been generally slow in exploring social outcasts in the material record (Little and

Papadopoulos 1998). In this, classical archaeology is not solely negligent. Despite an impressive and growing anthropological literature on exclusion and social marginality in the present (e.g. Dentler and Erikson 1959; Wilkins 1964; Erikson 1966; Lofland 1969; Glaser 1971; Scarpiti and McFarlane 1975; Gilman 1985; Sibley 1995), there has been little in the way of prehistoric literature on the subject, except for the seminal contribution of Shay (1985). In her study on the differentiated treatment of deviancy at death, Shay focused on what she refers to as a deviant social persona and, in defining social deviancy, she states:

> It has long been noted by sociologists that close similarities exist between various forms of social marginality (Dentler and Erikson 1959: 98). Nevertheless, sociologists find deviant behaviour hard to define. The difficulty arises from the fact that cases of deviancy have no objective properties which they share in common, even within the confines of a given group (Durkheim [1933] 1964: 71; 1966: 70: Erikson 1966: 5; 1975: 13). Thus it has been observed that behaviour which qualifies one person for punishment in a given society may qualify another for sainthood, depending on the circumstances under which the behaviour was performed and the type of audience by which it was witnessed. (Erikson 1966: 5–6)
>
> As deviancy is not a property inherent in any particular kind of behaviour, but is a property conferred upon a behaviour by the people who come into direct or indirect contact with it, many sociologists define deviancy as any extreme conduct that elicits explicit sanctions from the people of a group, who consider it to threaten them or to produce ambiguity regarding the limits of conduct.
>
> (Shay 1985: 222)

In order to distinguish normal from deviant social personae in the archaeological record, Shay formulated and tested a set of hypotheses on a broad cross-cultural sample of ethnographic examples of burial customs and in so doing added an important dimension to the study of ancient social systems.

The wealth of mortuary data from the ancient Greek world in terms of both physical remains (Kurtz and Boardman 1971; Laffineur 1987; Hägg and Nordquist 1990; Morris 1992), as well as literature and art (Boardman 1955; Ahlberg 1971; Alexiou 1974; Kurtz 1975, 1985; Vermeule 1979; Griffin 1980; Humphreys and King 1981; Gnoli and Vernant 1982; Humphreys 1993; Garland 1985; Sourvinou-Inwood 1995) is staggering. Some of this evidence has been harnessed in a variety of directions, to different ends. Particularly successful has been the use of death ritual to determine patterns of social structure, both in specific cases and more generally (Morris 1992; cf. Wason 1994: 67–102). A number of more critically reflexive avenues of investigating mortuary data (e.g. Thomas 1991: 103–7, 1999: 126–30) await to be applied to this vast body of evidence. Nevertheless, as stated in the Introduction, the search for recognizing social exclusion in mortuary evidence has not proved very fruitful. Indeed, it seemed clear, on the basis of ancient attitudes gleaned from early Greek authors, that the extreme action of refusal of burial was highly unlikely to have been applied to anyone except deviants (Morris 1987: 105; cf. Bremmer 1983: 89–94; Parker 1983: 43–8; Garland 1985: 101–3).

In Greek literature, however, we know that in Athens the bodies of criminals who died in captivity or those who were executed were either given to their relatives to be buried or were cast unceremoniously into the infamous pit, the *barathron* (Hager 1879; Rohde [1894] 1925: 163, 187). Those who were sacrilegious or traitors to their country were denied burial in the ground of that country (Hager 1879). Although the Athenian *barathron* has eluded discovery, it appears that the Spartan version, the so-called *Kaiadas*, may well have been found (Themelis 1982, 1985). The underground cavern near the modern village of Trypi (a name alluding to holes), plausibly identified by Themelis and his collaborators as the *Kaiadas*, is thought to have been used by the Spartans mainly for the corpses of Messenian captives, as well as for condemned criminals. Although the final analysis of the human remains has not been published, here is one example of what Morris would call informal disposal that is archaeologically visible.

Skeletons in wells

Another is the incidence of skeletons in wells. One such case, fully published, is that of the middle-aged male buried in the upper fill of a well in a quiet corner of Athens, north of the Akropolis, sometime around 900–850 BC in an area otherwise free of tombs (Little and Papadopoulos 1998). The individual had sustained a massive compound depression fracture on the left side of the cranium, a smaller, shallow elliptical depression fracture on the upper right side of the skull, as well as compression fractures to the first and third lumbar vertebrae (Figures 7.5–7.6). These fractures were well healed and remodelled, indicating that the individual survived both injuries by a number of years prior to his death. Putting it bluntly, this man had suffered a technically broken back, and a partially caved in skull and lived to tell the tale. Full details are provided in Little and Papadopoulos (1998), where it is further noted that the potential of his head wound to cause a transitory or permanent neurologic deficit was very high. Whatever the exact damage to this individual's motor or psychic well-being, Little and I suggested that the post-traumatic effects of his head wound may well have contributed to the unusual treatment he received after death and thus we labelled him a social outcast in Early Iron Age Athens.

What was immediately unusual about this burial was its location, in an area close to a number of contemporary cemeteries, but outside any formal burial ground, and the fact that the individual was neatly inhumed in a contracted position in the upper fill of the well. Both features were unheard of in contemporary funerary customs, at a time when cremation was standard for Athenian adults (Little and Papadopoulos 1998: 379–80). Most importantly, this was not a corpse hastily dropped into a well but an intentional disposal of the deceased. The example of this burial sparked a search for other burials in wells, which proved to be a significant category in their own right. Little and I assembled and discussed a number of burials in wells (Little and Papadopoulos 1998: 381–5); here the focus will be an important group of Aegean

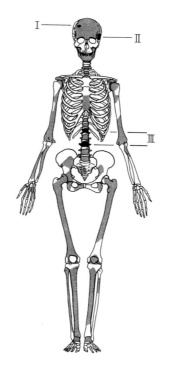

Figure 7.5 Athenian Agora skeletal specimen AA 288. Illustration of skeletal remains available for study. Stippled areas indicate preserved remains (rib fragments and unsided phalanges of the hands have been omitted). Black areas indicate location of traumatic lesions: (I) shallow elliptical depression fracture; (II) healed compound depression fracture at pterion; (III) compression fractures of the 1st and 3rd lumbar vertebrae. [Drawing by Anne Hooton]

Bronze Age wells, in addition to a much later, Hellenistic well in Athens specifically for the bodies of babies.

The occurrence of multiple burials in Bronze Age well shafts is documented at a number of sites, from the Early Bronze Age through the Late Bronze Age, c. 3000–1200 BC. Among the earliest is an Early Helladic well at Cheliotomylos at Corinth, excavated in 1930 and briefly noted in a preliminary report (Shear 1930: 404–6). The deposit was more fully published in 1949 by Waage (1949), with reports on the human and animal remains by Hrdlicka and Goodwin respectively (in Waage 1949; see also Pullen 1985: 113–15). The well, 1.0 m in diameter and 16.65 m deep, contained a deposit of Early Helladic II material, as well as the remains of about 30 individuals. These were mostly concentrated at a depth of 10.00–10.75 m, though human remains were sporadically encountered at depths above 10 m (Waage 1949: 421–2). The age and/or sex of the identified remains were given as follows: five males (two additional possible males), nine females, four children (aged 6–12 years at death), five adolescents/sub-adults, three young adults, five middle-aged individuals, three old individuals (Waage 1949). In his discussion of this well, Pullen noted that its

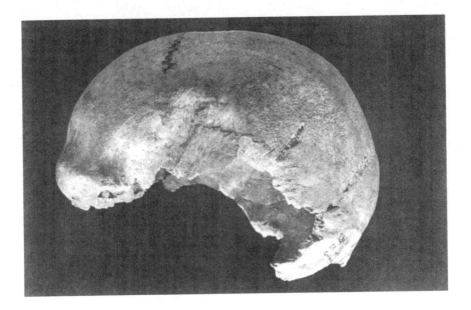

Figure 7.6   Athenian Agora skeletal specimen AA 288. Left lateral view of incomplete cranium showing healed compound depression fracture at pterion. [Photo: Craig and Marie Mauzy, by courtesy American School of Classical Studies at Athens, Agora excavations]

interpretation was problematic and went on to state:

> As the majority of the skeletal remains were found as a "mass of bones jumbled together", with the jawbones still articulated to the skull, within a space of less than one cubic metre, they must be considered as a multiple burial, not a feature prepared specifically for interment, but as a secondary usage of the feature.
>
> (Pullen 1985: 114–15)

Apart from these notes, Pullen was reluctant to speculate about the nature and social identity of the individuals found in this well. The fact that some articulation was noted between the bones established primary interment – not secondary burial – and the circumstances of the deposit indicate that the human remains were placed in the well either at one time, or during a relatively short period of time. Moreover, the well was located in close proximity to several contemporary tombs, in an area that was later to become one of the main cemeteries of the classical city of Corinth.

A similar situation was recorded in the west cemetery at Eleusis in west Attica, where two wells were uncovered. One of these (Figure 7.7), dating to the end of the Middle Helladic period (c. 1600 BC), contained the skeletons of four individuals at a depth of 6.10–7.90 m (Mylonas 1956: 58, pl. 9: b; Mylonas 1975, II: 158–60; III: pls. 168–9; Kritzas 1976–78: 178–9). The circumstances, like those of the Early Helladic well at Corinth and the Early Iron Age well at Athens, suggested primary inhumation

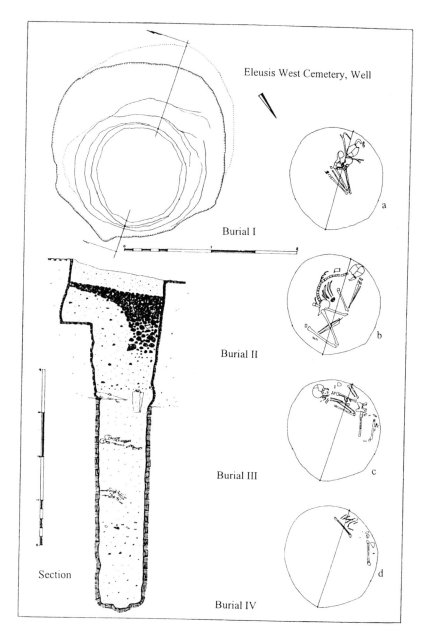

Figure 7.7 Eleusis, West Cemetery. Plans and section of Burials I–IV in Well Lp12. (After Mylonas 1975, Vol. II: 159, fig. 125, after a drawing by A. Petronotes. By courtesy Athens Archaeological Society)

close to a formal burial ground but somehow separate from it, and a manner of disposal atypical for the time.

At Mycenae, however, a well shaft with numerous skeletons, dating to the Late Helladic (LH) IIIA and IIIB period, was not located near tombs, but underneath the so-called Cyclopean Terrace Building or House of the Wine Merchant, located to the northwest of the Lion Gate and the citadel (Wace 1954). The excavation report, by Wace (1954: 273), is worth quoting:

> The shaft is roughly oval in plan and measures about 1.10 m by 1.25 m. The heavy fill came right down to its opening, but just above it in the fill were the skeletons of three women, one with a bronze ring, and of a very large dog. In the shaft itself at a depth of 1.10 m were two other skeletons, one with a bronze ring, apparently not laid out, and below them the remains of eight other skeletons at various depths. Fragments of a bronze brooch and a pair of bronze tweezers were found with these skeletons. The shaft continued downwards to a depth of 6.25 m, and has not been entirely cleared, though at this depth the soil and the rock sides of the shaft seemed to indicate that the winter water level had been reached. The pottery from the shaft was remarkably uniform, being LH IIIA and LH IIIB at all levels. It would therefore seem that this shaft was filled in at one time and not allowed to fill up gradually over a considerable period. The presence of so many skeletons substantiates this conclusion. It is possible that it was dug in search of water (for the great depth precludes the likelihood of its being purely a *bothros*), but perhaps insufficient was found and the cutting was filled up at the time of the construction of the Cyclopean Terrace Building itself.

In an appendix prepared by Angel on the human skeletal material (in Wace 1954: 288–9), the remains deepest in the well were the odd bones of a child (aged 7–10 years at death) and an adult (female?) over thirty; above these were fragments of 'middle-aged adults, male and female,' and two children (6–7 years old). Slightly higher were the scattered bones of a child (7–9 years old) and a middle-aged woman, and above these, the more complete remains of a woman (about thirty years old at death) and a child of six. The uppermost human remains were of three girls in their twenties. Angel also noted: 'Bones of domestic animals, including those of a large hound (of Great Dane size and massiveness), were at least equal to the human bones in number' (in Wace 1954: 288). As with the other similar prehistoric deposits, there was little speculation as to the social identity of the deceased, except that Angel was curious as to what meaning should be attached to the intramural occurrence of such individuals (in Wace 1954: 289). The question of intra- as opposed to extramural burial in the Greek world, and the reasons for it, especially in the case of children, has been discussed at length elsewhere and represents an interesting avenue for further inquiry (Young 1951; Sourvinou-Inwood 1983: 43; Nilsson 1955: 175; Burkert 1977: 295; Jordan and Rotroff 1999).

Slightly later than the well at Mycenae was that published in detail by Kritzas at the Mycenaean centre at Argos (Kritzas 1976–78). Referred to as the Xenake well, it was

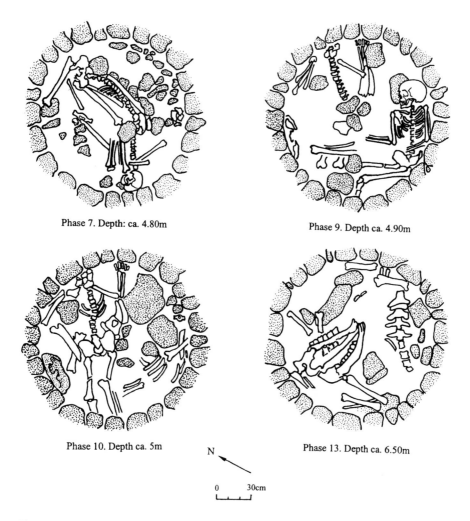

Phase 7. Depth: ca. 4.80m

Phase 9. Depth ca. 4.90m

Phase 10. Depth ca. 5m

N

Phase 13. Depth ca. 6.50m

0   30cm

Figure 7.8 Argos, Xenake Well, plans of phases 7, 9, 10, 13. [Prepared by Patrick Finnerty, after Kritzas 1976–78]

discovered in 1971 as part of a rescue excavation for a construction site in a private plot of land. The well was located on the southern slopes of the hill of the Prophet Elias, about 200–250 m southwest of the so-called Deiras Mycenaean chamber tombs. A solitary Middle Helladic pithos burial of a child represented the only material in the vicinity predating the well, while the remainder of the area was covered with poorly preserved traces of Mycenaean domestic structures (Kritzas 1976–78: 173). Carefully excavated and subdivided into fourteen vertical phases, of which only four are illustrated here (Figure 7.8), the well was built of dry rubble masonry averaging 0.74 m in thickness. It had an internal diameter of 1.35–1.40 m and a depth of 7.35 m. It was apparently used as a well and was subsequently filled at the end of the

Late Helladic IIIB or the beginning of the Late Helladic IIIC period. The top 1.60 m of the fill comprised soil with occasional sherds; from 1.60 m to a depth of 4.0 m, the fill was largely stones with abundant sherds. The first human remains were encountered at a depth of 4.0 m and continued to a depth of over 7.0 m. The skeletons of about twenty individuals were recovered from the well, as well as the skeletons of numerous animals. Poulianos, who studied the human remains, was able to identify ten males and six females; there were three infants (aged 1–5 years at death); the remainder were variously aged between twenty-six and eighty years at death. The animal remains were not studied at the time of publication, but special mention is made of the skeleton of a horse, including a very well-preserved skull, as well as the skeletons of bovine, pig, perhaps sheep/goat, and one dog (Kritzas 1976–78: 174).

In his detailed account of the Xenake well at Argos, Kritzas enumerated a variety of explanations as to why about twenty humans, in addition to numerous animals, made their way into this well. One possibility was that the well was used, instead of a more normal tomb, for the burial of paupers or slaves, although this interpretation was dismissed by Kritzas because of the presence of the animals, the manner in which the skeletons were found and the total lack of any offerings. Similarly dismissed was the possibility that the well served as a sacrificial pit (Kritzas 1976–78: 175), primarily on account of the lack of physical evidence for human sacrifice in the Greek world more generally (see Hughes 1991). Other possible explanations discussed, but also ruled out, include interpretations of the deceased as casualties of war, earthquake or famine (Kritzas 1976–78: 175). Plague or pestilence were considered by Kritzas as somewhat more likely possibilities, but here, too, the presence of the animals was worrying (Kritzas 1976–78: 175–6).

The final possibility discussed by Kritzas (1976–78: 176–8) and that preferred at the time of publication, though with some reservations, was that the deceased – humans and animals – were the victims of flood. Kritzas went on to discuss the geomorphological, as well as the literary evidence for floods in the plain of Argos, and could not help but raise the possibility of the flooding of the plain of Argos by the tidal wave associated with the Thera eruption. Despite the fact that several of Kritzas's tentative interpretations include people at the margins of society, the possibility that these skeletons in wells represent intentionally disposed bodies of deviants or social outcasts is never even considered. Moreover, the incidence of burials in wells in other parts of Greece at various times suggests a more complex reality than flood.

The final example of skeletons in wells to be discussed here is that of a Hellenistic well (Well G 5:3) on the north side of the Kolonos Agoraios, in the area of the Athenian Agora, that was closed sometime around 150 BC (Rotroff et al. 1999). The well contained the human remains of one adult male, one child aged about 11 years at death, and some 450 foetuses, neonates or infants. The well also contained the faunal remains of more than 130 dogs. In a preliminary report the authors speculated on various interpretations, including animal sacrifice and infanticide (Rotroff et al. 1999), in addition to listing other explanations canvassed in earlier scholarship, including epidemic, famine and siege. Rotroff, in particular, pointed out that this deposit may reflect normal rather than abnormal conditions, and went on to state that an 'infant was not accepted as a member of the family until the amphidromia, on the fifth or seventh day after the birth' and that children 'who died before that time would not receive formal burial' (Rotroff et al. 1999: 285).

Although the distinction between infants and children in various parts of the world can often be unclear, in ancient Greece such distinctions were quite precise. In classical Athens, for example, when a child was no longer a baby, at the age of three, it would be presented to the family clan, the phratry, and it subsequently participated in the choes festival for the first time that same year (Burkert 1972: 221; Hamilton 1992). The essential stages, the rights of passages, in the life of any Athenian are also recorded in an inscription dating to the AD second century

"Γάμων, γεννήοεως, χοῶν, ἐφηβείας."

Marriage, birth, choes, adolescence

(IG II/III,[2] 1368.130; Burkert 1972: 221, note 28)

Add death as the last in a long chain of social transitions (Metcalf and Huntington 1991: 108), as well as death before choes (or amphidromia), then an interesting pattern emerges in the study of Greek burial customs. Although bodies of adolescents and children over the age of three are commonly found in burial grounds along with adults, the incidence of infants under the age of $2\frac{1}{2}$–3 in Greek cemeteries is rare. Indeed, corpses of infants are commonly found buried within the home or settlement area, at least in the Bronze and Early Iron Age in Greece (Sourvinou-Inwood 1995: 433–9; and see above for intramural burial). The Athenian Hellenistic well G 5:3 is, therefore, similar to the Irish cillíní, designated resting places for stillborn and unbaptized children and other members of society who were considered unsuitable for burial in consecrated ground from early Christian times into the twentieth century (Murphy and McNeill 1993; Hurl and Murphy 1996; Donnelly et al. 1999).

The presence in well G 5:3 of an adult male and a child aged eleven only serves to emphasize the similarity and highlight the status of these individuals as non-normal social personae. The same is true in modern Greece, where unchristened children cannot be buried in consecrated Orthodox cemeteries. In a similar vein, references in ancient literature and modern Greek folk-songs make it clear that the funeral rites of the unmarried are different to those who were married in life, as the analysis of Lawson and others has shown (Lawson [1910] 1964: 556–7, 592; Rehm 1994).

CONCLUSIONS: SKELETONS IN WELLS AND BEYOND

Several of the scenarios discussed by earlier authors involved individuals – paupers, slaves, victims of catastrophe – at the margins of society, that would certainly qualify as deviant social personae in Shay's definition. This is particularly the case since 'deviancy is not a property inherent in any particular kind of behaviour, but is a property conferred upon a behaviour by the people who come into direct or indirect contact with it ...' (Shay 1985: 222). Building on the work of earlier scholars (Wilkins 1964; Saxe 1970: 11, 118–19; Binford 1972; Scarpiti and McFarlane 1975, esp. 5–8),

Shay (1985) formulated and tested a set of hypotheses on ethnographic examples of burial customs. Her first hypothesis suggests that mortuary practices reflect non-homogenous definitions of deviancy in different societies. The second proposes that there is a correlation between the different evaluations of deviant actions and circumstances and the level of complexity of the social persona of the deceased. The third asserts that because in traditional, simple societies volitional and non-volitional forms of deviancy are not distinguished, the individuals in question can be expected to be treated similarly at death.

Shay also distinguished between the particular conduct, behaviour or attributes of individuals in life, on the one hand, and persons dying under special conditions, on the other (Shay 1985: 223; cf. Binford 1972: 226). Examples of the former include deviant attributes, perpetration of crimes, being an alien, even participating in public service (Shay 1985: 223; cf. Glaser 1971). Examples of the latter include special conditions such as death as a result of violence, disease, suicide or battle. To the list of special conditions at death should be added those who died before effective initiation – those who did not attain a rite of passage, such as the *choes* festival in ancient Athens or baptism in Christian societies – as the case of the foetuses, neonates or infants in the Hellenistic well G 5:3 in Athens, and as the presence of *cillini* in Ireland establish. Moreover, as Shay (1985: 236) stresses, the 'property of deviancy' was conferred only upon a small minority of any given population. The examples of skeletons in wells presented in this paper are in keeping with Shay's hypotheses and provide an evocative glimpse of social outcasts in prehistoric and early historic societies.

Although skeletons in wells are a common feature of ancient Greek mortuary practices, they are not the only method of visible disposal of socially excluded individuals. The main cemetery of ancient Athens, the *Kerameikos*, was also the potters' quarter and, indeed, the location of potters' workshops on the site of an earlier cemetery, or the establishment of a burial ground on the site of earlier potters' activity is well known in the ancient Greek world (Papadopoulos 1996: 121–2; cf. Kurtz and Boardman 1971: 188–9; Morris 1987: 65). The term 'potter's field' in English tradition has come to mean a public burial place for paupers, unknown persons and criminals (Colman 1997: 113–14). Although this usage ultimately derives from the passage in Matthew 27:7, which refers to the purchase of a potter's field for use as a graveyard, the association of potters' quarters and burial grounds has a much older ancestry. The precept of the Biblical potter's field suggests that a sizeable number of socially marginal individuals may have been buried in formal burial grounds. In such a case, the distinction between normal social persona and deviant social persona is not at the level of the tomb, but rather at the level of the cemetery. That is, cemeteries for normal social personae as opposed to cemeteries for deviant social personae. Here, recent work by historical archaeologists on slave cemeteries in the United States is of special interest (particularly: Patterson 1982; Harrington 1993; Garman 1994; Jamieson 1995). For example, Garman has argued that although the physical separation of burying places for Euro-Americans and African-Americans remained fixed, it was the gravestones that carried the crucial information, which allowed an exploration of race, class, gender and death in American society and their intersection (Garman 1994; cf. Tashijan and Tashijan 1988: 190; Deetz 1996). In dealing with the messages carried by the tombstones, Garman showed that as texts they generated a wide range of meanings for those who stopped to read them (Garman 1994: 89; cf. Iser 1978).

Stressing the significance of the gravestones is of particular relevance given the amount and importance of gravestones in the Greek world, especially in the archaic and classical periods, and the fact that there are numerous gravestones of slaves and foreigners buried in cities such as Athens (Bäbler 1998). In looking at a broader sample of African-American burial practices, both contextually and diachronically, Jamieson (1995: 55) pointed to rapid shifts toward more European practices in various African-American communities at widely varying periods in their history, whereas in other communities, African-Americans continued customs which were not of Euro-American origin, despite the immense pressures to adapt to Euro-American cultural, religious and economic domination.

The studies by both Garman and Jamieson provide useful 'cautionary tales,' but important ones given the fact that Greek society relied heavily on slavery (Finley 1980; Ste. Croix 1981). Together, they suggest that rather than searching for strange or atypical forms of disposal of the deceased – such as skeletons in wells – it is important to begin by comparing and contrasting cemeteries or burial plots associated with the same site. Indeed, perhaps the majority of social deviants and outcasts have always been, at least in the Greek world, right under our noses all the time, in formal burial grounds.

ACKNOWLEDGEMENTS

I am grateful, in the first place, to Jane Hubert for inviting me to contribute to this volume, and for bearing with an author who never met any of the deadlines. For discussion of various aspects connected with this chapter, I am grateful to Charalambos Kritzas, Julie Laskaris, Lisa Little, Cameron Monroe, Ian Morris, Sarah Morris, Eileen Murphy and Susan Rotroff. Sources for the illustrations are acknowledged more fully in the illustration captions. Finally, I would like to thank all of the participants at the WAC 4 session for stimulating discussion and for their many insights.

REFERENCES

Ajootian, A. 1990. Hermaphroditos. In *Lexicon Icongraphicum Mythologiae Classicae* V: 268–85. Zürich and München: Artemis Verlag.

Ahlberg, G. 1971. *Prothesis and Ekphora in Greek Geometric Art*. Göteborg: Studies in Mediterranean Archaeology.

Alexiou, M. 1974. *The Ritual Lament in Greek Tradition*. Cambridge: Cambridge University Press.

Atkinson, R.J.C. 1968. Old mortality: some aspects of burial and population in Neolithic England. In *Studies in Ancient Europe: essays presented to Stuart Piggott*, J.M. Cole and D.D.A. Simpson (eds), 83–93. Leicester: Leicester University Press.

Bäbler, B. 1998. *Fleissige Thrakerinnen und wehrhafte Skythen: Nichtgriechen im klassischen Athen und ihre archäologische Hinterlassenschaft*. Stuttgart: B.G. Teubner.

Bahn, P.G. 1997. Bodies of the bogs. *Archaeology* 50, 62–7.

Barber, P. 1988. *Vampires, Burial and Death: folklore and reality.* New Haven: Yale University Press.

Binford, L.R. 1972. Mortuary practices: their study and their potential. In *An Archaeological Perspective*, L.R. Binford (ed.), 208–43. New York: Seminar Press.

Boardman, J. 1955. Painted funerary plaques and some remarks about prothesis. *Annual of the British School at Athens* 50, 51–66.

Boone, E.H. (ed.) 1984. *Ritual Human Sacrifice in Mesoamerica.* Washington, D.C.: Dumbarton Oaks.

Bremmer, J. 1983. *The Early Greek Concept of the Soul.* Princeton: Princeton University Press.

Brommer, F. 1985. Herakles und Theseus auf Vasen in Malibu. In *Greek vases in the J. Paul Getty Museum* 2: 183–228. Malibu: The J. Paul Getty Museum.

Burkert, W. 1972. *Homo necans: Interpretation altgriechischen Opferriten und Mythen.* Berlin: Religionsgeschichtliche Versuche und Vorarbeiten.

Burkert, W. 1977. *Griechische Religion der archaischen und klassischen Epoche.* Stuttgart: Kohlhammer.

Buxton, R.G.A. 1980. Blindness and limits: Sophokles and the logic of myths. *Journal of Hellenic Studies* 100, 22–37.

Clerc, M. 1893. *Les métèques athéniens: Étude sur la condition légale, la situation morale et le rôle social et économique des étrangers domiciliés à Athènes.* Paris: Bibliothèque des écoles françaises d'Athènes et de Rome, Fasc. 64.

Colman, P. 1997. *Corpses, Coffins, and Crypts: a history of burial.* New York: Henry Holt and company.

Dasen, V. 1988. Dwarfism in Egypt and classical antiquity: iconography and medical history. *Medical History* 32, 253–76.

Dasen, V. 1993. *Dwarfs in Ancient Egypt and Greece.* Oxford: Clarendon Press.

Dasen, V. 1994. Pygmaioi. In *Lexicon Icongraphicum Mythologiae Classicae* vol. VII: 594–601. Zürich and München: Artemis Verlag.

Dasen, V. 1997. Multiple births in Graeco-Roman antiquity. *Oxford Journal of Archaeology* 16, 49–63.

Deetz, J. 1996. *In Small Things Forgotten: an archaeology of early American life.* Rev. and expanded edn. New York: Anchor Books/Doubleday.

Dentler, R.A. and K.T. Erikson 1959. The function of deviance in groups. *Social Problems* 1, 98–107.

Donnelly, S., C. Donnelly and E.M. Murphy 1999. The forgotten dead: the *cillini* and disused burial grounds of Ballintoy, County Antrim. *Ulster Journal of Archaeology* 58, 109–13.

Dover, K.J. 1989. *Greek Homosexuality*, 2nd edn. Cambridge, MA: Harvard University Press.

DuBois, P. 1988. *Sowing the Body: psychoanalysis and ancient representations of women.* Chicago: University of Chicago Press.

Durkheim, E. [1933] 1964. *The Division of Labor in Society.* New York: Free Press.

Durkheim, E. [1895] 1966. *The Rules of Sociological Method.* New York: Free Press.

Eitrem, S. 1915. *Opferritus und Voropfer der Griechen und Römer.* Kristiana: Kommission J. Dybwad.

Erikson, K.T. 1966. *Wayward Puritans.* New York: Wiley.

Erikson, K.T. 1975. On the sociology of deviance. In *The Collective Definition of Deviance*, F.J. Davis and R. Stivers (eds), 11–21. New York: Free Press.

Evans, A. 1988. *The God of Ecstasy: sex-roles and the madness of Dionysos.* New York: St. Martin's Press.

Finley, M.I. 1980. *Ancient Slavery and Modern Ideology.* New York: Viking Press.

Garland, R. 1985. *The Greek Way of Death.* Ithaca, New York: Cornell University Press.

Garman, J.C. 1994. Viewing the color line through the material culture of death. *Historical Archaeology* 28, 74–93.

Gilman, S.L. 1985. *Difference and Pathology: stereotypes of sexuality, race, and madness.* Ithaca, New York: Cornell University Press.

Gilman, S.L. 1988. *Disease and Representation: images of illness from madness to AIDS.* Ithaca, New York: Cornell University Press.

Glaser, D. 1971. *Social Deviance.* Chicago: Markham.

Gnoli, G. and J-P. Vernant (eds) 1982. *La Mort, les morts dans les sociétés anciennes.* Cambridge: Cambridge University Press.

Golden, M. 1981. Demography and the exposure of girls at Athens. *Phoenix* 35, 316–31.

Golden, M. 1990. *Children and Childhood in Classical Athens.* Baltimore: Johns Hopkins University Press.

Gould, J.P. 1980. Law, custom and myth: aspects of the social position of women in classical Athens. *Journal of Hellenic Studies* 100, 38–59.

Griffin, J. 1980. *Homer on Life and Death.* Oxford: Clarendon Press.

Grmek, M.D. 1989. *Diseases in the Ancient Greek World.* Baltimore:

Hager, H. 1879. How were the bodies of criminals at Athens disposed of after death? *The Journal of Philology* 8, 1–13.

Hägg, R. and G.C. Nordquist (eds) 1990. *Celebrations of Death and Divinity in the Bronze Age Argolid. Proceedings of the sixth international symposium at the Swedish Institute at Athens, 11–13 June, 1988.* Stockholm: Skrifter utgivna av Svenska Institutet i Athen.

Hall, E. 1989. *Inventing the Barbarian: Greek self-definition through tragedy.* Oxford: Clarendon Press.

Hall, J.M. 1997. *Ethnic Identity in Greek Antiquity.* Cambridge: Cambridge University Press.

Halperin, D.M. 1990. *One Hundred Years of Homosexuality: and other essays on Greek love.* New York: Routledge.

Halperin, D.M., J.J. Winkler and F.I. Zeitlin 1990. *Before Sexuality: the construction of erotic experience in the ancient Greek world.* Princeton: Princeton University Press.

Hamilton, R. 1992. *Choes and Anthesteria: Athenian iconography and ritual.* Ann Arbor: University of Michigan Press.

Harrington, S.P.M. 1993. Bones and bureaucrats: New York's great cemetery imbroglio. *Archaeology* 46, 28–38.

Hughes, D.D. 1991. *Human Sacrifice in Ancient Greece.* London and New York: Routledge.

Humphreys, S.C. 1993. *The Family, Women and Death: comparative studies.* 2nd edn. Ann Arbor: University of Michigan Press.

Humphreys, S.C. and H. King (eds) 1981. *Mortality and Immortality: the anthropology and archaeology of death. Proceedings of a meeting of the research seminar in archaeology and related subjects held at the Institute of Archaeology, London University, in June 1980.* London and New York: Academic Press.

Hurl, D.P. and E.M. Murphy 1996. Life and death in a County Antrim tower house. *Archaeology in Ireland* 10(2), 20–3.

Iser, W. 1978. *The Act of Reading: a theory of aesthetic response.* Baltimore: Johns Hopkins University Press.

Jamieson, R.W. 1995. Material culture and social death: African-American burial practices. *Historical Archaeology* 29, 39–58.

Jentoft-Nilsen, M. and A.D. Trendall 1991. *Corpus Vasorum Antiquorum U.S.A. Fasc. 27, The J. Paul Getty Museum 4.* Verona: Stamperia Valdonega.

Jones, S. 1997. *The Archaeology of Ethnicity: constructing identities in the past and present.* London and New York: Routledge.

Jordan, D.R. and S.I. Rotroff 1999. A curse in a chytridion: a contribution to the study of Athenian pyres. *Hesperia* 68, 147–54.

Kritzas, Ch.B. 1976–1978. Mykenaïko pegadi me skeletous sto Argos [in Greek]. In *Peloponnesiaka Parartema 6. Proceedings of the first international colloquium on Peloponnesian studies, Sparta, 7–14 September 1975*, vol. 2, 173–80. Athens: Society for Peloponnesian Studies.

Kurtz, D.C. 1975. *Athenian White Lekythoi: patterns and painters*. Oxford: Clarendon Press.

Kurtz, D.C. 1985. Vases for the dead: an attic selection. In *Ancient Greek and Related Pottery: proceedings of the international vase symposium, Amsterdam 1984*, 314–28. Amsterdam: Allard Pierson Museum.

Kurtz, D.C. and J. Boardman 1971. *Greek Burial Customs*. Ithaca, New York: Cornell University Press.

Laffineur, R. (ed.) 1987. *Thanatos: Les coûtumes funéraires en égée à l'âge du bronze. Actes du colloque de Liège*. Aegaeum 1. Liège: Université de l'Etat à Liège.

Lawson, J.C. [1910] 1964. *Modern Greek Folklore and Ancient Greek Religion: a study in survivals*. New York: University Books.

Little, L.M. and J.K. Papadopoulos 1998. A social outcast in Early Iron Age Athens. *Hesperia* 67, 375–404.

Lloyd, G.E.R. 1979. *Magic, Reason and Experience: studies in the origin and development of Greek science*. Cambridge: Cambridge University Press.

Lofland, J. 1969. *Deviance and Identity*. Englewood Cliffs: Prentice-Hall.

MacMullen, R. 1987. Late Roman slavery. *Historia* 36, 359–82.

Metcalf, P. and R. Huntington 1991. *Celebrations of Death: the anthropology of mortuary ritual*. 2nd revised edn. Cambridge: Cambridge University Press.

Miller, M.C. 1997. *Athens and Persia in the Fifth Century BC: a study in cultural receptivity*. Cambridge: Cambridge University Press.

Minns, E.H. 1913. *Scythians and Greeks: a survey of ancient history and archaeology on the north coast of the Euxine from the Danube to the Caucasus*. Cambridge: Cambridge University Press.

Morris, I. 1987. *Burial and Ancient Society: the rise of the Greek city-state*. Cambridge: Cambridge University Press.

Morris, I. 1992. *Death Ritual and Social Structure in Classical Antiquity*. Cambridge: Cambridge University Press.

Murphy, E.M. and T.E. McNeill 1993. Human remains excavated at Doonbought Fort, County Antrim, 1969. *Ulster Journal of Archaeology* 56, 120–38.

Mylonas, G.E. 1956. Anaskaphe nekrotapheiou Eleusinos [in Greek]. *Praktika of the Athens Archaeological Society* 1956, 57–62.

Mylonas, G.E. 1975. *To dutikon nekrotapheion tes Eleusinos*, vols. I–III [in Greek]. Athens: Athens Archaeological Society.

Nagy, G. 1979. *The Best of the Achaeans: concepts of the hero in archaic Greek poetry*. Baltimore: Johns Hopkins University Press.

Nilsson, M.P. 1955. *Geschichte der Griechischen Religion*. Munich: C.H. Beck.

Ogden, D. 1997. *The Crooked Kings of Ancient Greece*. London: Duckworth.

Papadopoulos, J.K. 1993. To kill a cemetery: the Athenian Kerameikos and the Early Iron Age in the Aegean. *Journal of Mediterranean Archaeology* 6, 175–206.

Papadopoulos, J.K. 1996. The original Kerameikos of Athens and the siting of the classical Agora. *Greek, Roman and Byzantine Studies* 37, 107–28.

Papadopoulos, J.K. 1999a. Tricks and twins: Nestor, Aktorione-Molione, the Agora oinochoe and the potter who made them. In *Meletemata: studies in Aegean archaeology presented to Malcolm H. Wiener as he enters his 65th year*, P.P. Betancourt, V. Karageorghis, R. Laffineur and W-D. Niemeier (eds). Aegaeum 20, 633–40. Liège: Université de Liège et UT-Pasp.

Papadopoulos, J.K. 1999b. Archaeology, myth-history and the tyranny of the text: Chalkidike, Torone and Thucydides. *Oxford Journal of Archaeology* 18, 377–94.

Parker, R. 1983. *Miasma: pollution and purification in early Greek religion*. Oxford: Oxford University Press.

Patterson, O. 1982. *Slavery and Social Death: a comparative study*. Cambridge, Mass.: Harvard University Press.

Pullen, D.J. 1985. Social organization in Early Bronze Age Greece: a multi-dimensional approach. Unpublished PhD dissertation, Indiana University.

Rabinowitz, N.S. and A. Richlin 1993. *Feminist Theory and the Classics*. New York: Routledge.

Rehm, R. 1994. *Marriage to Death: the conflation of wedding and funeral rituals in Greek tragedy.* Princeton: Princeton University Press.

Richlin, A. 1983. *The Garden of Priapus: sexuality and aggression in Roman humor.* New Haven: Yale University Press.

Richlin, A. 1992. *Pornography and Representation in Greece and Rome.* New York: Oxford University Press.

Robertson, M. 1979. A muffled dancer and others. In *Studies in Honor of Dale Trendall,* A. Cambiglou (ed.), 129–34. Sydney: University of Sydney Press.

Rohde, E. [1894] 1925. *Psyche: the cult of souls and belief in immortality among the Greeks,* originally published as *Psyche: Seelenkult und Unsterblichkeitsglaube der Griechen.* London: Routledge and Kegan Paul.

Rotroff, S.I., L.M. Little and L.M. Snyder 1999. The reanalysis of a well deposit from the second century BC in the Athenian Agora: animal sacrifice and infanticide in late Hellenistic Athens? *American Journal of Archaeology* 103, 284–5.

Ste. Croix, G.E.M. 1981. *The Class Struggle in the Ancient Greek World: from the archaic age to the Arab conquests.* London: Duckworth.

Saller, R.P. and B.D. Shaw 1984. Tombstones and Roman family relations in the principate: civilians, soldiers and slaves. *Journal of Roman Studies* 74, 124–56.

Samson, R. 1989. Rural slavery, inscriptions, archaeology, and Marx: a response to Ramsay MacMullen's Late Roman slavery. *Historia* 38, 99–110.

Saxe, A.A. 1970. Social dimensions of mortuary practices. Unpublished PhD dissertation, University of Michigan.

Scarpiti, F.R. and P.T. McFarlane 1975. *Deviance: action, reaction, interaction.* Reading, Mass.: Addison-Wesley.

Shay, T. 1985. Differentiated treatment of deviancy at death as revealed in the anthropological and archaeological material. *Journal of Anthropological Archaeology* 4, 221–41.

Shear, T.L. 1930. Excavations in the north cemetery at Corinth. *American Journal of Archaeology* 34, 403–31.

Sibley, D. 1995. *Geographies of Exclusion: society and difference in the west.* London: Routledge.

Snowden, F.M. 1970. *Blacks in Antiquity: Ethiopians in the Greco-Roman experience.* Cambridge, MA: Harvard University Press.

Sourvinou-Inwood, C. 1983. A trauma in flux: death in the eighth century and after. In *The Greek Renaissance in the Eighth Century BC: tradition and innovation.* Proceedings of the second international symposium at the Swedish Institute in Athens, 1–5 June 1981, R. Hägg (ed.), 33–48. Stockholm: Skrifter utgivna av Svenska Institutet i Athen.

Sourvinou-Inwood, C. 1995. *Reading Greek Death: to the end of the classical period.* Oxford: Clarendon Press.

Suhler, C. and D. Freidel 1998. Life and death in a Maya war zone. *Archaeology* 51 (3), 28–34.

Tashijan, A. and D. Tashijan 1988. The Afro-American section of Newport, Rhode Island's common burying ground. In *Cemeteries and Gravemarkers: voices of American culture,* R.E. Meyer (ed.), 163–95. Ann Arbor: University of Michigan Press.

Temkin, O. 1991. *Hippocrates in a World of Pagans and Christians.* Baltimore: The Johns Hopkins University Press.

Temkin, O. 1994. *The Falling Sickness: a history of epilepsy from the Greeks to the beginnings of modern neurology,* 2nd edn. Baltimore: The Johns Hopkins University Press.

Thalmann, W.G. 1988. Thersites: comedy, scapegoats, and heroic ideology in the *Iliad. Transactions of the American Philological Association* 118, 1–28.

Themelis, P.G. 1976. *Frühgriechische Grabbauten.* Mainz: Verlag Philipp von Zabern.

Themelis, P.G. 1982. Kaiadas. *Athens Annals of Archaeology* (Archaiologika Analekta ex Athenon) 15, 183–201.

Themelis, P.G. 1985. Kaiadas. *Archaiologia* 15, 55–8.

Thomas, J. 1991. *Rethinking the Neolithic.* Cambridge: Cambridge University Press.

Thomas, J. 1999. *Understanding the Neolithic.* London and New York: Routledge.

Tsiafakis, D. 1998. *E Thrake sten attike eikonagraphia tou 5ou aiona p.Ch* [in Greek]. Komotene: Centre for Thracian Studies.

Ucko, P.J. 1969. Ethnography and archaeological interpretation of funerary remains. *World Archaeology* 1, 262–80.

Van der Sanden, W. 1996. *Through Nature to Eternity: the bog bodies of northwest Europe.* Amsterdam: Batavian Lion International.

Vermeule, E.T. 1979. *Aspects of Death in Early Greek Art and Poetry.* Berkeley: University of California Press.

Veyne, P., F. Lissarrague, F. Frontisi-Ducroux 1998. *Les Mystères du gynécée.* Paris: Gallimard.

Von Staden, H. 1992. The mind and skin of Herakles: heroic diseases. *Hautes Études Medievales et Modernes* 70, 131–50.

Waage, F.O. 1949. An Early Helladic well near Old Corinth. In *Commemorative Studies in Honor of Theodore Leslie Shear* (*Hesperia* Supplement 8), 415–22. Princeton: American School of Classical Studies at Athens.

Wace, E.B. 1954. Mycenae 1939–1953, part VI: the Cyclopean terrace building and the deposit of pottery beneath it. *Annual of the British School at Athens* 49, 267–91.

Wason, P.K. 1994. *The Archaeology of Rank.* Cambridge: Cambridge University Press.

Wilkins, L.T. 1964. *Social Deviance.* London: Tavistock.

Wolters, P. and G. Bruns 1940. *Das Kabirenheiligtum bei Theben* Vol. I. Berlin: Walter de Gruyter.

Young, R.S. 1951. Sepulturae intra urbem. *Hesperia* 20, 67–134.

8   Madness in the body politic: Kouretes, Korybantes, and the politics of shamanism

SANDRA BLAKELY

Madness may be constructed through a variety of media – arts, institutions, religious sanction or political act. The purpose of these constructions is to constrain the energies of the uncontrollable; their success is measured not by the destruction of the irrational, but its restriction by structures to which it is naturally antithetical (Burkert 1962: 54; Turner 1982: 104–6; Geertz 1972: 27). The more enduring and substantial the force constrained, the greater the strength of these devices of management. This makes such strategies a natural advertisement of political power, as the energies of insanity are harnessed for the definition of the acceptable. Such a civilization of energy lies at the heart of many ritual practices; the political dynamics of myth and religion are, therefore, a natural arena in which to view the social employment of psychological states (Douglas 1966: 1–7; Turner 1969; Jeanmaire 1951: 138; Ustinova 1992–98: 517).

One such ritual articulation of madness may be found among the more fragmentary personae of Greek myth. Myth is an anthropology – a tool for thinking about social structures, psychological need, and human mortality (Applebaum 1987: 1). It accomplishes this by providing models – intensified abstractions of social phenomena and psychic crises. As our access to these models is through those portions of antiquity which are best preserved, we tend to see only those that served civic or aristocratic ends. It is, therefore, the politics of madness and representations of its public uses, that have come down to us in the mythological record. The association, in myth, of madness with other functions, such as prophecy, healing and ritual, expresses the attempts to harness its energies.

The Greek figures who combine these characteristics are often candidates for the designation of 'shaman' – I say candidate, because the validity of this type for the Greek world has long been problematic. The discussion has often appealed to Eliade's universal type, a figure with more exceptions than examples in more closely conducted anthropological studies (Eliade 1974; Waida 1992: 215–39; Humphrey 1994: 191–2). So considerable, in fact, is the gap between his model and any number of examples, that many researchers finally dismissed the notion of a shamanic 'type', deeming it to be the reflection of academic need more than ethnographic reality, and a convenient catch-all for non-western spiritual experience (Atkinson 1992: 307–9; Howard 1993: ix–xi; Walraven 1992: 240–64).

Eliade's bricolage of ethnographies does provide a list of traits used to identify possible shamans in the Greek corpus: key among these are an extrasomatic journey, prophecy, healing, and dance (Eliade 1974: 376). Thus Abaris came out of the North either carrying or riding upon an arrow, a form of transportation used by souls in Siberia; he banished pestilence, predicted earthquakes, composed poems and taught the worship of the Hyperborean Apollo (Herodotus 4: 36; Dodds 1951: 141; Meuli 1935: 153–64). Epimenides, Aristeas, Hermotimos, Zalmoxis and Empedokles, Pythagoras and Orpheus provide similar combinations of prophecy, bilocation, attendance on Apollo and connections with Thrace, Scythia and the far North (Meuli 1935: 121–76; Dodds 1951: 135–78).[1] None of these provide enough ritual detail for our analysis – studies of all of them, moreover, ultimately address the limitations of the shaman in the Greek sphere. Sketchy attestation, the lack of conclusive vocabulary and of certain key elements of the Eliadic model, have helped make the Greek shaman a figure whose absence can be noted more fully than his function can be explored (Eliade 1974: 387–94; Burkert 1962: 37; Graf 1988: 80–106; Bremmer 1983: 24–53; cf. West 1983: 146–50).

A different anthropological model, and mythological corpus, may offer more insight into this elusive figure. Studies of the politics of shamanism – the potential antagonism between the ecstatic individual and the state – provide an avenue of investigation to which the limitations of ancient sources, which allow neither interviews with shamans nor observation of their performances, are not a hindrance. The ritual articulation of these myths, moreover, offers insight into performative dynamics in a way that none of the individual shamanic candidates do. Orpheus, Pythagoras, and Empedokles, three of the shamanic candidates, were all said to be initiated into the mysteries of a perplexing group of daimones, known alternatively as Daktyloi, Telchines, Kabeiroi, Kouretes and Korybantes (Porphyrios, *Vita Pythagorae* 17; Ephoros, FGrH 70 F 104; Apollonios of Rhodes, *Argonautica* 1.915–921; Diodoros Siculus 5.48-4–50.1; Plutarch, *Solon* 12.7; Diogenes Laertius 8.2–3.). As daimones, they are less than Olympian but more than mortal; never subjected to a pan-hellenizing syncretization, they are characterized, from their earliest attestation, by a polymorphous confusion, whereby the distinction between a Daktyl, a Korybant or a Kabeiros is never truly clear (Strabo, 10.3.7; Lobeck [1829] 1961: 1110; Hemberg 1950: 7–26, 328–354). It is evident, however, that they were widely known and long lived; they were sufficiently familiar to merit two Aeschylean plays, a Hesiodic epic, and a Telchinic history. Testimonia from a 2000 year span show remarkable consistency, whereby the daimones are all characterized, throughout their attestation, by ecstatic dancing, armed attendance on the Great Mother, and an irreducible confusion.[2] They invent iron, commit fratricide, protect travellers and work in magic; they are corporate, appearing in groups of various sizes and locations from Crete, to the Troad, Cyprus, Rhodes and Boiotia, often at sites famous for metal production and trade (Schachter 1979: 40 n15; Faure 1966: 45, 78; Morris 1992: 133, 157).[3]

The nature of the data must determine the form of the investigation; as the various daimonic entities overlap more often than they remain distinct, it is first necessary to consider the appearance of shamanic traits across all five types. Out of a wide range of similarities, three are especially striking: archaism, metallurgy, music and dance.

Shamanism is characteristically considered an elementary or primitive religion, most properly associated with archaic, tribal or non-centralized societies (Atkinson 1992: 316; Hamayon 1994: 76; Eliade 1974: 3–13, 438; Pentikainen 1996: 7). The daimones are similarly placed early in the ranks of divine beings; born directly from the earth as is typical of the earliest gods, they often appear alongside Titans, and are frequent candidates for the first men (Diodorus Siculus 5.55.1–3, 5.65–66, 5.70.2; fr 84,5 Bergk; Nonnos 13.135–57).

Important iconographic evidence of an association between the Kabeiroi and the first man is the Pratolaos fragment from the Theban Kabeirion (see Wolters and Bruns 1940: 96–7, pl. 5). Present at Zeus' birth, they are adult at the start of the current universal order, marking and recalling in their dance the defeat of barbarism and the onset of order (Euripides *Bacchae* 120–141; Strabo 10.3.19; Kallimachos *Hymn to Zeus* 45–53; Martial 9.16). They both resist and embody primordial transgressors, sent into subterranean exile for offences against the mother; such dungeons are the typical Greek loci for miscreants of earlier generations, such as Cyclopes and Giants. They are associated with metallurgy, as are Indonesian and Siberian shamans (Eliade 1974: 81–4): the Daktyloi invent iron, the Telchines the casting of bronze, the Kabeiroi are the sons of Hephaistos and metonymic smith's tongs (Hesiod fr. 176; Zenobios 4.80, 6.50; Kallimachos *Aitia* fr. 115, *Hymn to Delos* 31; Ammianus Marcellinus, 22.9; Strabo 10.3.22; 14.2.7–8).

The daimonic association with music and dance is perhaps their most widely familiar trait; accompanied by cymbal, drum and flute, their dances are military, kourotrophic, eastern and ecstatic, capable of invoking fertility, inducing madness or holding an audience spellbound (Lukian, *De Saltatione* 8; Plutarch *De Musica* 5, *Amatorius* 16.759 b; Seneca *Hercules Oetaeus* 1872; Lucretius *De Rerum Natura* 2.600–643; Plato *Laws* 7.796; Orphic Hymn 31). Missing from the shamanic type here are the journeys to retrieve the souls of the dead, although the most significant results of such journeys – healing, prophecy, and initiation – are indeed present. The daimonic association with the Great Mother does not have resonance in shamanic models, but the purpose of that association – fertility – is well attested (Hamayon 1994: 76–81).

The mere presence of these traits, however, fails to reveal the social and political dynamics of the shaman within the Greek mythic corpus: the myths assemble the ingredients of the shaman, but do not cook them into a cogent whole. For this more specific articulation, we may turn to a closer consideration of the relationship between the Kouretes and Korybantes. These are the two daimonic types most frequently deemed identical: they are distinct, however, in two important respects. The Kouretes function as seers, and are the patrons of rites of passage; the Korybantes, on the other hand, are known as healers, presiding over rites of healing and initiation that invoke and dispel an incomprehensible madness.

We begin by considering the narrative from which both rituals derive. The Kouretes and Korybantes serve the mother of the gods by helping her deceive Cronos: they emerge from the ground at Zeus' birth to dance around the infant, hiding him from his father's cannibalistic ambitions (Euripides *Bacchae* 120–141; Diodoros Siculus 4.80; Hyginus *Fabulae* 139; Ovid *Fasti* 4.207–214) (Figure 8.1). Their confusion of

SANDRA BLAKELY

Figure 8.1 Three Kouretes dancing around the infant Zeus. (From Roscher's *Ausführliches Lexikon der Griechischen und Römischen Mythologie,* Teubner, Leipzig, 1980)

Cronos signals their own command of the rhythms and choreography of civilized life. At issue in the protection of the infant king, who is metonymic for the state, is fertility: Cronos' perverse recycling, taking back into himself the offspring of his procreative activities, frustrates the proper energies of his spouse, the earth mother. The Diktaian Hymn to the Kouros makes explicit the centrality of this fertility for the Kouretes: Zeus is summoned as the Greatest Kouros to leap into winejars, flocks and crops, using a verb – *thorein* – used as well to describe impregnation, semen, and the birth of gods (West 1965: 149–59). This agricultural fertility leads to economic well-being, and with it prospering trade and a thriving citizenry. The connection between the infant king and the fertility of the state is a natural one – the peaceful continuation of civic order is dependent upon economic prosperity.

Cronos' crime can be seen as a twisted form of exchange between male and female, and exchange is an arena in which the shaman is a natural functionary. By eating his children, Cronos prevents the natural flow of reproductive energy, forcing Rhea into an uneven exchange whereby she must give all and receive nothing in return. The Kourete mediates between them, as the shaman may mediate between human and animal spirits to ensure the continuation of food supply: such shamans enter into a sacred marriage with the daughter of the game spirit in order to qualify them for this activity (Hamayon 1994: 77–84). The focus on food, divine mating, and exchange have strong parallels in the myth of Cronos' consumption of his children. At stake in both narratives is the life of a race, and the exchange, ideally, is deceptive and uneven. The art of the shaman is to take as much as possible and return as meagrely as he can – his power, that is, lies in his ability to deceive (Atkinson 1987: 342–55).

The shamanic figure is, thus, a natural one in the daimonic tale; less naturally necessary is the division of shamanic powers between the alternative daimones.

Both Kouretes and Korybantes are unique among the daimones in their emphasis on performance; enacting in their rituals the same mythic narrative, they achieve distinct ritual goals. The Kouretes preside over prophecy and rites of passage, two apparently different functions whose logical connection becomes clear upon closer examination. The Korybantes, on the other hand, function in rituals of healing, invoking and dispelling a fearfully distorted mentality; they add genuine madness to the tale of Zeus' nativity, a hyperbolic counterpart to the intensified perceptual acuity of the Kouretes.

The prophetic associations of the Kouretes have wide attestation. Minos was said to write his laws under divine inspiration in Zeus' cave on Mount Dikte; 'mouth of the Kouretes' was a proverbial expression of prophetic powers; a chorus of Kouretic prophets appears in Euripides' *Cretans* (Dionysius Halikarnassos 2.61; Zenobios 4.61; Hesychius s.v. Kouretes; Plutarch, *de Defectu Oraculorum* 42; Euripides *Kretes* f. 474). The relationship between prophecy and the rites of passage, however, is made most clear in the story of Glaukos, the son of the Cretan King Minos, and the seer Polyides. Unbeknownst to his father, Glaukos drowned, and a vigorous search for the boy ensued; Polyides, one of the Kouretes who were Minos' diviners, was selected to find him. He did so, and was then told he was to bring the boy back to life, a problem he solved by observing one snake revive another through the use of a herb. Forced by Minos to teach the revived Glaukos the secrets of his craft, Polyides tricked him by having the boy spit into his mouth when he departed from Crete: the saliva transferred with it all the prophetic powers back to their original owner.

Another Glaukos was a fisherman from Anthedon, 'The City of the Herb': seeing dead fish on the beach restored to life through the touch of a plant, he tasted it himself and became mad, leaped into the water, and became the Old Man of the Sea, a figure proverbial for his powers of metamorphosis and prophecy (Apollodoros *Library* 3.3.1). The Kouretic model of prophecy, thus, combines dance, inspiration, metamorphosis, the conquering of death, and initiation. The narrative, moreover, demonstrates in two ways the logical compatibility of their functions as seers and patrons over rites of passage, mental acuity, and public serviceability. The original Kouretic achievement – the protection of Zeus – relies upon their ability to scramble the perceptions of the father of the gods. This ability to negate mental clarity in others is balanced, in their prophetic garb, by a positive ability to secure it for themselves. In both positive and negative forms, moreover, these powers are used to perpetuate civic order, embodied succinctly in the personage of the infant king. This public serviceability accords with their wider functions as inventors, culture heroes, and eponymous divinities for Cretan cities (Lobeck [1829] 1961: 1124; Diodoros Siculus 5.65–66, 70.2; Stephanus Byzantius, s.v. Eleuthera, Itanos, Biennos). Kourotrophia is ultimately civic care, an appropriate theme for the myth that accompanied the ritual whereby young men became full citizens and soldiers.

The Korybantic rituals are distinct from these rites of passage. The subject of the rituals was 'chaired': ministrants would dance around him, using specific melodies and the music of pipes, cymbals or drums. This induced perplexity or possession: the subject was stirred in his emotions, rushed around in a tumult, and was, to all appearance, under a spell. Overwhelmed by divine power, he acted in a world unique to himself, hearing inaudible pipes and invisible drums, and moving in time to their rhythm (Linforth 1945: 121–62; Plato *Euthydemos* 277 DE, *Crito* 54D, *Ion* 533D–536D, *Symposium* 215E; Dio Chrysostom 13.387R; Origines *Contra Celsum* 3; Lukian, *Lexiphanes* 16). This movement is therapeutic: thus Plato describes Korybantic activity as *iamata*, Aristophanes' Philocleon is subjected to Korybantic rites to cure his mad infatuation with the courts, and the initiate's fears are dispelled and calm returned through a homeopathic treatment employing the very symptoms it sought to cure (Linforth 1945: 158; Aristophanes *Wasps* 119; Plato *Laws* 7.790D–791A).

This ritual activity shares with the Kouretic the use of ecstatic dancing, but its purpose is so distinct that we may wonder at attempts to syncretize the two. The purpose of Kouretic dance is the confusion of Cronos, a confusion so profound that a mock battle, suggested by the sound of the weapons, substitutes for a real encounter between the infant child and his cannibalistic father. The performers themselves are purposeful, moving together in a choreographed sequence that constitutes their military education. The civic orientation of the performance is clear in ritual, mythic, and literary evidence: ritually, it provides the passage to adulthood as granted by the community; mythically, it pantomimes the story of the protection of the king; and literary evidence, in the form of the Diktaian hymn to the Kouros, describes community benefits in the form of fertility for the fields and prosperity for trade brought about through this performance. Civic peace, citizen unity, and cosmic order are all achieved – as long as Cronos, the enemy, is successfully taken in by the performance of the dance.

The direction of Korybantic performance, however, is quite the opposite. The mere confusion of Cronos – engineered and controlled by Kouretic performers – grows in intensity and changes its subject in Korybantic dance, which is designed to invade and defeat the senses of the initiate. Neither Cronos nor the original dancers of the myth are said to be mad; in the ritual experience, however, mortal celebrants become mad when they approach the divine. The difference in the employment of the referent myth is striking: the Korybantic initiate in fact collapses all three roles into one. Encircled in the chairing ceremony, the centre around which the dancers move, he is the divine child and potential sacrifice. As the individual, bewildered and confused by the dance, he assumes the role of Cronos, the primordial foe; and as he yields himself to the infectious rhythm and joins in the dance, he plays the role of the kourotrophic warrior. This is a very different unity from the Kouretic civic band; more genuinely mystical, it is a hyperbolic assimilation of the participant to not one, but three divine figures. It signals, moreover, by the use of madness, the danger of approaching the divine.

This dangerous, divinely caused madness marks the difference between Kouretes and Korybantes; it also helps cast light on the social dynamics of Korybantic performance. Korybantic performances were therapeutic – a homeopathic cure, that seems to create the very symptoms it promises to expel. This reflexivity suggests that the act of healing was so vitally important that sickness could be invoked by the Korybantes in order to provide a subject to be acted upon. The real problem, that is, is less an odd epidemic of manic behaviour, but a lack of mania, and with it a lack of opportunity to articulate the social response to it. Ritual pathways, therefore, needed to be constructed precisely in order to grant access to untamed mentalities.

The success of Korybantic performance is measured by its effect upon an individual; if they are healed, the dance is a success. This contrasts strongly with the Kouretic dance, in which the emphasis is on a group of dancers who move together toward an ultimately civic benefit. This distinction between the focus on an individual and on a group has analogies in studies of the politics of shamanism, which note the tension between the anti-structural, charismatic power of the shamanic individual and the organizational designs of the state. The power of the shaman is so significant that it must be either incorporated into or expelled from the realms of power – it cannot be safely ignored. Demonstration of the latter is provided by numerous case studies in which shamanism provided an aegis for resistance to political organizations, and was consequently banned. Examples have been noted in Yugoslavia, Oceania, Korea, China, Columbia, and American Indian tribes (Lewis 1989; Taussig 1987; Overhold 1986: 16–17, 122–42; Bax 1991: 29–53; Humphrey 1994: 193–206; Hamayon 1994: 76–89; Atkinson 1992: 315–16). Returning to the mythic corpus, we should recall that the key daimonic myth does invoke political overthrow – the cessation of Cronos and the advent of Zeus, in which the Kouretes and Korybantes are the irreplaceable intercessors. But those possessed of genuine madness – the Korybantes – are excluded from the state-supportive rituals that turn youths into citizens and direct fertility to the public good. Approaching the god himself, the Korybantic initiate may be understandably less impressed by the mortal structures of kingship and order; the appealing infectiousness of his rites would make such a perspective widely accessible. His clear separation from the rituals of order is analogous to political ambitions to distance the shamanic type as the purveyor of potentially destabilizing sensibilities.

The splitting of functions and rituals is unusually neat for this particularly confused mythological corpus. The equation of one daimon to another may be read as an invitation to read them against each other, directing attention to the shamanic whole that, divided into two distinct entities, is perpetually referenced but never achieved. The longevity of this model of containment may derive from the persistence of the problem to which it responds – the need for the inscrutable to enable order to arise. Madness could no more profitably be erased from the realm of myth than that of experience: it compelled discussion, as a power too great to allow, but too substantial to forego.

NOTES

1 Plutarch *Solon* 12; Diogenes Laertius 1.114–115, 8.4, 12 21, 41, 60; Isokrates *Evagoras* 14, *Busiris* 8; Empedokles fr. 129D; Xenophanes fr. 7D; Iamblichus *Vita Pythagorae* 90–93, 140, 147; Suda s.v. Pythagoras; Aristotle fr. 191 R; Aelian *Varia Historia* 41.7; Herodotus 4: 94–5, 5.4; Strabo 7.3.5; Hesychius s.v. Zalmoxis; Ovid *Metamorphoses* 10.1–11.84; Strabo 7.330, fr. 18; Konon *Fabulae* 45; Euripides *Bacchae* 560, 650, *Iphigenia at Aulis* 1211–14, *Alcestis* 357–62 and scholia to 968; Hermesianax, fr. 7 Powell; Simonides fr. 567 Page; Aeschylus *Agamemnon* 1629–31; Pomponius Mela 2.17.

2 Hesiod fr. 176; Suda s.v. Hesiodos; Aeschylus fr. 46–48; Athenaios 7.282E; Strabo 10.3.7;
   Lukian, *De Saltatione* 8, *Dialogi Deorum* 12.1; Phoronis EGF 211 F 2 Kinkel; Hellanikos of
   Lesbos, FGH 4.89; Diodoros Siculus 3.55.8–9; Pausanias 8.31.3; 9.25.5–10; Pollux
   Onomasticon 2.156; Diomedes Grammaticus FHG 2.57.13; Euripides *Bacchae* 120–141;
   Lucretius 2.600–643; Vergil *Georgics* 4.62–66; Clement of Alexandria *Protreptikos* 2.14;
   Orphic Hymn 31; Johannes Stobaeus Eklogai 1.31; Oppian *Cynegetica* 3.7–19; Iamblichus *De
   Mysteriis* 3.9; Clement of Alexandria *Protreptikos* 2.14.
3 Hesiod fr. 176; Clement of Alexandria *Stromata* 1.15.132, *Protreptikos* 2.16; Strabo 10.3.22,
   14.2, 7–8; Phoronis EGF 211 F 2 Kinkel; Pherekydes FGH 3 F 47; Marmor Parium 11;
   Diodoros Siculus 5.55, 64; Zenobios 4.80; Aristides *Panegyrikos* 2.469; Apollonios of Rhodes,
   Argonautica 1.915–921; Scholia to Apollonios of Rhodes A 917, Wendel; Diodoros
   Epigrammaticus in *Anthologia Palatina* 6.245; Ephoros FGH 70 F 104; Plutarch, *Vita Numae*
   15; Kallimachos *Aitia* fr. 75; Nikolaos of Damaskos FHG 3.459 f. 116; Ovid *Metamorphoses*
   7.365–7; Suetonius *On Evil Speaking*: Hesychius s.v. Telchines.

REFERENCES

Applebaum, H. (ed.) 1987. *Perspectives in Cultural Anthropology*. Albany: State University of
   New York Press.
Atkinson, J. 1987. Shamans in an Indonesian ritual. *American Anthropologist* 89, 342–55.
Atkinson, J. 1992. Shamanisms today. *Annual Reviews in Anthropology* 21, 307–30.
Bax, M. 1991. Marian apparitions in Medjugorje; rivalling religious regimes and state-formation
   in Yugoslavia. In *Religious Regimes and State-Formation: perspectives from European ethnology*,
   E. Wolf (ed.), 29–53. Albany: State University of New York Press.
Bremmer, J. 1983. *The Early Greek Concept of the Soul*. Princeton: Princeton University Press.
Burkert, W. 1962. ΓΟΗΣ: Zum griechischen 'Schamanismus'. *Rheinisches Museum* 105, 36–55.
Dodds, E. 1951. *The Greeks and the Irrational*. Berkeley: University of California Press.
Douglas, M. 1966. *Purity and Danger: an analysis of the concepts of pollution and taboo*. New York:
   Routledge.
Eliade, M. 1974. *Shamanism: archaic techniques of ecstasy*. W. Trask (trans.). Princeton: Princeton
   University Press.
Faure, P. 1966. Les Minerais de la Crete Antique. *Revue Archéologique*, 7th ser., 1, 45–78.
Geertz, C. 1972. Deep play: notes on the Balinese cockfight. *Daedalus* 101, 1–37.
Graf, F. 1988. Orpheus: a poet among men. In *Interpretations of Greek Mythology*, J. Bremmer
   (ed.). London: Routledge.
Hamayon, R. 1994. Shamanism in Siberia: from partnership in supernature to counter-power in
   society. In *Shamanism, History, and the State*, N. Thomas and C. Humphrey (eds), 76–89. Ann
   Arbor: University of Michigan Press.
Hemberg, B. 1950. *Die Kabiren*, Uppsala: Almqvist & Wiksells Boktryckeri AB.
Howard, K. 1993. Introduction. In *Shamans and Cultures*, M. Hoppal and K. Howard (eds),
   ix–xi. Budapest: Korrekt Ltd.
Humphrey, C. 1994. Shamanic practices and the state in northern Asia: views from the center
   and periphery. In *Shamanism, History, and the State*, N. Thomas and C. Humphrey (eds),
   191–228. Ann Arbor: University of Michigan Press.
Jeanmaire, H. 1951. *Dionysos*. Paris: Payot.
Lewis, I. 1989. *Ecstatic Religion: a study of shamanism and spirit possession* 2nd edn. New York:
   Routledge.
Linforth, I. 1945. The Corybantic rites in Plato. *University of California Publications in Classical
   Philology* 13(45), 121–62.
Lobeck, C. [1829] 1961. *Aglaophamus*. Darmstadt: Wissenschaftliche Buchgesellschaft.
Meuli, K. 1935. Scythica. *Hermes* 70, 121–76.
Morris, S. 1992. *Daidalos and the Origins of Greek Art*. Princeton: Princeton University Press.

Overhold, T. 1986. *Prophecy in Cross-Cultural Perspective: a sourcebook for biblical researchers*. Atlanta: Scholars Press.

Pentikainen, J. (ed.) 1996. *Shamanism and Northern Ecology*. New York: Mouton de Gruyter.

Schachter, A. 1979. The Boiotian Herakles. *Teiresias*. Supplement 2, 37–43.

Taussig, M. 1987. *Shamanism, Colonialism, and the Wild Man*. Chicago: University of Chicago Press.

Turner, V. 1969. *The Ritual Process: structure and antistructure*. Ithaca: Cornell University Press.

Turner, V. 1982. *From Ritual to Theatre: the human seriousness of play*. New York: Performing Arts Journal Publications.

Ustinova, Y. 1992–1998. Corybantism: the nature, role and origins of an ecstatic cult in the Greek Polis. *Horos* 10–12, 503–20.

Waida, M. 1992. Problems of central Asian and Siberian shamanism. *Numen* 30(2), 215–39.

Walraven, B. 1992. Korean Shamanism. *Numen* 30(2), 240–64.

West, M. 1965. The Dictaean Hymn to the Kouros. *Journal of Hellenic Studies* 85, 149–59.

West, M. 1983. *The Orphic Poems*. Oxford: Oxford University Press.

Wolters, P. and G. Bruns 1940. *Das Kabirenheiligtum bei Theben I*. Erster Band. Berlin: Walter de Gruyter.

9 Impaired and inspired: the makings of a medieval Icelandic poet

LOIS BRAGG

Anyone interested in narratives depicting social exclusion finds the medieval Icelandic Family Sagas an embarrassment of riches. In this large and impressive body of anonymous, vernacular literature we find the social margins overflowing with Irish slaves, Saami sorcerers, Swedish goons, Hebridean witches, discarded concubines, disabled Viking veterans, paranoid old men, teenaged mass murderers, poor widows with half-witted sons, poets lurking around large estates to seduce farmers' daughters or wives, to name but a few.

The tenth- and early eleventh-century Settlement Era in which the Family Sagas are set was a grand social experiment in a stateless society. Law and order were effected, in theory, by consensus among propertied men, led by those who earned the widest respect for their judgement. By the thirteenth century, however, when the earliest Family Sagas were written, Iceland society was in collapse. The shrinking oligarchy that traced its origin to the great men of the settlement generation was unable to maintain social order or even personal safety, and eventually submitted the erstwhile Commonwealth to Norwegian rule. The Family Sagas, written by and for this foundering elite, are thus best regarded as a nostalgic enterprise, a wistful look back at the fancied origins of a society that ultimately failed. As such, they document a spontaneous endeavour to manufacture a palpable myth of origins, and it is in this light that the colourful social margins of the saga world are to be considered.

The myth-making function of the Family Sagas can be illustrated by their stereotypical ascriptions of ethnic origins to various stock characters. The prominent settlers to whom the elite of the saga public traced their lineages are said again and again to have been mighty landowners in south-western Norway, who emigrated to Iceland because of their fierce independence and proud refusal to submit to the nascent monarchy. In fact, however, we know that many of the prominent settlers came not directly from Norway but rather from northern and western coastal areas of the British Isles, where their fathers would have been landless Norwegian adventurers and their mothers local Celtic girls.

Even those among the settlers who came directly from Norway, however, were likely to have been of similar mixed ethnicity because south-western Norway had long enjoyed economic, cultural, and blood ties with the Celtic North Atlantic seaboard.

So, when the sagas depict blue-blooded Norse settlers heroically destroying treacherous Irish slaves and malign Hebridean witches, we properly read this social scenario in light of the anxieties of the latter-day Icelanders, who were struggling to come to terms with Norwegian hegemony while editing their genealogies. In other words, thirteenth-century Icelanders seem to have been salving their pride by mythically eliminating the historic Celtic elements in their society, and imagining a pure Norwegian ancestry that would explain their present submission to Norway as reunion with the putative homeland.

Modern readers of the sagas, when confronted with such unabashed classism and racism (not to mention the even more egregious sexism), are sometimes surprised when it is pointed out that motifs of physical impairment and disfigurement are not assigned exclusively to the lowly or the non-Norse, but rather are evenly distributed along the social scale, and often attach to saga heroes, the putative Norwegian ancestors of the saga writers and readers. Published scholarship rarely considers impairments at all, and does so only as mere individual eccentricities without any context of literary tradition, pattern, or semiotic value. And yet, the array of saga characters who are by present-day standards seriously disabled is so large and varied as almost to constitute the rule rather than the exception. Among the humble, the figures of the (prescient) blind old nurse and simpleton house-boy are commonplace and conventional, while among original settlers, the likes of Önund Wooden-Leg, who lost a limb in battle, and Bald-Grim, the son of Evening-Wolf, who shared his father's night-time madness, are familiar and unexceptionable.

One of the two best known and loved saga heroes is Njal, whose beardlessness suggests a sexual anomaly for which he is mocked by his neighbours. The other, Egil, is hideously ugly and, like his grandfather Evening-Wolf, experiences periods of madness, killing people without recognizing them and afterwards having no memory of what he has done. His later years are marked by suicidal depression and paranoia, played against the external impairment of his blindness. In sagas that feature more normative protagonists, impaired characters may serve as antagonists, such as the irascible disabled Viking Thorulf Crook-Foot in *Eyrbyggja Saga*, or may appear as mysterious strangers, such as the pseudo-mute Melkorka in *Laxdœla Saga*, or simply family members, such as the epileptic chieftain and kindly uncle, Thorir Goat-Thigh in *Vatnsdœla Saga*.

It is worth pointing out here that in medieval Icelandic narrative, characters who are mad, impaired, or disfigured are hardly unique to the Family Sagas, and in fact appear all along the generic gamut. The Legendary Sagas, which feature fantasy characters and situations, and which modern Icelanders call the Lying Sagas, are especially good sources for crippled heroes. Ivar the Boneless, for example, whose story is told in *Ragnar Shaggy-Pants' Saga*, is born with gristle in place of bones, and grows up to be the most outstanding of his brothers in the family enterprise of conquering England, accomplishing his many deeds from a divan chair. Some crippled legendary heroes are provided with prostheses made of precious metals or having magical properties, such as Egil One-Hand's sword, made by dwarfs and affixed to his stump (in *Egil's and Asmund's Saga*), while others, such as Walking-Hrolf (the hero of *Göngu-Hrolf's Saga*), have their own severed limbs magically reattached after a period of heroic crawling. One suspects, however, that in many of these sagas, the impairment is likely to be contributing to the fantasy effects, and perhaps also to a burlesque overlay, in contrast to the Family Sagas, in which such impairments are never comic.

Closer to the Family Sagas in their more integrated deployment of impairments are the myths. Of the thirteen male gods listed in Snorri's *Edda*, Odin is one-eyed (Figure 9.1), Tyr one-handed, Höd blind, Vidar mute (Figure 9.2), and Heimdall deaf, while Baldur seems to have been an albino, Thor drives a carriage pulled by a crippled goat, and Loki is transsexual, if one considers that a disability – medieval Icelanders certainly did. Nor are these divine impairments incidental. Rather, they are central to the characters and powers of each deity. The extant myths are etiological accounts (such as how Odin gave up an eye, Tyr a hand, Heimdall an ear) or deploy the physical anomaly to motivate the plot, such as Höd's blindness as a factor in the death of Baldur, or Loki's pregnancy (by a stallion) as the source of Odin's wonderful eight-legged horse.

Figure 9.1 A wooden sculpture of the head of a one-eyed, hanged man, thought to be a depiction of Odin. From the stave church at Hegge, Norway. (By courtesy Directorate of Cultural Heritage (Riksantikvaren) Norway)

Figure 9.2 The gods Höd, Týr and Vídar, depicted with their 'disabilities', in a seventeenth century manuscript of Snorri's *Edda*. It is not clear what Vídar is holding, or how this object indicates his muteness. [Photo: the Árni Magnússon Institute]

The evidence of the mythology strongly suggests that not only was an impairment or disfigurement no barrier to social status, but also that such conditions may even have had some kind of social cachet, marking and thus identifying the great man as different from his normative but lesser peers. However that may be, it is clear that while the Icelandic Family Sagas depict a large and diverse underclass, physical impairments and madness definitely do not serve as markers of, or rationales, for social exclusion, which is based rather on the lack of family connections and wealth.

A subset of the Icelandic Family Sagas, the so-called skald sagas, presents a variation on this general rule, however. There are six skald sagas: *Egil's Saga* (mentioned above), *Kormak's Saga, Gunnlaug Snake-Tongue's Saga, The Blood-Brothers' Saga* (whose hero is Thormod Kolbrun's-*Skald*), *The Saga of Björn the Hitardal Champion,* and *The Saga of Hallfred the Difficult Skald.* 'Skald' is simply the Iceland word for poet, but although many characters appear in their sagas as domestic satirists, composing occasional lampoons, the six saga heroes regarded as skalds all additionally spent a season of their lives composing under royal patronage back in Norway (or, alternately, Sweden or England), as many other historical Icelandic skalds are known to have done. In addition to various other plot similarities that will not concern us here, these six sagas demonstrate remarkable consistency in their heroes' social behaviour, for all of them, despite approbation and high status abroad, are anti-social outsiders back home in Iceland, flouting and thus threatening social norms from their positions on the margins of the saga social world. Furthermore, their individual impairments and disfigurements are presented as embodiments, even determinants, of this outsider status.

The figure of the skald, while somewhat anomalous in Icelandic narrative traditions, thus seems to be following a pan-European model of the poet as a physically marked, privileged, and near-inviolate observer and critic, a model still with us today and dating back at least as far as Homer and Æsop. Our present interest in the skalds is, therefore, not in the mere fact of their outsider status and its physical markers, which we may take as given, but rather in the culture-specific details of their marginality. But first, a few words about the art they practised.

Skaldic poetry is one of those unlucky literary genres whose considerable interest for the society that created it lay in intricate word play and cultural allusion. Consequently, outside its native milieu, which was the pre-literate, highly mobile, and socially volatile Viking culture of the North Atlantic, it discourages appreciation and defies translation. In fact, skaldic language was so far removed in diction and syntax from that of ordinary discourse, that by the time any of the verses were committed to written Icelandic, the genre as practised in its Viking heyday was just a fond memory. The thirteenth-century scholar and politician Snorri Sturluson took an antiquarian interest in the genre, however, and wrote a handbook he called *Edda* on its prosody and, luckily for us, its mythic allusions as well.

One of the myths that Snorri recounts in the *Skaldskaparmal* ('Poetic Speech') section of the *Edda* concerns the origin of poetry, a short synopsis of which will introduce many of the motifs associated with the skaldic personality. An all-wise being, created from the spittle of gods, was killed by dwarfs and his blood brewed into mead that would make whoever drank it a poet or scholar. These same dwarfs later drowned a giant who was their guest, and were attacked in revenge by the giant's son, Suttung, who put them out on a skerry at low tide and left them there to drown when the tide came in. To escape this death, they agreed to hand over the skaldic mead as compensation for their homicide. Suttung then stored the mead under a mountain in the protection of his daughter. To gain the skaldic mead for himself, Odin, travelling incognito, entered the mountain in the form of a snake and slept with the giantess, who then let him drink the mead. Assuming the form of an eagle, and with his belly full of the mead, he flew back toward Asgard, the home of the gods, with the giant Suttung, also in eagle form, in hot pursuit. Over Asgard, Odin spewed or vomited the mead into pots held by the other gods, but not before Suttung got so close to him that Odin

> cast some of the mead out at the rear, but this was disregarded. Whoever wants it can have it, and we call that the "poetaster's share". But Odin gave Suttung's mead to the gods, and to those people who understand poetic composition. This is why we call poetry "Odin's take", his "find", his "drink", his "gift" . . .
>
> (*Edda* chapter 6)

This complicated and clearly amalgamated myth associates skaldic poetry with trickery, treachery, cheating, disguise, and homicide, and attributes it to the agency of Odin, in whom the heathen Norse brought together features that we today might consider very disparate: the ugly, disfigured, sexually ambiguous, all-wise, and manic patron of the poet and the berserk. The myths in which he plays major roles show him as a lone traveller in pursuit of wisdom – in addition to the skaldic mead story, we find him undergoing ritual hanging to gain possession of the runes, and sacrificing an eye for a drink of wisdom from Mimir's Well – while he learned sorcery, the one type of occult knowledge associated exclusively with women, from the goddess Freyja. His cult was practised among the aristocratic warrior class, who believed Odin would paralyse their adversaries with battle terror and preside over his devotees, both in their battle fury ('going berserk') and after death in Valhöll. The common people, whose cults of Thor and Frey were focused on ensuring crop and herd fertility rather than battle success, seem to have feared encountering the one-eyed 'god of the hanged' as a mysterious traveller, his face shadowed by a large hat.

The more detailed study of the six skald sagas on which this present discussion is based suggests a conventional cluster of underlying, key features that attach to the skald hero. These are

(1) a physical appearance regarded as unattractive
(2) an adventitious impairment of some sort, acquired, in contrast to other saga heroes, under less than honourable conditions
(3) submissive or dependent postures toward women (grossly aberrant in this culture), along with
(4) errant and obsessive para-sexual practices that obviate normative marriage and children, all subsumed in
(5) a pattern of aggressive and violent behaviour regarded as puerile, ill-considered, or deranged, which cause the skald to be 'unpopular'.

The first and last, ugliness and anti-social behaviour, are always present, while the other components of the cluster (physical and sexual anomalies) appear in various forms and to varying degrees. It is important to realize that elsewhere in the saga literature these features are deployed, singly or in clusters, to identify a villain, not a hero, and that in the skald sagas, therefore, their use as a marker for the poet creates the kind of narrative tension we are more accustomed to finding in modern anti-heroes.

Egil, whose saga was probably written by Snorri Sturluson, is by far the most complex and interesting of the skald-protagonists. His father and paternal grandfather, as mentioned above, went berserk at night, the latter in one instance almost killing his son. Egil inherits this trait along with a hideous physical appearance, taller by a head than his fellows and so swarthy that he is described as a troll. In both looks and personality, he contrasts sharply with his handsome and popular brother. Although later in life Egil becomes a rich landowner and successful farmer, married to his childhood sweetheart and the father of several children, he remains an eccentric outsider in the district. He eschews community involvement and travels often to Norway and England, where he behaves with puerile violence (e.g. vomiting on a host or pretending to be a bear as part of a staged killing), and has many mishaps while in a berserk state. More in line with the typical saga hero, Egil contends with the Norwegian royal family and gains his skald status only under compulsion, when he is a prisoner of Eirik Blood-Axe in York. In contrast with other skalds, his most moving and accomplished poem is on the subject of fatherhood, a complaint to Odin on the death of a son who drowned as an adolescent. Mawkishly sentimental, ruthless killer, poet of incredible verbal artistry, Egil is the quintessential anti-hero, deservedly the favourite saga character of many readers today.

Kormak is a bit less complicated and much less appealing a character than Egil. With an Irish name and the dark curly hair deemed ugly by his neighbours, he, too, suffers by comparison with an attractive, popular brother and is known for outrageous behaviour and an ungovernable temper. Unlike the well-born Egil, however, Kormak is the son of a tenant farmer and, after his father's death, seems tied to his mother's apron strings. He falls in love with the feet and hair of the beautiful daughter of a wealthy householder, but, while roving the district as a juvenile delinquent, he makes serious enemies, one of whom (the most marginal, by the way – a poor widow) curses him with sexual dysfunction. Unable to marry, he is obsessed with badgering the first and second husbands of his beloved, and inflicting symbolic sexual humiliations on them, in the course of which he himself suffers similar humiliations symbolic of his phallic curse, including a debilitating swollen thumb, a near drowning by sea eels, a supine posture under a gigantic adversary and a loss of control over his ship when he breaks off the rudder.

Gunnlaug Snake-tongue has the expected black eyes and ugly nose, the contrasting brother, and the deranged behaviour that we have seen in Egil and Kormak. In addition, he is prone to leg injuries that serve as fulcra for the narrative turning points in the saga. In one such scene, Gunnlaug's bleeding foot affronts the king of Norway and clinches royal animosity against him, and in a second, a dislocated knee provides Gunnlaug with an excuse for missing out on his last chance to marry the girl he loves. Like Kormak, he devotes himself to obsessive harassment of her husband in Norway, whom he eventually kills, and is killed by.

This last trait of Gunnlaug's and Kormak's, the obsession with the beloved's husband, is most developed in the character of Björn the Hitardal Champion. Like the other skald-protagonists, Björn is insolent and unruly, and spends a good bit of time abroad killing people and composing verses for a royal patron. Also like the others, he falls in love with a woman he does not marry, and as with Gunnlaug, it is a leg injury that prevents it. Like Gunnlaug and Kormak, Björn pursues a preposterous obsession with the husband of his erstwhile sweetheart, plaguing the man with obscene verses and scurrilous gossip alleging unnatural acts with farm animals and even a seal, and to top it all off, a wood carving depicting the hapless husband buggered by Björn himself! The long-suffering husband finally succeeds in killing Björn, but only after the latter becomes blind.

Serving as the exception that proves the rule is Hallfred the Difficult Skald, who retains only the token beetling brows and ugly nose of his more typically troll-like colleagues. He limits his anti-social behaviour to interminable quarrelling with his father, marriage with a foreign woman, and lapses back into heathenism whenever he has the chance.

Of the six skald-protagonists, all but Hallfred are marked by physical anomalies or impairments that would be considered disabilities or pathologies today, but Thormod Kolbrun's-Skald, the left-handed protagonist of *The Blood-Brothers' Saga*, is the only one whose own narrative world regards him as disabled. The physical anomalies of the other four are recognized, certainly, in their sagas, but are regarded as consequences of bewitchment (Kormak), shape-shifting (Egil), or expected life-cycle complications related to youthful fighting (Kormak again, Björn, and Gunnlaug) or the effects of old age (Björn and Egil). In contrast, Thormod's crippled right arm is explicitly referred to by various saga characters as both a disability and a stigma. What this means for his outsider status will emerge in the discussion that follows.

The Blood-Brothers' Saga (BBS) has survived for us in two versions, both hard to date and one anomalous in its sententious comments on the action. We first meet the blood-brothers when they are still boys, Thorgeir 'big, strong, and contentious' while Thormod, the future skald, contrastingly of 'middling size' (i.e. short) with dark, 'kinky' hair (chapter 2). They perform the blood-brother ritual to seal their oaths of friendship, thus committing themselves to vengeance on the other's death.

The first third of the saga is then taken up largely with the juvenile exploits of Thorgeir, who 'wasn't much of a ladies' man; he said that it would be a 'disgrace to his manly vigor to go crouching around women' (chapter 3) and whose forte is rather homicide: he kills his first man when he is fifteen years old. Thormod's primary function in this section, in contrast, seems to be to praise and memorialize Thorgeir's killings in verse. On one occasion, the two forcibly appropriate a beached whale from a well-liked local farmer who is cutting it up, and Thorgeir kills the man in the process. Thorgeir is outlawed for the killing but escapes to Norway, where he enters the service of King Olaf Haraldsson. Thormod, meanwhile, spends the next few years at his father's house, relieving his boredom with what his blood-brother had called 'crouching around women', amatory adventures with poor local girls whose widowed mothers have little means to defend them except through sorcery. The first of these liaisons results in the crippling of Thormod's right arm when the exasperated mother conjures magical protection for her slave and sets him to ambush the unwanted visitor.

The second is with the girl nicknamed Kolbrun, 'smut brow' for her dark hair, a shamenka about whom he writes the series of verses that gives him his own by-name, 'Kolbrun's-Skald'. Meanwhile, the outlawed Thorgeir returns to Iceland and is killed in a continuation of the blood feud deriving from the original killing over the beached whale. Thormod's duty now as the surviving blood-brother is to avenge Thorgeir's death. After a short visit to the Norwegian court, where he is established as a court poet of King Olaf (and presumably secures his patron's support for his vengeance plan), he takes passage to Greenland in pursuit of one of the men involved in his blood-brother's death. This passage to Greenland is a liminal period for Thormod, during which he meets with a mysterious odinic figure. In Greenland, Thormod hatches and follows through on an elaborate plot of deception, involving playacting, disguise, and the exploitation of two local simpletons, Idiot-Egil and Louse-Oddi, to expedite his killing, not only of the man he was pursuing, but of all male members of his family as well. In the process, he is twice stranded on skerries with his legs disabled. Vengeance accomplished, Thormod returns to Norway and King Olaf, who has by now lost control of his kingdom to rebellious landowners. At the battle of Stiklestad in 1030 Thormod defends the king like a professional berserk – i.e. fighting without any body armour, and killing everyone in his path without incurring any wounds. But the king is killed nevertheless and, after the battle is over, Thormod is fatally wounded by a mysterious arrowshot. In a field hospital located in a nearby barn and staffed by a woman physician, Thormod's last actions are to defend the manhood of the wounded warriors and to die standing on his feet, with a freshly composed poem on his lips.

The more important, and now easily identified, motifs associated with Thormod Kolbrun's-Skald that place him squarely in the skald-saga tradition are the following: his distinctive hair, regarded as ugly; the crippling of his right arm under ignominious conditions; very submissive posturing (as we shall see, below) toward inappropriate female sex objects; and his monomaniacal killing spree in Greenland, which is regarded by other saga characters as deranged.

Thormod's distinctive 'black and kinky' hair (*BBS* chapter 2) is the most transparent of the literary symbols of his outsider status and predictors of his later anti-social behaviour. As with the other dark skalds, his colouring is striking in the context of a literary tradition that, in keeping with the myth of Norse origins, identifies the hero by his blond good looks. The ideal saga hero, Gunnar of Hlidarendi, 'had a handsome face, a light complexion, a straight nose that turned up at the tip, keen blue eyes, red cheeks, thick yellow hair' (*Njal's Saga*, chapter 19), while even the brainy Snorri *godi*, as small and every bit as clever the trickster as our hero Thormod, is a blond beauty, 'with regular features, a light complexion, pale ("bleached") hair and a red beard' (*Eyrbyggja Saga*, chapter 15). Thormod's striking Afro, like Kormak's black curls, derives from self-descriptions in his own verse, but whether it is therefore historical, or rather a part of a very old tradition for skalds to describe themselves in these terms, is an open question.

That Thormod was left-handed is another one of the details mentioned in his own verses, and is perhaps part of an old tradition for skalds rather than historically factual, considering how well-suited the universal cultural connotations of left-handedness – gauche, lacking dexterity – are to the ugly or impaired social misfit that the poet is so commonly thought to be. And the Old Icelandic word for 'left-handed' is in fact *ørvendr*, literally 'utterly lacking in fastidiousness or exactitude', therefore 'awkward'.

The story of how Thormod became left-handed, when his right arm was disabled by a poor widow's slave, must be an invention of a later period to 'explain' verse references. However, it is completely in line with the convention that the skald's impairment is a source of shame – as opposed to, say, a battle wound which would be a source of pride. Thormod's father, Bersi, calls the incident that crippled his son an 'ignominious affair' (BBS chapter 9), presumably because of the extreme social disparity between Thormod, a youth of the land-owning class, and his attacker, and the consequent impossibility of extracting any honourable compensation for the injury. However, the female and sexual context of the attack (seducing a sorceress's daughter, being attacked by a woman's slave) must also have been an embarrassing element in a society in which sex role reversal – willed or unwilled – was a shame and a scandal.

The humiliation of being effectively disabled by one's girl is brought out more fully in a later episode in which Kolbrun, enraged over the replacement of her name in Thormod's poems, visits him by astral travel and strikes him with excruciating eye pain. His father says, with dry irony:

> Those are a couple of unhealthy girlfriends you've got there – the one gives you a such lasting mark (ørkumbl) that you'll never be a fit man again, and now it looks like both of your eyes are going to pop out of your head. (BBS chapter 11)

Here, the injury to the right arm is regarded as a 'lasting mark', a mark that can never be healed either physically or socially, a 'stigma' in fact, and it is clear from Bersi's comments that Thormod's choice of sex partners is to blame for his injuries. What is especially interesting about these episodes is that Thormod is made to comply with the demands of poor women – he seems almost the battered shuttlecock of the two occultly powerful girlfriends – and even staid Bersi, focused as he is on male status and honour, advises Thormod to do as he is told by these girls.

But to return to the consequences of Thormod's crippled arm, Bersi makes a legal charge against the slave for 'damage', áverk, usually translated 'injury', a legal term applied to wrongs or damages that are the result of illicit encroachment on one's person or property. The charge interprets Thormod's disabled right arm as damage that is to be compensated, but no compensation is ever collected because the widow saves her slave from Bersi's legal tactics, and possible extra-legal revenge, by smuggling him out of the country. The disability is specifically that Thormod 'was laid up a long time and was ever after left-handed', ørvendr (BBS chapter 10). This same point about loss of strength and dexterity is made later by Thormod himself, albeit ironically, when, after splitting a man's head with one blow of his axe, he speaks a verse calling himself a left-handed man and then offers this explanation:

> 'It may be,' said Thormod, 'that it wasn't a very strong blow because it was dealt by a left-handed man, but I didn't strike more than once – I thought that was enough.' (BBS chapter 23)

Perhaps the most interesting treatment of this theme occurs during the liminal period in which Thormod sails to Greenland to avenge his blood-brother. He boards ship in Norway as a short, ugly, submissive-to-women, left-handed (weak, awkward) court poet and disembarks in Greenland as a powerful killer, focused on avenging his blood-brother and eschewing the company of women (evincing disinterest in a servant girl provided for him there, and later accepting female help only from an elderly married sorceress). In short, it is during the sea voyage that Thormod becomes a mad but methodical killer, a verse-spouting master of disguise and horror, who will be spending a good bit of his time stranded, seal-like, on skerries and none of it crouching around women. On board with Thormod was a mysterious stranger:

> His hood hung down low. He was a big man, broad shouldered, thick-set, and no one could see his face. ... He said he was called Gest. (*BBS* chapter 20)

The name Gest, literally 'guest', is a common pseudonym for anyone travelling incognito, but especially for Odin, the quintessential undercover traveller. At sea, Gest proves to have 'the strength of two men in everything he did', while Thormod, in explicit contrast, 'was no strong man' (*BBS* chapter 20). The two do not get along. During a storm, Thormod and Gest are bailing together, Thormod filling the buckets in the bilge and Gest dumping them overboard. Thormod does not have the strength to lift the buckets high enough for Gest, who complains about this for a time and finally empties a bucket on Thormod. Then the sail yard snaps and must be repaired so the sail can be raised again.

> Skuf [the trader who owns and operates the ship] saw that the men who came from Greenland with him were not very handy, but he had seen that Thormod and Gest were handy at carving. Skuf then spoke to Thormod: "Will you put our sail yard back together?" Thormod answered, "I'm not handy Ask Gest to fix the sail yard – he's so strong that he could just jam the sail-yard ends together."

> Skuf went to Gest then and asked him to repair the sail yard. Gest answered, "I'm not handy. Go talk to Thormod and get him to do it, because he's so eloquent [literally, 'handy with words'] that he could 'compose' the sail-yard ends back together so they'll stick. But since it's urgent, I'll trim one part of the sail yard and Thormod can trim the other."

> Now each of them took up his axe and each of them trimmed his piece. Gest looked over his shoulder a bit at Thormod. When Thormod had trimmed his piece of the sail yard, he sat on the cargo down in the hold, but Gest hewed a bit longer on the wood that he was working. And when he was finished carving, he put the two pieces together, and neither piece needed to be trimmed [further]. (*BBS* chapter 20)

Thormod's crippled right hand, which back in Iceland had been an uncompensated legal damage and a stigma, is now seen as fully compensated with verbal acuity. Gest makes the saga's point: a poet like Thormod can knit the pieces together with words. Gest is not being sarcastic: the two abilities are truly equal. And to prove it, he shows that when each of them, the poet and the strong man, trims one end, they fit together like magic.

The mysterious 'Gest' turns out to be a rather ordinary Icelander, some sort of cousin of Thorgeir's, but the Odinic persona he assumed on the passage out to Greenland is taken on by Thormod to effect his revenge. Thormod accomplishes his first killing on this spree while dressed in a reversible cloak, black on one side and white on the other, with the hood pulled down over his face. Immediately after braining his victim, he reverses the cloak and poses as a bystander trying to help, and thus is able to get safely away. The verses he speaks immediately following this killing include the comment on his left-handed blow that we have already noted and also remarks concerning his 'black hair' and 'great mark in speech' (verse 24), a reference to a stammer that had not been mentioned previously in the saga. 'I'm an easily recognized man,' he boasts, 'a dark man, kinky haired and stuttering. But I wasn't meant to die at that moment.' (*BBS* chapter 23). The stammering skald is a paradox on the same model as the left-handed killer (and the ugly Don Juan, as well), but the Odinic ability to pass unrecognized despite very distinctive features (such as being one-eyed, as Odin is) is Thormod's point in this verse.

The episodes in which leg injuries twice leave our hero stranded on Greenland skerries and mistaken for a seal are another rich source of symbolism referring to the underlying mythic narrative. Of course, being stranded on a skerry during a long swim or as the result of a shipwreck or fishing-boat accident would have been part of life for active men in traditional societies of the North Atlantic, and the scenes here are convincingly realistic in many respects. However, the doubling of the episode and its resonance with the mythic struggle over the ownership of the skaldic mead suggest some symbolic reference. Further, the seemingly gratuitous and repeated image of the poet as a seal recalls the thesis of the French anthropologists, Detienne and Vernant (1974), in their work on the Greek god Hephaistos, which posits strong archetypal connections among marine mammals, lame legs, cunning artificers, and left-handed sexual practices.

If we can accept that the skald was equivalent to the skilled craftsman – and we can accept that equivalence because we have just seen the saga spell it out in the scene with Gest – then we find the Detienne and Vernant study ready-made for explaining why saga-world seals, walruses, and whales so often appear in connection with sexual insult, lameness, and the skalds. Given the economic style of the sagas, in which no detail is ever truly gratuitous, the seal (whale, walrus) is often properly read as figuring a male character's deviation from normative sexual endowment or activity. Supporting this symbolism in the Icelandic tradition is the notion widespread among North Sea cultures that any given seal may actually be a dangerous woman in disguise, as exemplified by the folklore seal maiden or selkie wife, or the more hostile *ceasg* or *roane*, and, in the saga literature, by such figures as the mysterious Hebridean woman in *Eyrbyggja Saga* whose bedclothes are cursed and who appears after death in the form of a seal, or the sorceress who bewitched Kormak's phallus and later swims around his ship in the form of a walrus.

The beached whale that initiated the series of events leading to Thorgeir's death has also initiated the imagery pattern. The whale's appearance in the narrative was followed almost immediately (within a few sentences) by the break-up of the blood-brothers over a question of 'manhood' initiated by Thorgeir (chapter 7), the one who had been so concerned with his 'manly vigor' that he considered association with women a 'disgrace'. In a sense, Thorgeir's untimely death is the consequence of his interpretation of 'manhood' as the relentless measuring of himself against other men, a behaviour we have seen in Kormak, Björn, and Gunnlaug (and to some extent in Egil as well). The image of the marine mammal reappears at Thorgeir's death in the form of a strange figure named Helgi Seal-Nut, whose by-name must be a reference to an undescended testicle, on analogy with the retractable genitals of marine mammals. Helgi Seal-Nut seems a remnant of an older stratum of the story that may have puzzled the present saga author since, after a lengthy and elaborate introduction in which it is revealed that he is a marathon runner, Helgi's role is very minor, amounting only to running with the news of Thorgeir's death. He clearly belongs to a folktale tradition of asexual, mysterious, almost ethereal or incorporeal beings, the best known of which are the brother-sister pairs Haki and Hekja in *Eirik the Red's Saga* (chapter 8) and Thjalfi and Roskva, Thor's servants. Among many peculiar motifs associated with these runners is their near nakedness, set off by a garment that seems to expose their loins or buttocks and features fasteners in the genital area. In any case, Helgi's nickname, Seal-Nut, is echoed in an odd detail about Thorgeir's death: his killers 'split him to the heart, wanting to know what it was like because he was so courageous, and people say it was very small' (chapter 17). That the heart is a stand-in or even euphemism for the testicles will be plain in an adventure of Thormod's discussed below.

Once Thormod takes on the role of Thorgeir's avenger, he begins to attract motifs similar to those associated with Thorgeir. Back in Iceland, when Thormod was 'crouching around women', it was his girl who exhibited the leg anomaly, for Kolbrun is *útfoett*, perhaps meaning 'splay-footed' or at a minimum that her toes turn out as she walks. The cultural associations, if any, of the detail remain obscure, and all we can say for sure is that in distinction from the other skald-saga protagonists who fall in love with ideal blonde beauties (Kormak's Steingerd, Gunnlaug's Helga, Björn's Oddny), Thormod is attracted to the peculiar. But now it is his turn to experience leg anomalies. After killing the Greenlander who had been a party to Thorgeir's death and in the bloody process of eliminating all four of the man's nephews, he is struggling with a certain Falgeir, who lands an axe blow 'between Thormod's shoulders', presumably on the back. Thormod and Falgeir then tumble over a cliff and into the sea, where they continue to fight in the water. Thormod pulls Falgeir's breeches down over his legs and, the narrative tells us dryly, 'The swimming became difficult for Falgeir then' (*BBS* chapter 23) and he drowned. Thormod's method for dispatching this victim is thus to turn him into a kind of perverse seal whose melded legs cause him to drown rather than swim. Now, seriously wounded between the shoulder blades, Thormod manages to get to a skerry where he is found by a friend who is out in a boat looking for him but nevertheless mistakes him for 'a seal or else a walrus' and rows over to investigate (*BBS* chapter 23). In keeping with his seal-like appearance, Thormod is unable to walk for an entire year. Why a wound between the shoulders should lame him for a year is not explained – except by the seal imagery, of course. In any case, reading this new information back into his sea struggle with Falgeir, we see that while disabled legs caused Falgeir to drown, the same condition in the trickster Thormod enables him to wrestle successfully in the water and then swim for safety, like a seal, to a skerry.

In the second seal skerry episode, Thormod, resuming his killing spree the following year, is wounded in the leg and spends the rest of the day lying on the shore in a 'heap of seaweed', then takes a boat and tries to row away under cover of darkness, but is pursued (by the mother of all those dead nephews!) and abandons the boat to swim to a nearby islet that, like the skerry on which he was last stranded, is under water at high tide. He digs down between two stones and covers himself with seaweed, enduring in silence the taunts of the woman searching for him: 'Now if Thormod can hear my words, let him answer me if he has a man's heart rather than a mare's' (chapter 24). When she finally rows away, he swims toward shore stopping at skerries until he is too exhausted to continue and, for a second time, with a disabled leg, lies on a skerry to die. This episode is especially clear in its linking of leg wound, seal behaviour, and, as the woman so succinctly puts it, a 'mare's heart'. Thormod's seal-like flopping on the skerry supports the woman's accusation that he has no 'balls'. Looking back over the arc of marine mammal imagery, we see that Thorgeir regarded the beached whale as an opportunity to test his manhood (i.e. to fight and die), while Thormod, in contrast, adopts the seal's modus operandi to save his own life.

With the salient exception of Egil, the skald-saga heroes are remarkable for leaving no descendants, this in striking contrast to the typical dénouement of the Icelandic Family Sagas, the listing of descendants living at the time of the writing. This detail is of a piece with the archetype, for it clinches the skalds' outsider status and makes them, celebrities though they be, into but passing oddities in the history of Iceland. And this may be why sagas were written about them. While they seem unlikely candidates for hero status, they were not actually founding fathers, not the ancestors of the Icelanders now (in the thirteenth and fourteenth centuries) subjects of the Norwegian crown. On the one hand, all their ugliness and social gaucherie is safely buried with them. Even Egil, who does leave a vigorous family line, is survived only by those among his children who take after the blond, popular strand of the family while the dark, ugly, mad strand dies with him. Thus, the skalds' eccentricities are genetically and historically isolated, available for nostalgia because there is no-one with their anti-social traits left to have a destabilizing effect. At the same time, the skalds prefigure the larger social dysfunction that blossomed in the thirteenth century and lost Iceland's cherished independence. With no social role out in Iceland other than as maniacs creating social chaos, they find acceptable social niches only with the Norwegian king – just as Iceland's thirteenth-century chaos was resolved by incorporation into the Norwegian kingdom.

Thormod's death is as fitting as those of the other skalds, taking place back east and in ironic circumstances. The saga has no need to rehearse in detail what its intended readers knew perfectly well: Thormod's royal patron, the inept erstwhile monarch known in his own lifetime as Olaf the Fat, was St Olaf. Immediately after he was martyred at Stiklestad, Olaf's corpse began performing miracle cures among his surviving followers, while his wrath at his rebellious subjects was evinced by crop failures throughout Norway. Cowed by these signs of divine support for monarchy, the rebels submitted to God's will to keep Norway a hereditary kingdom and invited Olaf's son to rule them. St Olaf's burial site became the centre of a celebrated international cult, northern Europe's second most popular pilgrimage destination, and later, the seat of an archbishopric (present-day Trondheim) under which all of Iceland, even before its annexation to the kingdom of Norway, was ecclesiastically governed. So Thormod Kolbrun's-Skald, the disabled low-life Icelandic loser, not only found an arena of heroic action abroad and status in the Norwegian court, as all the skalds did, but he gained an important place in the foundational myth of the Icelandic church as well, ensuring his hero status among the clerics who wrote his saga and clinching his posthumous integration into Icelandic society.

Thormod Kolbrun's-Skald is *sui generis* in many respects, but nevertheless illustrates some typical features of the Icelandic saga skald. He appears in the saga literature as a historical character, the court poet of St. Olaf, but at the same time exhibits features associated with the archetypal poet of pre-literate European societies. Like Aesop, he is ugly; like Homer, impaired. Like any typical poet in a traditional society, his asocial status is figured in the lack of both wife and children. The figure of the skald in the Icelandic saga world draws not only on this common tradition of the ugly, disabled, asocial poet, but also on the distinctively Icelandic villain, antagonist, or dark figure. This type character is most often signalled by a narrative comment that he is 'unpopular', suggesting that the community in which he lives regards him as asocial, or even anti-social. While impairment has no moral dimension in the saga world, the unpopular figure, in sharp contrast to the saga hero, has been disabled under decidedly dishonourable conditions. His behaviour, again in contradistinction to that of the hero, is out of control; he is a madman, manic, subject to unreasoned rage. And his sexuality fits the same pattern: he is not only barren, like the archetypal poet, but engages in sexual or para-sexual behaviour that society regards as dishonourable and deranged. Nevertheless, the saga skald in general, and Thormod Kolbrun's-Skald in particular, is a genuine narrative and folk hero, the dark aspects of his anti-social character being somehow redeemed by his status as poet and historian of the Icelandic commonwealth.

REFERENCES

Note: All quotations from Icelandic texts are translated by the author.

The Blood-Brothers' Saga: Fóstbrœdra saga. 1943. In *Íslenzk fornrit* vol. 6, Björn K. Thórólfsson and Gudni Jónsson (eds). Reykjavík: Hid Íslenzka Fornritafélag.

Detienne, M. and J.-P. Vernant 1974. *Les Ruses d'intelligence: la metis des grecs.* Paris: Flammarionet Cie.

Eyrbyggja Saga 1935. In *Íslenzk fornrit* vol. 4. Einar Ól Sveinsson and Matthías Thórdarson (eds). Reykjavík: Hid Íslenzka Fornritafélag.

Njal's Saga: Brennu-Njáls saga 1944. In *Íslenzk fornrit* vol. 12. Einar Ól Sveinsson (ed.). Reykjavík: Hid Íslenzka Fornritafélag.

Snorri Sturluson 1931. *Edda: Edda Snorra Sturlusonar*, Finnur Jónsson (ed.). Copenhagen: Gylendal.

SUGGESTED TRANSLATIONS

Faulkes, A. (trans.) 1987. *Snorri's Edda*. London: Dent.
Hreinsson, Vidar (ed.) 1997. *The Complete Sagas of the Icelanders*. Reykjavík: Leifur Eiríksson Publishing.

10 'Strange notions': treatments of early modern hermaphrodites

RUTH GILBERT

Hermaphrodites . . . have been banished, tormented, abused, and employed in such Offices as were in themselves severe; cut off from the common Privileges and Freedoms enjoyed by the Publick wheresoever they have been; yea put to death in an inhuman and pityless Manner. But the Disgrace which hangs over human Nature, from Mens harbouring such strange notions of one another, is almost as bad.

(Parsons 1741)

How we treat intersexuals is not a medical matter. It's a political and social issue.

(Cheryl Chase, in Jackson 1999)

In the mid-eighteenth century, Parsons (1741), placed the hermaphrodite in the context of rationalist science to argue that a third sex could not logically exist. In an argument that seemed to advocate a sympathetic approach towards physical difference, he claimed that hermaphroditism was the error of ignorant and superstitious commentators who had misinterpreted those 'poor human creatures' who were 'distorted in some particular part' (Parsons 1741: xvi).

The particularity of this 'part' and the difficulty in speaking of, or representing it, did not, however, render hermaphrodites invisible. Indeed, just as their presence was denied as technically impossible and legally incomprehensible, the bodies of so-called hermaphroditic individuals were nevertheless repeatedly reproduced in various texts and images. Literary representations returned to Ovid's description of the mythical hermaphrodite as 'at once both and neither' (Ovid [43 BC–AD 17] 1955: 104). Or, as Beaumont phrased it in his Renaissance rewriting of Ovid's myth, 'neither and either' (Beaumont [1602] 1967: 191).

Such poetic constructions played with the conceptual incongruity of ambiguous sex, but many representations of hermaphroditism throughout the early modern period demonstrate how seriously the categorization of sex was taken. Whereas Renaissance artistic and philosophical works had often celebrated the idea of androgyny as a disembodied spiritual ideal, the reality of embodied sexual ambiguity was not so easily absorbed into the cultural life of early modern Europe. From medical tracts to legal treatise the hermaphroditic body was debased and debunked, and the individual involved sentenced to a life (or death) as a man or a woman.

What recurs in these texts is a social anxiety about the hermaphrodite's difference and their implicit and embodied challenge to a legal–medical tradition that enshrined the principle of the binary nature of sex. This tension, between a cultural imperative to mark out clear differences and the conceptual challenge posed by hermaphroditic anatomies, is still unresolved. As Cheryl Chase, an intersexual who was operated upon at birth in order to fix and define her sex, has very recently argued, genital ambiguity is found to be intolerable 'not because it is threatening to a child's life but because it is threatening to the infant's culture' (Chase in Jackson 1999: 19). This observation is the starting point for the following analysis of the way in which early modern Europe identified, interpreted and frequently vilified hermaphroditic individuals.

Hermaphroditism had both intrigued and appalled people for many centuries before Parsons declared that there was actually no such condition. From the ancient classical works of Pliny and Livy to Parsons' (1741) eighteenth-century revisionist account of intersexuality, hermaphroditic bodies stretched the limits of what seemed possible within the human form. They defied the conventional categories of sex, and therefore disrupted patterns of behaviour which policed sexual and gender identity. Hermaphrodites were compelling figures because, although they represented a deviation from the familiar form of the body, they also disconcertingly resembled it. The genital organization of the physical hermaphrodite constituted an over-determined confusion of parts which were anomalous in their formation but nevertheless recognizably human in themselves (Figure 10.1).

The following discussion focuses on cases and representations drawn from the late sixteenth and seventeenth centuries, to explore how individual hermaphrodites were treated and how the idea of the hermaphroditic body was presented. In particular, it considers three case histories which show how sexual indeterminacy raised questions about definitions, both in specific terms about medical and legal discourses and in more general terms about gendered identity and figurations of humanity. The chapter looks at the ways in which ambiguously sexed people were represented as monstrous births, signs to be read, puzzles to be decoded. But it also explores how ways of knowing, understanding, and interpreting the hermaphrodite body were closely implicated in a culture of spectacle, erotic titillation and popular entertainment. Parsons' (1741) treatise, quoted above, claims to distance itself from such associations, but it too, in its detailed discussion of anomalous genitalia, partially reproduces their effects. And in that it is by no means unique.

What emerges from a survey of the literature of the time is that no discourse was pure. In this period the distinctions that are now made between discourses such as science and pornography were not yet fixed (Gilbert 1999). The subject of hermaphroditism could not be confined to any singular discourse, and early modern representations of hermaphroditic bodies routinely straddled boundaries between prodigy literature and pornography, mythology and medical discourse. Supposedly scientific tracts from the Royal Society might also be marked by the salaciousness of the peep-show and entertainment could often pass for edification. In such a culture, the bodies of sexually ambiguous people became the objects of intense interest and scrutiny as they raised questions about how to define the borders between male and female, monster and marvel, the human self and its non-human other.

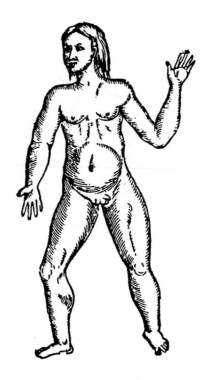

Figure 10.1   Hermaphrodite. (From Ambroise Páre 1573. *On Monsters and Marvels*. © Doz, 1971)

READING THE MONSTROUS BODY

Throughout the sixteenth and seventeenth centuries the monstrous body (whether real or imagined) was the subject of prodigy and wonder books, learned medical treatises, popular ballads and broadsides (Daston and Park 1981; Wilson 1993). Hermaphroditic individuals were thus absorbed into explorations of physical deformity which dehumanized their objects of study by describing them as monstrous births. Renaissance monsters were displayed, catalogued, and collected; they were interpreted as signs of divine judgement and as examples of the infinite variety of creation (Figure 10.2).

    The sixteenth-century humanist revival of classical literature had excavated theories of monsters and prodigies which, when inflected by medieval religious and popular folk-belief systems, effected a powerful hold on the Renaissance imagination. Medieval and Renaissance literature drew upon a vocabulary which distinguished (although not always clearly or consistently) between monsters, marvels, portents and prodigies. These terms structured a semiotic system that was based on the belief that signs were transmitted from God and mediated through nature. In the early fifth century, St Augustine had emphasized how these marvels were all inherently

Figure 10.2   A monster with two heads. (From Ambroise Páre 1573. *On Monsters and Marvels.*
© Doz, 1971)

connected to representation (demonstration), pointing out that the etymology of the
word monster 'evidently comes from *monstrare*, "to show", because they (monsters)
show by signifying something'. In this lexicon of representation, portents, 'show
beforehand' and prodigies derive from '*porro dicere*, to foretell the future' (St Augustine
1984: 588). As Cooper (1565: 4H2^v) put it, a monster was, 'a token or shewing: a
thing that signifieth').

In his 1579 translation of Melanchthon and Luther's anti-Catholic pamphlet, *Of
Two Wonderful Popish Monsters* (a 'Popish Asse' and a 'Moonkish Calfe'), Brooke (1579:
A2) explained that:

> There is nothing can stirre up the mind of man, & which can engender
> more fere unto the creatures then the horrible Monsters, which are
> brought forth dayly contrary vnto the workes of Nature. The which the
> most times doe note and demonstrate unto us the ire and wrath of God.

Monsters were to be read, he suggested, as God's 'advertisements'. The form, origins
and significance of the monstrous body invited interpretation and explanation.
Inevitably, images of monstrous bodies actually told stories not so much about
themselves but about those who viewed, analysed, and represented them.

In 1569 Fenton published *Certain Secrete Wonders*, an adapted version of Pierre
Boaistuau's earlier collection of monsters and prodigies. In his preface Fenton claimed

that the monstrous body was a uniquely thrilling spectacle which, as he phrased it, 'stirreth the spirite of man' and 'ravishest [. . .] his senses'. 'Misseshapen and deformed' bodies, he suggested, aroused powerful desires to, 'enter into our selves, to knock with the hammer of our conscience, to examine our offices, and have in horror our misdeeds' (Fenton 1569: Aiiij). Such introspection was particularly significant in the predominantly Protestant context of post-Reformation England. Calvinistic doctrine encouraged the searching of one's conscience and the contemplation of the monstrous sins which were held to be inherent within humanity. To view the monstrous body was, in these terms, to view the inner self. In this context, the hermaphrodite or disabled body was read as a materialization of social, political or personal corruption. As a 1562 ballad, which described a severely deformed child born in Essex, asserted, the monstrous body, 'declares what sinnes beset the secrete minde' (Anon [1562] Lilly 1867: 27).

This process, by which sins were represented through grotesque embodiments, was inflected by gender. Women were held to be especially responsible for the creation of monsters either because of their supposedly aberrant sexual desires which tempted them towards copulation with the devil or animals, or through the power of their imagination alone. Monstrous births were commonly attributed to the power of the maternal imagination in pregnancy to determine the shape of the infant in a literal act of misconception (Huet 1993). So, for example, in a case which was often cited in Renaissance studies of monsters and prodigies, the birth of a black child to white parents was explained by the mother having seen a picture of an Ethiopian at the moment of conception (Lupton 1579: 156). In these terms, female fantasy was a powerful force which inextricably linked representation and physiological processes. If the monstrous body was a kind of story, then the maternal imagination was able to circumvent biological paternal authority and write another, corporeal narrative.

In the early modern period the hermaphrodite figure was placed somewhere between horror and fascination. The 'real' and fictional monstrous hermaphroditic body inevitably merged in the images and stories about monsters which were energetically circulated in this period. Renaissance travellers' tales presented intriguing and exciting narratives of difference drawing upon Plinian images of the 'monstrous races'. The fantastic images found, for example, within the voyage narratives of John Mandeville and Leo Africanus were repeated as facts throughout a wide range of western European Renaissance literature (Wittkower 1942; Friedman 1981).

Paré's On Monsters and Marvels ([1573] 1982) illustrates the ways in which hermaphrodites were absorbed into diverse studies of monstrous births and bizarre occurrences. Paré's popular treatise consisted of a collection of anecdotes and images relating to anomalous bodily forms, which was largely culled from earlier works by writers such as Pliny, Galen, Aristotle, Hippocrates, Lycosthenes, and Boaistuau. Since the same stories and images of monsters were repeated and recycled so often it is impossible to establish how authentic such accounts were. However, in a moment of wry self-reflexivity, Paré noted in his own ambitious collection of such phenomena, 'I believe either fiction, or want of observation has made more monsters than nature ever produced' (Paré [1573] 1982: 434).

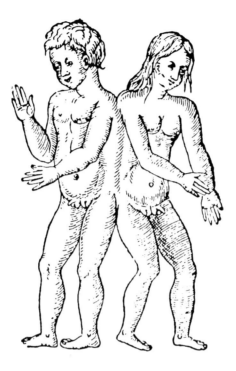

Figure 10.3 Hermaphroditic conjoined twin children. (From Ambroise Páre 1573. *On Monsters and Marvels*. © Doz, 1971)

Paré ([1573] 1982: 3) prefaced his text by distinguishing between monsters and marvels (*prodiges*). 'Monsters', he claimed:

> are things that appear outside the course of Nature (and are usually signs of some forthcoming misfortune), such as a child who is born with one arm, another who will have two heads, and additional members over and above the ordinary.

Marvels were, in contrast, 'things which happen that are completely against Nature' (Paré [1573] 1982: 3). Stories of women who gave birth to serpents and dogs were placed in this category and Paré included several chapters on fantastic celestial, terrestrial and sea creatures.

Paré listed thirteen causes of monstrous births, which ranged from the glory and wrath of God to the power of the maternal imagination, and the effects of demonic possession. The third cause he cited was 'too great a quantity of seed', and hermaphrodites, he claimed, like conjoined twins (Figure 10.3), 'come from a superabundance of matter' (Paré [1573] 1982: 26). In a chapter devoted to the discussion of hermaphrodites ('hommes et femmes') Paré defined four different types which were based on classic Galenic models of sexual gradation: the predominantly male, the predominantly female, those who were in effect neither, and those who appeared to be both. Such an interpretation of sexual indeterminacy drew on what Laqueur has termed the 'one-sex model' of sexual categorization that dominated pre-enlightenment ideas about human biology (Laqueur 1990: 8). This system understood sex as being based on a fundamental similarity rather than an absolute difference, so that male and female were not so much opposed categories as different points on a sliding (but still hierarchical) scale of sexual differentiation.

Paré's taxonomies of hermaphroditic possibilities highlight the hermaphroditic body as an extraordinary example of what was in effect a typical uncertainty within definitions of human sex. For Paré, hermaphroditism was not a singular sign but rather a collection of multiple signifiers which were always open to interpretation. He claimed, 'the most expert and well-informed physicians and surgeons can recognize whether hermaphrodites are more apt at performing with and using one set of organs than another, or both, or none at all' (Paré [1573] 1982: 27). What this statement highlights is that while, biologically at least, sexual difference might have been perceived as a fluid construct, there was also an overriding social and cultural imperative to fix ambiguous sex within the limits of binary oppositions.

DEFINING HERMAPHRODITES

The idea of hermaphroditism raised serious questions about the possibility and practice of social and cultural definition. How, for example, could someone who was neither clearly male nor female be properly defined as a person within the law. As Maclean (1980: 81) has argued, the Renaissance law 'consists of contraries (married/unmarried) or opposites of privation (able to succeed to a title/unable to succeed). There is little room for the "species relativa"'.

The legal history of hermaphrodites was constrained by a conceptual incongruity. According to Darmon (1985: 41) 'throughout the Middle Ages and up until the sixteenth-century, the situation of hermaphrodites seems to have been fairly ill-defined' (see Epstein 1990; Daston and Park 1995). Throughout history the judgements of folklore, if not the letter of the law, often led to the persecution of hermaphroditic individuals. From the early sixteenth-century both civil and canon European law drew upon the precepts which had been laid out in the third century Roman statute, Lex Repetundarum, which had pronounced that hermaphrodites were to be treated as either men or women, according to which sex predominated. This ruling formed the basis of most subsequent legal arguments. Hermaphrodites were attributed to whichever sex appeared to predominate and were given all the legal rights and obligations of either a man or a woman. They could marry, inherit, and enter into contracts in accordance with whichever sexual identity was decided upon, although in Renaissance France those hermaphrodites who chose maleness were still prohibited from holding positions as lawyers, judges and university rectors (Daston and Park 1995: 435). The fundamental tenet concerning hermaphrodites in ancient and Renaissance legal dictums was then, that they 'must be deemed male or female' according to which sex predominated (Anon 1632: 5).

As Coke (1628: 8) put it:

> Every heire is either male, or female, or an hermaphradite, that is both
> male and female. And an hermaphradite (which is also called Androgynus)
> shall bee heire, either as male or female, according to that kinde of the
> sexe which doth prevaile.

Coke's formulation signals the curious way in which the law recognized
hermaphrodites as a possible third sexual category only then legislatively to negate
their existence. The hermaphrodite could inherit only when s/he was no longer
hermaphroditic.

The legal solution to the 'problem' of hermaphroditism raised several difficulties.
Who, for example, defined the 'true sex' of the apparently hermaphroditic individual?
What would happen if neither sex prevailed? And, perhaps most significantly, how
could a legal judgement fix sexual identity? According to Foucault (1980), in the
Middle Ages the father or the godfather of an hermaphroditic infant was granted the
authority, within a patriarchal economy, to name, and thus define, her/his sex
(Foucault 1980: vii–viii). However, during the Renaissance there was, as Daston and
Park (1995: 430) have noted, an 'increasing reliance on outside testimony to
determine the hermaphrodite's predominant sex'. Throughout the sixteenth and
seventeenth centuries medical experts played a greater role in deciding the sex of
hermaphroditically ambiguous individuals. Commissions of renowned medical
authorities were gathered to establish the 'truth' in cases of doubtful sex. Where
neither sex could be proved to predominate, adult hermaphrodites were, in theory,
allowed to choose their own sexual identification, but having done so were legally
bound to stay within the prescribed social and legislative confines of that sex. Faultlines
emerged in these legal/sexual taxonomies when individuals were perceived to
alternate between sexual positions. Brillon noted in *Dictionnaire des arrêts* (1671–1736),
for example, that hermaphrodites who chose the male sex and then adopted a passive
role in sexual intercourse could be charged with sodomy (Epstein 1990: 102). The law
thus encoded a wider cultural anxiety about disguised and shifting sexual identities.

Such judgements implied a far more unstable picture of the hermaphrodite's place
within the law than had been articulated in the definitive legal formulations of *Lex
Repetundarum*. The difficulties of fixing sexual identity within medical jurisprudence
were highlighted in the French case of Marie/Marin le Marcis. Marie/Marin's story of
indeterminate sexual identification was made famous in the seventeenth century by
Duval's *Traité des hermaphrodits* (1612) and has become well-known to contemporary
cultural critics and historians through Greenblatt's (1986) discussion of Renaissance
sexual ambiguity.

Marie le Marcis was a servant who lived as a woman until she was twenty-one,
at which time she declared that she was actually a man and changed her name to
Marin. She renounced her female identity and stated her intention to marry Jeane le
Febvre, a widow with whom she was involved in a sexual love affair. Although
English law had no concept of female sodomy, France, and many other European
countries, legislated against penetrative sexual practices between women (Crompton
1980/1). The scandal that followed Marie/Marin and Jeane's declaration of their love

thus resulted in a charge of sodomy being brought against Marie/Marin. In 1601 the courts refuted her/his claim that s/he was a man and accused her/him of 'abusing' her/his lover with an unnaturally enlarged clitoris, and s/he was condemned to death. Jeane, who was viewed as the more innocent party (the penetrated not penetrator), was to be forced to watch her lover's execution, to suffer a whipping and to be exiled from the region.

Following Marie/Marin's appeal, a medical commission was appointed to define her/his 'true' sex. Jacques Duval probed within the doubtful subject's body, and aroused what seemed to be a latent penis to ejaculation, thus proving that Marie/Marin was not in fact guilty of sodomy. S/he was instead a victim of confused sexual determination. Greenblatt has hailed the moment of Duval's intervention in victorious terms, declaring that 'medical authority had masturbated Marin's identity into existence' (Greenblatt 1986: 32). However, as Gough (1994: 136) has argued, 'Duval's masturbation actually had quite the opposite effect. It robbed Mari(e/n) of the possibility of any proper legal identity at all'. Duval did not, as Greenblatt suggests, prove that Marie/Marin was really a man locked in a female form. He defined her as a thoroughly sexually ambiguous figure, a woman-man, or *Gunantrope*. As Gough (1994: 136) asserts, 'Duval's discovery does not make Mari(e/n) a man. It makes him/her a woman with a penis: an hermaphrodite'.

The appeal court's response to the medical commission's pronouncement was hesitant, and suggests the pressure that hermaphroditic identity placed on the boundaries of the legal system. The death sentence was withdrawn but Marie/Marin was still not free to follow her chosen sexual identity. S/he was instead ordered to live as a woman but to abstain from any sexual activity until she was twenty-five, at which time her/his sex might be more easily defined. The ruling indicates how the legal system, in effect, had no satisfactory response to such a case. Medical jurisprudence had made Marie/Marin more, not less, indeterminate and s/he was destined to live a liminal existence on the borders of male, female and hermaphroditic identities.

SCIENCE AND SPECTACLES

Stories about the case of Marie/Marin were recounted and recycled in both popular and scholarly literature throughout the seventeenth century and beyond. The case fuelled what was already an intense interest in accounts of ambiguously sexed people in this period. Such a fascination converged with the emergence of the seventeenth century 'new science' as well as with a developing culture in which the anomalous occurrences of the natural world were exhibited as public spectacles (Altick: 1978).

Whilst hermaphrodites may have been 'read' as signs from God, they were also often placed within a context of popular and commercial appeal. There is evidence to suggest that hermaphroditic individuals were shown as popular curiosities (at fairs and 'freak shows' as well as within texts and images) throughout the early modern period.

In Act III of Beaumont's *The Knight of the Burning Pestle* ([1607] 1969: III.273–274), the Citizen's Wife comments on the contemporary fashion for such shows, remarking that 'the hermaphrodite' was amongst the prettiest 'of all the sights that ever were in London'. Since topical allusion characterized such comedies, it is likely that Beaumont was referring to a popular spectacle of the time. Scientific discussions, anecdotal evidence and records of advertisements for shows, indicate that by the second half of the seventeenth century hermaphrodites were often displayed for popular entertainment.

The 'new scientific' desire to know and categorize the natural world in the seventeenth century focused a new scrutinizing gaze on to the anomalous and confusing spectacle of hermaphroditic bodies. Potentially, hermaphrodites were both intellectually intriguing and erotically stimulating sights. Many earlier representations of hermaphrodites, such as those depicted by Paré ([1573] 1982) in the late sixteenth century, were represented as anonymous bodies without social or cultural history. Duval's (1612) detailed account of the case of Marie/Marin le Marcis marked a shift in the representation of hermaphrodites. Throughout the seventeenth century hermaphrodites were increasingly depicted as specific and distinctive cases, rather than as universalized examples of God's wonder, or as the abstract signs of social or religious corruption. By the late seventeenth century the 'New Science' demanded names, locations, histories and most importantly ever more probing anatomical details.

Two particular cases of hermaphroditism which were related in letters published in the *Philosophical Transactions* of 1667 and 1686 characterized the ways in which the hermaphrodite became the focus of a developing scientific gaze in this period. 'An Exact Narrative of an Hermaphrodite now in London' (1667) was written in Latin by the physician Thomas Allen, who was a member of the Royal Society. It concerned the case of Anna Wilde, an hermaphrodite who had been born in 1647 in Ringwood, Hampshire. This account is characteristic of the mid-seventeenth-century scientific representation of hermaphrodites. Its preface in the *Philosophical Transactions* declared it to be fit 'for the view of the Learned'.

Allen's report was presented as the authoritative observations of a member of the Royal Society. But evidence suggests that his account was largely compiled from the stories of Anna Wilde's 'owner' who displayed her/him as freak in a travelling show. Such shows were evidently not unusual. In his diary entry for 22 August 1667, for example, John Evelyn ([1667] 1959: 513) mentioned that a popular spectacle was currently being shown in London:

> There was also now an *Hermaphrodite* shew'd both *Sexes* very perfectly, the *Penis* onely not perforated, went for a woman, but was more a man, of about 21 years of Age: divers curious persons went to see her, but I would not.

Evelyn did not elaborate on why he would not view this show, although it was clearly something of considerable contemporary interest. The hermaphrodite was viewed for entertainment by 'divers curious persons' and the 'facts' of her/his history were mediated through the stories told in this commercial context.

The early modern scientist was part of a viewing public who paid to look at such curiosities. An advertisement from the early eighteenth century, for example, announced that for one shilling an hermaphrodite could be viewed:

> Compleat Male and Female, perfect in both Parts, and does give a general Satisfaction to all Quality, Gentry, Physicians, Surgeons and Others, that have seen it, constant Attendance is given from One a Clock in the Afternoon 'till Nine at Night [...] There is a paper Lantern over the Door, with these Words upon it, *The Hermaphrodite is to be seen here without a Moments loss of Time.*
>
> (Anon 1680-1700)

Allen's description of his viewing of Anna Wilde for the *Philosophical Transactions* was clearly drawn from and implicated in this culture of curiosity and display.

The Dutch physician de Diemerbroeck (1689) reported viewing an hermaphrodite in Utrecht in 1668 (the year after Anna Wilde had been shown in London). Although s/he is unnamed in this account, the evidence suggests that Diemerbroeck was also describing Anna Wilde. Before he related the details of the case, Diemerbroeck signalled how hermaphrodites were presented as popular spectacles in street shows, as well as in specifically learned contexts. He recalled that he had previously seen a similar hermaphrodite in Anjou, who 'for a small matter turn'd up her Coats to any one that had a mind to satisfy Curiosity' (Diemerbroeck 1689: 183). However, the curious passer-by might also be the enquiring scientist. His anecdote demonstrated that the desire to fulfil the epistemophilic urge to know could be easily exploited as a money-spinning show and tell.

In December 1686, Monsieur Veay, a French physician, wrote a letter to the *Philosophical Transactions* about another sensational case of hermaphroditism which he had seen in Toulouse.[1] The case of Marguerite Malause which Veay related in his letter was widely discussed in early modern medical, paramedical and pornographic literature. The story of this young French woman, who might also have been a man, excited much contemporary interest. The case typified the way in which herma-phrodites were discussed within a variety of intersecting discourses. The medical reports of the case formed the basis of many popular stories about erotic transgression which circulated in texts throughout the late seventeenth and early eighteenth centuries. Veay's (1687) account gives a detailed description of the history and anatomy of Marguerite Malause. S/he was born in Pourdiac, near Toulouse, where s/he lived as a woman until s/he became ill in 1686 and was examined by Veay. He declared that s/he was an hermaphrodite, 'une chose fort extraordinaire' (Veay 1687).

Veay stressed that he would not have believed this possible if he had not seen it with his own eyes. He showed this extraordinary figure to several other doctors, who, in consultation with the governors of the hospital, declared her/him to be predominantly male and ordered her/him to change her/his name to the masculine Arnaud and adopt the clothes and life-style of a man. The testimony of Marguerite her/himself was not considered to be credible. Veay noted that there was no hesitation over the verdict because s/he was able to perform the functions of a man and not a woman (Veay 1687).

Later anecdotal evidence suggests that Marguerite/Arnaud did not live happily with this new male persona. S/he was the subject of considerable local curiosity and scandal and eventually left Toulouse and reverted back to a female identity. In 1691 s/he was arrested for transgressing the boundaries of the sex and gender which had been attributed to her and was ordered again to live as a man. In 1693 s/he came to Paris, where her case was considered by the famous physicians Helvétius and Saviard who concluded finally that s/he was in fact a woman.

In Saviard's (in Darmon 1985: 50) account of the case, which was published in 1702, he described how Marguerite/Arnaud had arrived in Paris:

> [. . .] in the guise of a boy, sword at his side, with his hair nonetheless hanging like a girl, and tied behind with a ribbon in the manner of the Spaniards and Neapolitans. She used to appear at public assemblies and allow herself to be examined for a small tip by those who were curious.

One anonymous pornographic work which typically shifted the emphasis of the case from medical curiosity to erotic titillation, also suggested that 'she got Mony by shewing herself' (Anon 1709: 17). The lines between science and spectacle could not be firmly drawn. Subtending these accounts are the untold stories of the ambiguously sexed people themselves. They were the objects of scientific scrutiny and sexual prurience, but we have little or no direct access to their own thoughts and feelings about their sexual identities. What emerges is a history in which their experiences of physical difference and sexual irregularity have been silenced and deemed conceptually and socially illegitimate. It is a history which reveals a fascination with the idea of hermaphroditic difference but which, in its repeated denunciation and dehumanization of the sexually ambiguous, demonstrates a decided lack of engagement with the marginalized themselves.

CONCLUSION

What such accounts demonstrate is that, above all, the hermaphrodite, whether depicted as a monstrous demonstration of divine judgement, an object of scientific scrutiny or a figure of erotic entertainment, was an absorbing figure. Ambiguously sexed individuals generated a particular curiosity which has arguably characterized representations of intersexuality up until the present day. Alexander Pope ([1714] 1956: 277) described an hermaphrodite who was currently being shown in London, as 'the most reigning Curiosity in the town'. He ([1714] 1956: 277–8) wrote of the hermaphrodite with palpable relish as:

> [. . .] a Person who is equally the toast of gentlemen and ladies, and is at present more universally admired than any of either sex. You know few proficients have a greater genius for Monsters than my self; but I have never tasted a monster to that degree I have done this creature: it was not, like other monsters, produced in the deserts of *Arabia*, nor came from the

country of the *Great Mogul*, but is the production of the joint-endeavours
of a *Kentish* parson and his Spouse, who intended in the singleness of heart
to have begot a christian but of one sex, and providence has sent them one
of two.

For Pope the hermaphrodite, who would 'expose her personal curiosities for a
shilling', represented a consummate opportunity for entertainment. Monsters were
objects to be 'tasted', savoured and digested with wit in an age which delighted in such
spectacles. The early modern meaning of 'taste' was associated generally with
perceptions of touching, feeling and experiencing an object, rather than its current
usage, which is focused more on specifically oral sensations.

The history of attitudes towards sexual indeterminacy is complex. Parsons' (1741)
defence of hermaphrodites from 'the strange Notions' which had led to their
persecution throughout history, which was the starting point for this discussion,
suggests a break with that cruel past. But his own dismissal of apparent
hermaphroditism, whilst ostensibly distancing itself from the playfulness of Pope's
account and the dehumanization which characterized many earlier treatments of the
subject, did not mark a point of liberation for the sexually ambiguous. Parsons'
argument that hermaphrodites were, in fact, women with enlarged clitorises was a
repetition of many other early modern accounts of ambiguous sex which presented
hermaphroditism as an eroticized spectacle. His thesis contributes to a history in which
embodied sexual ambiguity has repeatedly provoked confused and anxious responses.

It is, perhaps, too simplistic to focus on the ways in which pre-Enlightenment
culture was guilty of cruelly punishing those people with physical differences. In
presenting such a marked distance between that pre-Enlightenment culture and today,
we can fail to see our current society's equally troubled attitude towards intersexuality.
While western culture in the late twentieth century might, in many ways, celebrate
gender play and erotic ambiguity, actual genital irregularity is still a disturbing matter.
Despite the current preoccupation with accounts of transexuality and gender
dysphoria, the first question asked when a baby is born is still routinely 'is it a girl
or a boy?'. In a culture in which identity is organized around the binary of sex this is a
question that still insistently demands its answer.

NOTE

1 I am grateful to Jonathan Sawday and Bill Marshall for their advice on the translation of this
   letter.

REFERENCES

Allen, T. 1667. An exact narrative of an hermaphrodite now in London. *Philosophical Transactions
   of the Royal Society of London* 32, 624.
Altick, R. 1978. *The Shows of London*. Cambridge MA: Harvard University Press.
Anon. 1680–1700. *A Collection of 77 Advertisements relating to Dwarfs, Giants, and Other Monsters
   and Curiosities exhibited for Public Inspection*. London.

Anon. 1709. *An Apology for a Latin Verse in Commendation of Mr. MARTEN'S Gonosologium Novum.* London.

Anon. 1632. *The Lawes Resolutions of Womens Rights.* London.

Anon. [1562] 1867. The true reporte of the forme and shape of a monstrous Childe borne at Muche Horkesleye, a village three miles from Colchester, in the Countye of Essex, the xxi daye of Apryll in this yeare 1562. In *A Collection of 79 Black Letter Ballads and Broadsides, Printed in the Reign of Queen Elizabeth, between the Years 1559 and 1597*, J. Lilly (ed.), 27–9. London.

St Augustine. 1984. *City of God.* H. Bettenson (ed. and trans.). Harmondsworth: Penguin.

Beaumont, F. [1602] 1967. Salmacis and Hermaphroditus. In *Elizabethan Erotic Verse*, N. Alexander (ed.), 168–91. London: Edward Arnold.

Beaumont, F. [1607] 1969. *The Knight of the Burning Pestle*, M. Hattaway (ed.). New Mermaid. London: Ernest Benn.

Brooke, J. 1579. Unto the Christian Reader. In *Of two Woonderful Popish Monsters, to wyt, of a Popish Asse which was found at Rome in the River of Tyber, and of A Moonkish Calfe, calved at Friberge in Misne, Which are the very foreshewings and tokens of Gods wrath, against blinde, obstinate and monstrous Papists, Witnessed and declared, the one by Philip Melanchthon, the other by Martyn Luther.* London.

Coke, E. 1628. *The First Part of the Institutes of the Lawes of England: or, a commentary upon Littleton.* London.

Cooper, T. 1565. *Thesaurus Linguae Romanae & Britannicae.* London.

Crompton, L. 1980/1. The myth of lesbian impunity: capital laws from 1270 to 1791. *Journal of Homosexuality* 6, 11–25.

Darmon, P. 1985. *Trial By Impotence: virility and marriage in pre-revolutionary France*, P. Keegan (trans.). London: Chatto & Windus.

Daston, L. and K. Park 1981. Unnatural conceptions: the study of monsters in sixteenth- and seventeenth century France and England. *Past and Present* 92, 20–54.

Daston, L. and K. Park 1995. The hermaphrodite and the orders of nature: sexual ambiguity in early modern France. *Gay and Lesbian Quarterly* 1, 419–38.

Diemerbroeck, I. 1689. *The Anatomy of Human Bodies*, W. Salmon (trans.). London.

Duval, J. 1612. *Traité des hermaphrodits, parties génitales, accouchements des femmes, etc.* Rouen.

Epstein, J. 1990. Either/or–neither/both: sexual ambiguity and the ideology of gender. *Genders* 7, 99–142.

Evelyn, J. [1667] 1959. *The Diary of John Evelyn*, E.S. de Beer (ed.). Oxford: Oxford University Press.

Fenton, E. 1569. *Certaine Secrete Wonders of Nature.* London.

Foucault, M. 1980. Introduction. *Herculine Barbin: being the recently discovered memoirs of a nineteenth century French hermaphrodite*, R McDougall (trans.) vii–xvii. New York: Pantheon Books.

Friedman, J.B. 1981. *The Monstrous Races in Medieval Art and Thought.* Cambridge, MA: Harvard University Press.

Gilbert, R. 1999. Seeing and knowing: science, pornography and early modern hermaphrodites. In *At the Borders of the Human: beasts, bodies and natural philosophy in the early modern period*, E. Fudge, R. Gilbert and S. Wiseman (eds), 150–70. Basingstoke: Macmillan.

Gough, J. 1994. The Hermaphrodite: a study of its medical, legal, and philosophical status, and of its appearance in some examples of English renaissance literature. Unpublished D.Phil. thesis, Keble College, University of Oxford.

Greenblatt, S. 1986. Fiction and friction. In *Reconstructing Individualism: autonomy, individuality, and the self in western thought*, T. Heller, M. Sosna and D. Wellbery (eds) 30–52. California: Stanford University Press.

Huet, M. 1993. *Monstrous Imagination.* Cambridge, MA: Harvard University Press.

Jackson, K. 1999. Why should a John be a Joan? *Times Higher Educational Supplement*, 8 October.

Laqueur, T. 1990. *Making Sex: body and gender from the Greeks to Freud.* Cambridge MA: Harvard University Press.

Lupton, T. 1579. *A Thousand Notable Things of Sundry Sortes.* London.

Maclean, I. 1980. *The Renaissance Notion of Woman: a study in the fortunes of scholasticism and medical science in European intellectual life.* Cambridge: Cambridge University Press.

Ovid [43 BC–AD 17] 1955. *Metamorphoses,* M. Innes (trans.). Harmondsworth: Penguin.

Paré, A. [1573] 1982. *On Monsters and Marvels.* J.L. Pallister (trans.). Chicago: Chicago University Press.

Parsons, J. 1741. *A Mechanical and Critical Enquiry into the Nature of Hermaphrodites.* London.

Pope, A. [1714] 1956. To a Lady from her Brother. In *The Correspondence of Alexander Pope,* George Sherburn (ed.), 277–9. 5 vols. Oxford: Clarendon Press.

Veay 1687. An extract of a letter written by Mr. Veay, physician at Toulouse to Mr. de St. Ussans, concerning a very extraordinary Hermaphrodite in that City. *Philosophical Transactions of the Royal Society of London* 282, 282–3.

Wilson, D. 1993. *Signs and Portents: monstrous births from the Middle Ages to the Enlightenment.* London: Routledge.

Wittkower, R. 1942. Marvels of the East: a study in the history of monsters. *Journal of the Warburg and Courtauld Institutes* 5, 159–97.

11   The logic of killing disabled children: infanticide, Songye cosmology, and the colonizer

Patrick J. Devlieger

This study of the infanticide of children with a 'body difference'[1] explores the contrasting cosmologies of the Songye people who live in the East Kasai province of the Democratic Republic of Congo, and their colonizers. The practice of infanticide in African cultures, especially of twins, has been widely reported in the literature of colonial administrators, missionaries and social scientists during the pre-colonial and colonial eras. For example, Ploss (1911) writes that, traditionally, the birth of a deformed child (*Mißgeburt*) meant a great misfortune (*Unglück*) for the Basotho. If this child were to be left alive, hunger and war would result. Therefore, the Basotho argued that such children were to be drowned in a barrel with water, and the father would announce that the child was stillborn (Ploss 1911).

Early travellers and scientists claimed that, as a result of the practice of infanticide, they had not observed the presence of disabled people among Africans (Coussement 1935; Merriam 1974; Walk 1928). Colonial powers and religious organizations endeavoured to eradicate the practice, but remained doubtful of their success, partly because of a lack of quantitative data that could document the continued prevalence of the practice. Ethnographic data however does provide evidence of the distribution of the practice in Africa. Carreira (1971) argues that infanticide was practised in most of western and central Africa, and claims that the practice was not apparent in countries in Northern Africa, countries in the horn of Africa, parts of Western Africa, and the most southern African countries. Substantial evidence was produced that belief systems supporting infanticide may have been resistant to change (Coussement 1935; Leis 1965; Merriam 1974).

Few studies have examined African 'world views' that support the practice of infanticide, nor examined the impact of cultural contact on the practice. However, the oral and written records of the infanticide practice may yield to interpretations less elusive than attempts to describe the actual practice or the rates of incidence. The reason is that the actual practice of infanticide could hardly be observed and records of death from infanticide were not easily available. Future archaeological and ethnographic research may be able to rectify the dearth of knowledge of the actual practice.

The sources used in this chapter are ethnographic interviews conducted from 1983 to 1985 among the Songye and Luba peoples of the Kasai region of the Democratic

Republic of Congo. These interviews were conducted as part of an ethnographic field study on the conceptualization of disability in an African society. Comparative use of ethnographic literature and colonial records complement the current investigation of a cosmology that allows the practice of infanticide (the indigenous world view) or one that rejects such a practice (the colonial world view).

The historical and cultural study of practices such as infanticide are important to illuminate the interface between societies and people who are disabled. Disability studies is an emerging academic endeavour which researches disability in social and cultural contexts.

Within the context of pre-modern African and colonial-modern cosmologies it is now possible to consider practices such as infanticide and the rejection of the practice, and to recognize that within the current African independent post-modern times, both the traditional and the colonial cosmologies still linger. The post-colonial African context is characterized by a juxtaposition of remnants of pre-modern practices and beliefs, the management of disability through services in health, education, and employment that emanated from colonial and global initiatives, and post-modern, innovative hybrid solutions that, in the case of disabled people, involve participating in a global movement.

For the purpose of this chapter, only infanticide which is the deliberate taking away of life from a newborn or very young child with a disability is discussed; other forms are not considered (Scheer and Groce 1988). Disability is understood here as bodily differences that present a disorder in the world view of African peoples at a particular juncture in history. This includes conceptual categories that are not readily recognized as disabling in children from a western point of view. For example, the birth of twins, children who are born with teeth or whose upper teeth erupt before the lower, children who are born feet first, and other extraordinary conditions, are considered disorders that are sanctioned in the pre-modern African conceptions, including the sanction of death (Devlieger 1995).

DISABILITY AND COSMOLOGY

The need for a justification of disability at cosmological and symbolic levels is part of the discourse of disability (Ingstad and Reynolds Whyte 1995). The presence of a disability in a family is the object of many considerations by the parents and the social environment. Reflections on corporeal 'difference' are coloured by cultural elements of which an expectation of wholeness of the body and of the impact of sorcery are the most important in Africa. According to the principles of sorcery, a discourse is held to find a culprit, but also to exonerate the victim and his/her close relatives from blame or guilt. Naming a culprit provides psychological relief; it places the problem at another level.

Sorcery is a cultural system that attributes bodily difference to family and/or cosmological disharmony. Thus physical disability is not merely a corporeal problem, but is, above all, a relational problem with the physical environment, with family members and God (Devlieger 1995). At the birth of a physically disabled child, social and cosmological chaos results from the signs that conflict with the notion of a 'whole' child. The 'whole', child is both bodily complete and fitting in the cycle of life, as a returned ancestor. When a child is born who is not 'whole', the Songye go through a systematic examination at various levels: their environment, the ancestors, other (living) people, and ultimately God.

A first reaction to a child who is born with disabilities is to seek explanations in the physical environment, i.e. the non-observance of food and sexual taboos which a pregnant woman should observe. Food taboos are often a matter of contiguous or sympathetic magic, meaning that it is believed that some characteristics of the animal whose meat is eaten will be reflected in the child. For example, Carreira (1971) describes how eating turtle meat may result in a child with a humpback, eating monkey in a mischievous child, jaguar in a restless child, porcupine in a child with a bad skin, white ants in a child that is covered by blisters, etc.

Explanations at the level of social or family life are often excluded because it is assumed that a sorcerer does not have access to the womb. However, when a disability presents itself immediately, without a period where the child is sick, the parents cannot understand this, and since no one else could have caused it to happen, it is attributed to God, who is an absolute and unknown force. No known person could have caused 'this', so it must be God. God, the all powerful, also has the power to send a child who is different from other newborns. Thus, according to this conception of God, people may be mistaken about God, and God may deceive them (see Wauters 1949). The parents will, therefore, be convinced that the observed difference is an intervention of God and that the healing of the child depends completely upon the volition of God. The relation with God is also present in the practices of the ancestors.

From this perception of life and of God follows the belief that the spirit of the child who is killed does not die. This is a very widespread belief that is also found in the appeasement of the spirits, for example, by the killing of a white chicken and attaching this chicken to the neck or feet of the child. In addition, the throwing of the child into a river is accompanied by lecturing the spirit not to return but to be reborn elsewhere (see also Merriam 1974). The need to appease the spirit of the child who is killed is found in other African cultures as well. Higgins (1966) distinguishes between the normal birth and a Godly birth (jok anywala) in Uganda, of twins, children with minor deformities and those with unusual deformities.

In the past, if the mother was convinced that the deformities of her child were so great that it would be unable to live a useful life, she took it on her back and dropped it into the water pretending that this was done accidentally. Custom decreed that she must search for the child. If it was dead, it would be buried, if it was still alive, it would be allowed to live. Pretending that the death is an accident and searching for the child are done in order to appease the spirit. Nunley (1981) reports that in Sisala land in West Africa, even while Sisala twins are 'born to die' because, in their cosmology, there is no other option, the death of one twin demands the making of a carving to appease the hostility of the deceased twin spirit.

In the literature on infanticide a number of different hypotheses have been proposed (Nunley 1981). A variety of different approaches that range from convenience to adaptation have been proposed (Hausfater and Hrdy 1984). More recently, it has been argued that twin infanticide should be reconsidered as an adaptive strategy to deal with children who have a low potential for viability (Scrimshaw 1984). Such approaches do not take into account the cultural justifications and practices that society develops. Rosenblum and Budde (1982: 4) argue that in societies of 'Judeo-Christian heritage serious contradictions were raised between social arrangements that protected human life, on one hand, and encouraged infanticide on the other'. Dehumanization as a process to justify infanticide has been proposed for Western societies, defined as 'pseudo-speciation' (Ball and Hill 1996). The standard work on infanticide in the social and cultural contexts of classical antiquity was developed by Delcourt (1938) but new perspectives have recently been put forward.

Bodily difference is interpreted as a sign that demands an interpretation. At the time of birth, the particularities of the body are very carefully examined. Of special congenital characteristics (certain malformations, special pigmentation), it is sometimes said that they are divine marks which predestine the child to a special vocation. But what are the signs that predestine a child to death? There is much variation regarding this in Africa, but it can be said that physically deformed children, twins births, and children who are born in particular positions (such as breech birth) were, and may, in certain areas, still be candidates for infanticidal death.

Among the Songye, an 'abnormal' child was formerly killed by being buried in the forest in a termite hill. The child needed to be buried in a place that was already 'dead'; it could not be buried in another space because the earth would be polluted and be prevented from 'giving'. Among the Luba people, the child was thrown into a river with the verbal injunction that it should be born elsewhere.

According to Coussement (1935) who conducted research among the Kaonde, a group neighbouring the Songye, there are four cultural categories of disorder, or types of children who were prescribed to die. The first is called *kisheta*, this is a child that is observed not to be walking within the so-called normal age span. In such a case, the child is taken into the forest, i.e. away from the village, to an isolated space where there is no grass (this again symbolizes a dead space). The child is left to die. In other areas, the child is ritually drowned at a specific place called *kielwa bishieta*, a place reserved for this ritual, and where nobody would bathe.

The second category is *Katangwa*, the name of a child that is born from a young girl; when this is known, both she and the father of the child would be chased from the village and be forced to live outside. The pair would not be assisted with food nor with the birth, and after giving birth, the woman had to abandon her child, after which the couple were allowed to be reintegrated in the village through an elaborate ritual. The third is a child named *Mlombe*, which is born to a woman who has not been initiated. Both she and her lover would be chased from the village where they, too, would construct a hut awaiting the birth of the child. Again, nobody could assist the couple, and after the birth, the parents had to throw the child into a river or bury it in a hole in the forest. The couple could only return to the village after being purified by a traditional healer.

Finally, *Lutala* is the name given to a child in whom the upper front teeth appear before the lower teeth. In such a case the mother would carry her child on her back towards the river, where she would turn round and let the child glide and fall into the water. When returning to the village, she could not look back in the direction of the river. Coussement (1935) states that it is believed that if a *Lutala* or *Kisheta* child were to stay in the village this would cause the death of its parents, the chief and others.

African cosmologies explain the nature of life and death, and the role of humans in managing life and death, and their relationships with spirits and with God. Within this worldview, it is necessary to explain infanticide in the context of the cycle of life and relation between God and humans, as well as its social and political management.

COSMOLOGICAL MANAGEMENT: 'RETURNING' DISABLED CHILDREN

The return of disabled children to another world in the act of infanticide reflects a cyclical vision of life. The notion of return also applies to children born into this life: they too have returned. The cyclical vision of life is relevant to the practice of killing disabled children, because the Songye believe that although the body is dead, the spirit of the child never dies.

The geographical places in which infanticide occurs are significant. All the accounts have a common factor, that is that the killing cannot occur within the village. In the Kasai region of Congo, drowning the child in water, burying it in an anthill, or leaving it in an area in the forest 'where the grass is not growing' indicate considerations to facilitate return. Water in the cosmogony is the passive element that unbundles vital forces, as opposed to the active earth that brings these forces together. The anthill works in the same manner, as it facilitates death, since the earth in the anthill is dead. Equally, a dead area in the forest allows the decomposition needed to facilitate death.

Other reports place the killing of the child at a crossroads in an area between two villages, in order to confuse the spirit as to where to go (Merriam 1974). Some would be buried at a special cemetery. In some instances, specific areas are designated in the forest or in the river, and people will be told not to go into these areas. For example, Leis (1965) reports that the Ijaw disposed of twins 'born bad', or 'two born', regardless of their sex, immediately after their birth. They were thrown into the river or were placed in fishing baskets and allowed to die of exposure in a special part of the forest – the 'bad bush'.

SOCIAL AND POLITICAL MANAGEMENT

While a justification of infanticide may be understood in the context of African cosmologies, carrying it out demands social and political considerations. In the social management of infanticide, the ethnographic record seems to indicate a gerontocratic social and political system rather than a state-operated system. This was so among the Ben'Ekie, a Songye subgroup, prior to 1700, but it was threatened around 1700 by external encroachment, leading up to the development of an Ekie state in the eighteenth century (Fairley 1989). In response to this political centralization, a secret religious society (*bukishi*) emerged among the Ben'Ekie. This has also been reported to exist among other Songye groups (Stappers 1950; Weydert 1937). According to comparative research conducted by Scheer and Groce (1988), the Songye were reported to be the only people where the decision-making was recorded.

When a deformed child was born among the Ben'Ekie the elders of the village would ask the father: 'What kind of problems are you causing?' A discussion of the behaviour of the husband would ensue. They would request two chickens and a goat from him, as a fine for the social disharmony that he had caused by the birth of this child, and the elders would make incantations. When the child died, it would be taken into the forest and buried in a pit dug from a termite hill, and told not to come back. Merriam (1974), writing about a different Songye group, contends that no child in the village of Lupupa Ngye is killed at birth and only 'insanity, Mongoloidism, or other highly visible malfunction' is a reason for killing. The father of the child goes to the notables to explain the situation when he has given up all hope of the child being normal. The notables visit the child, and may first counsel the father to wait to see whether the condition improves. If no improvement takes place, the father again importunes the notables, who then usually give their permission to have the child killed. The father then pays a fine of 500 francs (Merriam 1974).

INFANTICIDE AND THE COLONIZER

In the colonial courts, the practice of infanticide was treated as homicide and the beliefs sustaining the practice as superstition. In 1781, the penal code of France assimilated infanticide as murder, and in 1810 assigned it the death sentence. The colonization of Africa is said, by some scholars, to have diminished the practice of infanticide. Coussement (1935: 136), for example, states that since the European occupation, these 'crimes' are no longer widely practised and that his 'informants' told him that the practice was no longer observed. However, they were also horrified at the idea that a *Lutala* child (a child whose upper teeth erupt first), would be in their midst. A court order relating to the infanticide of a *Lutala* child was published at that time, and the court of the district of the Lualaba in Jadotville charged the mother with 'having committed a homicide with the intention to result in the death of a child' (Coussement 1935: 136). He reports that the court heard that this child's upper teeth had erupted first and that:

> the indigenous consider it a disaster and source of problems to see the upper teeth erupt before the lower teeth; that in the past these children were put to death by the maternal grandmother; that, while this custom had fallen into disuse by the European occupation, the memory is still alive especially where the people are backward.

The court ruled that since the custom had fallen into disarray, and that in the village itself many such children have grown up, the mother killed her child under pressure of the father, whose pressure was so great that her maternal instinct failed. The original punishment was three years jail for the mother and five years for the father. These charges were reduced months later to one and three years, respectively.

In the case above, it is clear that a state system prevailed over a gerontocratic system and that the world views sustaining the decision made by the court considered infanticide as murder in the context of the modern state. For the history of disabled people in Africa, the establishment of the colonial system may have meant the legitimization of the very existence of disabled people who were disabled from birth. However, according to oral history throughout sub-Saharan Africa, popular proverbs admonish people not to laugh at disabled people, and to respect them (Devlieger 1999). Part of this respect is dictated by the recognition that laughing at disabled people could cause disability to happen to you (Batukezanga 1981).

In the post-colonial Senegalese context, Diop-Vertu (1987) argues that infanticide is generally thought to be practised by young women of rural origin who naively become pregnant in the city. Infanticide, then, is the result of the conflict with traditional beliefs, including scandal, social taboo and social isolation. The legal debate then centres itself around the question of the nature of the delinquency. Diop-Vertu calls these mothers 'occasional delinquents' because the episode is limited to the particular infanticide. The penal code of Senegal qualifies infanticide as voluntary homicide and murder. In each case the question needs to be resolved as to whether the killing was intentional, and to appreciate the circumstances of the cause. Medical examination of the child may determine whether the child died from voluntary violence or negligence. The Senegalese penal code punishes infanticide with indefinite forced labour or with the death sentence according to how the child died. In most cases, it is possible to soften these sentences by time served in prison.

DISABILITY IN AFRICA: IN PRE-MODERN, MODERN, AND POST-MODERN TIMES

A review of the practice of infanticide in the context of Songye cosmology raises questions about the social construction of disability in Africa. The traditional practice of infanticide, sustained by a gerontocratic political system, could not be tolerated under a colonial state system.

Perhaps it is useful to distinguish between killing and murder. 'Killing' seems to be an appropriate term in the context of an emic perspective, a cosmology and justification couched in terms of a perspective on life and personhood. 'Murder', on the other hand, seems the appropriate term within the perspective of the laws of a state. I would suggest using the word 'killing' as part of a pre-modern, indigenous perspective on disabled children, and 'murder' in the context of modern, colonized Africa.

Post-modern Africa is characterized by liberation from colonial oppression. The voices of African people are emerging through the rejection of Africa's recent history. As in the rest of the world, the voices of disabled people are also emerging in Africa, and they are rejecting the practice of infanticide as one that denied them their very existence. The disability rights movement also rejects the beginning of institutional development under the colonial state as one that was controlling, not liberating, for people with disabilities. However, a more even assessment of the history of disability may recognize the justification of infanticide from an emic perspective as well as see the contributions of the colonial system to preserving the very existence of disabled people.

Contemporary post-modern conditions are not only characterized by the emergence of new perspectives, but also by the juxtaposition of many discourses and practices. These may include infanticide, and other radical practices of exclusion, such as institutionalization, but also radically liberating organizations. However, out of the sharp disjunctures of African history, one also sees the emergence of hybrid forms and practices that may present alternatives in the African context. Some recent initiatives, for example, provide work and shelter for disabled people in the context of world views based on both Christian and traditional beliefs. Such combinations of practices and beliefs fit the expectations of new social, economic and political forms in Africa.

ACKNOWLEDGEMENTS

An earlier version of this paper was presented at the Annual Meeting of the Social Science History Association in Chicago as part of a session entitled 'Different Bodies and their Societies'. I would like to thank the participants in this session for interesting exchanges. In particular, I would like to thank Pam Block for her assistance with careful editing of the manuscript.

NOTES

1 The term 'body difference' rather than 'disability' or 'handicap' is used because the latter terms now tend to refer to certain specific categorizations. For the same reason, the term 'deformity' is not used because what would be considered a deformity as a deviation from the norm in the African context, may not be perceived as a deformity in the Western context. Thus, the term body difference intends to convey a meaning that is stripped of such connotations.

REFERENCES

Ball, H.L. and C.M. Hill 1996. Re-evaluating twin infanticide. *Current Anthropology* 37(5), 856–62.

Batukezanga, Z. 1981. *Guérir le Malade et la Maladie: l'infirme et son univers en Afrique noire.* Kinshasa: Kikesa.

Carreira, A. 1971. O infanticídio ritual em África. *Boletin Cultural da Guiné Portuguesa* XXVI, 101, 149–216; 102, 321–76.

Coussement, G. 1935. Crimes et superstitions indigènes chez les Kaonde. *Bulletin Juridique Indigène* III, 6, 135–7.

Delcourt, M. 1938. *Stérilités mystérieuses & naissances maléfiques dans l'Antiquité classique.* Paris: E. Droz.

Devlieger, P. 1995. Why disabled? The cultural understanding of physical disability in an African society. In *Disability and Culture*, B. Ingstad and S. Reynolds Whyte (eds), 94–106. Berkeley: University of California Press.

Devlieger, P. (1999). Frames of reference in African proverbs on disability. *International Journal of Disability, Development and Education* 46(4), 439–51.

Diop-Vertu, S. 1987. Propos sur l'infanticide au Senegal. *Présence Africaine* 141, 37–40.

Fairley, N.J. 1989. Ritual rivalry among the Ben'Ekie. In *Creativity of Power: cosmology and action in African societies*, W. Arens and I. Karp (eds), 289–311. Washington: Smithsonian Institution Press.

Hausfater, G. and S.B. Hrdy (eds) 1984. *Infanticide: comparative and evolutionary perspectives*. New York: Aldine.

Higgins, S. 1966. Acholi birth customs. *Uganda Journal* 30(2), 175–83.

Ingstad, B. and S. Reynolds Whyte 1995. *Disability and Culture*. Berkeley: University of California Press.

Leis, P.E. 1965. The nonfunctional attributes of twin infanticide in the Niger Delta. *Anthropological Quarterly* 38(3), 97–111.

Merriam, A.P. 1974. *An African World: the Basongye village of Lupupa Ngye*. Bloomington: University of Indiana Press.

Nunley, J.W. 1981. Sisala twin surrogate sculpture as a response to an infanticide practice. *Uomo* 5(1), 65–84.

Ploss, H. 1911. *Das Kind in Brauch und Sitte der Völker*. Leipzig.

Rosenblum, V.G. and M.L. Budde 1982. Historical and cultural considerations of infanticide. In *Infanticide and the Handicapped Newborn*, D.J. Horan and M. Delahoyde (eds), 1–16. Provo: Brigham Young Press.

Scheer, J. and N. Groce 1988. Impairment as a human constant: cross-cultural and historical perspectives on variation. *Journal of Social Issues* 44(1), 23–37.

Scrimshaw, S.C.M. 1984. Infanticide in human populations: societal and individual concerns. In *Infanticide: comparative and evolutionary perspectives*, G. Hausfater and S.B. Hrdy (eds), 439–63. New York: Aldine.

Stappers, L. 1950. De geheime sekte van de Bukishi by de Beena Milembwe. *Kongo-Overzee* XVI, 73–96.

Walk, L. 1928. Die ersten Lebensjahre des Kindes in Südafrika. *Anthropos* XXIII, 38–109.

Wauters, G. 1949. *L'Ésoterie des noirs dévoilée*. Bruxelles: Editions Européennes.

Weydert, J. 1937. Le bwanga "bukishi" chez les Ba Musolo. *Bulletin du Cercle Colonial Luxembourgeois* 8(1), 3–5.

12   Leprosy and social exclusion in Nepal: the continuing conflict between medical and socio-cultural beliefs and practices

Jeanette Hyland

This chapter explores the expectations of a rural community in southern Nepal with regard to people affected by leprosy, how these views are expressed in community life, and the historical roots of these attitudes and expectations.[1] An attempt is made to understand the background of the social exclusion of people with leprosy in Nepal, and why it persists.

COMMUNITY SURVEYS

Origins and causes of leprosy

Two surveys carried out in 1980 and 1990 in Nawal Parasi revealed that people affected by leprosy were expected to isolate themselves, or to be isolated by others, from normal society. Although medical beliefs and practices regarding leprosy have totally changed in recent times, community beliefs have not changed to the same extent.

The community notions of the origin, source, or aetiology of leprosy provide clues to the reasons for contemporary attitudes and behaviour towards leprosy sufferers. The surveys show that there are a wide range of supposed causes for leprosy, including such things as fate, curses, spirit (*bhut*), bad blood, a bite, germs (dirt, contagion, filth, bad food), heredity and failure to do one's religious duty. It is also believed that leprosy may occur spontaneously. While 'germs' and 'heredity' are given relatively frequently as causes of leprosy, it is significant that only a small proportion identified 'germs' as the *only* possible cause. The vast majority of respondents held multiple, and multi-layered notions of the origin or cause of leprosy. Over a third were uncertain about the cause(s).

That most people held multiple notions of the origin of leprosy reflects the nature of Nepal's Hindu reality, which demonstrates an 'amazing plasticity which allows it to adapt to new situations, and yet remain true to its ancient assumption' (Burnett, 1990: 87). New ideas are accommodated while old ones can still be retained. This accommodation is a feature of Nepal and provides an important background to the understanding of contemporary beliefs. In such a context, people often hold seemingly contradictory or conflicting ideas.

Figure 12.1 Staff receiving patients at a rural clinic in Nepal in 1995. [Photo: J. Hyland]

Social responses to people affected by leprosy

Findings from the community survey are enlightening. Answers to questions about understanding and expectations of leprosy showed that there was little change in these expectations. In spite of an intensive public education and treatment campaign (Figure 12.1) conducted between 1980 and 1990, the responses from the two surveys were very similar.

In the 1980 survey, 162 respondents were asked what they would do if a member of their family got leprosy – would they 'separate' them, 'place them apart' or 'put them out of the village'? They were then asked the same questions with regard to a non-family member in the same village. The majority said they would separate or place apart a family member found to have leprosy, while only a third said they would put them out of the village. With regard to non-relatives with leprosy, 69 per cent said they should be separated and 45 per cent said they should be put out of the village.

The English terms 'separate' and 'place apart' are used to render *nachune* and *chutyaune* which literally mean 'not touch' in a ritual sense, separate, divide off, or set apart. Both *nachune* and *chutyaune* can take place within the household, where the person, thus separated, will eat and live, isolated from human touch, and not be allowed to take part in any normal household duties connected with food and drink. *Chutyaune* can also mean placing in a separate dwelling, but remaining as a family responsibility to feed and shelter. The term 'put out' is the more drastic act of expelling from the household and from the village. In some cases the family might still feed the person once a day, but others were literally sent away and had to try to survive as outcasts from the community.

In the 1990 survey, the 'separate' and 'place apart' options were incorporated in the concept of 'not touching'. This also indicated ritual pollution and restriction placed on social interaction within the family, particularly connected with physical contact and the handling of food and drinking water. The majority stated that the reason why they feared getting leprosy themselves was because people with leprosy were not touched, were ritually separated and were likely to be 'put out' of the village.

Answers to other questions on possible means to cure leprosy add to the complex picture of community expectations related to the disease. Those who expressed a belief that leprosy was caused by 'fate' and could be cured by *puja* (religious ritual) were found to be significantly more likely to expect negative social consequences of leprosy than those who did not hold such beliefs. However, holding the belief that leprosy was caused by germs, and could be cured by medicine, made no significant difference to expectations about social exclusion. Whether believed to be caused by fate and curable by ritual, or by germs and treatable by medicine, over 70 per cent still considered leprosy to be both ritually polluting and socially ostracizing.

ROOTS OF EXCLUSION IN RELIGION AND LAW

The practice of separation or social exclusion of leprosy patients in Nepal has a long history. It is a reflection of a religious tale, taken up and encoded in the Nepal Legal Code of last century, which, in part, mirrored the worldwide practices of quarantine at the time. Some of the roots of the contemporary beliefs and expectations are thus found in the 1600 year-old popular religious writing *Swasthani Brathkatha* and also in the legal code of Nepal, the *Muluki Ain*.

The Swasthani Brathkatha

This religious book, dating from about 1600 years ago and revised by Sri Budhisagar Parajuli (1990), is read in orthodox Hindu homes across Nepal during a certain month every year. It contains a story of leprosy 'falling upon' a queen as a curse because she had offended the gods. It tells of the dreadful things which happened to her before she was restored to her husband and the court through ritual prescriptions. Many Nepalis hear this story repeatedly from infancy and believe it to be a true story about real events.

Muluki Ain

The first Nepal Legal Code was enacted at the end of December AD 1853. This first *Muluku Ain* contained certain provisions regarding *Maharog* (the 'great disease' or leprosy). Those with *Maharog* were not permitted to enter Kathmandu: 'because *Maharogi* men are not permitted into the city they are to be put outside and provided with food and two sets of clothes per year . . . by the *Guthi* [community committee]'. There was also provision for a man to return any betrothal gifts and leave his espoused if the girl was a *Kustha Rogi* (leprosy sufferer).

In 1886 the *Muluki Ain* underwent a major revision. It provided that '. . . people with *Maharog* were to be placed in a place assigned by the government, given food and clothing by the (decision of) *Guthi* members'.

In a 1933 *Ain*, *Maharogi* men were still not permitted into the city, but in a 1935 revised *Ain*, the provision does not mention the city, merely stating that 'people with *Maharog* are to be put in a place appointed by the government'. In this *Ain* there is also provision for *Maharogi* (and those blind in both eyes) to be given first place by those in charge of alms. There is also provision that at a marriage, if either the girl or boy is found to be *Maharogi*, then no wedding tax will be charged. While in the 1853 *Ain* there were different punishments set down for transgressions by different *Jat* (castes), the provision in the 1935 *Ain* did not differentiate between castes.

The 1935 *Ain* was promulgated in 1963. Here the provision for *Maharogi* people to be sent to a place appointed by the government was still present, and it was the duty of the local ward leader or magistrate to do this. People with leprosy were still to have first place in distribution of free dry food. There was also provision for marriages to be cancelled if arranged for either a *Maharogi* boy or girl, if leprosy had been concealed; in these circumstances the husband could leave his *Maharogi* wife and take another.

By 1978 a further revision to the law saw *Maharogis* still being sent to a place designated by the Chief District Officer, but such places had to have medicine and treatment available.

In an unpublished paper given in 1978 at a seminar in Kathmandu, Das recommended that the law be changed because 'it had become unnecessary and harmful'. He wrote:

> It is clear that the aim was to keep leprosy patients in a separate place, apart in leprosaria, two of which had been provided, as there was no effective medicine. In its aim the *Ain* showed inspiration. But it is known that one kind of leprosy is not infectious, and leprosy itself is less infectious than other infectious diseases. The *Ain*, however, had an opposite effect; it 'backfired' as far as leprosy control is concerned. In the *Ain* provision was made that the police could take and forcibly send a *Kustha Rogi* (person with the disease of leprosy) to one of the leprosaria. Consequently the diseased were hidden and untreated. According to the Ain *Kustha Rogis* were to be put out of their villages and provided for physically.

Das argued that *Kustha Rogis* can be treated and should, therefore, remain in their home and families; there is no need to send them to a leprosarium, since leprosy improves with scientific medicines. These days, just as with other infectious diseases a husband cannot marry again, so, with leprosy, a husband should not be allowed to leave his wife (Das 1978).

The law was subsequently changed to no longer require mandatory detention of people affected by leprosy. Up until the 1970s, the *Muluki Ain* had required people with leprosy to be kept in leprosaria where they were provided with shelter, clothing and food. When mandatory detention was withdrawn, these provisions were also withdrawn. The beliefs and expectations of the general public did not change with the closure of the leprosaria. Consequently people affected by leprosy are still socially excluded and now have to survive without any mandated provisions to fall back on. As a result of further revisions, the *Muluki Ain* which was still in force in 1990–91, at the time of this research, only mentioned leprosy as a ground for marriage annulments, and then only if those arranging the marriage on either side had hidden the fact of leprosy.

THE CULTURAL TIME LAG

Community expectations that leprosy should be isolated are not surprising when understood against the background of religious stories and the legal provisions of Nepal reviewed above. In any case, before effective antibiotics were found for leprosy, isolation was believed, in many parts of the world, to be the best means of control, and many other infectious conditions were controlled in the same way. While isolation may have provided protection from the believed danger of contagion, its application was not always humane, and people hid their condition rather than be sent away for ever.

Changes in the law relating to leprosy in Nepal are not yet reflected in community expectations. As Macdonald (1984: 281) wrote, with regard to items which had recently been omitted from the Legal Code of Nepal, the law's 'prescriptions and . . . omissions have not yet been incorporated into the customs of the people'. Scientific advances in treatment, and policies based on modern knowledge about leprosy, are not yet reflected in rural Nepal, and concealment remains the most attractive option (Figure 12.2).

Thus village people with leprosy try to guard their privacy in their community by silence and concealment. However, as Miller (1990) suggests, there is a lack of privacy in village life, and thus it is difficult to keep anything really secret; silence does not work in a social setting where questions are always being asked. So, when silence does not work, people invent stories to divert attention away from the real issue. Words are used as a shield, until such time as there is imminent danger of the matter being discovered, when some sort of action has to be taken.

Most of the people affected by leprosy in the studies documented in this chapter followed this pattern: they kept silent, but when questions began to be asked they used stories to divert attention from the issue. When they felt that their condition was about to become known, some withdrew from attending clinics, and even left their village. In a new environment they would again try to conceal their condition, in order to protect their social integrity and avoid exclusion. This process has been called the 'concealment cycle' (Hyland 1993: 271). There appear to be a number of stages in the process: private curiosity, then suspicion, followed by gossip, and then private slander. Eventually, the slander comes out into the public arena and the individuals concerned

Figure 12.2 A woman affected by leprosy has small wounds on her arm, and her hand and forearm are numb as a result of nerve damage; she is concealing her identity with a blanket. [Photo: Melvas Truchanas]

hear it, and may be confronted. Isolation or expulsion of the individual from the village community may be used to resolve the ensuing conflict. In some cases, those with leprosy may choose to withdraw from their village, or seek treatment at a distant clinic (Figure 12.3) in order to preserve their social integrity. Thus the process or cycle of protection through concealment is continued.

The pattern of social separation of people with leprosy can be viewed in the context of the more general concept of ritual pollution and the maintenance and restoration of ritual purity in Hindu society. People affected by leprosy experience a similar progression to social exclusion as people who are ritually polluted for other reasons. However, unlike the general provisions for restoration of ritual purity, there seldom seems to be a way back for people with leprosy once they have been socially excluded. The excluded queen described above, however, was able to become ritually 'pure' again.

THE LIFE EXPERIENCES OF INDIVIDUALS AFFECTED BY LEPROSY

As has been seen, having leprosy is considered something to be quiet about. It is an issue which, if outsiders are aware of it, may be used to the disadvantage of the

Figure 12.3 A woman with leprosy being interviewed by the author. She receives treatment away from the village, and has managed to conceal the fact that she has leprosy from her family. [Photo: Melvas Truchanas]

individuals and their families, and may lead to social exclusion. Of those leprosy sufferers whose condition was widely known, all but one were excluded in some way. By contrast, those who had succeeded in keeping their condition concealed had maintained their social integrity, and were living with their extended family in the village community. A few had either separated themselves or been separated by family members, but still remained in the household. In some cases this kind of separation seemed to have been sufficient to safeguard their family's position and to retain the co-operation of their neighbours at essential times of planting and harvest. For others, separation was closer to exclusion, living in a separate shelter, undertaking farm duties in return for food, but having no physical contact with their family.

Others were expelled from the village in a more distant and permanent form of separation. This level of exclusion may be seen as tantamount to being told to go and kill yourself: one woman excluded in this way said she had been on her way to jump in the river when the leprosy control staff encountered her and brought her to the hospital. In a rural society where members of the community are inter-dependent, being expelled from the village is equivalent to social, if not physical, death. Staff at the leprosy hospital related a number of anecdotes about people with leprosy who had either attempted or actually committed suicide following their diagnosis.

Some leprosy sufferers, in order to avoid this social and physical exclusion, had left their village with their nuclear families, to start a new life in another place. Yet others had left their family, their village, and even their country, in order to protect the social integrity and status of their families. A number were living isolated lives away from their family and village. Other individuals, who had been on the brink of being exposed, decided to stop treatment rather than risk this exposure and consequent exclusion.

Some case histories

A teenaged boy

One boy had learned about leprosy from his school books, and a patch he developed on his arm was like the descriptions he read. He knew that medicines were effective for leprosy, and he was told that his type of leprosy was not infectious and needed only six months' treatment. He attended the clinic regularly, completed his treatment, and had no disability or visible signs of leprosy whatsoever. His parents knew that he had leprosy, but he concealed his condition from his school friends and village neighbours. Thus, his social integrity was preserved, and he avoided social exclusion.

A middle-aged woman

A woman who developed skin patches and weakness nevertheless managed to conceal her condition. She said leprosy was a curse from God, and was doubtful about the idea of a micro-organism, but when asked why she took medicines she was given, she replied that perhaps she would get better. She was medically cured after forty-three months, but was not fully well, and has some persisting disability and psychological problems. Her family and friends did not know that she had leprosy, and only a son who lived at a distance knew. She bore her secret anxiously and alone for years before being able to speak about it with the interviewer, and when she did, she wept. In spite of everything, she has preserved her place in her home and village community, and her social integrity, because she managed to conceal her leprosy.

A Brahmin priest

Two members of the same family reported as new patients on the same day. The elder of the two had waited at least two years after being first recommended to the leprosy hospital by a neighbour who was a Leprosy Control Programme worker. He came to the hospital with his son two weeks after another son had died there. As a Brahmin priest he had made a vow to the gods but had not yet been able to fulfil it, and he believed his condition was a curse, written in the stars. He came with the hope that medicine would help his problems and both he and his son continued treatment regularly.

When he came to the hospital he had swollen patches, a weak foot and eyelid, a watering eye, and was unable to work. His treatment continued for twenty-three months, during which time he was hospitalized at times, and operated on. Some disability persists. His wife and family knew about his leprosy, and the community were said to be 'curious', but they did not say anything, and his public role as a priest continued. Thus, even though his village neighbours knew about his diagnosis, and his disability and deformity may be permanent, his social status as a Brahmin priest has ensured that he is not socially ostracized or excluded.

A deserted woman

One woman had been ill for almost a year before her husband consented to seek help, albeit outside the village. By that time her feet and legs were so swollen that she could no longer walk or work. He took her to Pokhra, where she was referred back to the leprosy hospital. Her husband, who was her third husband and not of her caste, left her there and went off with another woman, and now lives in another part of the country with his new family. The deserted woman was hospitalized at first, then attended regularly and was cured after forty-three months, but remains unwell and suffers from depression. She has no lasting disability but she has not been able to conceal her disease, and she now lives alone, and is isolated from other people. Her situation is precarious as she has no land to live off, only savings and what work she can get; her situation has little hope of change. She had gone against the mores of her society by marrying out of caste, and although her leprosy is cured, and she has no deformity, she remains socially excluded.

A mountain policeman

One man was medically 'cured' of leprosy, but his physical condition nevertheless grew progressively worse throughout his treatment. He was in hospital for half of the forty-four months it took for the disease process to become inactive and his smear to revert to negative. At interview he asked us: 'Why am I getting worse? I have done everything the doctors told me'. He had repeated severe 'reactive' episodes which the medical staff of the hospital were unable to control effectively. The medical officer used all possible drugs, yet could not arrest or reverse the disabling process.

This man used to be supremely physically fit. He was a disciplined professional man with a future and a career. Now he has extensive disability (both eyes, both hands and both feet are involved). Although he may have been able to conceal the disease at first, in the end his family, the village community and his work colleagues all knew. As a result his wife left him, he lost his job, and he lived an isolated life with his parents. Thus he ended up publicly exposed, disabled and socially excluded.

A Muslim farmer

A man who had tingling in extremities, fever and swollen skin patches, was brought to the hospital by a family friend. He attended four times, but although he got well, he was not cured. Only his wife, family and one friend knew that he had leprosy, but the medication caused black skin discolouration, which triggered curiosity among community members, and they started asking questions. However, when the medicines were stopped for a few months the skin colour returned to normal.

He had been late once at the clinic and been received in a disrespectful and demeaning way, he had to pay a fine and was warned and shouted at for being late. He had also witnessed similar treatment of others who were late for their appointments. Next time, when he could not go on time, he did not want that to happen again so he did not go. A further problem was that he had been told to take the medicines during the day and after a meal, and during the Muslim festival of Ramadan he could not do so because he was required to fast during the hours of daylight. Consequently he did not take the medicines for a month. His physical problem was resolved, although he still had some tingling in his extremities. His withdrawal from the clinic had the effect of deflecting public curiosity, and of restoring the skin to normal colour. Thus by withdrawing from treatment he avoided public exposure as a *Kushtharogi*.

A hill ploughman

One man attended only once and was not cured. He remained anxious, and disabled, but only his wife and brother knew of his leprosy. However, the disability meant that he began to eat with a spoon and, in a village where everyone eats with their fingers, such an unusual practice triggered talk. To avoid confrontation, he decided to go away to get work to protect his family's social standing. He left and went to India to work. It is relevant in this, and other cases, that if he had been labelled *Kushtharogi* it is unlikely that suitable marriage partners could have been found for his children.

A fisherman

This man's symptoms were severe, but subsided after bouts of treatment. Once released from hospital he did not return, although he was not yet cured. As a fisherman, he travelled round the country to various rivers, and effectively withdrew from his own village, which was not aware of his leprosy. He perceived his illness as separate, distinct acute episodes of illness, not as flare-ups of a long-term chronic illness (see Neylan *et al.* 1988).

From these case studies it can be seen that the relationship between social exclusion and disability is not simple or consistent. Social exclusion seems to have more to do with the ideas associated with *Kustharog* than simply with the fact of disability or fear of contagion, and whether someone is excluded or not will depend, in part, on their social status in the village.

CONCLUSION

It has been seen that the beliefs and social expectations relating to leprosy are multiple and multi-layered. It is significant that those who believe that germs are at least part of the cause, and believe that the disease can be cured by medicine, are nevertheless just as likely to believe that they will be socially isolated, i.e. that leprosy is both ritually polluting and socially ostracizing.

The cultural beliefs and practices relating to leprosy were well known when the Leprosy Control Program was implemented in 1974, and formed the basis for part of the public health education programme at that time. It was hoped at the time that the beliefs that resulted in social exclusion and expulsion from the village would be reduced as a result of this education. These hopes have not been fulfilled and, given the deep traditional roots of exclusive practices, it may have been naive to hope that such changes could take place so quickly. Furthermore, what had not been foreseen was that by changing the law many people affected by leprosy would become even more socially and physically vulnerable, because there was no mandated source of food and shelter for them. Even now, newly diagnosed leprosy sufferers may have few options; in order to remain a full member of society, it is still necessary to conceal the disease from those who may use the knowledge to apply social sanctions, and thus jeopardize the future welfare of themselves and their family.

There remain many unanswered questions. Not least of these is whether there can be a return to social health, or social integration, after medical cure of leprosy. What would the mechanism be, if any, that would bring people with leprosy back from social death? Could there be a ceremony, an appropriate ritual cleansing, which could restore those with leprosy to a state of ritual purity. The answers to questions must be answered if leprosy is to become a socially acceptable disease.

NOTE

1   The chapter draws on data gathered between 1990 and 1995 during doctoral and post-doctoral field work in Nepal – research which built on the author's twenty years experience in general health and leprosy programs in Nepal. Community surveys among 160 people were also carried out in 1980 and 1990 in the district of Nawal Parasi in southern Nepal, and the accounts of thirty-four people affected by leprosy were also recorded.

REFERENCES

Burnett, D. 1990. *Clash of Worlds*. Eastbourne: MARC.
Das, G.S. 1978. Legal arrangements and provisions for and about *Kustha Rog* (leprosy). Unpublished paper.

Hyland, J.E. 1993. A socio-cultural study of leprosy in Nepal: compliance, patient illness career patterns and health education. Ph.D. Thesis, University of Tasmania.

Macdonald, A. 1984. *Essays on the Ethnography of Nepal and South Asia*. I. 1984 edition. Bibliotheca Himalayica Series III vol. 3 (Ratna Pustak Bhandar, Kathmandu, Nepal).

Miller, C. 1990. *Decision-Making in Village Nepal*. Kathmandu, Nepal: Sahayogi Press Pty. Ltd.

Neylan, T.C., K.E. Nelson, V. Schauf and D.M. Schollard 1988. Illness beliefs of leprosy patients: use of medical anthropology in clinical practice. *International Journal of Leprosy* 56, 2.

Sriswasthani Brat-Katha. Revised by Sri Budhisagar Parajuli. BS 2047 (1990). Nepal: Ratna Pustak Bhandar.

13   Between two worlds: the social implications
of cochlear implantation for children born deaf

KATHRYN HOLLINS

The use of cochlear implants in children born deaf has the potential to create a marginalized group, which is neither Deaf[1] nor hearing. With the recent introduction of the use of cochlear implantation as a response to deafness in prelingually deaf children, it is timely to clarify the key issues and explore the main social implications. This is not without controversy, due to the differing frames of reference used to understand deafness, which makes it distinct from other 'disabilities'. It has sparked off demonstrations and fierce debates, television interviews and broadcasts, articles in newspapers and medical journals and worldwide discussions on the Internet.

DEFINITIONS OF DEAFNESS AND COCHLEAR IMPLANTATION

In Britain, there are about eight million people with some form of hearing loss. The group of people to whom this chapter refers are those who are totally or profoundly deaf from birth, also known as prelingually deaf. The incidence of permanent deafness in infancy is between one and two per thousand, which means that about 240 of the infants born each year in Britain are profoundly deaf. This includes 60,000 of the total population, the majority of whom now use British Sign Language as their first language. Infants who are born profoundly deaf receive no benefit from hearing aids, but the majority are considered suitable, by medical criteria, for cochlear implantation (Daniels 1995). The first paediatric implant programme in Britain was in 1989 with the first prelingually deaf child implanted as recently as 1991. By 1995, 5000 children worldwide had received the most frequently prescribed cochlear implant system, Nucleus (Nucleus 1995).

A cochlear implant attempts to replace the function of a damaged cochlea, otherwise known as the inner ear. Cochlear implants provide an electrical current that bypasses the damaged parts of the inner ear and stimulates the auditory nerve directly. A 25 mm long wire, which contains electrodes, is inserted into the coiled inner ear during an operation, which lasts three to four hours. A device is inserted into a hole drilled into the mastoid bone, just behind the ear. After a month the person returns for initial fitting of the external microphone and tuning of the device, which is known as 'switch on'. For a child, a process of intensive 'rehabilitation' begins which continues over the following few years.

FRAMES OF REFERENCE USED IN UNDERSTANDING DEAFNESS

In order to explain why the use of cochlear implants in children is controversial and only one of the responses to deafness, one needs to examine how deafness is constructed in three contrasting models.

The medical model

In the medical model, deafness is seen as an impairment, or as a deficit of one of the senses. Deafness is viewed as a pathological condition, with the main priority being to recover hearing. As stated by Frank (1995), this is the majority view within Western medicine, where a 'restitution narrative' is formulated in response to illness. An example of this would be, 'yesterday I was well, today I am ill, but tomorrow I will be better'. This has been extended into the field of disability such that the 'natural' reaction to a disabled person is to attempt to search for a cure, remove the deviation and recreate 'normality'.

The medical model implies that the problem is located in the individual rather than in any societal construction. Within this model, deafness becomes an illness that requires treatment. The primary aim is integration of the deaf person into the hearing world. Cochlear implantation fits with this model, as any degree of hearing is assumed to be better than no hearing at all. The understanding of childhood deafness put forward by one Ear Nose and Throat surgeon is as follows (Hollins 1997: 24):

> To some extent deafness is not a medical condition in an adult who is part of the signing Deaf community, but it could be said to be the medical model if you look at a newborn without any hearing, in that there are things that medicine can do which will remodel the child's brain, make it mature differently from a child who didn't have [deafness].

There is a strong assumption that follows on directly from the medical model, with regards to what it means to communicate as a normal human being: 'Inadequate sensory input during these periods [of early childhood] leads to lifelong linguistic and communicative deficits' (O'Donoghue 1999: 73). The implicit assumption is that if one cannot respond to an auditory sensory input, one will automatically suffer from a communication deficit. This minimizes the potential role of sign language in providing an alternative method of communication via a visual sensory input.

The social model

The World Health Organisation (WHO) follows a scheme which seeks to recognize that there are not only individual dimensions to disability but also social dimensions, with its definitions of impairment, disability and handicap. In this framework, impairment is defined as any loss or abnormality of structure or function. Disability is described as any restriction or lack of ability to perform an activity considered normal for a human being, due to the underlying impairment. Finally, handicap is defined as a disadvantage for a given individual, resulting from an impairment or disability that limits or prevents the fulfilment of a normal social role, depending on age, sex, and social and cultural factors. In this scheme, deafness due to a damaged cochlea would be seen as an impairment and the consequent inability to understand spoken English as a disability. An example of a handicap that results from this in our society is the inaccessibility of most theatre performances to deaf people due to the lack of sign language interpretation.

The social model of disability goes a step further than this by arguing that although the WHO scheme of impairment, disability and handicap recognizes that there are social dimensions to disability, it fails to see that disability actually arises from social causes (Oliver 1990: 6). As Woodill (1994: 216–17) writes:

> The emerging minority group metaphor shifts the analysis from sickness to discrimination ... This is a far different prospect for a person with a disability than playing the sick role. Yet the power of the medical metaphor is such that this change will not come easily.

Disabled people have proposed a twofold classification, which defines impairment as 'lacking part of or all of a limb, or having a defective limb, organism or mechanism of the body'. Disability is defined as 'the disadvantage or restriction of activity caused by a contemporary social organization, which takes no or little account of people who have physical impairments and thus excludes them from the mainstream of social activities' (Oliver 1990: 11). Rather than viewing disability as an individual or medical problem, this view states that disabled people experience disability as social restriction. An example in reference to deaf people would be that the inability of the general population to use sign language restricts deaf people's access to mainstream society (Oliver 1990: xiv).

Oliver (1990: 1) argues that most theorizing about disability has a grand theory underpinning it, 'characterized as "the personal tragedy theory of disability"'. Two audiologists can illustrate this approach: 'there is no greater disability than the calamity of total deafness' (Ballantyne and Martin [1960] 1984). Disabled people themselves, Oliver suggests, have therefore to construct an alternative, which could be called 'social oppression theory' (Oliver 1990: 1). The logical outcome of defining disability as social oppression is to see disabled people as 'the collective victims of an uncaring or unknowing society rather than as individual victims of circumstance' (Oliver 1990: 2). Social policies that aim to alleviate oppression rather than compensate individuals, fit with the social model of disability.

Lloyd (1992) points out that there are two main axes which are emphasized in the development of the social model of disability: the medicalization of disability and its relationship to healthcare, and socio-economic discrimination. A social model argues that the medicalization of disability can have various consequences, for example (Lloyd 1992: 211):

> The narrow defining of disability as a clinical condition results in an all-pervasiveness of doctors' power over disabled people's lives, of which the power to make decisions about fitness for work and entitlement to welfare benefits are but examples.

If this perspective is taken, careful consideration must be made of the role of professionals in decisions concerning cochlear implants. The term 'audism' has been coined to describe the corporate institution that deals with deaf people; it is the way that the hearing world dominates, restructures and exercises authority over the deaf community (Lane 1992: 43). Audism is a paternalistic undertaking similar to the philosophy of colonization:

> Their beneficiaries have no language, culture, institutions – or none worth considering – and the benefactors have the burden of supplying them with their own. Ethnocentrism is one way, an intellectually unreflective way, of coming to grips with the diversity of humankind and human culture.
>
> (Lane 1992: 44–5)

Lane (1992: 48) further illuminates this ethnocentrism by explaining the social and economic rewards gained by the 'audist' establishment as a result of their 'beneficence'. He estimates that there is a two-billion-dollar market in America for services and products aimed at hard-of-hearing and deaf people, and that a significant proportion of this is not related to educational value. The second main axis of a social model, as described by Lloyd, considers the socio-economic context of disability. Understanding the history of disability in the context of the rise of capitalism is seen as vital:

> It is not necessary to be a Marxist to recognize that economic conditions have a significant impact on social behaviour and on relationships between different groups of individuals in society.
>
> (Harbert 1988: 12)

Finkelstein suggests three evolutionary phases within a materialist framework, which shows the position of disabled people in relation to the rest of society (Finkelstein 1980). Phase 1 describes agriculture as the dominant economic base, to which disabled people were able to make a contribution as part of society. Davis suggests that 'one could go as far as to say that disability, in our sense of the word, did not exist in such a world' (Davis 1995: 73). The point being made here is that agricultural society can be flexible in accepting different types of individual contribution. Phase 2 describes the rise in factory-based employment, which required stricter adherence to inflexible production rules, thus excluding all kinds of disabled people. This resulted in a special segregated group which was seen increasingly as both stigmatized by their families and a burden on the State, which contributed to the rise in institutions and further segregation. As Davis (1995: 74) points out:

> by the mid-nineteenth century, the body *an sich* had become the body *für sich*[2] and the impaired body had become disabled – unable to be part of the productive economy, confined to institutions, shaped to contours defined by society at large.

Finkelstein (1980) postulates that phase 3 will see an end to segregation, primarily due to technological advances, and disabled people and professionals will work together with shared purpose. This remains to be seen.

The socio-economic context of being deaf in current society has some important implications. In the West, if one accepts a label of being disabled one can qualify for various material benefits. These include special disability allowances, bursaries, equipment and many other potential monetary gains. But if one views oneself as culturally Deaf then this may well be unacceptable. The economic benefits may sit uneasily with a person's ideological reasons for rejecting such special rights. Having said that, the recent disability bill in Britain enables people to qualify for additional benefits without necessarily being called disabled. Need is recognized without any strings attached.

A 'post-modern' stance can be taken within a social model of disability. Woodill (1994: 202) argues that in recent years there has been a growing dissatisfaction with the positivist images of modern science, leading to a shift in how people comprehend the world from a: ' "realistic world view" to a "constructivist" one in which all reality is "mediated" by human perception and interpretation'. The implications for how one understands disability is, he says, far reaching:

> From this stance one does not speak about "having a disability", in the sense that one actually possesses a particular condition, but rather of the "emergence of physical differences" or the "invention of handicaps", indicating the view that these "conditions" are social creations of a given culture.
>
> (Woodill 1994: 202–3)

The cultural-linguistic model of deafness

The cultural-linguistic model of deafness sees the society of Deaf people as a distinct group with its own organization and traditions, rather than emphasizing what is lacking in deaf people, as seen in the medical model. Although the social model of disability shifts the perspective on disability, it has been argued that it does not seek valid alternative ways of being. The cultural-linguistic model recognizes the Deaf world in its own right, with its own language, sense of identity and way of life. Up until the eighteenth century in Europe deaf people were not generally part of identified groups but tended to be isolated from each other within hearing families, without effective forms of communication. With the creation of residential schools for deaf children during the eighteenth century, a community of deaf people first became self-aware with their own language (Davis 1995: 82). Since then, Deaf communities have developed in many countries, with their own complex sign languages and cultures. For these communities, being Deaf is an alternative way of being, with its own rich form of communication and customs (Figure 13.1). The 'discourse of nationalism' of the twentieth century impacts on what Davis suggests could be called the 'nationality of Deafness', and by extension disability (Davis 1995: 76). The emergence of Deaf people as a group could be likened to the formation of nation states. Indeed an annual international conference on Deaf issues is named the 'Deaf Nation Symposium'.

Lawson (1981) suggests that sign language is the core feature of membership of the Deaf community. Certainly the recognition by linguists of British Sign Language (BSL) as a language has important implications for the Deaf community and distinguishes the Deaf movement from the mainstream 'social model of disability' movement. Higgins suggests that belonging to the Deaf community is about choosing to identify with the Deaf world and being involved in shared social activities, along with a certain degree of hearing loss (Higgins 1980: 175). This is both a self-ascribed status and an ascription given by the group. Thus it requires others in the community to recognize a person as Deaf; it is not simply an individual construction. Johnson and Erting (1982: 234) argue as follows:

> Our theoretical position is that deafness is an ethnic phenomenon. It is not primarily a physical disability; rather, it is fundamentally a way of behaving. While some degree of hearing loss is necessary for a person to be ethnically Deaf, the loss of hearing per se is not the critical variable.

Figure 13.1   Deaf communities have their own complex sign languages and cultures; for these communities, being Deaf is an alternative way of being. [Photo: R. Galloway/Photofusion]

Many individuals have only a minor hearing impairment in audiological terms but still are recognized as Deaf persons according to social and cultural criteria. On the other hand, some people with very profound hearing losses are not considered to be Deaf according to those same criteria.

It is often argued that a vital factor in the formation of ethnicity is the process of interaction between groups, which leads to the following viewpoint: 'Deaf people can only be understood in relationship to their position to the hearing world. To view them outside that context is to fundamentally distort their experiences' (Higgins 1980: 175). If a Deaf culture acts as a completely separate group, without acknowledgement of its interaction with the hearing society, one has to question whether this simply isolates Deaf people further and narrows opportunities for access to mainstream possibilities.

Johnson and Erting (1982: 244) argue that an ethnic group can persist, even if the cultural symbols and rules change. In the same way, even if an ethnic group shares much of the cultural content of the wider society, 'much of that content may have little relevance for the actual constitution and maintenance of the ethnic group'. Deaf culture in Britain shares certain features with British culture and so in that sense could be argued to be a variant of British culture. For example, French Deaf people would greet others in the same way as French hearing people by kissing each cheek, whereas British Deaf people would shake hands in greeting like British hearing people. Yet there are also differences between Deaf and hearing people's rules and values, and the values of Deaf cultures are sometimes seen to overlap. Of note is the fact that 90 per cent of deaf unions involve two deaf spouses even though 90 per cent of deaf children are born to hearing parents.

In addition, the divorce rate is lower for marriages between two deaf partners, compared to one deaf and one hearing partner, which is presumed to be due to a higher level of shared experience and easier communication. A recent newspaper article reported on the possibility of the new millennium bringing, 'children born deaf at the request of deaf parents' (Meek 1999: 1). This raises the issue of whether parents can actively choose for their child to be deaf, and join the Deaf ethnic group, as opposed to trying to remove deafness by a procedure such as cochlear implantation.

There are many stories of Deaf children of Deaf parents 'discovering' their 'deafness' late on: 'Would you believe . . . I never knew I was deaf until I first entered school?' ('Howard', in Padden and Humphries 1988: 17). It was not that Howard was unaware of being unable to hear sounds, but rather that, until then, the sign 'deaf' had meant 'like us', whereas in school he met others who used 'deaf' to mean 'not like us'. His deafness became a topic of debate: 'Even his language has ceased to be just a means of interacting with others and has become an object' (Padden and Humphries 1988: 18). Howard's interaction with the hearing world was significant in creating his Deaf identity, with the 'oppression' of his native language being part of that process.

Some members of the Deaf community recognize both a cultural-linguistic and a disabled element to their experiences. For example:

> Deaf people are different, we have our own separate, visual language, sign language, which other disabled people do not have. That's why we prefer

to call ourselves a linguistic minority. But we can't escape the fact that we are disabled as well. We have tried to remove the label of disability and see ourselves solely as a linguistic minority because we see ourselves positively and don't consider ourselves disabled.

(in Hollins 1997: 31)

Summary

The medical model is the majority view on deafness, as well as the stereotypical view of the medical profession. 'Deafness as deficit', is the most common perspective on deafness, especially amongst those with no personal knowledge of deafness or deaf people. The interests of the majority are that the individual should adapt to society rather than society adapt to the individual. In the social model of disability, it is society's attitudes and practices that create problems for deaf people rather than deafness itself. The cultural-linguistic model recognizes Deafness as another valid way of being, with its own language, culture and community. Those who favour the social or cultural-linguistic model often tend to be advocates through personal experience of deafness, either through being deaf themselves or through knowing a deaf person. The meaning and model of deafness for children born deaf and their families affects the way that they respond to deafness.

THE CONCEPT OF NORMALITY AND COCHLEAR IMPLANTATION

As well as looking directly at the construction of deafness in this discussion, one needs to examine the construction of normality, for as Davis (1995: 24) asserts, 'the "problem" is not the person with disabilities; the problem is the way normalcy is constructed to create the "problem" of the disabled person'. Cochlear implantation could only become a viable option because society has such a strong sense of what is 'normal'.

The use of the 'norm' and 'average' only entered European languages in the nineteenth century as a branch of statistics. Davis shows how the social implications of this included the idea of the 'average man', used by Marx in his postulation of an average worker who will perform 'one day of average social labour' (Marx [1867] 1970). With a society based on the concept of norms one has the existence of deviations or extremes, and thus disabled people become the deviants. This contrasts markedly with societies that are based on a concept of the ideal, such as the ancient Greeks, where the general population occupied a non-ideal status. There is an expectation that norms are attainable for the average person whereas ideals are clearly unattainable. Davis (1995: 29) argues that individual humans could:

never embody the ideal since an ideal, by definition, can never be found in this world. When ideal bodies occur they do so in mythology. So

Venus or Helen of Troy, for example, would be the embodiment of female physical beauty.

In a norm-led society, there is a continual pushing towards the norm, and away from the potentially contaminating effects of deviations from the norm. A grave consequence of the rise of the concept of the norm at the turn of the century was the eugenics movement, which sought to create the perfect human body in the quest of social improvement. Alexander Graham Bell ([1883] 1969), a eugenicist, gave a paper entitled 'Memoir on the Formation of a Deaf variety of the Human Race', in which he spoke about the 'disastrous possibility' of a Deaf race being formed due to the common practice of marriages taking place between deaf people. In effect, the practice of avoidance or removal of 'abnormal' genes takes place in today's medical practice, through the use of genetic counselling for 'at risk' expectant mothers.

Western rehabilitation services for a person with physical disabilities could be viewed as trying to recreate 'normality'. A successful response to rehabilitation is judged by whether the process enables the person to gain closer proximity to society's norms of physical, mental and social capability. Finkelstein (1988: 4–5) describes the rehabilitation process he underwent following a spinal injury, in which many hours were spent

> trying to approximate to able-bodied standards by "walking" with calipers and crutches ... Rehabilitation philosophy emphasizes physical normality and, with this, the attainment of skills that allow the individual to approximate as closely as possible to able-bodied behaviour.

Another attempt to create physical 'normality' is the current interest of some parents of children with Down's Syndrome, in surgically altering their child's facial features, for example by shortening the tongue. Will a more invisible appearance make life easier for a child with Down's or does their noticeable appearance have advantages? An article in *The Independent* (10 June 1997) suggests that if you see a person with Down's Syndrome packing shelves in a supermarket: 'you know not to ask them a complicated question about stock levels or launch into a complaint about the points on broccoli under the store's loyalty card scheme ...'.

Aiming for invisibility is certainly one way of approaching the difference of deafness. Drawing on Stiker's work, Reynolds Whyte (1995: 273) points out that the modern Western discourse on disability is such that, 'rehabilitation emphasizes integration into a society of similar people through individual effort and social compensation, and the unspoken agreement to identify difference and pretend it does not exist'. African-Americans who attempted to minimize their stigmatized status by their denial of membership of a minority group were an example of this, seen in a process called 'passing'. In the United States a person was legally considered Black if he or she was genetically $\frac{1}{32}$ Black. Due to the presence of racial discrimination, some people who physically appeared to be white chose to deny their African heritage.

Parents who choose implantation for their child could be described as trying to make them 'pass' as hearing, which, within the cultural-linguistic model, is seen as a denial of the child's Deaf heritage. There are no doubt some advantages to being invisible, but one has to consider whether the gains outweigh the losses. The quest for invisibility via cochlear implantation could, in fact, create greater visibility, both physically through the wearing of an implant and socially through not being able to fit into either the Deaf or the hearing world. The use of cochlear implantation can be seen as society's attempt to mould a deaf person into a hearing person, a denial of difference and an attempt to recreate 'normality'. Is this ideology of normality helpful, where the individual is changed rather than the environment? Must the deaf child be implanted instead of society learning sign language?

THE CREATION OF A MARGINALIZED GROUP

Cochlear implants are here to stay. How widespread their use will become in children born deaf remains to be seen, but the growing number of implant users needs to be recognized. By using implantation, deaf children are being more clearly identified as disabled people rather than as members of the Deaf community. Neither fully Deaf, nor fully hearing, they occupy middle ground, limbo, a liminal position. What does it mean to be between two worlds? Is it possible to become rooted and content in a marginal land? Murphy (1995: 154) describes the 'suspended state' of the disabled as being 'neither fish nor fowl; they exist in partial isolation from society as undefined, ambiguous people'. Each society and each age creates a different selection of marginalized people and one could argue that implanted children born deaf are forming a new marginal group within society. Their own identity as a group, their relationship to the hearing and the Deaf communities, and thus the social implications, cry out for consideration.

During the process of learning to decipher spoken language with the use of a cochlear implant, one could describe a deaf child as occupying a transitional state. Murphy (1995: 153) argues the following:

> it is during the transitional phase from isolation to emergence that the person is said to be in a liminal state – literally, at the threshold – a kind of social limbo in which he or she is left standing outside the formal social system.

A transitional state suggests something precarious and unstable: at the moment of transition, one 'wavers between two worlds' (Van Gennep [1908] 1960: 18). Yet Van Gennep goes on to note that there is '... the existence of transitional periods which sometimes acquire a certain autonomy. Examples of these are seen in the novitiate and the betrothal' (Van Gennep [1908] 1960: 191–2). A transition can go on to become a reality in its own right as shown by Goffman (1974: 3), who stated that William James

> made a stab at differentiating the several different "worlds" that our attention and interest can make real for us ... Each of these subworlds,

according to James, has "its own special and separate style of existence," and each world, whilst it is attended to, is real after a fashion.

An alternative discourse is seen in Devisch's (1990: 125) description of the 'cults of affliction' amongst the Yaka of south-western Democratic Republic of Congo (former Zaire). Difference is dramatized, resulting in the disabled person being regarded with respect and awe due to occupying a transitional space between society and the supernatural. The disabled person still occupies an in-between place but, in this instance, it is socially defined:

> As a result of the initiation, the disabled person no longer dwells in the twilight zones of social indefinition. Through the initiation and the permanent cult, the marginalising effects of the bodily defects and other disabilities are symbolically transferred to the figurines. These provide a liminal zone and a juncture with the society at large and its belief system.
>
> (Devisch 1990: 125)

There are a number of groups that are situated in a middle ground between the Deaf and hearing worlds, with their own experience of marginality. These groups include oral deaf people, hard-of-hearing people and Deaf people with disabilities or mental illness. Can the experiences of these other groups be useful, in considering the experiences of implanted children? An oral deaf person who does not use sign language has to work hard to be accepted within a Deaf club, as he or she is often seen as rejecting sign language and Deaf culture by using oral language (Kyle et al. 1996: 68). In the eyes of the Deaf community, oral deaf people sit uncomfortably between the Deaf and hearing worlds and implanted children who are exclusively taught oral language may be viewed in a similar light. Hard-of-hearing people are visibly labelled as hearing impaired through the wearing of hearing aids. Within the hearing world, hard-of-hearing people are continually at a disadvantage yet they are no better off in the Deaf community due to their lack of knowledge of sign language and of Deaf culture. Implanted children who become exclusively reliant on the technology of cochlear implants in order to communicate may find themselves similarly disadvantaged. Another marginalized group is Deaf people with mental health problems, who are not always welcomed in Deaf clubs and are doubly stigmatized in the hearing world (Kyle et al. 1996: 81).

SOCIAL IMPLICATIONS OF COCHLEAR IMPLANTATION

The marginality that may be experienced by cochlear implant users can lead to social exclusion. The Social Exclusion Unit, set up recently by the British government, sees social exclusion as including the linked problems of poor physical and mental health, low income, family breakdown, few skills, high crime environment and bad housing (Peatfield 1998: 34). Key areas of development for an implanted deaf child, just as for any child, that would reduce the likelihood of the problems of social exclusion, are good linguistic, psychological and educational development.

Linguistic development

The acquisition of language is believed to be one of the main aims for a child's early development. This needs to take place in the first few years of life in order for full linguistic development to occur. Pinker (1994) points out that Deaf children of Deaf parents learn sign language at the same rate, and in the same way, that hearing infants learn spoken language, thus showing the comparability of oral and sign languages as methods of language acquisition.

The first few years of life are a critical period during which the developing nervous system is particularly receptive to laying down the pathways necessary for language use, and is also particularly sensitive to auditory stimulation. The Department of Health in Britain recommends that the optimal age for cochlear implants in prelingually deaf children is between two and seven years old, and that after the age of ten, there is unlikely to be a significant benefit. Yet it is important to note that there is still no evidence of a child acquiring oral language with an implant (Lane et al. 1996: 397). There is some evidence of improvement in speech (Nucleus 1994: 9), but no evidence of language acquisition.

A study looking at speech intelligibility amongst sixty-one implanted children showed that it took two years before any intelligible speech was heard, and after three and a half years, these same children only had an average speech intelligibility score of forty per cent (Robbins et al. 1995: 399–401). Even if the technology improves such that this becomes possible, all studies so far suggest that it would take five years for a child to acquire the full benefits of implantation (Nottingham Paediatric Cochlear Implant Programme 1996). If a child is implanted as early as the age of two, this could mean not having functional spoken language until the age of seven.

If an implanted deaf child does not learn language skills through sign language while the potential benefits of the implant are acquired, the chance of them ever fully acquiring good language skills is reduced. The limited achievement of prelingually deaf children with implants in oral language learning is probably, in part, due to being deprived of any form of language in the first two or more years of life (Lane et al. 1996: 407).

Deaf children do not need to have deaf parents in order to benefit from a signing environment. If deaf children from hearing families have regular contact with culturally deaf adults and can communicate with them, they will have similar benefits to those who have deaf parents (Watkins et al. 1998). There are clear advantages to a deaf child in finding a place in both Deaf and hearing communities, with fluent use of both a sign language and an oral language. A similar situation occurs for a child raised both as a member of an ethnic minority and as part of the majority culture. In Wales, Welsh children are now educated both in Welsh and in English. Immigrants to Britain often choose to bring up their children in a bilingual environment, which respects that both the minority and the majority culture are valid parts of the child's identity.

Psychological and educational development

Little research has yet been carried out regarding benefits or risks to psychological and educational development. Proops (1996: 40) states that 'the enhancement of the patients' quality of life is so great that it offers an excellent return for medical pounds spent'. This may well be true for deafened adults but there is no such evidence as yet for prelingually deaf children. As stated in the National Institutes of Health Consensus Conference (NIHCC 1995: 1957): 'Data on cognitive and academic development are not yet available [and] Comparatively little research has been conducted on the long-term psychological and social effects of implantation'.

What effect will the implant have on the development of the child's sense of identity? Will an implant create a confusing identity for the individual? In one bilingual school for deaf children, the head-teacher reported that among those who become more oral, whether it be via implantation or hearing aids, many keep hold of their Deaf identity. She says,

> we have children here ... who are making progress orally who are still "Deaf", they still exhibit that Deaf identity ... with their peers, with their friends and they want to be part of the Deaf community, go to Deaf youth club.
>
> (in Hollins 1997: 27)

In terms of psychological development, the British Deaf Association (1994: 9) states that it has

> grave concerns that implantees may suffer psychological damage from their failure to live up to unrealistic expectations. This position is not taken in reaction against hearing culture; it is based on the painful first-hand experience of many Deaf people, (including those who are partially deaf) who have throughout their childhood worn hearing aids, which have contributed little or nothing to their speech and development, but which are seen as essential tools in the battle to assimilate Deaf people into a hearing world.

Educational achievement in deaf children is recorded as being very low, with the average American high school graduate only reaching a grade 3 standard (age eight). The assumption made is that the lack of access to a spoken language is damaging, and that sign language does not give the necessary linguistic skills required for good academic achievement. The Canadian Association of the Deaf rejects this traditional explanation for deaf illiteracy and attributes the problems to three factors: first, the impaired communication environment, second, the deficit model orientation of early intervention and educational programmes and third, the lack of qualified deaf professionals (Carver 1990).

A comprehensive study is being carried out within the Nottingham paediatric cochlear implant programme, which is looking at a number of outcome measurements in implanted children over a period of several years. Language acquisition and psychological and educational development are included in this study.

CONCLUSION

> Ethnic background, while present and part of the self, is not the essential constituent of the individual as a human being. Transcendence of narrow ethnicity is desirable if we are to live together in some degree of harmony with others different from ourselves. Such transcendence is to be distinguished from passing.
>
> (DeVos 1977: 241)

This chapter has argued that the use of cochlear implants in children born deaf is not the only response to deafness, and may, in fact, be more damaging than helpful, resulting in the creation of a new marginalized group. Seeing deafness as a deficit that needs to be cured is the viewpoint of the medical model. Yet there are alternative ways of seeing deafness and thus of responding to it. The social model of disability suggests that society's response to deafness is problematic rather than deafness itself. The cultural-linguistic model views Deafness as another way of life.

For those who do choose implantation for their child born deaf, the benefits are, as yet, unclear. Research so far is weighted towards recording improvements in speech production and speech perception and must be widened to look at language acquisition, educational, psychological and social development. Even if cochlear implantation becomes more effective in its aim of restoring hearing, it raises important ethical questions regarding mainstream society's perception of quality of life. Research is needed which systematically examines what makes a life worth living, including research carried out by disabled people (Oliver 1998).

Marginalization or social exclusion damage a child's opportunities for developing a strong identity, good psychological health and fluent linguistic ability. If cochlear implantation takes place at the expense of a child's deaf roots, it could lead to the further social exclusion of a deaf child, rather than the assumed re-integration into mainstream hearing society. To reduce the social exclusion of implanted deaf children, both mainstream society and the Deaf community need to take an active role. Society must recognize how its inequalities help to create the problems experienced by deaf people. The Deaf community has an important role in enabling implanted children to become healthy and well-integrated adults:

> There is a danger that, if the role of Deaf people is neglected, implanted children will find themselves in a limbo between the Deaf and hearing worlds, with inadequate support from either, having had expectations of their improved ability to hear and speak quite falsely raised.
>
> (British Deaf Association 1994: 14)

The group of cochlear implant users will form its own reality and style of existence, relevant to the experiences of the individuals within it and its interaction with the Deaf and hearing worlds. Support from both cultural traditions is crucial in forming a strong and positive sense of identity. Central to this is the promotion of a bilingual environment with both a sign language and an oral language. This recognition of both settings means that instead of becoming further marginalized, implanted children born deaf could become healthy members of both mainstream society and the Deaf community.

NOTES

1   The convention proposed by James Woodward (1972) will be used: the lowercase deaf refers to the audiological condition of not hearing, and the uppercase Deaf refers to a particular group of people who share a culture and a language, e.g. British Sign Language in Britain or American Sign Language in the United States.
2   Davis (1995) explains *an sich* and *für sich* as follows: 'The body as such is probably a Utopian idea, a vision of a pristine, univalent communication based on body language alone. The body for a purpose is certainly the rule in the early modern world'.

REFERENCES

Ballantyne, J. and J.A.M. Martin [1960] 1984. *Deafness*. London: Churchill Livingstone.
Bell, A.G. [1883] 1969. *Memoir upon the Formation of a Deaf Variety of the Human Race*. Washington DC: Alexander Graham Bell Association for the Deaf.
British Deaf Association 1994. *Policy on Cochlear Implants*. London: British Deaf Association.
Carver, R. 1990. Cochlear implants in prelingual deaf children: a Deaf perspective. In *Cochlear Implant and Bilingualism: a workshop report*, 3–8. Kimpton, Hertfordshire: Laser.
Daniels, S. 1995. Cochlear implants in the UK. In *Cochlear Implant and Bilingualism: a workshop report*, 15–21. Kimpton, Hertfordshire: Laser.
Davis, L. 1995. *Enforcing Normalcy: disability, deafness and the body*. London: Verso.
Devisch, R. 1990. The Mbwoolu cosmogony and healing cult among the Northern Yaka of Zaire. In *The Creative Communion: African folk models of fertility and the regeneration of life*, A. Jacobson-Widding and W. van Beek (eds), 111–28. Stockholm: Almquist & Wiksell.
DeVos, G. 1977. The passing of passing: ethnic pluralism and the new ideal in the American Society. In *We, the People: American character and social change*, G. DiRenzo (ed.), 220–54. Westport, Conn.: Greenwood Press.
Finkelstein, V. 1980. *Attitudes to Disabled People: issues for discussion*. New York: World Rehabilitation Fund.
Finkelstein, V. 1988. Changes in thinking about disability. Unpublished paper.
Frank, A. 1995. *The Wounded Storyteller: body, illness and ethics*. London: University of Chicago Press.
Goffman, E. 1974. *Frame Analysis*. Middlesex: Penguin Books Ltd.
Harbert, W. 1988. Dignity and choice. *Insight* 25.
Higgins, P.C. 1980. *Outsiders in a Hearing World: a sociology of deafness*. Beverley Hills, California: Sage Publications.
Hollins, K. 1997. An exploration into the meaning of deafness and the use of cochlear implants in children. Unpublished M.Sc. dissertation, University College London.
Ingstad, B. and S. Reynolds Whyte 1995. *Disability and Culture*. Berkeley: University of California Press.
Johnson, R.E. and C. Erting 1982. Linguistic socialization in the context of emergent Deaf ethnicity. In *Social Aspects of Deafness* vol. 1. Deaf children and the socialization process, C. Erting and R. Meisegeier (eds), 234–97. Washington DC: Gallaudet College.

Kyle, J., L. Allsop and M. Griggs 1996. *Deaf Health in Scotland: issues for deaf people in health promotion*. Bristol: Centre for Deaf Studies.

Lane, H. 1992. *The Mask of Benevolence: disabling the Deaf community*. New York: Alfred A. Knopf.

Lane, H., R. Hoffmeister and B. Bahan 1996. *A Journey into the Deaf World*. California: Dawn Sign Press.

Lawson, L. 1981. The role of sign in the structure of the deaf community. In *Perspectives on BSL and Deafness*, B. Woll, J.G. Kyle and M. Deuchar (eds), 166–77. London: Croom Helm.

Lloyd, M. 1992. Does she boil eggs? Towards a feminist model of disability. *Disability, Handicap & Society* 7(3), 207–21.

Marx, K. [1867] 1970. *Capital* vol. 1, S. Moore and E. Aveling (trans.). New York: International Publishers.

Meek, J. 1999. Morality tales. *The Guardian Saturday Review*, July 31 1999, 1.

Murphy, R. 1995. Encounters in the body silent in America. In *Disability and Culture*, B. Ingstad and S. Reynolds Whyte (eds) 140–58. London: University of California Press.

National Institutes of Health Consensus Conference, 1995. Cochlear Implants in Adults and Children. *Journal of the American Medical Association* 274(24), 1955–61.

Nottingham Paediatric Cochlear Implant Programme 1996. Paediatric Cochlear Implant Workshop, Nottingham: Circus Design.

Nucleus 1994. *Nucleus 22 Channel Cochlear Implant System: Parent Guide*. Colorado: Cochlear Corporation.

Nucleus 1995. *Nucleus Cochlear Implant System: Issues and Answers*. Colorado: Cochlear Corporation

O' Donoghue, G.M. 1999. Hearing without ears: do cochlear implants work in children? *British Medical Journal* 318(7176): 72–3.

Oliver, M. 1990. *The Politics of Disablement*. London: Macmillan Press Ltd.

Oliver, M. 1998. Theories of disability in health practice and research. *British Medical Journal* 317, 1446–9.

Padden, C. and T. Humphries 1988. *Deaf in America: voices from a culture*. London: Harvard University Press.

Peatfield, Z. 1998. Social Exclusion. *YoungMinds Magazine* 34, 8.

Pinker, S. 1994. *The Language Instinct: how the mind creates language*. New York: Morrow.

Proops, D. 1996. Cochlear implants: a modern miracle. *The Practitioner* 240(1558), 38–40.

Reynolds Whyte, S. 1995. Disability between discourse and experience. In *Disability and Culture*, B. Ingstad and S. Reynolds Whyte (eds), 267–91. London: University of California Press.

Robbins, A.M., K.I. Kirk, M.J. Osberger and D. Ertmer 1995. Speech intelligibility of implanted children. *Annals of Otology, Rhinology and Laryngology* 104(166), 399–401.

Van Gennep, A. [1908] 1960. *The Rites of Passage*. Chicago: The University of Chicago Press.

Watkins, S., P. Pittman and B. Walden 1998. The deaf mentor experimental project for young children who are deaf and their families. *American Annals of the Deaf* 143(1), 29–34.

Woodill, G. 1994. The social semiotics of disability. In *Disability Is Not Measles: new research paradigms in disability*, M.H. Rioux and M. Bach (eds), 201–26. Ontario: L'Institut Roeher Institute.

Woodward, J. 1972. Implications for sociolinguistics research among the Deaf. *Sign Language Studies* 1, 1–7.

14 The social, individual and moral consequences of physical exclusion in long-stay institutions

JANE HUBERT

The prestigious *American Journal of Psychiatry*, as recently as 1942, published a paper which proposed that, if a child with severe disabilities reached the age of five years, then 'it is a merciful and kindly thing to relieve that defective – often tortured and convulsed, grotesque and absurd, useless and foolish, and entirely undesirable – of the agony of living'. (Kennedy 1942: 14)

In Britain, although there has not been a 'eugenics policy', there has been a long history of shutting away the 'tortured and convulsed, grotesque and absurd, useless and foolish' from sight, and in spite of 50 years of government policy to close the old mental institutions, some remain open. It is not surprising, therefore, that the emotive and prejudiced view quoted above, which equates physical and mental disability with grotesqueness and uselessness and the 'entirely undesirable', still reflects the attitudes of many people. These attitudes are likely to persist if people with intellectual disabilities continue to be segregated, and remain socially and physically invisible.

The policy of segregation in Britain existed in some form or another until the creation of the National Health Service in 1948. Even then it took a number of scandals and enquiries in the late 1960s into what were then called mental 'subnormality' hospitals, to provide further impetus to close them down. As recently as 1998, Normansfield, one of the hospitals involved in a major enquiry in the 1970s, finally closed. The introduction of idiot asylums in England in the nineteenth century had been seen as a forward-looking move. They were intended to be places where 'idiots' would be educated, and then return to their homes. But, in fact, they usually stayed for life, because their families did not take them back and, as a result, the asylums grew and 'developed into the repressive and custodial institutions whose legacy is with us now' (Ryan and Thomas 1987: 97).

In spite of Government policy, there are still people with intellectual disabilities living in institutions today. The men and women who are still segregated from the rest of society in the wards of old mental handicap hospitals, in the worst conditions and with the poorest quality of care (Shepherd *et al.* 1996) tend to be those with multiple or severe disabilities, and those who are perceived as 'dangerous'.

This chapter focuses on this so-called category of people, who have been labelled as having severe intellectual disabilities. Most of them also have additional characteristics which others in society tend not to want to see or confront in daily life, or even 'catch' (Hubert unpublished), such as epilepsy, mental illness, behaviour problems ('challenging behaviour'), physical disabilities or physical deformities.

People who live in institutions are conceptualized and perceived by others very differently from similar people living in the community. Douglas (1966: 97) writing about purity and danger, and concepts of pollution and taboo, draws attention to this difference in perception of those who live among normal people in normal households and social environments, and those who live in institutions. She suggests that as long as they stay at home 'their peculiar behaviour is accepted' but 'once a patient is admitted to a mental hospital, tolerance is withdrawn'. When people move into a mental hospital, they enter a 'marginal state'. They no longer have a place in the social system, and are left out of what Douglas (1966) calls the 'patterning of society'. People who enter this marginal state are then perceived as both vulnerable and dangerous.

What is the symbolism of being institutionalized? Why is it that once someone crosses the threshold into an institution, people's perceptions of them change, attitudes to their behaviour are different and they become ideologically as well as physically excluded? We know that any physical threshold can symbolize new beginnings and new statuses (Douglas 1966). Bridegrooms carry new brides over the threshold in order to symbolize these new statuses, a new relationship, new rights and responsibilities. The crossing of the threshold of a mental institution certainly implies a change in status, if not such an optimistic one.

However, moving into an institution is not just like moving house. Interwoven with the transition are other strands of change: there is an element of abandonment, of the relinquishment by the family of their responsibilities, and of rejection by society. At the same time, there is the yielding up of the confined person's own responsibility for themselves, not only for their own bodies, but also for their own minds. They begin to live in a closed environment in which place and time are forever intertwined (Goffman 1961), and an environment in which social existence and relationships are replaced by the constant testing, diagnosing, assessing, classifying and organizing that have become integral to institutional life.

What happens to people when they are segregated in this way – left out of what Douglas calls the 'patterning of society' from childhood onwards?

LIFE IN A LOCKED WARD

In 1997 a social anthropological research project was set up in an old 'mental handicap hospital', to document the process of transition from a locked ward (referred to hereafter as 'Bracken'), or 'challenging behaviour unit', from the perspective of the twenty men who live there, and based on extended periods of fieldwork over time.

All the men in the ward have been categorized as having severe intellectual disabilities and challenging behaviour, and most of them are said to have autism, or to fall within the spectrum of autism. Most have no speech, or perhaps just never speak. As children they lived at home with their parents, but their behaviour became, or was deemed by someone inside the family, or in the services, to have become too difficult for the parents to manage. They were admitted to children's hospitals on a long-term basis, and eventually ended up on a locked ward of the hospital where they still live.

The hospital is finally to be closed down, and the residents are to be moved into smaller units. The current plan is that the ones who are considered to have the least problems are to move into houses in community settings, whereas the ones with the most severe difficulties, especially those with very challenging behaviour, are moving into a new unit, purpose-built in the existing hospital grounds. It remains to be seen whether their lives will change in any radical way.

It is a truism to say that, in order to try to understand people – who they are, what their hopes and fears are, and the nature of the lives – it is necessary to get to know them. But most of the men in Bracken have no speech, and the perception of them by others who have contact with them, mainly care staff and doctors, seems to be that the men are essentially unknowable beyond the superficial sum of their impairments, basic needs and challenging behaviour. There is little acknowledgement of their human qualities, which are indeed often masked by their 'strangeness', and there is little evidence that staff (with a few notable exceptions) have tried, or even thought it feasible to try to build up meaningful reciprocal relationships with them.

In order to try to comprehend the men's own experiences, it was also important to get an understanding of the ethos and culture of the environment in which they live, to determine the individual relationships within it, and the accepted group (staff) attitudes towards each individual, which seriously affect how each one is treated. These are the sorts of things that Goode (1994: 49), has called 'the lived realities of everyday life', which are beyond the reach of quantitative methods of research.

One of the most obvious differences between the men and all the people involved in their lives, is that the ward *is* their life. For all the others who come in and out of the ward, it is only a fraction of their lives. However involved care staff and professionals may be, the main part and, to most, the real part of their lives is lived outside the institution.

The plan to carry out social anthropological research in Bracken had a mixed reception. Although there were some professionals who welcomed the idea of a qualitative study, there were others whose reaction was 'but we know everything about these men'. It is true that they have been constantly investigated, described and assessed *ad nauseum* by psychologists, psychiatrists, external assessors and others. But these quantitative measures only describe certain aspects of people's behaviour or needs, they do not describe the whole person, and most of the assessments in fact amount to catalogues of impairments. Little was really known about the men as individuals or as whole human beings. Apart from quantitative clinical assessments, each man had a huge file, or set of files, containing his medical notes, starting with the first step over the threshold into an institution, in many cases very early in childhood. These sad files, and the results of the constant assessments, were the main sources for the perceived identity of each man. As most have no speech, they cannot present their own pasts, thus their identities are constructed by others: their families (who often no longer really know who they are in any meaningful sense), care staff, and professionals who come briefly in and out of their lives. Their personal histories are lost, and are replaced by other people's records, made for other people's purposes.

In fact, most of the time they are not actually considered as individuals who have a 'past' at all. Their lives since they came into the institution are not really seen as sequences in time, or as consisting of development or change. They are, and always have been in a sense, only what they are *today*. The constant assessments have not recorded the changes in them as human beings, nor have their bulky volumes of medical notes. The men emerge from these as objects who have been bitten or punched by others, or who have themselves bitten or punched others, whose drugs have been upped and downed and upped again, whose teeth have rotted, cataracts enlarged, hearing deteriorated, and so on. They do not emerge as social beings.

All this makes the nature of their experience quite unlike those who seemingly started out with similar disabilities and problems, but who were kept at home as children, and have lived with their families all their lives. As a recent study carried out with families has shown (Hubert 1991) the people who stay at home do have pasts and futures, and reciprocal relationships. Parents perceive their own children who live at home very differently from the way they perceive those who lived in institutions, however similar they appear to be to others. These parents, who accept as 'normal' the way their own children look and behave, regard the same kinds of appearance and behaviour of institutionalized people as bizarre and dangerous (Hubert 1991: 26). Their children, though they may to some extent live socially isolated lives even at home, have not been totally excluded from society.

Because of the strength of the relationship between parents and their adult children living at home, it was possible for a mother of an adult son with profound intellectual disabilities to say (Hubert unpublished): 'I never really think of Tony as being a handicapped person until someone asks me to speak about it. He's just Tony, I don't know how else to put it'. Whereas, with regard to similarly disabled men living in the local institution, she said: 'They're awful, they are so different, my son isn't like them'. Parents feel this particularly strongly, but social attitudes generally towards people who live at home, ostensibly 'in the community', are to some extent less negative than towards those who live in institutions.

The views that parents have of institutions, and of the people who live in them, make many of them adamant that their sons and daughters will not go into any sort of residential care, and attempts by professionals to plan for the future are often met with hostility. One mother said (Hubert 1991: 44): 'To the parents of mentally handicapped children [the hospital] is a bit like Dachau ... I'd top me and him rather than him go there'. And another (Hubert 1991: 57): 'I think I'd rather kill him, quite honestly, I'd rather give him an overdose, than see him go in there ... he'd be better off dead'.

Their feelings were so strong that 75 per cent of mothers who participated in the study (Hubert 1991: 113) hoped that their son or daughter would die before they did, so that they would be able to care for them to the end. Their lives have been devoted to their disabled child, and, in a very important sense, they perceive them simply as ordinary people with extraordinary needs. This is very far from their attitudes and preconceptions, or anyone else's, about people who live in institutions.

One of these mothers, speaking of her son, who has severe physical and intellectual disabilities, illustrates the nature of relationships that can exist in a family environment (Hubert unpublished):

> I really do love his company ... we have a good thing going, me and Davey ... I don't see it as a burden, it's a positive relationship, we enjoy each other's company. He's twenty-one this year, I am so proud of him that he's reached twenty-one.

Another mother, whose son's appearance provokes hostile stares and sometimes laughter in the street, said:

> It's upsetting, I get hurt because of him, and I think, well, he doesn't look like a monster from outer space, I mean he's beautiful ... he's hard work, but he's worth it ... I wouldn't part with him, I'll look after him till every breath in my body goes.

Compare this with a typical institutional assessment of Rob, who lives in Bracken, the locked ward:

> Physical health: good. Psychiatric diagnosis: autism. PIMRA scores low. Medication: Clopixol, Procyclidine, Chlorpromazine, with Diazepam and Promethazine when necessary. Adaptive Behaviour Scale: tenth decile. Brief ability/disability assessment scale: fully ambulant. Unable to read, write or count, very few spoken words. Said to enjoy television. Aberrant Behaviour Checklist: high in irritability. Physically aggressive. Seeks attention. Injures self. Screams when agitated e.g. he tends to repeat the word "blind" and if staff don't repeat it after him he will start screaming.

That may be because Rob *is* blind, and this is seldom acknowledged, and no concessions are made to his needs in the institutional environment. Only one member of staff did acknowledge it, and when he said to her, in his desperate way, 'blind, blind, blind', she would hold his hand and say 'I know', and he would be quiet.

Although it is parents who have the most positive perceptions of their children, other people's attitudes to people with severe intellectual disabilities who live at home is tempered by the fact that they have not been physically excluded. The families themselves may often feel socially isolated, but to some extent, at least, their adult children are perceived by others as sons or daughters, siblings, grandchildren, nephews and nieces, and thus have some degree of social identity (Hubert unpublished). Men and women who have been segregated for most of their lives, on the other hand, are not perceived to have any social identity, and this has led to a degree of both desocialization and dehumanization.

This is very apparent in the group of twenty men who live in Bracken, and one of the most powerful ways in which they are dehumanized is by representing them as sexually dangerous (and, at the same time, sexually vulnerable). At the beginning of the research project, before the fieldwork in Bracken had begun, the female psychiatrist in charge described all the men in the ward as either perpetrators or victims of sexual abuse (or both), and added that the ward 'smelled of sex'.

Subsequent experience in the ward did not bear out any of this: it smelled of faeces, and urine and drug-laden breath, but not of sex. What she was really suggesting was something quite different – that these men were sexually uncontrolled, polluted and polluting, a common fantasy about the ward. What this psychiatrist was saying could often be heard in the voices of other professionals, especially those who did not actually work directly with the men. There were clear undercurrents of fear, and prurience, in the way they spoke of them: fear of potentially uncontrollable sexual activity, of violence, ugliness, the unknown, and of the undefined power of people who are perceived as almost totally 'other'. As Young (1990: 123) writes:

> When the dominant culture defines some groups as different, as the Other, the members of those groups are imprisoned in their bodies. Dominant discourse defines them in terms of bodily characteristics and constructs those bodies as ugly, dirty, defiled, impure, contaminated or sick.

Bracken was known as the 'worst' ward in the hospital, partly because it was physically large and grim, but mainly because of the exaggerated reports of the nature and behaviour of the men who lived there. It was considered a 'punishment block' for staff, and for someone to enter voluntarily, as a researcher, was difficult for many to understand or accept.

Part of the fear and disgust that is felt in relation to people who differ so markedly from what is considered to be 'normal' is the failure to see beyond the immediate images that are presented. Going into Bracken for the first time, at the beginning of the fieldwork, was a chastening experience, confirming the existence of one's own fears and prejudices – emotions that would have been violently denied before going in:

> Some of the twenty men were sitting rocking in padded metal chairs that were bolted to the floor; others ran up and down, or round in circles; one sat at a table, almost naked, his clothes ripped to pieces, pulling his lower jaw down and roaring loudly; another banged his head over and over again against the wall; another leapt and twisted and threw himself at the wall and floor with great force. A blind man rocked back and forth in a chair, screeching; yet another ran backwards and forwards, whooping and clapping, and then squatted in the corner of the room, watching me. There was a continuous blend of unfamiliar movement and noise, which seemed to go on and on. I couldn't see any member of staff, I thought I was alone in the ward, and I was paralysed by fear.
>
> (Extract from journal)

The statement: 'I thought I was alone in the ward' indicates, at the very least, acquiescence in the concept of the men's social invisibility, for, of course, the room was full of people. In that first moment I was excluding them from my social world, because of the way they looked and moved and sounded, because of the deprived and disempowering environment in which they were – and because of sheer terror. This experience is a graphic example of how people tend to react when confronted by those who are 'different', however 'inclusive' they consider themselves to be.

Only by getting to know the apparently unknowable do perceptions change. Gradually, the strange shapes and movements and sounds in Bracken turned into individuals, and the initial shock and fear soon evaporated. But at one level the horror remains, because within this institution, and in spite of vast improvements in treatment and conditions over the years, the men continue to live segregated, deprived, and, to some extent, dehumanized lives. Their segregation, their social death, has been complete – and until recently those who physically died were also segregated in death. Within the grounds of the cluster of hospitals there is an area of mass graves, containing some 2000 bodies, where residents were buried, one upon another, until only forty years ago. Death is, in fact, not the ultimate exclusion – where and how a person is buried can continue their exclusion beyond death.

The men who are living in the locked ward today, since they entered the institution in childhood, have become socially invisible, and this physical and social exclusion has had further repercussions. It has led, through the actions and non-actions of those responsible for them over time, to more subtle exclusions from normal social and gender categories. This is illustrated by the following story of David, who lives in Bracken.

David

David has lived in institutions for some 30 years, since early childhood. He is very tall, and his physical appearance is both strange and threatening at first sight. He strides around the ward for most of the day, often roaring loudly.

The most striking thing about him, however, is that when he is on the ward – which is for almost every hour of his life – he has no clothes on, or at most a symbolic, narrow strip of torn cloth tied around his middle, which serves no practical purpose. No one else in the ward is allowed to walk around without any clothes on (though the degree of 'undress' that is tolerated varies from one man to another), but with David it has become accepted, because if he is put in clothes, he tears them up, so he tends not to be given any. And it is true, he does tear up his clothes. David's situation is a very graphic illustration of what is true for everyone else, to a greater or lesser extent, in the locked ward. In 'normal' society, we do not accept nudity in the everyday social environment. The ward may not be a very 'normal' environment, but there are nineteen other residents, and there are also about forty male and female staff members who work on shifts. There are also others who come in: domestic staff, psychologists, maintenance men, psychiatrists, day centre staff and so on, and they see him, and everyone knows: 'David never has any clothes on'.

In this way he is, therefore, not perceived as a social adult; he is excluded from this normal social category. But he is also excluded from the category of adult males, in spite of his obvious adult maleness. To all intents and purposes his sexuality is denied.

He is de-sexed and de-gendered. The general staff attitude towards David is particularly significant because there is much concern about sexual abuse within the locked ward, and any touching or feeling or signs of sexual arousal are discouraged between residents. If sexual abuse is observed (and again the definition of this will vary widely according to the attitudes of staff to the individuals concerned), there is an immediate set of responses. The event is taken very seriously. And yet, sitting with the other residents, walking around among them, is a naked man.

What effect does his nakedness have on the perceptions of him – of staff, residents or others who enter the ward, and on his own self-perception? Because the staff members no longer perceive him as a male, then it seems to be assumed that the other residents do not either, and will not be affected by his nakedness.

To most people who come into Bracken, David is seen simply as someone who is always naked, who roams the ward, bellowing loudly, who has no useful speech, has cataracts, epilepsy, and who is on anti-convulsant and powerful anti-psychotic drugs. However, David is far from being a non-person, and the following extracts from fieldnotes describe a very different David from the diminished image of him that is held by those who work with him:

> I had visited David's parents, and when I went into the ward I told him that I had seen his mother and father, and talked about them to him, and about the house where he had lived as a child, and I said that I expected that he missed them. He stopped roaring, and sat and looked at me as I spoke, and then suddenly he said, out of the blue, quite clearly: "Bless you". I had never before heard him say anything spontaneously before that was not a one word demand. I was taken completely by surprise. But those two appropriate words, dredged up from somewhere, indicated that he understood, and emphasized the fact, usually ignored, that he has feelings as well as needs, and I know now that he has memories too.
>
> (Extract from journal)

And on another occasion:

> I had been talking to David, and then he said "David crying". Although he had no tears his eyes looked incredibly anguished. I said "Why are you crying?" and "poor David", and stroked his head and rubbed his shoulders until he looked less unhappy and walked away.
>
> (Extract from journal)

David epitomizes all the men in the locked ward. They are not considered or treated as full human beings, and this concept of them is continually reinforced by staff who ignore (and sometimes even encourage) ways of behaving that constantly push the men further into the category of 'other'. More significant, perhaps, is that although their sexual dangerousness is often used as a justification for controlling them within a locked environment, at the same time, not only are they denied normal gender roles, but also their sexuality is mocked.

OTHER EFFECTS OF INSTITUTIONALIZATION

For whatever reasons these men were confined to an institution as children or adolescents, the overall effect has been to bring them to a state in which they fulfil the popular stereotype of mad people in institutions. One of the men in the ward, for example, was described when he was first admitted as a four-year-old as a loving and appealing child. Two years later, at the age of six, he was described as miserable, withdrawn and disturbed, and three years later, at the age of nine, was said to wipe faeces over himself, and to have become restless, violent, and self-injuring. It is pointless to try to imagine what this child, and all the others, would have become if they had not been shut away in a total institution. What Sinason (1992) has called 'secondary handicapping' must have been multiplied many times for them.

The effects of life in any kind of total institution are profound. In *The House of the Dead*, Dostoevsky's account of his years as a political prisoner in the 1850s, he described his own reactions to living constantly among other prisoners (Dostoevsky [1860] 1950: 20): 'Besides the loss of freedom, besides the forced labour, there is another torture in prison life, almost more terrible than any other – that is, *compulsory life in common*.' He also describes the intense effects on others (Dostoevsky [1860] 1950: 232–233):

> All the convicts lived in prison not as though they were at home there, but as though they were ... at some temporary halt. Even men sentenced for their whole life were restless or miserable ... This everlasting uneasiness ... sometimes found involuntary utterance, at times so wild as to be almost like delirium, and ... often persisted in men of apparently the greatest common sense.

In a letter to his brother, Michael, he wrote: 'To be alone is a necessity of normal existence ... otherwise, in this forced communal life, you become a hater of mankind' (Carr 1931: 60).

It is not surprising, perhaps, that young children with intellectual disabilities who were locked away in institutions became restless and miserable, even, perhaps, 'haters of mankind', and began to give voice to wild, involuntary utterances.

CLOSURE OF THE INSTITUTIONS

It would be fair to say that nowadays no five-year-old in Britain would be subjected to the way of life that the men in Bracken have had to bear. It is now acknowledged that it is unacceptable to house, or warehouse, large numbers of people together in institutions in this way. The policy to close the institutions was clearly, in terms of moral and human rights, a welcome step forward, yet attitudes to the closure of these large Victorian hospitals are, in fact, very mixed. Many families of the men and women who are to be moved out of long-term institutions are opposed to the closure, and to their relative being moved into a community environment, whatever the assumed benefits to the people themselves. Staff at all levels also have mixed reactions.

A graphic example of such negative attitudes was the move to close the notorious 'Colony of Mentally Ill' on the Greek island of Leros, in Greece. The closing down of the colony, in which men and women were living under conditions which had provoked an international scandal, was initially opposed by those most involved, including the doctors, staff and families of residents, in spite of the appalling standards of care (Tsiantis *et al.* 1995). In spite of the undeniable improvements in the 'quality of life' of at least some of the patients, the attitudes of the staff who had worked with them apparently still did not change radically (Kourdoutis *et al.* 1995). Recently it has been reported that some of them were, in fact, dispatched to another asylum, on a different island.

The reasons why families of mental patients who had been confined on the island of Leros did not want them back, or living in or near their communities, are obviously very complex, and included powerful concepts of stigma and 'bad blood'. In Britain the reasons why many families are opposed to the closure of institutions are also complex. But there is one clear thread. Once a child, or adult, has been committed to a long-term institution, to this marginal, socially and physically excluded existence, how can they, years later, be brought back into society without indicting the family, the wider kinship and social group, and society as a whole? Such a move must carry with it the uncomfortable and, perhaps for some, unbearable implication that this person was not, and thus had really never been, beyond the social pale, was not too morally, emotionally or physically dangerous to be incorporated into the social group.

Parents, even some thirty or forty years after their child went to live in an institution, still have strong and unresolved emotions about the disability and what happened in the past, and about the child. Their young children, when they entered the institution, died a social death. For the parents who remain, this may sometimes be harder than a real death. There is an incompleteness: there has been no burial, no closure to the mourning of the parents who let them go. Even those who never visit their children mourn them still. One mother said that she thinks about her son every day, and has done so for thirty years. She asks why her first-born son was born like this, what had she done to make it happen? Why did it happen to her? Was it a punishment from God? Her son is lost to her, but there is no relief from her bereavement. She has never told her neighbours or friends that she has a son. It is as though he were dead, a child to remember and mourn - but not to lay to rest. She, and many other parents, now oppose the closure of the institution. They would prefer that their adult children remain segregated, because the alternative, to bring them back into the social world, is too painful to contemplate. No one really wants to resurrect their dead.

THE FUTURE

However segregated the Bracken men's lives continue to be, what is left of their future will at least be in more acceptable environments. But it is not enough simply to change the physical surroundings. Research has shown that this is only the first step.

Johnson's (1998: 186) conclusions, from her Australian study of women who had been moved out of a locked ward, are depressing: 'Deinstitutionalization ... did not succeed in changing the fundamental ways in which they were viewed. It was overwhelmed by the existing discourse which objectified the women'.

Also, concepts of 'dangerousness', and of pollution do not vanish overnight. This is very clearly illustrated by Jodelet (1991), who relates that in France, in the 1970s, about 1000 patients from the local mental institution (all far more able than the men in Bracken) were moved out into the local community, to live with local families. Research, some twenty years later, has shown that, even now, very few families let their lodger eat with them. They are given separate cutlery; their washing-up is done in a separate bowl, and they themselves are not allowed to put their hands in the bowl because they would pollute the water. Thus, in spite of twenty-five years of cohabitation, the families involved still believe that they can be polluted by people who have mental illness or intellectual disabilities.

The fear of difference, and the multitude of negative images that cling to people who have been segregated from society, will not just disappear. It is difficult to believe that the men and women in locked wards such as Bracken will not carry with them, wherever they eventually live, a legacy of separateness and stigma, reinforced by the continuing perceptions of them as 'others', defined, as Young says, as 'ugly, dirty, defiled, impure, contaminated and sick'.

REFERENCES

Carr, E.H. 1931. *Dostoevsky: 1821–1881*. London: George Allen and Unwin.

Dostoevsky, F. [1860] 1950. *The House of the Dead* (trans. Constance Garnett). London: William Heinemann Ltd.

Douglas, M. 1966. *Purity and Danger: an analysis of concepts of pollution and taboo*. London: Routledge and Kegan Paul.

Goffman, E. 1961. *Asylums: essays on the social situation of mental patients and other inmates*. London: Penguin Books.

Goode, D. 1994. *A World Without Words: the social construction of children born deaf and blind*. Philadelphia: Temple University Press.

Hubert, J. 1991. *Home-bound: crisis in the care of young people with severe learning difficulties: a story of twenty families*. London: King's Fund.

Jodelet, D. 1991. *Madness and Social Representations: living with the mad in one French community*. California: University of California Press.

Johnson, K. 1998. *Deinstitutionalizing Women: an ethnographic study of institutional closure*. Cambridge: Cambridge University Press.

Kennedy, F. 1942. The problem of social control of the congenital defective – education, sterilization, euthanasia. *American Journal of Psychiatry* 99, 13–16.

Kourdoutis, P., G. Kolaitis, A. Perakis, P. Papanikolopoulou and J. Tsiantis 1995. Change in care staff's attitudes towards people with learning disabilities following intervention at the Leros PIKPA asylum. *British Journal of Psychiatry* Supplement, 56–69.

Ryan, J. and F. Thomas 1987. *The Politics of Mental Handicap*. London: Free Association Books.

Shepherd, G., M. Muijen, R. Dean and M. Cooney 1996. Residential care in hospital and in the community – quality of care and quality of life. *British Journal of Psychiatry* 168, 448–56.

Sinason, V. 1992. *Mental Handicap and the Human Condition*. London: Free Association Books.

Tsiantis, J., P. Kourdoutis, G. Kolaitis, A. Perakis and H. Assimopoulos 1995. The psychosocial dynamics of change at Leros PIKPA asylum. *British Journal of Psychiatry* Supplement, 46–55.

Young, I.M. 1990. *Justice and the Politics of Difference*. Princeton: Princeton University Press.

15   *Exclusion from funerary rituals and mourning: implications for social and individual identity*

Oyepeju Raji and Sheila Hollins

All human societies have their own beliefs, practices and rituals surrounding death and mourning. What, then, are the implications for the social identity and sense of individual identity of those individuals, or groups, who are excluded from these practices and processes? This chapter examines the implications in relation to one such group, those people who have intellectual disabilities (labelled variously as people with mental retardation, mental handicap or learning disabilities), and who have a long history, in many parts of the world, of social and, in some cases, physical exclusion.

PEOPLE WITH INTELLECTUAL DISABILITIES

Intellectual disabilities start before adulthood and have a lasting effect on development; they may be of varying levels and people with intellectual disabilities have many different talents, qualities, strengths and support needs. A minority have major difficulties in communicating their ideas and preferences, but most struggle with abstract concepts and need help to understand complex ideas.

In many societies around the world, people with intellectual disabilities are considered undesirable or are even feared, and different cultures deal with these attitudes and feelings in different ways. Some cultures are more paternalistic or give spiritual explanations which allow control to rest with a superior being, while others attempt to understand and control the lives of those who are different.

In Europe, medieval Christianity explained the working of the psyche by objectifying evil. Demonic forces were implicated in the workings of the disordered mind, and 'idiots' were, at different times, believed to be fathered by the devil, or to be incarnations of the devil himself. Therefore, demons were exorcized as treatment for insanity and affected people were thrust out of society (Stockholder 1994). By the sixteenth century the devil was no longer considered directly responsible, and the parents themselves were blamed for the birth of an 'idiot' child. People with intellectual disabilities have continued to be stigmatized over the centuries, culminating in the nineteenth century with their wide-scale confinement in institutions.

The hospitalization of this population continued to increase during the first half of the twentieth century, thus creating almost impenetrable barriers between open society and people considered inferior and contaminating.

Throughout recent years the balance of the relationship between medicine and disability has changed, with profound implications for the understanding of disability and disabled people. Policy and practice frameworks now emphasize social inclusion as a fundamental priority. However, in day-to-day life, both within the remaining institutions and in the community, social exclusion is still a reality for people with intellectual disabilities in some significant aspects of their lives.

DEATH AND DYING RITUALS

The context of death and dying is one in which the reactions and role of people with intellectual disabilities are frequently ignored or denied. It is relevant to begin, therefore, with a brief discussion of the significance of rituals associated with death and mourning in different cultures and different faith groups, and to consider the human experience of bereavement.

The way in which people dispose of the dead, and the meaning they give to death, varies from culture to culture. In different parts of the world, and even in neighbouring parts of the same town, the actual rituals used, their timing, and the identity of the key participants, vary enormously. Such rituals have a range of different functions, including to help the spirit on the way to another life, to separate the body and soul, to prepare for resurrection, and so on. Whatever they are or do, in some way they change the status of the person who has died, and at a different level also change the status of the people left behind. They construct boundaries between life and death, or between this life and the next life, not only for the dead themselves, but also for the living, so that each one, as they participate in, or observe the funerary rites and the disposal of the body, can internalize the separation, and the finality of death – at least for the living.

The role played by different family members varies. In some societies, such as those governed by Islamic faith, only men attend the public rituals involved in the disposal of the body. Women may, however, prepare the body first, and may weep publicly, or display some other outward sign of grief, for a defined period. In Western culture the son often has a key role, whereas in parts of South East Asia, a woman's brother has responsibility for his widowed sister and her children (Clamigirand 1980).

In some societies, funerary rituals are completed within days of a death, whereas in others some rituals will be carried out at prescribed intervals weeks or months or even years afterwards. Sometimes the rituals take place on the anniversary of the death a year later. Hertz (1960) describes how dividing the funerary rituals into two parts, sometimes separated by several years, first helps the survivors to mourn and adjust to the changes or disruptions in their own lives, and then, at a later stage, encourages them to celebrate the new status of the deceased as an immortal ancestor. This is particularly true in South East Asia but has also been described in many other parts of the world.

On the island of Timor in eastern Indonesia, a funeral feast is held every few months for all members of the community who have died since the last feast (Clamigirand 1980).

The ritual is held in the core house, the space rendered sacred by the presence of the heirlooms that have come from the ancestors, and other objects used in rituals. These rituals are said to mark the definitive separation of the dead from the living.

In south-western Nigeria, from where one of the authors (OR) originates, followers of traditional beliefs will visit a 'priest' for a 'spiritual post mortem' to understand the cause of death and obtain guidance on the necessary sacrifice to be made. The traditional belief is that a spirit world or realm exists, and the funerary ritual is to help the spirit on its journey from this world to the next to join the ancestors. It is also believed that the peaceful repose of the spirit will prevent it from coming back to haunt the living. The spirit is powerful and can still communicate with the living in a protective and prosperous way if it is happy, or in disastrous ways if it is sad or angry. The spirit of the dead is shown respect by the way the funeral is performed, and it is feared that disrespect would cause the wrath of the spirit of the dead on the living. The spirits of the ancestors are significant in all spheres of life, and are invoked in rituals for other important events, such as fertility and harvest.

Anyone thought to be spiritually impure, or who is emotionally immature or physically unable is not allowed to participate in traditional south-western Nigerian funerary rituals. In some parts of Nigeria this may be, at least in part, because physical and intellectual disabilities (and mental illness) are believed by some to be caused by negative spiritual influences (evil forces) direct from the gods, or invoked by one's enemies, and such people may be subjected to spiritual cleansing and healing. The scientific explanation of these conditions as understood through Western influences, that they are biological in origin rather than spiritual, is not accepted at the local level, and segregation from 'normal society' and efforts at purification persist. Christian and Islamic spiritual influences prevailing in different parts of Nigeria have modified practice to some extent, but the traditional spiritual focus largely remains.

In Britain, Anglican Christian funerary rituals appear to have merged with middle class British culture in the latter half of the twentieth century, and funeral directors have largely taken over the planning of funerals from the church. Cremation is widely preferred to burial in Britain, and many funerals, particularly in cities, are carried out in crematorium chapels by ministers who know nothing of the family or the dead person (Blanche and Parkes 1997). Funerals are often one of the few occasions when the wider family is brought together, and are usually private affairs, only for those invited. The bereaved tend to keep their emotions in check to avoid embarrassing themselves and those present. This is in contrast to some other cultures where the death of a person affects the whole community, where mourning is a public affair and the bereaved are encouraged to display their grief openly.

In Roman Catholic practice, the dying person will seek forgiveness for their sins in this life so that they will live in peace in the next world. When possible the priest will anoint the dying person, giving them the Sacrament of Extreme Unction to prepare them and help them move from this life to the next. Thus the death rituals begin before death. After death, the coffin is brought into the church the day before the funeral, and prayers are said around the coffin. The next day the mourners gather in the church for a Requiem Mass before the coffin is taken either to the cemetery or the crematorium. Masses for the Holy Souls are said every November when prayers for deceased relatives and friends are said to hasten the souls of deceased relatives and friends to heaven. Hockey (1990) wrote about death as a rite of passage, or transition – not an end point. This concept of an inter-relationship between life and death is one which probably helps both those struggling with letting go of life, and those adjusting to an internalized relationship with the deceased.

Muslims prefer to perform their own funerals in preparing the soul for the life hereafter in a fit state. Non-Muslims, who are considered spiritually impure, do not touch the body, which has to be made pure before embarking on the final journey to meet The Creator. Ritual washing and prayer are performed in a prescribed way before burial. Women do not participate in the prayer and do not accompany the body to the graveside. The body is not dressed, but is wrapped in white cloth and buried without a coffin in recognition of the fact that a person enters this world with nothing and must leave with nothing. The body is never cremated, because by Islamic law the body must be returned to The Creator as whole as possible. It is believed that the body will be visited by angels in the grave. The rituals continue at intervals for forty days and a widow remains in mourning for 110 days. There is some change in attitude and belief among Muslims who have migrated to western societies, linked to a decline in the status of established religion there. The move away from extended family and community networks also means that they may have little to do with death and bereavement before they become directly affected.

Muslims believe in submitting to the will of God, and death at any age is accepted as the fulfilment of life, the term of which is only known by God. Wailing and public display of emotion is discouraged and women and people with intellectual disability, who are said to have 'emotionally weak hearts', do not attend funerals (Muslim leader in South West London *pers. comm.*). People with intellectual disabilities (both children and adults), like children as a whole, are not expected to understand what has happened, and are not allowed to participate. It is assumed, on this basis, that they will forget things quickly, and they are not encouraged to ask questions. Islamic faith encourages acceptance of ones' fate without question, and this is not thought to be possible for weaker members of the community.

The importance of funerary rituals, and of witnessing the laying to rest of a relative, has over recent years been emphasized and highlighted by the demands of indigenous, and non-indigenous, peoples from all parts of the world, to have the human remains of their ancestors returned to them from museums, laboratories and anatomy departments in their own and other countries (Hubert 1992). People not only need to bury their dead, but also to see them buried, with appropriate rituals, so that some acceptance and closure can be brought about.

THE NON-INVOLVEMENT OF INTELLECTUALLY DISABLED PEOPLE IN FUNERARY RITUALS

In Britain, it is common practice for close adult relatives and friends to attend the ceremonies connected with burial or cremation, and to take part in the surrounding mourning process. However, people with intellectual disabilities tend to be excluded from these rituals, even when children are included. They are denied the right to take part in the funerary rituals of someone close to them, and to take their place among the mourners, and sometimes may not be told about a death, even of a close relative. They will, of course, observe all the changes around them, but they are not helped to make sense of it by being allowed to share fully in the experience. They are often left bewildered, and have no role in either the formal, or informal processes and rituals that surround death and dying.

The experience of death is universal, it is an integral part of the human condition, but, in spite of this, each death has an incalculable impact on the individuals left behind, and on the social group within which it has occurred. However quickly the life of the group settles into its new social and emotional shape, nothing is ever the same again. But people with intellectual disabilities, unlike everyone else in the family or social group, are not thought to notice the emotional tensions, outbursts and discussions about the past and the future that surround a dying person. They are thought to be unaware of the abrupt disappearance of someone that they have lived with, and who may have cared for them for the whole of their life. They are expected to be able to understand the finality of the end of a relationship without having had a chance to say goodbye, or to see their family and friends say goodbye to the one who has died.

Whatever the implications of exclusion from death and dying, and the surrounding practices and rituals, the fact that this happens has its own implications for the perception and treatment of people with intellectual disabilities. There may be many reasons why people exclude them: their cognitive functioning may not be considered sophisticated enough to recognize the changes in their relationships and roles; the people around them may perceive them as perpetual children, unable to take full responsibility for themselves, and needing to be protected from the harsher facts of life; they may be thought to lack emotional feelings because they do not express themselves adequately (Oswin 1991). Sometimes it may be thought to be for their own good, sometimes for the benefit of others who are finding it difficult to deal with their own emotions, let alone someone else's grief.

It is sometimes the case that parents suppress the inevitability of their own death, and any reminder of their own ageing and mortality, or that of close relatives and friends. These are among the secrets which they typically keep from a son or daughter who has intellectual disabilities. Some parents may try to deny their own mortality because of their own fears about what would happen to their son or daughter if they predeceased them.

The exclusion of people with intellectual disabilities from participating in death and mourning is particularly significant because, for them, the death of a parent may bring about other related losses. For example, their support network may change radically, and they may have to leave the family home. Many parents of people with intellectual disabilities will have rejected institutional care for their sons or daughters and preferred to continue to care for them at home themselves. But when a parent dies, the remaining parent, or other relatives, will face a new dilemma. Their son or daughter is often taken out of the household into short-term residential care and is, thus, absent while the other relatives and friends grieve, receive solace from others and participate in the funerary rituals. The surviving parent may accept or even encourage this and typically say that they cannot cope with their son or daughter being upset at this time, for once putting their own needs first. Often, the son or daughter will be sent away to live permanently in residential provision with paid carers who may well be strangers. In addition, they will be expected to carry on with their normal daily routine, and will not be excused from attending their day centres or 'work', let alone have their grief acknowledged.

BEREAVEMENT AND GRIEF

Grief is a dynamic, psychological reaction to loss and bereavement. Normal grief has been extensively described (e.g. Bowlby 1961; Parkes 1972, 1998), suggesting a progression through several, non-discrete stages with some overlap or return to earlier stages. There is great variation in the quality and length of grief; however, normal grief does resolve over time. There is an initial phase of shock and numbness, which may be short-lived. This is often followed by physical or psychological distress and protest, the expression of which is influenced not only by culture but also by personality (Parkes 1972). As the reality of the loss begins to sink in, there may be a sense of emptiness, despair or a feeling of depression at the realization that the deceased person is never coming back. The final phase is one of recovery or reorganization when the bereaved start to adjust to life without the deceased. Some factors have been identified as contributing to a poorer eventual adjustment to loss (Parkes 1972; Oswin 1991), and these include inhibition of the expression and experience of grief. Changes in behaviour, which occur during the early phases of 'yearning and protest', as described by Bowlby (1961), and understood as part of grieving, are often labelled as 'challenging behaviour' when they occur in people with intellectual disabilities (Parkes 1972), and attributed to causes other than bereavement. Some people with intellectual disabilities may have a different style of grieving and different ways of communicating their needs, and these may not be understood, and thus may be ignored. The reactions of people with intellectual disabilities to bereavement has received little attention until recently.

Two case studies

An autistic man whose father was terminally ill became angry with the nurse who was trying to relieve his father's pain. He also hit and punched his father and insisted household routines should remain the same. His parents had to choose between sending their son away, or arranging for his father to be admitted to hospital, and they decided that their son should have short-term care away from home. When his father died, his mother decided to make all the funeral arrangements herself, and not to involve her son. As he had his own advocate, it was possible to intervene and support him in choosing the level of his own involvement. He decided to see his father's body, to buy flowers for his father and to attend the service in the crematorium. He took his place beside his mother, thus playing the high status role expected of an only son in his community, and his behaviour was impeccable. This example demonstrates that people with quite profound disabilities are able to participate, benefit from and contribute to the rituals surrounding death, and to the grieving process (Hollins and Sireling 1999).

Contrast this story with that of the daughter who was sent away for a few days after her father died – until everything had been sorted out. Her mother decided not to tell her that her father had died in case she was upset. Her daughter had limited language, but asked "Where's my Dad?" at regular intervals (Hollins and Sireling 1999). To begin with she was told that Dad was at work. Still the question was asked every day. After three years it had become wearing, dealing with this persistent questioning ten or twenty times a day. But now there were no funerary rituals to support any other explanation, and the abstract explanations available had no meaning to someone with such limited cognitive ability. Exclusion from the funeral and the physical reality of her father's death had had exactly the opposite effect to that intended. Instead of being upset at the funeral, this woman remained confused and upset years later.

Grief, if denied expression, is potentially pathological, and bereaved people with intellectual disabilities may develop severe emotional problems. Two recent studies (Hollins and Esterhuyzen 1997; Bonell-Pascual et al. 1999) followed up fifty men and women with intellectual disabilities who had lost a parent through death, first at up to two years, and then again five years later, to determine their involvement in rituals surrounding a death, and to try to understand more about the natural course of grief in this group. The data available included information about whether they were able to visit their parent in hospital, attend the funeral or choose mementoes. At up to two years, over a third had a memento, but only half had been included in funerary rituals and an even smaller number (16 per cent) had been given an opportunity to visit their parent in hospital during their last illness (Hollins and Esterhuyzen 1997). At the time of the second follow-up, it was found that few of the staff caring for the bereaved people had known them at the time of their parents' death, which in itself is an indication of the repeated 'losses' incurred by people with intellectual disabilities. However a common theme in their responses to questions about how the person had grieved was that of continuing non-involvement. Some people had been prevented from attending a funeral despite asking to go, or had only been enabled to visit a parent's grave six or seven years later (Bonell-Pascual et al. 1999).

Raji and Hollins (unpublished) carried out a study of funerary rituals and the involvement of people with intellectual disabilities in different cultural and religious groups in south-west London. Information was collected from funeral directors and religious leaders, on the assumption that they would have most involvement with families following bereavement, and would be the best source of information about local practice. It was found that there was a general non-involvement and lack of awareness of the special needs of this group. Some groups were reluctant to be interviewed, and it was only those religious leaders and funeral directors who already had contact with professionals teaching and carrying out research around the subject of bereavement, who were aware of the importance of involving people with intellectual disabilities in funerary rituals. Furthermore, those interviewed suggested that it was familiarity with people with intellectual disabilities in a particular cultural or religious group which would affect inclusion in rituals, rather than any fixed cultural or religious belief. In the local Muslim community, intellectual disabilities and mental health problems were apparently associated with stigma.

A person with intellectual disabilities is often a disenfranchised mourner, excluded from the knowledge of the death, and from being present at associated rituals (Doka 1989). Their relationship with the deceased is denied at the point of death. It could be argued that to do so is an attempt to change the status of the deceased, and to relieve them of the perceived burden carried in their lifetime. It could also be that, at some level, the exclusion of someone from the funeral of a person who was close to them is an attempt to force a belated separation, recognizing the distorted pattern of attachment which often exists when unusual dependency needs persist beyond childhood (Esterhuyzen and Hollins 1997). Some adults with intellectual disabilities lead very private lives with elderly parents in their family home, and are not well known in their local community. Sinason (1992), Bicknell (1983) and others suggest this is due to the shame felt by many parents following the birth of a child with a severe disability. Although many younger parents have more open and accepting attitudes, the task of enabling a child's individuation and separation from the mother may still be hampered by dependency needs, and a lack of alternative carers.

Factors described as predictors of depression following a bereavement in adult life include insecure attachment patterns in childhood, and a profound disruption of meaning to one's life because of the bereavement (Marris 1991). To face life without a parent who was not only one's carer, but also a friend, confidant and breadwinner must be devastating. To adjust to a new life over which one, in any case, has little control, while not understanding why things have changed, must be even more so. The research by Hollins and Esterhuyzen (1997) showed that the grief of people with intellectual disabilities is not recognized as such. As a consequence, this grief, which may often be expressed behaviourally, is often attributed to the cause of their intellectual disability, described as a behavioural problem, or just seen as part of their personality. Only years later were some of the study group receiving bereavement counselling or similar interventions. Parkes (1998: 1524), quoting Bowlby (1988), points out that 'the most important thing that we have to offer frightened or grieving people is a "secure base", a relationship of respect'.

Since the late 1970s, the theme of the importance of respect runs through the writings of influential advocates for the rights of people with intellectual disabilities (Wolfensberger 1987). Within some cultures the stigma associated with intellectual disability is a reason why people are excluded from social occasions, ceremonies and celebrations, with affected relatives being kept hidden to avoid embarrassment. To be a liminal person, not fully belonging, no longer a child yet not recognized as an adult, excluded from full membership of the community which one was part of as a child, is the fate of many people with intellectual disabilities. It is not surprising, therefore, that so many with mild and moderate intellectual disability try to 'pass' as normal (Edgerton 1993), denying or hiding any difficulty or disability which might contribute to their exclusion from the social group.

CONCLUSION

Rituals contribute to cultural identity and are a source of valuable social support. They reinforce group ties and reaffirm group memberships, which can be supportive in both practical and emotional terms. The exclusion of people with intellectual disabilities from funerary rituals and mourning customs excludes them from this valuable source of community support. Although different religious and cultural groups have various explanations for this, it would appear that people with intellectual disabilities are seldom fully accepted as members of society with meaningful social roles and relationships.

REFERENCES

Bicknell, D.J. 1983. The psychopathology of handicap. *British Journal of Medical Psychology* 56, 167–78.

Blanche, H.T. and C.M. Parkes 1997. Christianity. In *Death and Bereavement Across Cultures*, C.M. Parkes, P. Laungani and B. Young (eds), 131–46. London: Routledge.

Bonell-Pascual, E., S. Huline-Dickens, S. Hollins, S. Esterhuyzen *et al.* 1999. Bereavement and grief in adults with learning disabilities: a follow-up study. *British Journal of Psychiatry* 175, 348–50.

Bowlby, J. 1961. Process of mourning. *International Journal of Psychoanalysis* 42, 317–40.

Bowlby, J. 1988. *A Secure Base: clinical applications of attachment theory*. London: Routledge.

Clamigirand B. 1980. The social organization of the Ema of Timor. In *The Flow of Life: essays on eastern Indonesia*, J.J. Fox (ed.). Harvard: Harvard University Press.

Doka, K. (ed.) 1989. *Disenfranchised Grief*. Lexington, MA: Lexington Books.

Edgerton, R.B. 1993. *The Cloak of Competence*. Berkeley: University of California Press.

Esterhuyzen, A. and S. Hollins 1997. Psychotherapy. In *Psychiatry in Learning Disability*, S. Read (ed.), 332–49. London: W.B. Saunders.

Hertz, R. 1960. *Death and the Right Hand*. London: Cohen and West.

Hockey, J. 1990. *Experiences of Death: an anthropological account*. Edinburgh: Edinburgh University Press.

Hollins, S. and A. Esterhuyzen 1997. Bereavement and grief in adults with learning disabilities. *British Journal of Psychiatry* 170, 497–501.

Hollins, S. and L. Sireling 1999. *Understanding Grief: working with grief and people who have learning disabilities*. London: Pavilion Publishing.

Hubert, J. 1992. Dry bones or living ancestors? Conflicting perceptions of life, death and the universe. *International Journal of Cultural Property* 1, 105–27.

Marris, P. 1991. The social construction of uncertainty. In *Attachment Across the Life Cycle*, C.M. Parkes, J. Stevenson-Hinde and P. Marris (eds), 77–90. London: Routledge.

Oswin, M. 1991. *Am I Allowed to Cry? A study of bereavement amongst people who have learning difficulties*. London: Human Horizons.

Parkes, C.M. 1972. *Bereavement: studies of grief in adult life*. London: Tavistock Publications.

Parkes, C.M. 1998. Coping with loss: facing loss. *British Medical Journal* 316, 1521–24.

Sinason, V. 1992. *Mental Handicap and the Human Condition: new approaches from the Tavistock*. London: Free Association Books.

Stockholder, J.E. 1994. Naming and renaming persons with intellectual disabilities. In *Disability is not Measles: new research paradigms in disability*. M.H. Rioux and M. Bach (eds), 153–79. Ontario: L'Institut Roeher Institute.

Wolfensberger, W. 1987. *The New Genocide of Handicapped and Afflicted People*. Syracuse: Syracuse University Division of special education and rehabilitation.

16   *Social exclusion in northern Nigeria*

MURRAY LAST

A central problem in an archaeology of madness and disability (and of social exclusion more generally) is how can the people we would now put in those categories – the ill and the impaired – be identified in the historical record? How can we identify those people that another society has put in such categories which seem so similar to ours, but, in fact, are not? Furthermore, social categories vary over time even within a single community; our own past can be 'another country'. Using an all-embracing term like social exclusion compounds the problem. This broader category revolves around stigmatization. Here we must ideally distinguish between stigma actually experienced by the stigmatized, and externally imposed on them by others (and so, in principle, observable), and stigma internally imposed by the stigmatized themselves, who then pattern their behaviour to avoid the (possibly imagined) stigma of others. The latter behaviour is much harder to observe and to attribute confidently to stigma rather than to any other factor (or to a trait like 'shyness'). Yet anticipated social exclusion, in being firmly in the sufferer's mind, can be as devastating to social competence as any overt act of excluding – but much harder to cancel. The challenge is to find ways of identifying that anticipated exclusion, and to see more generally if there are surrogate markers of stigma, whether in the historical record or today, that we can rely on to render visible what is commonly invisible.

Comparative ethnography allows the identification and testing of possible surrogate markers. If societies are placed on a scale from less to more developed or complex, (as used commonly to be the practice) then the assumption is that the past of a more complex society can be seen in the present of a simpler society. For those of us concerned with the history of relatively new nations like Nigeria, their past is of intrinsic interest, and not merely for the light it might throw on the past of more developed states. Nonetheless we can recognize practices there (such as some kinds of physical restraint in 'traditional' asylums) that have ceased in Europe – and from these practices get insight into how they may have intimately affected those involved. The past of these traditional asylums, however, is elusive. One cannot assume, of course, that 'things have always been like that' – not least because half a century of colonial rule transformed much of everyday practice. A first step, then, is to outline the ethnography of social exclusion in a contemporary culture like that of Muslim northern Nigeria, to offer the reader an example of 'another culture' and to suggest ways research might go further in finding solutions to the central problems mentioned above. Muslim northern Nigeria is sufficiently different from Europe or North America to call into question some of the assumptions that underlie our categories, yet not different enough to be put aside as exotic. However, my account of northern Nigeria is itself open to question – any generalizations about a society of over forty million people can only be partially true.

SOCIAL EXCLUSION

Before we start on the Nigerian ethnography, however, let us look briefly at a minute item in British ethnography – the term 'social exclusion' – since it, too, needs to be situated within its specific 'moment' in British politics.

'Social exclusion', as a standard term in British sociological writing, dates to the mid-1980s (Alcock 1997: 92). A pamphlet published by the Child Poverty Action Group set out the ideas behind their new term, which was to be used for a wider category of people than had been covered by such earlier terms as 'poverty' or 'handicap'. You could be 'excluded' without being poor and without having some impairment. Being identified as one of a stigmatized minority might lead to exclusion from the resources commonly available to the majority, or from the rights taken for granted in 'mainstream' society. It was linked, therefore, to issues of 'citizenship' in multicultural communities. With the new Labour government formally establishing a 'Social Exclusion Unit' the term has gained official recognition in Britain, and it has gained still wider currency with United Nations' agencies now using the term. But the term is still placed within inverted commas by London-based journalists writing for *The Economist* (5/12/98: 36) and *The Independent* (20/12/99: 5), for example, as if the term, however familiar to specialists, was one that even their readership could not be expected quite to accept.

Though the term has yet to appear in textbooks of general sociology, the underlying idea is as old as sociology itself – and older: both Durkheim and Weber analysed the ways groups are formed by including some individuals and social categories and excluding others. Long before them lawyers had designed principles of exclusion from inheritance or power; similarly, systems of stratification, social class and caste all have at their core the notion of 'closure'.

The current usage of social exclusion has clearly negative connotations. The British government's Unit is to construct policies to eliminate social exclusion – though not, it seems, to open the door to immigrants. For the focus is on the process of exclusion and its elimination, not on the excluded themselves (or their elimination?). It is not they who are to be transformed, nor any specific attribute of theirs altered – they are all right as they are, even if it is an impairment (such as deafness) that has been until now the reason for their being outside the 'mainstream'. The broad implication is, nonetheless, that the excluded should be brought in 'from the cold', or enabled to come in, should they so wish. It is not, however, a Social Inclusion Unit. In either case, it is society that does the excluding, and not the excluded themselves; and it is society's practices that require reform, not any particular characteristic of those excluded.

The concept of social exclusion seems, perhaps paradoxically, to reaffirm the idea of closure, the idea of a barrier which will still keep out some while ensuring that others exercise their right of access to whatever is lawfully theirs as 'citizens'. It is recognized that boundaries exist and that means are to be found by which individuals can cross those boundaries. The boundaries, however, are to remain or even be strengthened: not just so that those not entitled to benefits stay excluded, but so that deaf people should retain their own social exclusiveness (and their own [sign-]language), those who are disabled should not seek to 'pass' as normal. The model is that of ethnicity; deaf people form a cultural group of their own. Whereas in the past, ethnic difference might have counted as a kind of impairment, now impairment offers a kind of ethnicity of its own, one that need not be given up for the sake of becoming 'normal'. The term 'social exclusion' is a response to this shift in models.

Only poverty sits awkwardly in this model, not least because the 1960s notion, developed in the USA, of a distinct 'culture of poverty', suggested that the poor had a characteristic subculture that inhibited them from ever becoming better off (Lewis 1965). No one really argues that poverty should not be alleviated, or that the worse-off should not cease to be so poor. They are not a separate underclass but rather relatively 'deprived', for it is their very lack of the usual items of consumption, common in the average household, that excludes them and their children from partaking in the normal social exchanges of their neighbourhood.

'Social exclusion', then, has a much wider remit. While the constituency embraced by 'the excluded' is now made larger and its political potential obvious, there is surely a danger that the political will to remedy the serious inequalities suffered by those at the extremes of exclusion will be so watered down that nothing effective is achieved. It may not in practice help the 'ultra-poor' to be included within a broader category of the 'socially excluded', only to find the limited funding diverted to other, more articulate or popular out-groups.

I have emphasized here the almost parochial nature of the current, British use of 'social exclusion' so as not to impose unwittingly yet another concept deriving from 'western' politics. We need to assess how useful the term proves to be. But, initially at least, I think we need, as an experiment, to try to identify what categories of people were shut out from what aspects of mainstream society in the past; and to try to determine what in the archaeological record can be taken as evidence of exclusion in a specific context. We may find, in the ethnography of contemporary communities, that a set of narrower categories – for instance, of people who are ultra-poor, impaired or stigmatized – may be a more useful, albeit more complicated, starting-point than a simplifying term like 'social exclusion', that lumps together different groups.

'SOCIAL EXCLUSION' IN NORTHERN NIGERIA: A CASE STUDY

'Social exclusion', then, is embedded in a particular matrix of ideas and politics that have relevance for reform in a changing Britain. This does not mean that the term or the ideas behind it have universal currency even in Britain; to some extent the term is restricted to the social knowledge of specialists. In the discussion that follows, however, I am shifting to another level of social knowledge: I am outlining for northern Nigeria ideas that seem to me to be common to the general public. I am not quoting thoughts current in Nigerian Ministries or universities among welfare professionals or theorists. In this context, once we move out of the British milieu, some general questions need to be raised. For example, how different are people's implicit understanding of themselves and their surroundings? The data for my answers to these questions are based on some forty years' work on northern Nigeria, first as an historian and then as an anthropologist, living there or visiting almost annually. It is a synthetic account, but the core material on spirits derives from living in a deep rural farmstead for two years, 1969–1971, and thereafter from keeping in regular touch with my hosts there. On madness and disability, the detailed material dates from teamwork with colleagues in urban Kano over the last fifteen years (Last 1991a, 1991b).

The body and the self

We cannot assume, first, that people in northern Nigeria wholly identify their selves with their bodies. In a sense, people's selves are *in* their bodies, temporarily; a person occupies, as it were, only a room in the 'house' that is their body. The archetypal instance of the body-as-housing is pregnancy, but other beings – worms, parasites, even invading spirits – can enter the body-as-housing and live within it as a normal, even necessary part of the body's 'household'. A case of madness, then, can be seen as when a spirit takes charge of the 'house', and acts madly (for a human, that is, if not for a playful spirit). Your self is not mad, though it can be cross or sad, in which case your self may have locked itself into its 'room' (as in depression). Therapy for the mad can be aimed at 'domesticating' an invasive or restless spirit, and then returning control of your 'house' to you. It may not necessarily be to drive out the spirit (as in exorcism). The body, from this perspective, belongs not to you but to your parents, your lineage or the community. It is they who initially made 'your' body and improve it through various ritual operations (circumcision, for example). It will be they who will dispose of it when, in death, you have abandoned your 'room' in the body. Otherwise it is up to you to keep it in good repair; your body is on loan to you.

But it is not always clear whether 'you', the lodger in this body, are to be trusted – or indeed that you are what you seem to be. The making of a body during pregnancy is hazardous: a troublesome water spirit, for example, may slip in when your mother is washing and pretend to be 'you'. There are, therefore, tests to see if 'you' are really human, and tests later ('initiation') to see if you are really strong or sensible enough to be entrusted with a piece of the lineage's 'housing' stock. Finally, rituals and medicines seek to ensure your 'house' is kept locked and safe from unwanted intruders. It is the duty of the body's owners, as well as yourself, to keep intruders at a distance. But given the number of openings or orifices in a body and the travelling away from home that is essential for everyday life, closure can fail, and result in disabilities of various kinds.

This notion of the body as housing distinct from your self extends beyond madness. It also means that physical deformities do not diminish the rights and recognition of your 'self' as a full person in the community. Once adult, you are not categorized, when disabled, as a permanent 'social child', as happens sometimes in Britain (e.g. with Down's syndrome): you have rights to sexuality (and to parenthood); you have money and property. A spirit may have crippled you, but stigma is not attached to 'you', though the spirit who wounded you or is possessing you (and causing you to behave oddly) may be stigmatized. Once rid of the spirit, you are socially acceptable again, albeit still perhaps to be considered vulnerable. If, as with a disability, there is no recovery, so be it: your 'housing' is defective, but 'you' are not.

Secondly, since the causes of disability and the sources of madness lie outside one's self, the environment in which one lives is seen as inherently dangerous. The prevalence of danger outside, therefore, accentuates the importance of having a secure sanctuary inside – a home, a room of one's own. Much cultural energy is spent in keeping 'home', one's 'inside', safe and in removing all potentially dangerous objects or persons away from it (hence the significance of boundaries). The outside is the appropriate place for whatever is dangerous, since the dangerous cannot be destroyed. You cannot escape danger – it is ever-present danger, not risk-taking, that keeps an individual vulnerable. To try and remove altogether the dangerous from its place outside is simply to invite its relocation inside. In short, the dangerous has its place, and its rights, too. Inevitably, then, everyone, once the sanctuary of home is left behind, is moving in potentially dangerous space – to the fields, to the well or river, to a neighbouring farmstead or village market. It is quite possible, when on an ordinary errand, to bump into a spirit by pure mischance – and be rendered, quite suddenly, lame or crazy; or perhaps invisibly contaminated so that you take the pollution unwittingly home with you, and harm someone in your family. The landscape is criss-crossed by spirit 'highways'. Fields that lie on these pathways are more hazardous; farmsteads are not built across their line. Though I learnt to 'read' this landscape, it was often the smaller, scarcely visible signs that were important – not the dramatically obvious features. Spirits are not in any way exotic; people hear them rather than see them (I have even found a passage of spirit-speech transcribed in a serious eighteenth century Arabic manuscript). However, spirits usually prefer to play with children, especially at certain times of day and in certain places, for example where there is dirt or cast-offs. You tell their presence by the effects they have on things, animals or people, the metaphor for them being a light 'wind' or 'breeze' (iska).

In this context, just as home is the essential sanctuary, so too trust is the all-important social characteristic: what or who is trusted is taken to be danger-free even if you are not absolutely certain. For danger is largely invisible (were it visible one could easily avoid it). The skill that renders the invisible visible, the inaudible audible, is the skill of the healer, diviner, priest: they have learnt how to have risk-free relations with the 'super-social' whereas everyone else just needs the social skills of everyday life. Only the old, as their social skills decline, sometimes gain this super-skill. It is they – the elders, the healers – who provide you with the necessary protection to rely on, day in day out. 'Witches' and 'sorcerers', though, are those who, especially when as young ambitious adults, have acquired this super-social skill for their own gain but hide it, though they live in the same house or community with you. They betray the essential trust within the home; the evidence of their betrayal is a series of otherwise inexplicable deaths or illnesses within the household.

Exclusion, then, is of those whom you cannot trust; those who are deformed or mentally ill are not the problem – it is the seemingly well whom you cannot trust that must either be killed or driven far away. Their hidden violence is especially unacceptable because it is invisible until too late. Hence sorcery and witchcraft are the most heinous of crimes. As an ex-witch, however, I was considered safe to have within the house; I had already sated my appetite for human flesh elsewhere, and was no longer evil. But my rival in the house, a witch still 'on the make', was driven out while I was there by the house's youths who would have killed him if they could. Yet there were limits to his 'exclusion'; he was allowed to build a house and farm his fields less than a mile away, where he remained an isolated figure, socially broken. Only nineteen years later, on the death of his father (also a suspected sorcerer, a *mai dodo*) was he allowed to return to our farmstead with his one still-loyal wife; he died soon after, and was buried normally.

In marked contrast to the 'evil' of witches and sorcerers, there are men and women with chronic psychoses who live for years under a tree festooned with their bits and pieces. Others wander the high roads regardless of the passing traffic. The latter, in fact, keep to a specific route, and are given shelter, water and food at their regular stops. Neither have a 'home' but are subsumed within the category of beings who occupy the 'outside', apparently oblivious of any danger and causing harm to none. But were they to get violent, threatening lives or even just carrying a sword, they would be summarily killed, people say. They apparently value their freedom, and resist attempts to make them wear clothes or settle; yet they offer a sort of parodic sociality towards those they are familiar with, rarely going off the roads into the bush on their own. They are not so much 'excluded' as wryly tolerated (and teased by the young).

As an individual permanently occupied by spirits, a vagrant's proper place is, therefore, outside along with all the spirits that are not in human-bodily form; he or she will come to no further harm there. In talking with them, one does get an occasional sound of their 'real' self that has been dispossessed by the intrusive spirit. The neighbours who provide them with food and water seem to recognize this real self, and the courage the 'real' person must have to continue to live like this. Self-harm and suicide are very rare, though it is recognized that not all accidental deaths are quite as accidental as they seem (falling down wells is the most common 'accident', especially for women). Again the real self will usually not be blamed, and the body will be buried normally.

Third, social interest lies not in the poor or the sick; misfortune is so readily met with that it scarcely holds people's attention except perhaps briefly as a 'horror story'. What is of much greater interest is how people actually get wealthy and prosper: that is the real challenge facing everyone – becoming poor is too easy. Poverty, then, is not seen as a virtue, a misfortune that renders you in some sense holy. Although Muslim scholars and their students are rarely rich and, as Allah's servants, should not pursue wealth, they do not scorn all wealth. Wealth, if it comes, is a blessing from Allah, and should be received as such – then shared with others. It is the hoarding of wealth for oneself that is questioned: miserliness suggests the wealth came not from Allah but through some evil pact or witchcraft. Poverty then implies either failure in attracting Allah's blessing or a pact that went wrong; the poor are not specially beloved of Allah. So to serve the poor and the meek earns little honour. There are no charitable foundations, no *waqf*, in northern Nigeria and even the distribution of 'tithe', *zakat,* is often informal; the poor are not the preserve of institutions (cf. Iliffe 1987). Charitable welfare is not a primary category for political action; politics is about prosperity, not poverty, and the academic study of the extremely poor (or the politically weak) generates little enthusiasm.

Giving alms (*sadaka*) to the unfortunate is not so much for their relief as a 'sacrifice', a gift to earn protection for the donor from the powers that cause the misfortune. The victims of these powers are not, though, seen as a sort of visible surrogate for the powers themselves. People who are mad or impaired are fed and given shelter anyway; they (especially their real selves) are part of the household and provided for, house by house, personally. They are not a special category. The general disinterest suggests not stigma so much as neglect; victims are unfortunate rather than dangerous or evil. By contrast, the external forces that cause misfortune and the deities or ancestors that ensure (or block) legitimate prosperity are both matters of real concern to the powerful who are responsible for the well-being of their households or communities. Any failure to protect their dependants and ensure their health calls into question their right to power. It is the powerful, then, who are in danger of summary 'exclusion' if madness or injury strikes not them but their dependants once too often.

To many readers these ideas about the self and the body will be reminiscent of similar notions in Christianity about the soul, with Satan as the archetypal intruder and source of evil. In northern Nigeria, however, there is no sense that the body is inherently a source of sin; the division between body and soul is not quite as Descartes had envisaged it. Very different, too, is the particular emphasis that Christian theology puts (or once put) on suffering as the experience through which the soul grows: the ill, it was said, are going through a process of God-induced soul-growth and are therefore in need of special care during that sacred process (Orme and Webster 1995; cf. Tyndale [1528] 2000: 11). Caring, under the symbol of the cross, is thus a holy act. Suffering in northern Nigeria has nothing holy about it: little good comes of it, the body's travails are not a source of the self's development. The possible meaning of pain is similarly not elaborated: it is simply horrible, to be avoided if possible, endured silently if not. It is punishment given and taken as a deterrent, rather than punishment that somehow purifies or corrects, as has been argued theologically within European cultures. Pain arises primarily out of anger, not love; and the remarkable stoicism with which pain is borne has a different purpose – sustaining the silence of self-control in the face of a humiliating attack.

In short, the categories of 'mentally ill' and 'impaired' – and the suffering they imply – have rather different dimensions in northern Nigeria from those in, say, Britain as well as bearing significantly different meanings. Such differences in ideas, current at the popular level, leave very little trace in the historical record except perhaps in the absence of formal institutions of the kind set up by the colonial authorities in the twentieth century. Yet these differences need emphasizing, if we are to understand how 'social exclusion' in the pre-colonial past may have been experienced. Yet it was never just a social experience. Consider very briefly the ecology of exclusion. We should not assume, for example, that the physical environment in northern Nigeria is that much more benign, and neglect less lethal, simply because it has a tropical climate. The diurnal temperature range for instance on the savannah plains can be as much as 70° Fahrenheit, reaching over 100° by day and then down to 30° at night, and making those without shelter feel unbearably cold. In the late dry season, scavengeable food and water are rare; malaria, sleeping sickness, tropical ulcers compound the suffering of the uncared for, and there are hyenas to attack the sleeping. Social exclusion can be both tough and terrifying.

The process of social inclusion and exclusion

Social exclusion is more than a system of categories and boundaries; it is also a series of processes that require negotiating. If we wish to compare such processes cross-culturally it can be useful to draw a graph that plots the gradual acquisition of rights on one axis against the passage of time (in terms of social or biological 'age'). The graph would show at what ages an individual begins to acquire what rights and assets within the community, and at what points in old age are these rights taken away and by whom. Such a graph may begin well before birth, especially in societies where a foetus' 'right to life' may be in doubt. Different graphs need to be drawn for women and for men, as well as for those of markedly differing social rank; such a graph could show, for example, how widely do people with Down's syndrome vary in what rights and responsibilities they get access to at different points in their lives. Over a lifespan, there is usually an extended period of maximum rights ('adulthood'; 'maturity') when people are at their most free in making decisions both for themselves and for those who in some way depend upon them. These rights will vary, but in any one community they constitute a bundle of social assets whose acquisition is readily anticipated. People know what they are – the bundle is not an observer's construct; commonly they relate to such items as fitness for marriage and access to property (such as land, a house or room, tools) which, taken all together, enable an individual to acquire dependants and then to care for them. It is this relationship, rather than the simple ability to work, that is crucial for defining maturity: socially either you have dependants (and are adult) or you are yourself dependent.

Seen as a process, social exclusion is (1) the failure to gain or be granted various assets and rights at the times you would expect to have them – that is, when your peers acquire them, or (2) being deprived of those assets when all your age group still have them, or (3) having the assets you once enjoyed transferred to another – to your son or daughter for example – because you are deemed socially incapacitated. Acquisition or loss can be either a gradual process in which incremental gains are made with or without a series of ceremonies to mark the changes, or they can occur at a specific point – such as 'initiation' or 'retirement'. Failure to go through such initiations – one of which is usually marriage – results in exclusion; or else is itself a consequence of exclusion.

The conceptual model in use here is that of childhood as a status of exclusion – temporary in the case of a real child, permanent in the case, say, of a slave who will continue to be a 'boy', a social child all his life. Indeed dependants of any age who are in need of care from other adults are apt to be assimilated into the social category of 'child' – and may well resent the patronizing entailed. It is thus often possible to identify 'social children' by the way others speak to them. Notoriously, in the 'West', the aged who have started to lose their full status as humans are addressed (and treated) more like children than adults, may not be trusted with money and may be laughed at if they seek sex. Old age as a second childhood is not just a joke. Disabled people report being spoken down to in a similar way; servants or employees, by contrast, were addressed in a rather different tone of voice, even when treated or talked about (by the social class that employed them) as if they were in some way childlike. Even pet animals can be assimilated into the category of 'child'.

I suggest, however, that in northern Nigeria those with severe learning difficulties rarely leave the status of 'child', whereas those adults who fall mentally ill revert only temporarily to being treated as a child – a reversion made easier by the fact that the spirits causing madness are conceived of as childlike. Psychotic vagrants are similarly treated as almost-children, their childishness evidenced by their nakedness and lack of all social sense (wayo). However, those with such impairments as blindness, deafness or paralysis due to polio can acquire rights and assets similar to the unimpaired; and the aged are rarely spoken down to as if they were a kind of child, though they may be neglected. Nor are domesticated animals spoken to in this way. By contrast, slaves were forever socially 'young', even when they took partners and had children; like a child, they were the property of another person, a special kind of domestic animal rather than a full human. Not even the apparent possession of dependants made them adult, if only because those dependants were not in law truly theirs. Only on emancipation might they 'grow up'. Yet at the same time we know household slaves often did, in fact, become important confidantes and companions in their owners' families. In short, the formal model of 'social childhood' could be contradicted in practice; personal status, even for a slave, was negotiable.

Social exclusion can also be seen as a denial of a 'career', of a 'future', as the community conventionally defines it. Just as one definition of being old is no longer to have a future, so too the excluded can be seen not just as perpetually young but as prematurely old: they are now what they will always be, and no one will ask them, as one might of a child, 'what are you going to be?'. There is no 'process' to go through. In fact, the situation is usually more complex: it is possible to see such individuals negotiate access to different futures, to explore what is socially possible in terms of work or marriage. Women, for example, who are known to be infertile or to have vesico-vaginal fistulae (and are therefore incontinent), have managed to develop lives that turned out not to be quite so 'finished' as they once seemed. Similarly, individuals stigmatized with albinism or apparent leprosy have made niches for themselves within their communities. The course of a life is not always so readily prescribed.

Given this degree of variability in practice, any failure to pass through the transition into social adulthood can also be seen as a failure of negotiation. Often, however, failure is not total; people can become partial adults, with some rights and assets if not the whole bundle that others have. This is especially true where patients recover only partial control over their mental health or where neighbours find a way of accommodating to a person's disability (like learning to sign). Furthermore, the immediate community develops attitudes towards a specific social difference that are not necessarily those to be encountered in a distant town: there is a topography of stigma, with popular stereotypes having contours of their own. It is, therefore, through treating social exclusion as a process that we can identify the compromises that moderate exclusion or modify its effects over an individual's lifetime. Yet the archaeological or historical record is unlikely to retain traces of these negotiations and compromises, crucial though they are to individual experience.

The spatial dimension of 'exclusion'

The metaphor underlying the term 'exclusion' is based, of course, upon notions of space and closure. It is to this dimension of 'exclusion' – archaeologically perhaps the most promising – that we now turn, to see if historically any signs of social exclusion might possibly show up spatially in patterns of separate settlement or burial. But it is necessary first to consider the question of 'boundaries' or 'closed doors'. In northern Nigeria, politics have traditionally been centripetal: power is established at a centre point, and relies less on control or surveillance than on attraction. Power draws people to it, recruiting especially the young and 'masterless' who are willing to subordinate themselves in anticipation of later reward. Frontiers, such as they were, were therefore left open to incomers, as centres of power competed with each other for adherents. All eyes were focused, then, on centres, not on borders (Figure 16.1). Only after the *jihad* of 1804–1808 was there a formal closing of the state's frontier, in an attempt to keep non-Muslims out and to create an Islamic utopia within (Last 1967). But this closure only meant that the ambitious incomer had to become Muslim to enjoy, at least in theory, the same access to potential power as other Muslims. Exclusion in this context, then, can be spatially ambiguous; frontiers are represented more by distance from the centre than by any line on the ground; the further you are from the centre, the less powerful you are seen to be. Conversely, the further from the centre you are, the freer you are to live the life you chose to live.

There is, however, another aspect to northern Nigerian space. Within walled cities, as in walled farmsteads, there is a spatial inclusion that dictates where you live. The poor and socially weak are out on the margins where the visitor scarcely sees them. The powerful are close to the core, similarly hard to see or hear but, in the case of the great city, the invisibility is deliberate since it is also an attribute of power. A great city is also unusual in that those even at its margins have usually sought to be urbanites: for the disabled people as for the more obviously ambitious, there are far more opportunities there than in rural areas. In short, those who are disabled and those who are ultra-poor can create, or can hope to create, an urban career for themselves that is distinctly different from what they could expect if they stayed at home.

Figure 16.1 The power of Muslim scholarship at the centre: the learned Waziri of Sokoto, Alhaji Dr Junaidu, setting off on his stallion Danda for Friday prayer with his staff and the emblems of his office. [Photo: M. Last 1963]

Exclusion in the urban context

Space in an ancient city like Kano remains structured though its structure has greatly changed over the forty years since I first stayed there in 1961. The basic dichotomy is still plainly visible, between the City (*birni*) of the older, respectable households and the 'barracks' (*bariki*) and 'new town' (*sabon gari*) of the younger residents, whether local or people from elsewhere in Nigeria. The old City, though, has in recent years become very cramped, the rich and powerful have largely moved out to newer housing. The overall population has grown by perhaps six times in the last forty years; with more than two million now, the scale of Kano's economy means that there can be a distinct sub-economy of the ultra-poor. As the region's political and commercial hub for the last 500 years, Kano has long attracted the poor, the young, the ambitious, and those who are disabled and impaired. Metropolitan centres with their ruling class and their great merchants, the armies of soldiers and servants, the demand for transporters and suppliers of food and other services, have always offered both jobs to the able-bodied and alms to those who are disabled. Surpluses from the urban economy provide a mass of material for recycling: cooked foods, cast-off clothing and wrappings, broken utensils (clay pots, calabashes, wooden and metal bowls) and tools, waste of all kinds whether domestic rubbish or garbage left on the street, dead livestock ranging from camels and horses to dogs, cats, snakes, lizards and birds (valuable for their skins, feathers, fats, etc.). The list of recyclables is long, and varies with current needs or fashions.

As certain city quarters decline, so multi-occupancy and population density rises. Rooms that were once used for washing are turned into bedrooms, with corresponding stress on the people living in them (the smells and, above all, the damp cling to such rooms, as do the spirits who cluster there, delighting in 'dirty' places). The destitute and runaways find shelter around the markets or in these new city-centre slums – women from a forced marriage, young children from an abusive home, youths addicted to marijuana and amphetamine with minds blown through continued overdosing. Other venues, on the outskirts of the city, are the motorparks where lorries and buses unload passengers from rural areas. In recent years, the political structures that controlled them and monitored those passing through them have been dismantled: porters, pimps and 'brokers' specializing in strangers remain to offer help to those at a loss. Here, too, are the buildings that combine the services of brothels, beer parlours, 'hotels' and 'restaurants', both catering for transients and providing menial work or left-over food.

Identifying the socially excluded, either as individuals or as categories in an urban setting, requires knowing the often implicit social barriers that divide up a town. The 'excluded' thus live on the other side of a road or a stream. A market may be sited exactly on the dividing line; the barrier becomes a meeting place, just as the market outside the walls enables another category of 'dangerous' to have dealings without endangering the home community. The location of market-places in and around a city, therefore, reflects not only the city's commercial geography but also, very significantly, the social categories of those involved. With purdah the social norm in Kano city, one central market-place, for example, became reserved de facto for women, but in this guise it could also operate as a site for pickpockets to sell off stolen goods. Butchers are a particularly low-status, if very rich, group: livestock markets and their associated slaughter slabs are normally sited in the western section of the market-place, which is itself west of the town, preferably beyond any residential area. Spirits, attracted like flies to all the blood, can satisfy themselves and then pass on westwards on their daily journey, without endangering any humans. Hence, if there is housing west of a shambles, it is likely to be shanty-style, casual or temporary.

Better shelter is found in the city market-place: the homeless can sleep there overnight, in part because the market sheds offer a little protection from the cold or wet, in part because it is no-man's-land. Waste or hilly ground, by contrast, is shelterless and, being regularly used by neighbouring houses as a public lavatory, is an unpleasant site for sleeping – and the presence of strangers there is especially unwelcome. Even the lairs of the outlaw, urban 'hunters' (yan daba) are seldom sited on such ground; they prefer the edges of built-up areas or housing that is ruined or still under construction.

The key sites of urban inclusion are archetypically the prisons, hospitals and private reformatories for delinquent boys. Whereas in the countryside miscreants are driven off (or, if caught thieving in the market, summarily killed by a market mob), in the great cities they are locked up or shackled with leg irons. Pre-colonially, a prison was simply a part of the official gaoler's house where men awaiting trial were held; no one was sentenced to prison. Colonial authorities built new prisons and used them not only for the new category of sentenced convicts but also to hold (and keep safe) mentally ill people who were deemed potentially violent. Today, psychiatric hospitals house the ill that are brought in to them, using both drugs and chains to restrain the violent, with prisons as clearly separate establishments. But men recognized as criminals can have places of their own in which to live by informal arrangement with the authorities. For example, young sons of the rich who are deeply involved in drugs are often sent for three or more months to private reformatories to be shackled by the ankles in pairs, two boys together twenty-four hours a day in total silence, and given a strict, intensive Qur'anic education. Graduates from this regimen act as teachers. The buildings are reinforced against attack.

Archaeologically, then, many of these premises might puzzle later researchers when they uncover the ground plan or come across the rusted remains of restraints. Asylum, prison, school – located as they often are near the centres of power at the city's core – share many features. Furthermore in their scale, they reflect styles of building and use of rooms that might otherwise only be found in the great houses of the City's elite. In the huge compounds are spaces where servants or children might be disciplined, livestock corralled and those who are very poor and disabled might find left-over food and shelter overnight. Indeed the entry-room (*zaure*) of any substantial house serves as the sleeping quarters of the house's boys and their friends.

Disabled people gravitate to the great cities, both to form communities of their own and to participate in a sub-economy of poverty that is peculiar to the great cities, urban levels of wealth and population density providing an economic scale and diversity that smaller towns cannot match. In a sense, the choice for them is between staying at home in the countryside or emigrating to the great city (or its immediate hinterland): there is nothing in-between. Thus, in Kano city today, the blind people form a dispersed community under a recognized head, the *Sarkin Makafi*, and often beg on set 'beats', having hired a young guide (*ja gaba*) who will take a share of the alms. Blind informants say that beautiful girl guides earn more than boys, but take more too; and different communities in town are more generous than others – patterns of giving apparently vary widely.

There is another category of blind people: these are (and were, pre-colonially) the singers of classic religious poetry, in Arabic, Fulfulde and Hausa; one of their songs that I recorded lasted over two hours. Such singers attend Friday mosque, and on weekdays travel round markets or call on private houses to recite sacred or moral poetry, and in doing so receive alms from men and women alike (Haafkens 1983). Islamic scholars who have become blind late in life (through diabetes, for example) can continue to teach in the traditional manner, with a student reading the text aloud and the scholar then commenting on the text's meaning.

Deaf people also have a recognized head, the *Sarkin Bebayi*, who organizes them *vis-à-vis* the city authorities. In one city I lived in, a deaf-mute served as a key informant for the palace; he spied on government officials who scarcely noticed his presence in their residential area. Deaf people in the big cities, being a large enough group, have their own long-established traditional sign language, which their hearing neighbours use with them (Schmaling 1997). In the countryside, my experience is that signing is more rudimentary and less widespread, and deaf people are more isolated from each other. Two young deaf people I know have now married, whereas in the past each would probably have married a hearing partner. With a few deaf schools in operation, people even in rural areas know there are opportunities if only they can get access to them. Cities offer that access. Otherwise, deaf people work in more or less the same range of crafts as do the hearing, and they marry in the normal way (though they have the reputation of divorcing more often than the average Hausa woman, who will divorce some three or more husbands in a lifetime).

Finally those who are 'crippled' who beg in the city have organized themselves – or been organized. Pitches are controlled and allocated; interlopers are driven off. In one city I knew well in the 1960s, Zaria, the beggars paid protection money to able-bodied patrons who recruited young disabled people. Today in Kano, beggars' leaders have Mercedes of their own and make pilgrimages by air to Saudi Arabia (where Mecca and Medina, especially during the *hajj* and the *umra*, offer alms on a scale sufficient to start up a business back home). Physically disabled young people may live together in sheltered housing in the suburbs, and daily share a taxi in to their 'pitches', especially by traffic lights at road junctions. There the more mobile of them will direct traffic, in the exaggerated manner of a policeman, whenever the electricity fails and traffic lights go blank. Thus, they have become a recognized part of daily life, familiar as individuals albeit with only a constricted social role to live out, at least when young. Elderly people with physical disabilities may leave street life to the young; if they survive, they become largely invisible to all but their close community.

Skeletal material would offer the archaeologist few clues. The great cemeteries, clustered round a saint's tomb, have been used and re-used since the fifteenth century for women and men, young and old, stranger and local alike. Those who are mad or physically disabled are buried in the same ground as everyone else. Exception was made for the bodies of the leading men of every major family; they were buried in the backyard of the house, but the simple mode of Muslim burial was the same for all. Only the bodies of slaves and decapitated convicts were literally thrown away, dumped in the borrow-pits (Figure 16.2), the ponds from which building earth was dug and in which crocodiles lived and scavenged (the last ones died *c.* 1930; such 'urban' crocodiles, often of great age, were apparently quite tame, coming out of the water and being ridden by children). Otherwise exclusion in death seems to have been less sharply imposed than exclusion in life.

The peripheries of towns and villages

For some specialist groups, however, although it is either unacceptable or imprac-ticable that they live within a city or even a village, their relationship to large conventional settlements is essentially symbiotic. They live in camps or isolated houses built amid the fields, outside a village or town. The most common of these are the temporary camps (*tsangaya*) of Muslim scholars and students. With cornstalk frames sometimes plastered with mud, and sited so as to be far from the distractions and pollution of everyday life, these camps are made for sleeping and teaching in, or for extended periods of meditation. The Qur'an, the focus of study in the *tsangaya*, is itself considered dangerously powerful. Furthermore, to the powers-that-be, students can be as troublesome as their teachers are critical. There is thus an element of exclusion at work here: the radically pious are best kept out of town. Nonetheless they cannot stay too far away since students and their teachers rely on alms from villagers and townspeople for whom they can perform religious and other services.

Figure 16.2 The permanence of urban residence: ancient houses within the 15th century walled city of Kano – in the foreground, a 'borrow' pit (*kududduhi* – for quarrying earth) that once housed the crocodiles which cleansed the city of carrion and the corpses of slaves. [Photo: M. Last 1963]

Similarly symbiotic are the traditional asylums for the mentally ill. Healers specializing in the possessed have often large compounds, just outside a country town. Here in isolation they can house twenty or more patients (one exceptionally large asylum had close to a hundred at its peak), both men and women. Brought to the healer by their kin, the ill people are usually first shackled to the trunk of a felled tree, or, if less violent, to a large log which they can carry with them. The extremely violent are first dosed with a strong laxative which disables them, sometimes for days (one patient I knew of became so dehydrated that he died). Over several months the patients are treated with both herbal medicine and rituals, but the healer may also administer drugs he has obtained (whether by deception or by purchase) from a government hospital or pharmacy. The advantage in being in the neighbourhood of a town is that his patients, as they get better, can wander into town looking for food or even doing the odd job for money.

Neighbours are used to the healer and his patients, and therefore, in offering those who are ill some access to normal life, they are an informal part of the process of recovery. Furthermore, the patients' kin can easily make visits, as it is the kin who fund the costs of living and treatment. Currently, the majority of men in asylums, both traditional and modern, are there through overdosing on amphetamines; being young, on their own (often as migrants) and extremely poor, they have tried to earn more money through working longer or faster by taking amphetamines [one labourer I knew well regularly took fifty tablets a day]. Similarly students in asylums had taken stimulants to stay awake in order to study longer (especially before exams). Others have used marijuana and, more rarely (except among sons of the rich), cocaine to excess. By contrast, few, if any, of the women patients have overdosed, presenting instead with the stresses of unbearable social lives. For them, often city-dwellers, the periods in an isolated farmstead, with its rural diet and its cold, constitute a hard, strange regime from which they often want to escape, if only they could.

Another category of symbiotic yet separate settlements in the hinterland of towns are villages of thieves (usually under a recognized head, the *Sarkin Baraye*, if they are on the margins of a great city), to which a victim of robbery goes to buy back stolen property. Thieves' villages in this form may date only from the twentieth century, though we know of professional highwaymen who were based just beyond some of the city's gates. In the nineteenth century there were also 'villages of the blind' just outside the city. Blind people have traditional crafts – making ropes, weaving straw mats – and therefore can support themselves if they do not wish to (or physically cannot) go round begging. At the same time, they are close enough to the city to attend Friday mosque or participate in the major religious festivals. Deaf people, however, did not have such distinct residential settlements in the nineteenth century.

In the pre-colonial period, in some areas, it is possible that people with smallpox or with leprosy were excluded from villages and forced to live in special camps (as occurred, for example, in east Africa), but there is no evidence for this in Hausaland until the colonial period when mission-run leprosaria were established. Had such camps existed, they would have been sited near enough to other settlements so that food and other necessities could be left for them to collect without spreading infection.

The deep rural refuges

In frontier zones, usually the higher ground between rich river basins, a range of communities or individuals seeking separation from the centres of power, though still lying ultimately within their jurisdiction were (and still are) to be found. They are socially excluded in the sense that they are objects of fear and contempt to mainstream society – yet, as such, have a role as 'the wild' within the wider regional culture (Figure 16.3). Traditionally they seek, however, to be self-sufficient rather than symbiotic with the rest of the economy; they were too far away for any but extended journeys to a metropolitan centre. Some frontier communities, though, were predators on mainstream society, while others were only temporary or seasonal residents of the frontier.

In these zones, then, there are traces of old mining settlements, in use only in the dry season, and also remains of the shelters used by charcoal burners, hunters and some specialized pastoralists with a particular breed of cattle. Here too, especially in the past, there were the larger bandit villages that preyed upon travellers passing through the bush on the main 'roads'. Only certain of the frontier forests are notoriously dangerous (on the Kano-Sokoto road, the *dajin rubu* was famously feared in the nineteenth century; now it is the woods that fringe sections of the Kano-Jos road). Then, it was

Figure 16.3   The authority of embodied spirits in the 'bush': a deep rural healer, Mai BaGwari, finalizing, with a sacrifice at the tamarind tree, a woman patient's initiation into the spirit cult (*bori*); the hoe (*galma*) in her hand is an emblematic miniature. [Photo: M. Last 1972]

armed caravans who were as likely to be attacked as solo traders with their donkeys; now it is cars or buses, with the bandits having AK-47s. Woodland, with its low branches, remains the great equalizer; then it was effectively impassable to escorting warriors on horseback, just as today it is largely impenetrable by police or army vehicles even with four-wheel drive.

However, it is the fear of hyenas or lions that deters most travellers from sleeping in these areas; it is the natural home of spirits too. It has, therefore, a reputation for special diseases against which the townsman has no immunity – diseases that affected the limbs (especially knees) as well as the mind. To live with impunity on the frontier suggests the possession of special powers. It is one of the few cultural 'resources' excluded communities can lay claim to – and is sometimes cited as a reason for their exclusion.

When walking in parts of northern Nigeria to locate ancient settlements and coming across farmers to ask about their history, I have, nonetheless, found few places that could truly be said to be 'empty': pools, caves, long-abandoned wells are associated with names of people (or peoples) that are not just myths. An oral tradition might tell about who once lived in this or that bit of scrubland (*duhu*). Indeed, place names reveal layers of languages in sites where the ecology seems now so unwelcoming that it is easy to assume that the people who lived there briefly were in flight from the new, expanding Muslim cities (and their raiding armies) by the rivers on the plains. Though such places are palimpsests of exclusion, it is not these micro-settlements that concern me here. I want to focus briefly on categories of places whose inhabitants sought exclusion or who had it forced upon them collectively.

The most deeply rural are the settlements of sectarian communities (such as the *Salihawa* and *Digawa*) who are seeking to create utopias in the 'desert' beyond the reach of the authorities. They consider the government to be heretical (a view the government reciprocates) and so will deal with it at best only through an intermediary. Like the bandit villages of the past, they have reason to stay hidden from view, yet they interact with their neighbours even when they are non-Muslim: they say the non-Muslim on the frontier is provably more God-fearing than the rich Muslim on the plain.

The other category of people, then, associated today with the deep rural area are the non-Muslim Hausa (*Maguzawa*) living in their large isolated farmsteads (Last 1993). As pagans – and therefore, to Muslims, drinkers of beer, eaters of reputedly unclean meat, physically strong and sexually powerful – they are stigmatized, attracting a certain hostility, mixed with curiosity. Their reputation for strength does not redound to their credit: hard labour was reserved for slaves and pagans (and women should, therefore, be better at carrying burdens than men). As specialists in extensive, labour-intensive agriculture, *Maguzawa* need large polygynous families in large farmsteads – and the scale of their settlements (two hundred or more in a single compound) is matched only by those of former slaves (*rinji*), who are also primarily farmers. [By contrast, craftwork and trade require brain, not brawn, and are of higher status and the speciality of Muslims, whose often monogamous households, in villages and towns, are very small by comparison.]

Maguzawa, both as pagans and denizens of the bush, are reputedly close to the world of spirits. Their healers specialize in serving Muslims afflicted by spirits and other illnesses caught when travelling. For Muslims, residence in a pagan house alongside other mentally ill people, is usually a last resort against an intractable illness. *Maguzawa*, given their intrinsic connection with evil, are considered the ultimate 'laundrymen'; by leaving the cleansing of extreme evil to them, Muslims do not have to launder such evil themselves. *Maguzawa* share this reputation for special powers with certain other groups, such as conjurors, who play on their association with the wild when they come as visitors to markets on the edge of villages or towns, announcing their wares by a peculiar roar and wearing distinctive clothes. Some conjurors carry snakes or lead hyenas; others claim to make things change their shape or disappear at will. As 'witches' (*mayyu*) they say they carry in their stomachs a hailstone (*kankara*; the one I handled was, in fact, a red-flecked glass marble), and can thus be coolly capable of great evil. Today, people say, we may not perhaps believe in them, but we certainly are wise to fear them. Children are taught to be scared of them, in case they are lured and kidnapped to be sold off south or sacrificed (to redden the nuts of kola trees). Conjurors are, therefore, not only dangerous but can delude townsmen and cost them money. So while they are not formally excluded, they are certainly stigmatized socially.

The deep rural, frontier areas, then, provide a site both for those who want to be beyond the reach of mainstream society and for those regarded as too dangerous to have as neighbours even when their services – such as healing the deeply deranged – might, on occasion, be required. The only exceptions to this pattern of settlement are, first, the residents of the key fortresses (*ribat*), built in the nineteenth century to close the frontiers, in which young Muslim elite warriors were settled as a religious duty; second, the early twentieth century villages of pioneers settling the newly opened-up lands after the establishment of colonial peace. The latter are a new style of Muslim frontiersman – in so far as the 'frontier' still exists, with roads now enabling lorries and bicycles to reach even remote settlements, and radios playing urban music and reporting news from the centres of power.

In these deep rural areas, disabled or mentally ill people remained as part of the larger household. They would marry and rear children; there was usually some craft work or tasks they could do (such as keeping a 'shop'). The ill might even become healers in their turn. The social costs could be carried by the wider economy of the farmstead. Too many such people in one place might bring it the reputation of being a house troubled by spirits – and therefore not one a young girl (or indeed a divorcee on the lookout for a good household) would wish to marry into. In that case, the whole farmstead would be rebuilt on another, more auspicious site (Figure 16.4). Such large farmsteads need to attract incomers no less than a rising state does; its very openness towards strangers – men or women – ensures it has the necessary labour power and the social diversity to make it prosper. Witches apart, social exclusion is counter-productive in this context.

Archaeologically or historically, it is often extremely difficult to identify which settlement ruins in the deep countryside might have been occupied by the excluded.

Figure 16.4   The transience of farmsteads in a deep rural community: moving house to a more auspicious site after the death of the blind head-of-house (*mai gida Mayau*); the entire rebuilding and relocation was completed within a single, long day. [Photo: M. Last 1972]

A nineteenth century *ribat* is the most readily identifiable, if only because it had close links to the central power. Otherwise we can readily distinguish only between settlements that sought to hide and those secure enough to be seen from afar. Thus the presence of a market site, usually outside the village wall, is often taken as one sign that it was a 'normal' village. The existence of several clusters of really old baobabs tells of a well-established past settlement as does the presence of one or two tall silk-cotton trees, once carefully sited by gates to be climbed as communal look outs. More ambiguous is a small, planted wood of acacias that once acted as a screen and made a village almost invisible; similarly ambiguous is a lone strip of woodland once left as an escape route for those running from the fields in to a place of shelter. Both, though, suggest long-occupied sites, and not the transient camps of refugees in flight.

More significant, in this context, is knowing which walled towns women ran to when raiders were in the offing, and which towns or villages were temporarily abandoned. In these circumstances, blind or disabled people – like aged people – might simply not be able to flee; in which case one must assume that, in the raiding season, such people moved to the safer cities if they could. The only evidence I have, though, is for elderly people to be left behind to defend the house or hide as best they might, listening to the earth to hear the raiders coming. We know elderly women relatives were ransomed back after such raids; but I have no evidence regarding disabled people.

In this brief survey, I have tried to indicate the range of kinds of social exclusion and inclusion that are to be found in northern Nigeria. This shows how mentally ill and disabled people are juxtaposed with other categories of people seeking either sanctuary from, or limited access to, the wider community as it was then politically organized. What I think has been shown by this survey is that the degree of exclusion, the distance from the centre of power (whether defined in the terms of urban or domestic space or measured regionally), is more significant than a simple dichotomy of 'in' or 'out'.

The problem is made more complex by the fact that nineteenth century, pre-colonial northern Nigeria experienced both political unification and an economic boom, accompanied by a quite widespread peace. As a result, people moved to and fro as emigrants and immigrants, with strangers and refugees finding a welcome as well as runaway slaves setting up 'maroon' communities on inaccessible hills. Social exclusion and inclusion were occurring continuously on many levels. In material terms, town walls were left to decay and suburbs grew up beyond them. With the onset of colonial rule, countryside that raiders had made too dangerous to settle became available, with emancipated slaves, ex-soldiers and other marginal men and women moving in to farm there for the first time.

The changes in social categories brought about by colonial rule have been considerable: slavery carries little stigma now; rural villages have become culturally more bourgeois, imitating the styles of the city, with purdah and Islam practised more assiduously; wealth is now expressed in money, and can be acquired, accumulated and spent in many more ways than before. The pattern of who can marry whom – the most obvious test of social exclusion and inclusion – has changed in several, quite subtle ways. But certain core categories of the excluded have remained, and by their very stability have taken on, perhaps, an extra significance. I would include in these core categories those of people who are mentally ill, and those who are physically impaired: their chances of 'marrying well' are no greater than before, indeed perhaps worse. The growth of government, and offer of state welfare, may well have resulted in more neglect rather than less. And with the current failure of effective administration, what social welfare there ever was is now much reduced. Instead, the socially excluded today again depend primarily on their kin or the moral commitment of the local Muslim community wherever it is they choose to live.

CONCLUSION

By focusing briefly on only three aspects of social exclusion – the problem of categories; exclusion as a process; the ambiguities of spatial distribution – and by offering northern Nigeria as a non-western illustration of these aspects, I have tried to give some idea of how complex a study of poverty, disability and mental illness can be even in another contemporary society, let alone in that society's pre-colonial past. The kinds of indicators we need – if we are to go beyond the obvious, and understand, say, intimate experience of exclusion – require the level of knowledge that only local people, long-term neighbours (and often only women), usually have. Any archaeology, history or even ethnography of social exclusion must be a collaborative effort, and reports, such as this one, are meant to prompt further thinking about how social exclusion, in all its diversity, is best researched. It is a relatively new field. But the field itself is changing now.

In the last twenty or so years in Africa, a wholly new dimension of disability has been developing, on a scale unheard of for most of the twentieth century. The civil wars in many states since Independence have resulted in large numbers being deliberately maimed, whether as a strategy of terror against fellow citizens and civilians under 'enemy' rule, or through soldiers' unrestrained quest for extra-magical powers to lessen their own terror over their own chances of survival.

Whereas wars eventually end, the disabilities they have caused last a lifetime. At the polling booths for Mozambique's recent election, observers were astonished by the numbers of people missing ears, noses, lips – disfigured in wars that ended over a decade ago. In Uganda, many women in the Luwero triangle were rendered infertile by repeated rape two decades ago (Giller 1998). Women have lost their breasts in machete attacks in Angola, in wars that are still unresolved after nearly thirty years (Brinkman 2000). More recently, hundreds of children and women in Sierra Leone refer to themselves as 'useless' because RUF fighters cut off their arms (*The Independent* 21 December 1999: 12). Finally, there are the thousands who have lost a limb or two to exploding mines; and many thousands more will lose theirs before the millions of mines have been finally cleared from fields that have to be farmed nonetheless (McGrath 1994).

The twenty-first century, then, will have new categories of disabled people, this time not brought about by disease or spirits, but deliberately by men involved in the evils of war. Apart from the many who have been left physically disabled, there are those whose minds have been traumatized by what they experienced, or saw, or even did. To limblessness that prevents work are added the nightmares that prevent sleep; then add to this the humiliation brought about by rape, the loss of hope that results from infertility. These are new categories of the 'socially excluded'. Their sheer numbers may give them a certain social solidarity and their real needs earn them recognition from the unscathed; the wider world community may offer them short-term help. But it will remain for each local community to live with the long-term consequences of the social devastation, and devise means of coping with it.

A final category of the new 'socially excluded': those who as young men or boys committed these acts of maiming and rape. Their home communities, in Sierra Leone for example, no longer wish to have them back in their midst; they committed acts that their victims or the victims' kin cannot forgive. Many are accustomed to drugs; most lack jobs, they have missed out on any education other than that of bush fighting – and who will marry them? Who will bear and bring up their children? There is here the making of another category of social outcast, men polluted by their past and with no way to live, except by further unacceptable violence. Even if retrained as soldiers in a new army, the stigma may well still cling to them and to the institution that takes them on (Peters and Richards 1998; Richards 1996).

For archaeologists of the future, there will be traces that indicate these new categories of people who are disabled and those who are socially excluded. War and broken bodies leave their mark, even if the intimate horrors that broke those bodies and ruined their lives, may be lost. It is the task of ethnography to record now, not in the manner of formal archives but as the testimony of witnesses, what these bones will not tell the coming centuries.

REFERENCES

Alcock, P. 1997. *Understanding Poverty*. 2nd edn. Basingstoke: Macmillan.

Brinkman, I. 2000. Ways of death: accounts of terror from Angolan refugees in Namibia, *Africa*, 70(1), 1–24.

Giller, J. 1998. Caring for 'Victims of Torture' in Uganda: some personal reflection. In *Rethinking the Trauma of War*, P.J. Bracken and C. Petty (eds), 128–45. London: Free Association Books.

Haafkens, J. 1983. *Chants Musulmans en Peul*. Leiden: E.J. Brill.

Iliffe, J. 1987. *The African Poor*. Cambridge: Cambridge University Press.

Last, M. 1967. *The Sokoto Caliphate*. London: Longmans Green.

Last, M. (ed.) 1991a. Youth and health in Kano today. *Kano Studies*, special issue. Kano: Bayero University.

Last, M. 1991b. Spirit possession as therapy: Bori among non-Muslims in Nigeria. In *Women's Medicine: the Zar-Bori Cult in Africa & Beyond*, I.M. Lewis (ed.), 49–63. Edinburgh: Edinburgh University Press.

Last, M. 1993. History as religion: deconstructing the Magians ('Maguzawa') of Nigerian Hausaland. In *L'Invention religieuse en Afrique: histoire et religion en Afrique noire*, J.-P. Chrétien (ed.), 267–96. Paris: Karthala.

Lewis, O. 1965. *Children of Sanchez*. Harmondsworth: Penguin.

McGrath, R. 1994. *Landmines: legacy of conflict*. Oxford: Oxfam.

Orme, N. and M.Webster 1995. *The English Hospital 1070–1570*. New Haven & London: Yale University Press.

Peters, K. and P. Richards 1998. 'Why we fight': voices of youth combatants in Sierra Leone. *Africa* 68(2), 183–210.

Richards, P. 1996. *Fighting for the Rain Forest: war, youth and resources in Sierra Leone*. Oxford: James Currey for the International African Institute.

Schmaling, C. 1997. *Maganar hannu*, 'language of the hands': a descriptive analysis of Hausa sign language. Dissertation zur Erlangung der Würde des Doktors der Philosophie der Universität Hamburg.

Tyndale, W. [1528] 2000. *The Obedience of a Christian Man*. D. Daniell (ed.). Harmondsworth: Penguin.

Index

Abaris: shamanic character of 120; *see also* Greece

Abingdon: archaeological evidence of social care of the disabled 53–4

Africa: cults of affliction of 190; disabled, differential burial of 75; disabled, infanticide of 159–60, 161, 162, 163–4; drug abuse 228, 229, 232; infanticide, colonial response to 159, 164–5; infanticide, cosmological justification of 160–1, 163; sorcery, its explanation of disability 160–1; twins, infanticide of 161, 162, 163; violence, social exclusion of the perpetrators of 238; warfare and disability 237–8; *see also* Nigeria, Songye

albinos: Nigeria, social role of 225; Yoruba, differential burial of 75

Amba: differential burial of the afflicted 75; *see also* Africa

American Psychiatric Association 10, 14, 20

anaemia: skeletal evidence of 50

Anna Wilde: public displaying of 153, 154; *see also* hermaphrodites

Apollo: shamanic character of 120; *see also* Greece

archaeology: archaeologically invisible burials 96–7; care of the disabled, archaeological evidence of 53–4, 56, 57, 73–5; child abuse, apparent absence of evidence for 32, 34; disability, archaeological evidence for 32, 34, 36–9, 40, 41, 47–52, 54, 60–76, 81–6, 104, **2.3**, **2.4**, **3.1**, **3.2**, **3.3**, **4.1**, **4.2**, **4.3**, **4.4**, **4.5**, **5.1**, **5.2**, **5.3**, **5.5**, **7.5**; dwarfism, Palaeolithic evidence of the social care of 54, 56; infanticide, evidence of 104, 105, 108, 110–11, **7.5**; Palaeolithic social care of the disabled 54, 56; social

exclusion, archaeological correlates of 2, 5–6, 7, 101–3, 111–12, 230, 236; *see also* Aymyrlyg, skeletons, wells

Argos: Late Helladic well burials 108–10, **7.8**; *see also* Greece, wells

Aristeas: shamanic character of 120; *see also* Greece

Aristophanes: Korybantic rituals, description of 124; *see also* Greece, Korybantes

Arkansas: intellectual disability, legal definition of 15

Astarte: invocation of in the Roma stela 90, **6.2**

asylums: commitment legislation 9, 12–17, 18, 19, 20–2; establishment of 196; history of 12, 196; Nigeria, their peripheral location in 231–2; *see also* commitment legislation, institutionalization, physical exclusion

Atkinson, R. 96

audism 183

Australia: commitment legislation 14, 17; Mental Health (Treatment and Care) Act (1994) 17; mental illness, lay definitions of 19; mental illness, legal definition of 14, 15, 16–17; Murabit, archaeological evidence for the care of the disabled 57; New South Wales 1990 Mental Health Act 17

autism: bereavement, response of autistic individual to 213–14; institutionalization of people with 197–8, 200

Aymyrlyg: care of individuals with physical abnormalities 73–5; chronology of 60; clubfoot 66, 76; developmental defects 61–71; differential burial of the afflicted 75; dysplasia of the hip 63–4, **4.2**; frontometaphyseal dysplasia 71, 76, **4.5**;

169–70; *Muluki Ain* 170–2; Nepal Legal Code 170–2; *Swasthani Brathkatha* 170
Netherlands: dangerousness, legal definition of 18
neurofibromatosis: characteristics of 68; skeletal evidence of 67–8, 76, **4.3**
New South Wales: dangerousness, legal definition of 18; Mental Health Act (1990) 17, 18
New York: Blackwell's Island hospital 55; Mental Hygiene Law 15, 17
New Zealand: mental illness, legal definition of 17
Nigeria: albinos, social role of 225; alms-giving (*sadaka*) 223; amphetamine abuse in 228, 229, 232; asylums, peripheral location of 231–2; blind, communities of 229, 232; body, concept of 220–1, 223; colonialism, its effects on traditional social categories 236–7; danger, concept of 221; deaf communities 229–30; differential burial of the afflicted 75; disability, spiritual causes of 210; disabled, their incorporation in rural settlements 235; disabled, their treatment in Islamic funerary practices 230; drug abuse 228, 229, 232; exclusion, concept of 222; funerary practices of 210; house, concept of 220–1; impairment, concept of 223; infertile women, treatment of 225; intellectually disabled, child-like status of 225; intellectually disabled, incorporation in rural settlements 235; Islamic scholars, economic status of 222–3; Islamic scholars, temporary camps of 230–1; jihad of 1804–1808 226; Kano, social exclusion in 227–30; landscape, concept of 221; lepers, pre-colonial exclusion of 232; lepers, social role of 225; madness, causes of 221; madness, concept of 223; madness, ritual treatment of 220; madness, toleration of 222; miscreants, treatment of 228–9; misfortune, social response to 222–3; old, treatment of 225; poverty, social response to 222–3; power structures of 226; psychotic vagrants 222, 223, 225; self, concept of 220, 222, 223; slaves, status of 225, 226; social exclusion in 2, 228–9; social exclusion, process of 224–5; sorcerers, power of 221–2; spatial correlates of social exclusion 226–7; spirit possession, its association with madness 220, 221, 222; spirits, concept of 221, 222; thieves' villages 232; *tsangaya* 230–1; urban opportunities for the disabled 226–7; wealth, social

response to 222–3, 236; witches, power of 221–2
Njal: portrayal of 129; *see also* Family Sagas
normalcy: medical construction of 187–9
Norway: medieval hegemony over Iceland 128, 129; psychiatric approaches to mental illness, critical attitude towards 19–20
Norwich: St Margaret in Magdalen Street, evidence of scoliosis in the skeletons from 41; St Michael-at-Thorn, evidence of scoliosis in the skeletons from 40–1

Odin: Blood-Brother's Saga, role in 138–9; Egil's Saga, role in 134; portrayal of as disabled 130, 131, **9.1**; skald sagas, portrayal of 132–3; *see also* skald sagas
Old Man of the Sea: Greek myth of 123
Ontario: dangerousness, legal definition of 18
Önund Wooden-Leg: portrayal of 129; *see also* Family Sagas
Orpheus: shamanic character of 120; *see also* Greece
osteomyelitis: skeletal effects of 48, **3.2**
osteoporosis: skeletal effects of 49–50
otherness 1: danger, attribution of to 2–3, 12; perception of people with intellectual disability as 'other' 197–203; social construction of 2–3
Ovid: hermaphrodites, poetic representation of 144; *see also* hermaphrodites

Paget's Disease: skeletal effects of 48
Pakistan: Lunacy Act (1912) 14
Palaeolithic: social care of the disabled, archaeological evidence of 54, 56
Paré, A.: *On Monsters and Marvels* 148–50, **10.1, 10.2, 10.3**; *see also* hermaphrodites
Parsons, J.: hermaphrodites, writings on 144, 145; *see also* hermaphrodites
Pennsylvania: dangerousness, legal definition of 18
physical disability: accommodation of the disabled in Dynastic Egypt 87, 94; Ancient Greek social attitudes towards 98; archaeological evidence of 32, 34, 36–9, 40, 41, 47–52, 54, 60–76, 81–6, 104, **2.3, 2.4, 3.1, 3.2, 3.3, 4.1, 4.2, 4.3, 4.4, 4.5, 5.1, 5.2, 5.3, 5.5, 7.5**; *Eddas*, their portrayal of gods as physically disabled 130–2, **9.1, 9.2**; Family Sagas, their portrayal of 129–34, **9.2**; Icelandic mythology, its deployment of 130–2, **9.1, 9.2**; Medieval evidence of 29–31; political

Lightning Source UK Ltd.
Milton Keynes UK
UKOW04f0858180314

228313UK00003B/55/P